Battle Imperial

Charles William Vane
3rd Marquess of Londonderry

Battle Imperial
The Campaigns in Germany &
France for the Defeat of Napoleon
1813-1814

Charles William Vane

*Battle Imperial: the Campaigns in Germany &
France for the Defeat of Napoleon
1813-1814*
by Charles William Vane

Originally published under the title
Narrative of the War in Germany and France, in 1813 and 1814

Leonaur is an imprint of Oakpast Ltd

Text in this form and material original to this edition
copyright © 2008 Oakpast Ltd

ISBN: 978-1-84677-540-6 (hardcover)
ISBN: 978-1-84677-539-0 (softcover)

http://www.leonaur.com

Publisher's Notes

The opinions expressed in this book are those of the author
and are not necessarily those of the publisher.

Contents

Introduction	9
The Continent in 1813	11
The Battle of Lutzen	22
Towards Bautzen	34
The Battle of Bautzen	44
The Swedish Forces	68
Armistice	80
Dresden	94
Battle at Toplitz & Kulm	109
The Armies Manoeuvre	123
Contest at Mockern	136
Leipzig: the Battle of the Nations	151
Retreat & Pursuit	164
Hanau	177
Holland & Denmark	190
Switzerland	205
Into France	232
Genius at Bay	246
Paris Falls	256
Aftermath	268
Poland	281
Opinions	295
Appendices	317
Addenda	363

To the Officers of the British Army

Redeeming the pledge I gave in my *Narrative of the Peninsular War*, to introduce to the public a *Second Volume*, relative to the Campaigns of 1813 and 1814, provided my first efforts should be supported by the indulgence of my brother-officers; I now offer this additional tribute to those who have kindly considered my first book as not unworthy of their notice.

Vane Londonderry
Lieutenant-General Colonel 10th Royal Hussars

Introduction

The following pages will be found to record, in an unbroken narrative, all those important military operations which came under my immediate notice during the campaigns of 1813 and 1814. I felt that this could be done without compromising my own official responsibility, or breaking through the regard and consideration due to others. That which the soldier's eye has witnessed, surely the soldier's pen may fairly describe ; for, as I have already stated in my Advertisement to a former work, I was constantly in the habit of writing detailed statements of every occurrence. I did this, not merely in fulfilment of my public duty, but for the information of that individual to whose wise and dignified policy, not Great Britain only, but every nation of the civilised world, is, in my estimation, largely indebted.

I am free to own, and proud to record, that his affection was the solace—his good opinion the glory of my life; and it is a source of honest pride to me at this moment that my communications, such as they were, and prepared always on the spur of the occasion, were considered by him worthy to be preserved. My letters to him form not merely the groundwork, but almost the entire substance, of the following pages. I have given them nearly verbatim, with the difference only of adopting a connected form, to avoid the inconvenience of those repetitions which must of necessity occur in detached and occasional communications. By doing this, I am aware that I forego, in some degree, the advantage of that internal evidence which the letters in their original form would have carried with them. This, however, is a sacrifice which I am content to make, as it regards myself personally.

No one, I am certain, can impeach the accuracy of the facts, or the sincerity of the opinions recorded in this *Narrative*; though it is possible some question may be started as to the share of literary distinction to be awarded to the writer.

In reference to my former *Narrative of the Peninsular War*, I stated very explicitly the obligation I was under to a gentleman for the arranging my letters, and thus aiding my first efforts in submitting them to the press. In the present case I have no such statement to make. This work, such as it is, is written and compiled wholly by a soldier, not by an author; and, whatever the amount of its deficiencies may prove to be, I must take them upon myself. There will probably be no occasion to wait long for an estimate of them, as that vigilance which exercises itself in weighing the claims of any individual to be considered a writer of military history is always in full activity.

There is another point upon which I wish also to be explicit. Many may suppose that some of the opinions advanced, or documents produced, might arise out of papers belonging to my late lamented relation, which may have fallen into my possession since the period of his decease. But the fact is, on the contrary, that all these valuable records are still in the hands of his executors, from whom his family have never hitherto received them.

CHAPTER 1

The Continent in 1813

The successful progress of the allied armies against the Emperor of France, in the north of Germany, at the commencement of the year 1813, induced the British government to decide upon taking active measures in aid of the common cause in that quarter. It was therefore deemed expedient, not only that the Prussian and Swedish efforts should be connected in one combined operation, but that His Majesty's Hanoverian dominions should be roused into action, and a fair opportunity afforded them of displaying that zealous attachment to the real interests of Great Britain, for which, on former occasions, they had been so eminently conspicuous.

The most direct method of affording the desired assistance was obviously, in the first instance, to furnish military *attirail* in arms and stores; and with these the Swedes, Prussians, and Hanoverians, were promptly supplied, in great abundance and variety. The next step was to place the several levies, for whose use these supplies were intended, under effective superintendence. For this service the writer of the following pages was selected; and his instructions were to proceed forthwith to the north of Germany, charged, on the part of his Sovereign, with all the correspondence relating to the Prussian, Swedish, and Hanoverian armies, including an auxiliary corps of Russians attached to the forces, which, under the Prince Royal of Sweden, were about to commence a new series of operations from the southern shores of the Baltic.

The Prince Regent, acting in the name and on behalf of His Majesty, had determined at this period, when the powers of Europe were at length rousing themselves, and about to shake off the intolerable load of French oppression, to seize the first opportunity of renewing his ancient alliance with Prussia; and by accrediting a minister at the court of Berlin, to manifest his desire that the friendly relations between the two powers should be restored.

Lord Cathcart at this time filled, with great zeal and ability, the high and important situation of His Majesty's ambassador at the court of Petersburgh. To him, therefore, and the writer of this memoir the charge was assigned, (in their capacity of accredited ministers at the head-quarters of the armies of the Sovereigns of Russia and Prussia,) of making the British government acquainted with all the details of military arrangements and movements, including those of His Royal Highness the Prince Royal of Sweden, to whom Sir Charles Stewart had especial letters of authorization as to all matters of a military nature, although the political and diplomatic affairs connected with the court of Stockholm were conducted by Mr. Thornton, who, as the British minister at that court, attended the Prince Royal's head-quarters.

It is not to the present purpose to enter into any statement of diplomatic transactions; it is enough to say of those which preceded the treaty of alliance between Great Britain and the courts of Russia and Prussia, that they were brought to a conclusion in a manner highly satisfactory to His Royal Highness the Prince Regent, whose anxious purpose was solely to sustain the common cause, and not to pursue objects of separate aggrandizement. It would, indeed, be unfair and improper so to characterize the efforts which were made to remedy the inconvenience resulting from the intersection of different states; an inconvenience which had been long felt and complained of in the Electoral dominions. No time, undoubtedly, could be more proper for procuring a redress of this grievance than that, in which England was making efforts of such magnitude and importance in behalf of the allies. There could, indeed, be but one opinion as to the importance of the object and the fitness of the occasion; and the transaction is adverted to for the sake of bearing testimony against the gross and shameful misrepresentations by which it has been sought to impress an opinion, that the great object of the grand alliance had been lost sight of, for the sake of securing His Royal Highness the Prince Regent's personal gratification in a point which was supposed to interest his private feelings.

I will not assert that these were the most flagrant misrepresentations ever attempted; for unhappily many such have gone abroad, and with but too much success, as will appear whenever the diplomatic history of Europe for the last twenty years shall be honestly written. My province, however, lies beyond the limits of diplomatic discussion. Duty indeed would forbid the necessary disclosures, even had I the inclination to unravel these state intricacies. But it better suits my taste and habits to confine myself to the single object of a military narrative.

I sailed from Yarmouth on the 13th of April, 1813, in the *Nymphe* frigate. The winds being adverse, it was not until the 16th at noon that we made Heligoland. The return of the pilot-boat gave me an opportunity of communicating with the governor, Colonel Hamilton; but the news he was able to furnish fell very short of the demand suggested by our anxiety to be made acquainted with the actual position of affairs on the mainland.

The following day we ran up the Elbe. Off Cuxhaven I had an interview with Major Kinsinger, the commandant of a detachment which had been sent by Colonel Hamilton from Heligoland, to take possession of the batteries, after the town had been evacuated by the French. From Major Kinsinger I received the most encouraging reports of the success of the allies, and of the good disposition of the people in all quarters.

The universal cry was for arms; all ranks were animated with one spirit: for while the disasters which the French armies had experienced in quick succession emboldened the peasantry in planning and executing measures of annoyance, the wanton excesses committed by the retreating columns, especially in the neighbourhood of Bremen, had roused a spirit of retaliation which could not be restrained. The actual state of affairs in Hamburgh at this moment was both critical and complicated. The town was occupied by a force of 2000 men, under the command of an officer in the Russian service, Baron Von Tettenborn, who having been detached from the division of Count Wittgenstein, immediately after the Russian troops had established themselves in Berlin, pressed forward with such ardour and boldness, as to compel General Morand to retire from Swedish Pomerania. Hamburgh was thus left open; Baron Tettenborn having entered it on the 18th of March, was welcomed by the inhabitants with every expression of delight, and proceeded forthwith to restore the ancient government.

No event could have been more favourable for the furtherance of the operations then in progress. An opening was thus afforded for direct communication between Great Britain and the north of Germany, of which our ministers lost not a moment in availing themselves: so that I found a British consul already in the full exercise of his functions, and the shores of the Elbe beginning to resume an aspect of commercial bustle and importance. Still it cannot be denied that this success of the Russians was the result of a lucky concurrence of circumstances, rather than of any well-concerted combination. The advantages obtained by the forward movement of Tettenborn's corps were, however, numerous and important; and though its consequences were eventually disastrous, and most unfortunately compromised some of the best citizens of Hamburgh, it may perhaps be doubted whether the arrangements for opening the campaign could, under any other circumstances, have been carried forward with so much spirit and success.

The general position of the allied armies, at the moment of my arrival, was as follows. General Blucher's corps, about 30,000 men, were at Zwickau, in Saxony; General Winzingerode, with 15,000, was on the right of the above, between Merseburg and Altenburg, his parties extending to Weimar. General Wittgenstein and D'Yorck having formed a junction, had crossed the Elbe at Dessau, and were known to be moving in the direction of Halle, with a force of not less than 40,000, in contemplation of an immediate attack on Wittenberg, in which there was a garrison of from 4 to 5000 French. General Bulow, with a corps of about 10,000 men, was observing Magdeburg. Such may be regarded as the general operations in this quarter at this period of the campaign; but detached from, and in a certain sense independent of these, were the new formations under General Dornburg, on the Aller and Weser, that had already distinguished themselves in a very brilliant manner. Add also among the latter General Tettenborn, who had pushed forward towards Celle, in the neighbourhood of Bremen, with a force of about 4000 infantry and 3000 cavalry, having four regiments of cossacks and two of dragoons. This officer proved himself a sanguine and active character, always ready for a movement *en avant;* and being by birth a German, he brought into the cause his full share of that national sentiment with which every German bosom now seemed animated.

A combined object was now given to these desultory operations, as General Walmoden had arrived for the purpose of taking the command of all the new levies on the Lower Elbe; General Tettenborn, and the zealous and indefatigable General Chernicheff, were placed under his orders: an arrangement highly favourable to the active system of operations, as I found that General Walmoden had already concerted with General Tettenborn to press the enemy's left; and calculating upon their force in cavalry, of which the French had none in this direction, they were sanguine as to the result.

The members of the regency of Hanover, assembled at this moment in Hamburgh, with Count Kilmansegge, a nobleman of much weight and importance in that country, at their head, were employed in re-establishing the civil authorities in the different towns as fast as the French left them. If to the details thus given, I add, that 7000 Swedes occupied Stralsund, Rostock, &c, and that the Prince Royal was daily expected with 10,000 more,

I shall nearly complete the picture, which, with reference to the military objects of the allies, the north of Europe exhibited at the moment of my arrival.

On the side of the French, affairs wore a very different aspect. Beauharnois, the viceroy of Italy, had failed in an offensive movement from Magdeburg; and the failure seemed likely to lead to important results. General Vandamme had thrown himself into Bremen with 5000 or 6000 men, and proceeded to strengthen the fortifications; but if the Viceroy retired from Magdeburg, it seemed improbable that a position could be held so far in advance, and that Davoust would persist in maintaining himself on the Aller, or attempt any line of operation beyond that of falling back, so as to ensure his communications with the great mass of their force, which, to the amount of 70 or 80,000, was concentrated in the neighbourhood of Frankfort and Wurtzburg under Marshal Ney.

The force under Davoust and the Viceroy might be estimated at 40,000. Concentration was now obviously their policy: for finding themselves harassed in all directions by different bodies of Russian cavalry, their communications, if not wholly cut off, were rendered every where uncertain. Their garrisons also were completely shut up in the several fortresses where they had been left, and the *morale* even of their best troops became affected. Thus while the boldest and ablest of the French commanders found full employment in concerting measures of defence, and securing their retreat, the word along the whole line of the combined armies was "forward!" and the most intelligent soldiers did not scruple to express a confident expectation that the French would be driven across the Rhine before the month of June.

That England was in no respect wanting in exertion, is obvious from quantities of arms, ammunition, and military stores, ordered for the Russian, Prussian, and Swedish governments, and actually supplied for their use within the incredibly short space of two months. Great care was exercised in regulating their distribution, both as to their kind and degree; so that no want should occur which had not been provided against. So ably were the energies of the government at home, seconded by the officers appointed to the several departments of this service, directed, that it is not too much to affirm that all the objects proposed by this extensive aid were fully accomplished; and urgent, as the emergency appeared, and general as the excitement of the public mind against the French proved, so that the call for arms was little less than universal, that call was nevertheless so well replied to, that no individual was left without a weapon who had the strength or the desire to wield one. Brigadier-General Lyon was now entrusted with the command of the Hanoverian and Hanseatic troops; and received orders to place himself at the disposal of the Prince Royal of Sweden, for the purpose of aiding in training the new levies. The Brigadier took with him about 460 men of the King's German Legion, with a large proportion of officers. The business of the storekeeper's department was conducted with praiseworthy activity; and the several agents stationed at Stralsund, Colbergen, and the other places to which the consignments were addressed, showed a laudable zeal and ability.

With regard to myself, my attention was called, in the first instance, to the formation of the Hanoverian levies. It had been intended to have fixed one general point of *rassemblanent*; but it was foreseen that it would be attended with much inconvenience and expense, thus to bring nearly all the population of the country to one quarter. As the neighbourhood was now comparatively clear of the enemy, it appeared much more expeditious and advantageous to raise the corps in different places, and to conduct the business or training and arming on the spot where the recruits were obtained. My suggestions to this effect were immediately acted upon. Another object, but of much more commanding interest, was the movement of the Swedish corps, that already occupied Stralsund in considerable force, to a forward position; and this, it was conjectured, would be increased by the arrival of the Prince Royal to about 11,000 strong.

Of the negotiations and discussions which had led to this

decisive step of His Royal Highness, I shall say nothing; but the presence of such a body of troops, under a commander so celebrated as Bernadotte, could not fail to have a powerful influence on the events of the campaign and the state of the country, more especially as I am bound here to remark, that throughout the Hanoverian dominions he had contrived to render himself popular, and enjoyed a high reputation.

It next became my duty to ascertain, as speedily and accurately as possible, the military state of affairs at the Prince Royal's head-quarters, after his landing on the continent. I determined, therefore, to detach Lieutenant-Colonel Cooke for this purpose: an officer of much zeal and talent, who, I had no doubt, would be able to recommend himself both to the Prince Royal and Mr. Thornton; or if Mr. Thornton should not have arrived from Stockholm, to make his own way through the difficulties with which such a mission was surrounded.

Notwithstanding all my anxiety to get forward to Berlin, the first and main object of my attention, I was obliged to remain a day or two in Hamburgh. The time, however, was not unemployed; for, at the pressing solicitations of General Tettenborn (acquiesced in by Count Kilmansegge on the part of the Hanoverian regency), I was induced to use my influence with General Lyon to augment the issue of arms to General Tettenborn from 3000 to 5000 stand. It appeared that the general could make use of these 5000 forthwith; and that the Hanoverian levies, for whose use they had been originally destined, were at that moment by no means in such a state of forwardness as to require them. I was happy to find that this arrangement could be acceded to on the part of General Lyon, without prejudice to the service especially entrusted to him. I had thus an opportunity of obliging General Tettenborn, whose active exertions had afforded the greatest advantage to the common cause; it being almost incredible how much he had done, and what a force he had brought under arms by a month's exertion.

My journey to Berlin was performed with as much haste as possible; and prevented all observation on the state of the country, or the disposition of the people. I arrived there on the 22nd of April, late at night; and found a strong expectation prevailing that the King of Prussia would join the Emperor of Russia in a day or two at Dresden, having set out from Breslau for that purpose. I determined, in consequence, to continue my route immediately to head-quarters. An official communication had just been received, announcing the capitulation of Thorn to General Langeron on the 16th. The garrison, partly French and partly German, consisted of about 3000 men: the latter were allowed their parole, the former were made prisoners of war. It was farther said, that a very fine park of artillery had fallen into the hands of the allies. But an object of more immediate and pressing interest was Spandau: its locality made it of immense consequence to Berlin, and its fall was anticipated with great anxiety. The garrison had made proposals to surrender, and were at this time waiting for General Wittgenstein's answer; but if the terms were rejected, an immediate assault was to be made on the place by the troops surrounding it, aided by those which could be collected in Berlin.

The subject for General Wittgenstein's consideration was not, however, entirely of a military nature. An opinion prevailed, founded on the statements of the French themselves, that ah enormous quantity of plunder was lodged in the place belonging to the Viceroy of Italy. If the garrison were allowed to go out with their baggage, all this would be retained and secured; whereas the general was very desirous that his Russians should get the booty. Under these circumstances, there was little room to expect that any terms proposed would be assented to; and the assault was daily looked for with no small interest by the inhabitants of Berlin, who would gladly have been relieved, at any cost, from so dangerous and troublesome a neighbour.

These circumstances afforded a good opportunity of convincing the allies, practically, what were the real principles and feelings with which Great Britain had entered on the contest. Intimations were not wanting, that the only rapid and certain mode of effecting an object of the greatest importance to the safety of Prussia, *viz.* the recovery of her fortresses, was by money; and it certainly was reported from different sources, that some of the commanders would not be proof against large offers. In reply, it was at once declared that such measures on the part of Great Britain would be wholly out of the question ; that if the allied armies could drive the French over the Rhine, the fortresses would not long hold out; and that we had now but one object to look to, which was to annihilate Buonaparte by force of arms, and not by treachery or gold.

My nearer approach to the scene of operations, served to convince me that their actual aspect was somewhat different from that which, the sanguine anticipations of my Hamburgh friends had ventured to predict. At Stettin, the allies had met with a slight reverse; and it was believed that the French armies were advancing, as an intercepted despatch from the Viceroy to Marshal Ney disclosed a plan of attacking General Blucher's corps, which was advanced to Altenburg, where it was unsupported. General D'Yorck had, in consequence, made preparations to meet Beauharnois; and General Blucher was ready to encounter Marshal Ney, who was known to be at Eisenach; while General Sebastiani's corps, chiefly cavalry, was at Coburg. The whole force under these two generals was not less than. 50,000 men; and it was evident that their main army was *debouchéing* by the passes and defiles of the Thuringian forest. This forward movement could scarcely fail to lead to important results; and it became probable that within a few days the plains of Jena and Auerstadt would become the scene of a tremendous conflict; and if the allies were victorious, that the French must pass the Rhine.

My arrival at Dresden was very happily timed. The two Sovereigns had entered the town on the preceding day: an event most propitious, inasmuch as it enabled me to carry into immediate effect the first and most important object of my instructions. His Majesty the King of Prussia having been with the Emperor the greatest part of the morning, as well as having attended a long service at church, it was not possible that he could grant me an audience on that day; but Baron Hardenberg, the chancellor and first minister of state, gave me an appointment, and entered into a general communication in every respect satisfactory.

It was at the moment of this reunion at Dresden that the weight and importance of the grand military combination became developed. The career of Russian successes had enabled the army to march in the most rigorous winter from the banks of the Moskwa to the shores of the German Ocean. The barriers of the Oder had been passed, and the Rhine was now beginning to be considered as the probable limit of its victorious operations. Prussia was now incorporated in the consolidation of power against France. The King, whose courage and prudence had of late shone forth in a manner worthy of the descendant of the great Frederick, had been rescued by the affectionate loyalty of his people and army from the thraldom prepared for him; and he now came forward from his comparative retirement at Breslau, to place himself at the head of the greatest national efforts which our, and it may perhaps be said any, age had witnessed.

Of the share which England was prepared to take in this great confederation, some faint idea has already been given; and the immediate effect of her wise and liberal policy was found to be, that British commerce and British enterprise had now a channel again opened to them in the north of Europe. Our efforts were not alone limited to the supply of military stores, as before enumerated. The circumstances of the allies were such, as made it a case of absolute necessity that they should look to England for what has been truly called "the sinews of war;" and it may not be amiss to state, what was then well known, that in addition to 500,000*l*., which was the charge of the Russian fleet, two millions sterling were destined to sustain the military operations of the Prince Royal of Sweden in the north of Germany, and two millions more were given as a direct aid to Russia and Prussia. In return for efforts of such magnitude, it was. agreed, on the other hand, by the allies, that Russia was to employ (exclusive of garrisons) 200,000 men, and Prussia not less than 100,000, in active operations against the enemy.

CHAPTER 2

The Battle of Lutzen

To resume the detail of occurrences on my arrival at Dresden, it must be remembered that the Foreign Office in England at this period attached intelligent officers to the different head-quarters and corps of the allied armies; amongst them, Sir Robert Wilson was throughout the war conspicuous for his ability and gallantry. At the period I am now alluding to, when he was with the advance at Chemnitz, an officer, despatched by him, arrived at Dresden on the 27th; and announced that the enemy was moving on our left, and that their advance had reached Jena. In consequence of their approach, the allied army was concentrating itself on the Saale, between Merseburg on the right, and Altenburg on the left. Buonaparte was supposed to have reached Erfurth; and it was in expectation that he would forthwith risk a battle in the plains, that the allies now effected this concentration. Marshal Kutusoff was unfortunately taken ill at this moment; but there were many able officers to supply his place, so that the general interests of the army were likely to be fully maintained. General Count Wittgenstein had removed his quarters from Dessau, while General Miloradovitch's corps was thrown forward to Plauen to strengthen the left.

Every moment gave indication of a serious conflict, but there was no feeling of apprehension as to the result: for though the amount of French force assembled on this side of the Rhine was not estimated at less than 160 or 170,000 men, numerically much superior to that of the allies, yet in their *morale* and composition they were so decidedly inferior, that a French general-officer had been heard to say, when looking at the new troops, "*Que ferons nous de ces cochons de lait?*" Their cavalry, too, was in every respect deficient. Still it was impossible not to perceive that the Emperor of the French did not play for so large a stake as the allies in risking a battle. If beaten, the Thuringian mountains were in his rear, and would enable him to escape without being annihilated by the superior cavalry opposed to him; while the allies, if worsted, would find great difficulty in drawing off, having only one good bridge across the Elbe, at Dresden; while the commanding point of Magdeburg was in the hands of the enemy. These considerations, however, did not check the forward movements of the allied troops; and on the 25th, a corps of 15,000 infantry and 8000 cavalry defiled through Dresden in very fine order.

On the 27th I was admitted to an audience with His Majesty the King of Prussia, and had the honour of presenting my credentials. It was not possible to be received in a more gracious or satisfactory manner. In adverting to the position of military affairs, His Majesty dwelt much on the extraordinary efforts the Prussians had made: observing, however, that the effective force *en campagne,* at the moment, fell far short of the number to which his army would be ultimately brought by levies, now actually raised, though not yet entirely armed or fully disciplined. His Majesty concluded a very gracious conversation, by renewing the assurances of his devoted regard and high consideration for His Royal Highness the Prince Regent. The morning of the 27th brought us likewise the agreeable news of the surrender of Spandau. By the terms of the capitulation, the garrison was allowed to return to France, under an engagement not to serve against the allies for the space of six months. The artillery and every thing else contained in the fortress were to be given up.

A point of considerable moment to the commercial interests of Great Britain came at this time under discussion. Amongst the immediate advantages to' which we had a right to look as a requital for our great exertions, the destruction of Buonaparte's favourite continental system held the foremost place. An edict of the Prussian government, bearing date the 20th March, had formally declared the abolition of all those restraints under which the commerce of the north of Europe had so long suffered; but it was hardly to be expected that the remedies applied could be such as to prove at once equal to removing the evils. Representations were made to me that a tariff of duties had been issued at all the Prussian ports of the Baltic, so oppressive in its provisions as to destroy British trade altogether, and especially to put an end to any exportation of corn from the Prussian territories. The chancellor, Baron Hardenberg, paid immediate attention to my remonstrance on this subject; and I had the satisfaction of receiving his assurance, that the regulations of the tariff should be suspended, provisionally, until an arrangement conjointly with Russia could be agreed upon.

The indications of offensive operations on the part of the enemy were not confined to the main army in front of Dresden. General Sebastiani, with about 8,000 or 10,000 infantry, 3,000 cavalry, and a proportion of artillery, moved to the Elbe; while Marshal Davoust advanced from Bremen, in the direction of Rotenbourg, on Harburg. These changes of position made it necessary for the detachment, dispersed throughout the Electorate of Hanover, to cross the Elbe: which was effected at Boitzenburg, Altenburg, and Harburg, without the smallest loss. Measures were taken to secure the navigation of the Elbe, and artillery and infantry were posted at all the points most capable of defence; so that a strong opinion was entertained at the Russian head-quarters that the enemy would find it difficult to press his advance, and impossible to maintain himself permanently at the mouth of the Elbe.

The allied Sovereigns removed their head-quarters to Grimma on the 19th. Lord Cathcart on that day informed me it was his desire, as he was under the necessity of following His Majesty the Emperor of Russia, that I should remain at Dresden; for the purpose of commencing with Baron Hardenberg, the Prussian chancellor of state, and the Russian plenipotentiaries, the previous discussion of the important objects of the subsidiary convention with Great Britain. I was thus precluded from taking a personal share in the active operations of the following days.

The details of these important occurrences reached me through the reports of those who directed or witnessed the movements. In giving them, however, I may observe, that my position afforded me some facilities for procuring as extensive information as I should have enjoyed had I been myself present, or stationed in any particular part of the field.

A short recapitulation of the leading points in the positions of the opposing armies, at the close of the month of April, will make it more easy to give a clear account of the movements which followed ; and will impress more distinctly on the minds of my readers the progress of the combined operations. The general position of the allied army was between the Elbe and the Saale: the grand head-quarters being at Altenburg. Count Wittgenstein, with the Russians, had his head-quarters at Zwickau. Kutusoff's corps was some miles in front of Dresden; General Miloradovitch, forming his advance, at Chemnitz. Next, as regards the Prussians, General Blucher's, attention was directed to the mountains which bound Saxony on the side of the Thuringian forest, with his head-quarters at Altenburg. General D'Yorck was farther to the right, towards Dessau; and still farther northward, General Bulow was observing Magdeburg. On the other side, the French army occupied the line of the Saale, from Saalfeld to the Elbe. The Emperor was at Naumburg on the 29th, and directed the operations in person. He was known to have brought all his available means to bear on this point of advance. The corps under the Viceroy of Italy (which had retired from Berlin); Marshal Davoust, who had abandoned Hamburgh and the Lower Elbe; General Bertrand with reinforcements from Italy; and detachments of cavalry which had been ordered from Spain, and newly-mounted: all combined to swell the total of the French force, and joined themselves to the main army, which the Emperor's astonishing activity had re-organised, and which had accompanied him on his return to the scene of fresh operations. The estimate of the total amount of the several corps, which placed the French force somewhere about 150,000 men, was certainly not exaggerated; though, to say the truth, it is very difficult to come at any precise grounds of calculation.

Napoleon's policy, at the moment, was to strengthen the impression which his sudden combinations were so well fitted to produce; and with this object he spared no effort to amplify his apparent resources. Those writers who have since recorded his exploits have taken an opposite line: they have thought to aggrandize their hero, by representing his means of offence considerably below my impression of their amount. Making due allowances, however, for opposite representations, I think we may take the number I have given as a fair medium; and say that, including the reserves which were a few marches in the rear under Marshal Oudinot, the Emperor of France commenced his operations with a force of 150,000 men actually in the field. The reputed numerical strength of the allies would exceed this number; but in that estimate were included the raw levies, but newly starting into military action; and even from the troops which were in a comparative state of discipline, large deductions ought to be made for the corps left in observation of the several fortresses. The best opinions coincide in estimating the total force advanced beyond the Elbe at about 85,000 men: of which 55,000 were Prussians, and 30,000 composed the Russian grand army.

A strong opinion prevailed at head-quarters, that the movement now about to take place of passing the Elbe by the allies was both critical and false: critical, as a defeat would involve circumstances of great disadvantage; false, as in the case of a victory the enclosed country of defiles and gorges bordering the Saale, through which the enemy must retire, would prevent our superior cavalry from reaping the fruits of success. The more prudent plan of operations, in the opinion of many, would have been that of a defensive camp (as pointed out in the King of Prussia's memoirs) established between Wittemberg and Torgau. To force the enemy to pass the river, if he would fight with you, and thus compel him to a battle in the plains stretching from Wittemberg to the sea, would have been the direct advantage of this plan of operations; besides acting on a temporary defensive one of this nature, would have given the Russian reinforcements, which were known to be within fifteen days' march, time to arrive; and thus the means for future offensive movements would be much increased.

Such were some of the views maintained by those whose aversion to the plan of operations resolved upon was a matter of notoriety. Amongst these were so many names of eminence, that it is impossible not to suppose that political rather than military considerations had been allowed to influence the decision which had been taken. The position of Saxony directly, and Austria remotely, must have influenced the councils of the allied Sovereigns: there were elements in the combination which lay too deep for mere military reasoning, founded on a superficial or partial view of affairs.

No reasoning, however, could have anticipated that any considerations would have induced the allies, whose chief superiority was in cavalry, to have withdrawn from the plain where that cavalry would have been available, to contend in villages flanked by masked-batteries, and strengthened by entrenchments and every aid of art. Both sides, however, were resolved on assuming the offensive; and, while the French Emperor made his advance on the road from Erfurth to Dresden by way of Leipsic, the allies were making a parallel movement on the direct road from Dresden to Jena. The French army crossed the Saale on the last day of April, possessing itself of Weissenfels and Naumburg; and on the same day the Prussian army was collected at Borne. On the 1st of May it was at Köthen; Count Wittgenstein, with the Russians, at Zwickau; General Winzingerode observed and kept the enemy in check on the Flossgraben.[1]

In the night of the 1st of May, the allied armies *en masse* crossed the Elster at Pegau. General Miloradovitch had under-

---

1. This operation was rendered memorable by the death of the Duke of Istria (Marshal Bessières), who was killed on the 1st by a cannon-shot, in a smart conflict in advance of Weissenfels, near Posen.

taken to watch the enemy on the road from Chemnitz while this movement was effected on the right, as there was reason to apprehend he might push forward a strong corps in this direction, and thus get into the rear of the allied army. The remaining part of the Russian grand army had advanced from Dresden, by way of Rochlitz, to the Elster, and taken up a position to the rear of Wittgenstein; and Blucher, with his Prussians, on the morning of the 2nd of May, moved in the same direction to act as reserves. The allied Sovereigns, who had changed their headquarters on the 29th from Dresden to Grimma, were with the reserves. Their own conspicuous courage and spirit of enterprise would, under any circumstances, have led them forward; but at this moment the Emperor of Russia's presence in the field was a matter of no ordinary importance, as it served to allay certain feelings of annoyance which appeared amongst some of the older officers of the Russian army, in consequence of the nomination of Count Wittgenstein as commander-in-chief upon the death of Kutusoff.

It would be idle and improper in me to enter at large into the military feelings of a great power, who took at this period the most prominent and effective part in the war. In making the above allusion, I have only recorded it to show that so early as the period in question, it was necessary for the Emperor Alexander to use all that firmness, intrepidity, and tact, which pre-eminently distinguished the latter period of his brilliant career.

The imperfect sketch above traced may be sufficient to give a correct idea of the relative position of the hostile armies on the morning of the 2nd of May. It will appear from the annexed plan, that the leading divisions had passed each other in opposite and nearly parallel directions. Buonaparte, in his eagerness to make a dash on Leipsic, had extended his columns along the line of march; so that while his advance was close upon Lutzen, his rear had scarcely cleared the deep valley of Grümsbach, on the road from Weissenfels to Leipsic.

The united armies of the allies, which, as I have stated above, had crossed the Elster the preceding night at Pegau, were thus manoeuvring on his right flank; and may be said to have had the choice of time, place, and manner of conducting the attack. The plan of it was nearly as follows: the enemy, it was perceived, occupied in force the villages of Gross Görschen, Klein Görschen, Rahno, and Kaya, which lie near each other, somewhat in the form of an irregular square, in the plain between Lutzen and Pegau. The advance of the allies was intended for the purpose of driving the enemy from these villages, and bringing the brunt of the attack on the right of the enemy's position, which appeared to be parallel to the main road from Weissenfels. If the endeavour to turn his right wing should prove successful, the cavalry, it was expected, would have an opportunity of acting with advantage; and the result would have been decisive, inasmuch as the line of communication with the rear would have been cut through. The plain is traversed by the deep channel of a rivulet, called the Flossgraben, which was crossed by the whole combined army in small compact columns; and it served as a support to the right after these columns had deployed.

It was now noon, and some of the Prussian troops had been for thirty-six hours on the march; a halt was therefore ordered behind the heights, about a mile and a half from Gross Görschen. These heights afforded a view of the enemy's columns in full march towards Leipsic, by the way of Lutzen. The appearance of our battalions disconcerted this design ; and their foremost troops, hastily recalled, could be observed retracing their steps, and drawing towards the villages in their centre, against which the main attack was now to be directed. The first line of the assailants was formed by the Prussians under General Blucher; the second by the corps of Russians, which had been under the immediate command of Wittgenstein; the Russian guard and grenadiers were in reserve, together with the cavalry of both armies. After an hour's rest the attack upon the villages was begun; and after a desperate resistance, Rahno and Klein Görschen (which lie about a cannon-shot to the right and left of Gross Görschen) were carried by two brigades of Russian infantry under General Ziethen.

For several hours this success was maintained; and our columns pushed forward, driving the enemy before them beyond Kaya, which was in flames, and left unoccupied by both parties. It was now about six o'clock, p. m., and the allies had gained, by hard fighting, more than a mile of ground. The village of Staarniedal, on the enemy's right wing, was evacuated; but the want of sufficient force prevented the allies from occupying it, although the second line had been brought into action. It was obvious Napoleon considered that the fate of the battle would be decided by the possession of the five villages, and the obstinacy of the defence proved the importance he attached to them. By this protracted struggle the issue was in fact determined, as it afforded time to bring up General Bertrand's corps in support of the right of the French line; while on the left, the Viceroy of Italy, who had brought back his troops almost from the very gates of Leipsic, was in sufficient force to baffle an effort made by Prince Eugene of Wirtemburg, with a corps of Prussian infantry, to turn the enemy's position by its left flank. This movement failed altogether: Prince Eugene, instead of outflanking the enemy, was himself outflanked, and kept his place in the line only by an exertion of the greatest bravery.

This was the state of things when the day closed: doubtful and hard-earned success in the centre was counterbalanced by the threatening aspect of both wings of the enemy's army, which was steadily advancing; while no adequate force could be brought forward to resist them, formidable as they were both from numbers and from the comparative freshness of their troops : it thus became necessary to give up the point to which the attack of the morning had been directed.

Before the resolution was taken to draw off the troops, a very gallant effort was made to snatch from the enemy the fruits of his success. As soon as the darkness of the night afforded a cover to the attempt, the whole force of cavalry, which had scarcely been engaged at all during the day, was ordered forward with the hope of effecting a surprise, and driving the enemy from his ground at the moment he thought himself secure in its occupation. The attempt did not succeed: in the first instance, the advanced-posts of the enemy's line were driven in without difficulty; but the dense masses of infantry which were next to be encountered, and the confusion caused by a deep ravine, in which several squadrons found themselves entangled, occasioned the failure of the plan. The assailants were soon dispersed in all directions; and the allies were not only unsuccessful in their immediate object, but lost the services of their cavalry at the critical moment when it became necessary to withdraw their columns, in the very front of a daring « and successful enemy. The retreat was effected early in the morning of the 3rd upon Borne and Altenburg.

During these important events, from the 29th of April to the 2nd of May, I had continued, most reluctantly on my part, at Dresden, in the preliminary diplomatic negotiations before detailed. I had made vain efforts to get away on the 1st; but it was not till the evening of the 2nd that my wishes were so far accomplished as to enable me to set out for the Prussian headquarters, which it was said were at Borne.

I had the mortification to find, on my arrival the morning of the 3rd, that the battle had been fought. I was met on my road by all the equipages and *attirail* of the army proceeding to the rear. Much confusion was observable. The roads were choked up with the immense train of carriages and baggage of every description. Precautionary measures were immediately adopted to protect the allied army from being hurried across the Elbe. Of the ten thousand remarks and observations to which such a battle gave occasion, amongst those who had been personally engaged in it, I shall mention only that the best opinions were agreed in considering that the French had, in a certain degree, been unprepared for the attack; and were indebted for the result to the steadiness with which the villages in the centre were maintained, and time thus afforded for calling in the force from the extremities of the line.

The allies certainly had an advantage throughout the day; but the appearance of the Viceroy on the right at the close of the evening, when there were no more reinforcements to bring up, changed the face of things. Night came on before any advantage was reaped, and the allies remained on the field of battle. It was observed, too, and the fact was of importance, that the greater part of the enemy's corps actually engaged were German troops, Westphalian and Bavarian. Some of the more sanguine calculators indulged an expectation, that these would lay down their arms; but all accounts agreed that they fought with most desperate bravery. The question of comparative force was next the subject of much debate. The most probable conclusion at which I could arrive was, that Buonaparte had brought up about 110,000 men; the Viceroy 30,000, with 2500 cavalry and 1300 artillery; making about 140,000 men: this agrees nearly with the estimate given before. The French infantry was described as good, and the artillery well served; but they had no flying artillery, and only little cavalry.

With respect to the allied troops engaged, the corps of Wittgenstein, D'Yorck, Blucher, and Winzingerode, would amount to near 60,000, including 20,000 cavalry: to these we must add, 9000 under Bulow, 10,000 with Miloradovitch, and General Massenbourg's division of about 25,000: making, something more than 80,000 men disposable in the field. I had, however, reason to believe, that not more than 20,000 Russians and 50,000 Prussians, if so many, were engaged. The loss of the allies in killed and wounded did not fall short of 10,000 men, amongst whom were some names of note. Prince Leopold of Hesse Hombourg was unfortunately killed: the Prince of Mecklenburg Strelitz, and the deservedly celebrated Prussian General Scharnhorst, (whose services in organising the *landwehr* had been so conspicuous,) were amongst the wounded. The Prince died the next day at Pegau. General Scharnhorst lingered till the 28th of June: his loss was universally regretted; and his country has since done homage to his merits, by the erection of a public monument. General Blucher himself received a slight wound. Both the allied Sovereigns displayed the greatest courage. Not a single piece of artillery was lost, and but few prisoners were taken. Several of the enemy's guns and tumbrils, with about 6 or 800 prisoners, were carried off as the trophies of this day.

That the actual superiority during the battle had been on the side of the allies, may be inferred from the fact that the villages from which their columns were withdrawn, on the morning of the 3rd, were not occupied by the enemy till late in the day. I returned to Dresden on the 5th: our operations for retreat were conducted without haste. The allies marched on the 4th from Borne and Altenburg to Rochlitz and Colditz; on the 5th to Dobeln and Nossen; on the 6th to Meissen and Willsdorf. The rear-guard, under Miloradovitch, was engaged on the 5th at Teffersdorf; on the 6th at Ertzdorf: and General Blucher had a very smart affair at Colditz, in falling back upon Meissen. Count Wittgenstein's head-quarters were established in Dresden on the 5th; and the train of the *attirail* continued passing without intermission. Some idea may be formed of the number, when it is stated that on one road 13,000 wagons passed in succession. It became now very evident that the line of the Elbe was to be abandoned. But before we enter into an account of the events which followed this resolution, it will be necessary to cast a glance at the state of affairs on the Lower Elbe, and to trace the immediate effect of the battle of the 2nd upon the operations in that quarter.

We left General Sebastiani in movement from his position on the Aller, and Marshal Davoust advancing from Bremen. The precautionary measures, which were there rendered necessary to keep the navigation of the river unmolested, proved unavailing. Marshal Davoust with 10,000 infantry, including the division of Vandamme, possessed himself of Luneburg, Harburg, and Stade; and established his posts at intermediate points along the left bank of the Elbe. A corps also, in number about 2500, was pushed forward to Cuxhaven; which they entered, though not without considerable loss from the fire of some English gunboats which opened upon their column in its advance. An attack on the island of Wilhelmsburg was, in the first instance, unsuccessful; but it was renewed the next day with better fortune, and Hamburgh was in consequence exposed to the danger of bombardment.

CHAPTER 3

Towards Bautzen

The allies having considered it expedient, after the battle of Lutzen, to repass the Elbe, it may not be irrelevant to discuss a little the plan of operations then thought best to be pursued.

By the most authentic accounts, it appeared that Buonaparte's army comprised a force of 110,000 men, including 10,000 to 15,000 Bavarian contingents; the Viceroy's corps, composed of four divisions, amounted to 41,000; Ney's corps, to 30,000; Davoust, Sebastiani, and Vandamme, to 24,000; the garrison of Magdeburg and Wittemberg, to 12,000: making in the whole a disposable offensive force of nearly 200,000 men; allowing out of the gross number, garrisons for the fortresses.

In addition to the above may be enumerated, the Saxon army at Torgau of 13,000 men. With so powerful a force, although its composition might be very inefficient, yet if aided by the advantages of his strong fortresses on the Elbe, Oder, and Vistula, there was little doubt of Buonaparte's attempting to retrieve by offensive movements his late disasters.

To calculate next the numerical force of the allies, and their means of carrying on the war, or making resistance between the Elbe and the Oder, becomes important. From the best information I could obtain, Wittgenstein's force, composed of Russians and Prussians now concentrated, amounted to little more than 60,000 men, though increased to 80,000 by the arrival of Barclay de Tolly with his *corps d'armée*; Bulow's corps, stated at 13,000, might have been raised by the militia, *landwehr*, and Count Woronzoff's division, to 40,000: to which may also be added, the armaments on the Lower Elbe, about 15,000; but then their composition could not be reckoned upon, or accurately stated.

Of any means of increasing this force by that which could be derived from the blockades of the garrisons there appeared no prospect, as in general the garrisons of the enemy in the fortresses were nearly double the blockading force. The reinforcements arriving from the interior of Russia were highly estimated: Labanow's at 40,000; Tolstoy's at more than that amount, besides other corps.

Having considered the general numerical forces of the contending armies, it may be right to make a few remarks on their composition and state of efficiency. The French army was chiefly formed of young troops, but possessed experienced and excellent officers. They had little cavalry; but, to all appearance, an imposing and well-served artillery. Their old soldiers were distributed into 20,000 guards with Buonaparte, 10,000 with the Viceroy, and the same number between Ney and Davoust. In addition to the celerity of movement which always distinguishes a French army, their possession of so many strong places, both on the Elbe and the Oder, gave them a peculiar facility and security of operations; while the allies were reduced to a state of fluctuating uncertainty and difficulty with respect to their communications, in whatever direction their movements might be carried on.

It was impossible not to observe that the state of the Russian army was, at this period, somewhat on the decline, from the incredible fatigues and hardships it had gone through during two campaigns. The battalions were so weak, that three or four scarcely formed a regiment, and seldom exceeded 250 or 300 men. The cavalry was fine and commanding. The horses, subsisting in a country abounding with forage, were in good condition: yet, in a retreat of some extent, no advantage was taken of this superiority over the enemy; nor did it seem politic so to do, as the plains were avoided, and the grand army (excepting indeed Bulow's corps, which was then in a situation likely to be obliged to seek its safety in retreat on the shores of the Baltic,) buried in the mountains and defiles that separate Saxony from Bohemia. A considerable portion of the Russian cavalry was composed of the Cossacks.

It would be unbecoming in me to speak disparagingly of a description of troops which, on many occasions, signalized themselves greatly, especially when well commanded: nor is it my opinion that they are an inefficient body, when applied in a particular manner, on certain occasions ; for instance, in following up, harassing, and living upon the flanks and rear of a retiring army. From the observations I have made of these troops (which may be nearly assimilated to the Guerillas in Spain), I conceive that they are not formidable when a bold enemy advances; and being no longer buoyed up by their spoliations and hopes of plunder, they become careless and indifferent in their exertions. Having little discipline, they spread much confusion and disorder along the line of march; roaming in *pelotons* every where without control; and lastly, being dispersed as bat-men and orderlies with every officer throughout the army. I should suppose it quite impossible to ascertain at any time, or with any accuracy, their effective amount.

The regular heavy cavalry are undoubtedly very fine; the men gigantic; horses good; equipments superior, and in perfect condition. The light cavalry are less striking in point of horses and general appearance; but some of the hussars and lancers are good. The artillery seems particularly fine and well appointed: the horses to the brigades belonging to the guards are more round, compact, and perfect, than those in any other service.

There is, however, a wide difference between the staple of the Russian army and the Emperor's guards. The latter are very select, both cavalry and infantry; nothing, indeed, can be superior. The grenadiers of the guard are generally very tall men. The cuirassiers are equally large and stout: the discipline and well-dressed state of these men are very imposing. The whole appearance of a Russian army denotes hardihood and bravery, inured to any privations. They subsist well on black bread: few cattle are seen following the army. Their commissaries have little to do; and the great burden of managing the commissariat, which is so irksome a task to a British commander on service, seems perfectly light and easy to a Russian chief.

Before I dismiss this hasty sketch of the Russian army, I cannot, as a military man, refrain from offering some remarks upon the enormous unnecessary *attirail* by which it is attended. The numerous baggages, wagons of all descriptions, &c. &c. exceed belief; and no general officer has less than eighteen or twenty orderlies, cavalry and infantry, which always follow him. In fact, I am persuaded the men out of the ranks, and the followers and military attendants in a Russian army, amount at least to one-fifth of the total number.

With regard to the officers, they are certainly brave men, and some of superior abilities; but the generality of them did not at this period possess those talents and resources found amongst their opponents, so long initiated in the school of Buonaparte.

The general tone prevalent throughout the military officers of the Russian army was of a desponding nature. They thought they had done enough, especially as Austria had not declared herself, and Saxony continued to oppose them. The tide of their success seemed to them arrested, and they eagerly looked to their own frontiers.

The soldiers of the Prussian army had, at this crisis, a higher and more animated feeling: they were fighting for their existence; and every mile, if in retreat, raised a murmur of discontent. Their state of discipline was good, and their superior officers most efficient; their cavalry fine, and artillery excellent.

Had the enemy overran their states, the means of increasing their army would not only have been doubtful, but, on the contrary, there must have been a considerable diminution of effective force for their garrisons. Colberg, Konigsberg, Spandau, &c. &c. must each have been supplied with a strong force; and no strong reinforcements could have been looked for to the Prussian armies.

Again, the Poles required consideration; and from the information I received, there was every reason to fear the enemy would have had an additional force from them of 30,000 or 40,000 men; and we should have had a hostile country to contend with, as Poland became independent.

To return to the state of the campaign.—It must be considered that the enemy had a superior numerical force immediately manoeuvring upon the positions of the allies, supported by two lines of fortresses, which could secure all their operations: and under such circumstances, it would have been impolitic to have contended against them with inferior means, between the Elbe and the Oder, and thus risked the loss of the Russian army, by its being possibly cut off from his own frontier. For although it is to be remarked that, upon the *noyau* of this Russian army, they could raise one in their own country of 300,000 men; yet, in the event of the loss of it and all the experienced officers, the military power of Russia might have been crushed for a generation. Was it possible then for the allies, without a fortress on either of the two rivers, and with inferior armies, to act on the offensive? Were they so to act, what would be their attempts, in which, from the nature of their position, they would not be foiled—in which they would not expose their line of communications? And under such circumstances, what rational hopes of success could be entertained?

It is a melancholy truth, that the allies, with the same fearless but incautious rapidity that urged Buonaparte to Moscow, hastened on to the banks of the Elbe and to the shores of the German Ocean; calculating on the spirit of the countries they hoped ultimately to deliver, and on the chance of uniting Austria, Sweden, and Denmark, in one common cause: thus reckoning on the destruction of the French army to such an extent, that it would be impossible for Buonaparte to assemble another before the month of June at the earliest. Calculating with every sanguine view on these events, they rushed from the boundaries of Russia into the heart of Germany, leaving nearly all the powerful fortresses in their rear (two only of inferior notice having as yet capitulated); and now, too late, they found that Buonaparte, even in May, assailed them with nearly double the force they had collected. According to military calculations, indeed, should Austria not continue a decidedly hostile party, she would probably aim at compelling them to extinguish the flame in the confederate states of Germany, which they had too prematurely and too rashly kindled.

Even the policy of departing from Kalish was very doubtful; but as to that of passing the Elbe, unsupported with barely the means of fighting one battle (for want of ammunition was given out as the reason for retreating), there can be but one rational opinion of its extreme hazard.

The enemy having passed the Elbe at Dresden, Meissen, Wittenberg, and Torgau, and having a direct line of only a few leagues to their main fortresses, Custrin, Stettin, and Glogau, could advance with security and rapidity. The allies having collected on the Breslau road had no alternative, if their flanks were turned, or if Berlin, and Glogau, and Custrin, were the enemy's line of march, but to attack them in flank, and risk every thing; or make for Silesia, and as soon as possible station themselves behind the Oder. Had they fallen on the enemy immediately on their passage of the river, they might have occasioned them a momentary check. Had they collected their army in a central point at Torgau (instead of bringing every thing on the river Spree to a mountainous country, where the superiority of their cavalry was lost), and moved from right or left, as they might have been threatened, making their retreat, if necessary, on Frankfort, thus connecting their whole line of operation by having a central position, the advance would certainly have been more safe and advantageous. A *tête du pont* could have been thrown up at Frankfort: from thence to the Vistula they might have retired under the protection of Marienberger, Plotyk, and Thorn, thus keeping the shortest and most direct line, they could certainly with less risk attempt any considerable affair with the enemy; but by the movement executed, it was to be feared that the enemy bearing in force on the right would leave no alternative but a direct and rapid retreat.

The allied army passed the Elbe on the 8th of May. The headquarters of the Emperor and King of Prussia were established at Bischoffswerde; and General Wittgenstein, with the main body of the army, was marching on the great roads leading towards Bautzen. The corps of General Blucher passed the Elbe at Meissen (General Kleist's corps having put itself in communication with him), while General Bulow's corps still remained on the left bank of the Elbe at Dessau to watch the enemy's movements.

It redounds infinitely to the credit of the allied army, that during the passage of so formidable a river, with the enemy advancing upon it towards his own fortresses, the operation was conducted with perfect order, and that not even a carriage or *attirail* of any kind was left behind. Some works, indeed, had been thrown up on the left bank to cover the bridges; and these, when the enemy had passed, it was thought proper to abandon.

It was not accurately ascertained upon what points of the river the enemy was directing his principal corps; and as he possessed the support of the strong fortress of Wittenberg on his flank, and it seemed uncertain what line of policy the Saxons would now adopt at Torgau, it may be easily imagined how difficult, if not impossible, it would have been, with the aid of these places in the enemy's favour, for the allies to have prevented his forcing the passage of the river under a heavy fire of well-appointed artillery.

On the night of the 8th, the enemy made attempts to re-establish the arches of the main bridge at Dresden; but the Russian artillery was so well directed, that he failed in his object; but succeeded on the 9th in passing near Raditz. The ground being very commanding on the left bank, and favouring their establishing batteries of heavy guns, they passed in boats, and covered themselves advantageously.

The passage was very bravely disputed by General Miloradovitch's rear-guard; and the Russian artillery, after displaying the greatest coolness and courage, was only withdrawn from the impossibility of contending against the superior position and fire of the enemy.

From the best authenticated accounts, Buonaparte had entered Dresden in person; while Eugene Beauharnois' corps and Marshal MacDonald's were stated to be immediately opposed to us. On the 10th, the allied army continued its march on Bautzen ; and as it was deemed advisable to concentrate the forces, General Blucher was ordered to Camenz, and General Kleist's corps to fall back upon him From Muhlberg, while General Bulow's retreat, if necessary, was directed on Roslitz. General Kleist's corps was attacked by an advanced-guard of the corps of the enemy which had crossed at Meissen, and moved by Konigsbruck; and a sharp affair took place, in which the enemy made no impression.

The spirit of the rear-guard of General Miloradovitch's corps was also very conspicuous on this day at Weissig, where the enemy suffered considerably from the charges of the Russian cavalry.

About this period, it was unfortunately ascertained that the Saxons remained favourable to the enemy. General Heilman was deposed from his command, and the fortress of Torgau delivered up to Marshal Ney and General Regnier. The head-quarters of the allied army were moved on the 12th to Herrnhut, on the road to Gorlitz; and the army took up a position near Hochkirch, a field already so celebrated in the Seven Years War. General Miloradovitch's corps was again engaged, during the whole of this day, with the enemy, who sustained a very severe loss.[1]

The whole army was in position on the night of the 13th, except General Bulow's corps, which still remained on the right; and was in readiness to assist the *landwehr* and levies of the Prussian states, which amounted to above 40,000 men, and were

---

1. I cannot here refrain from giving publicity to a report made to me by Sir Robert Wilson on the 10th, in the following terms, of a most meritorious individual, and a much esteemed and dear relative of mine, the son of Sir Walter James, Bart., who was serving as a volunteer and *attaché* to my mission with the armies:—"Mr. John James has merited and gained great credit for his gallant zeal in yesterday's affair. All the generals, and particularly Miloradovitch, express great admiration of him, and will state his good service to the Emperor." I afterwards learnt that General Miloradovitch recommended Mr. John James to His Imperial Majesty for an Order of Merit, which he obtained.

daily increasing. General Miloradovitch was still in advance of Bautzen. General Barclay de Tolly's reinforcements were expected to arrive in a day or two : several new corps of Prussians were come up, and the Russians received an accession of several thousand convalescents. The allied army remained in position on the 14th. The enemy made no apparent movement. General Sebastiani and Marshal Davoust were reported to be moving on Magdeburg. General Miloradovitch having been pressed by the enemy in force, passed the river Spree on this day, and the enemy had taken up a position within cannon-shot of our advance.

Up to the 17th, the respective armies had remained in presence of each other, without the occurrence of any event of importance. The allies had strengthened the position they had taken up by many strong field-works and entrenchments; and seemed determined, in ardent hope and unabated confidence, to await the enemy's attack. The recent arrival of General Barclay de Tolly's corps in the position, added considerably to their strength. The enemy had been reconnoitred on both flanks; and it appeared that the great body of his army was assembled in this quarter, as no force had been stationed between' the range of mountains which separate Saxony from Bohemia, and which bounded our left flank, though it was certainly possible for reinforcements to be passing on routes bearing on Custrin and Frankfort on the Oder; but as yet there had been no such intelligence.

It was difficult, from the nature of the country, to ascertain the force the enemy might have in motion. They occupied all the villages around. Patrols had apparently been made with a view to an attack, but it was delayed much longer than appeared to be necessary.

On the night of the 17th and 18th, the enemy *debouchéed* in the direction of Luckau and Lubben on our right: the force was stated to consist of Regnier's corps. Intelligence having been also received that General Lauriston, with 9000 men, would march to reinforce this detachment. Generals Barclay de Tolly and D'Yorck, with a strong corps, were sent to intercept and fall upon General Lauriston. General Barclay de Tolly fell in with the enemy about six o'clock in the evening of the 18th, in the neighbourhood of Konigswartha; and a sharp contest ensued, which was put an end to only by nightfall, and in which the allies were completely successful. They drove back the enemy at all points: took upwards of 1500 prisoners, a general of division, and eleven pieces of cannon; besides the enemy's loss in killed and wounded, which was considerable.

General D'Yorck was engaged more on the right, and encountered a strong force (supposed to be Marshal Ney's) stationed for the support of General Lauriston's corps. He was in action from daybreak on the 19th till eleven o'clock at night, and with considerable success, though engaged against very superior numbers. A very brisk attack was also made on the same day by the enemy, who endeavoured to possess themselves of the town of Bautzen. They manoeuvred on the left, but in reality aimed at General Miloradovitch's right, who sustained the attack most gallantly, with the assistance of General Kleist's corps, which was sent to his support. The conduct of the troops engaged was highly commendable; but two brilliant charges of Russian light cavalry were particularly conspicuous.

CHAPTER 4

The Battle of Bautzen

After the military movements on the 20th, and the attack on Bautzen by the enemy, his intention appeared to be to force the river Spree, and pass to some heights on the right of the allies: thus threatening General Miloradovitch's rear, and gaining advantageous ground from which his artillery could sweep the main position of the allies, and cover by its fire the dispositions for the general attack. The conflict which ensued was bravely supported. A Russian battalion and some Prussian lancers, under cover of a battery, boldly advanced alone, and contested the heights in spite of the enemy's powerful efforts, until they were supported by General Kleist's corps.

In the mean time, on the extreme right, the enemy's corps followed Generals Barclay de Tolly and D'Yorck in their retrograde movement from their expedition against General Lauriston.

General D'Yorck's corps entered the position in the evening of the 19th, but the night was spent before the whole of General Barclay de Tolly's division was on the ground.

General Miloradovitch repulsed the repeated efforts made by the enemy to force him on the left; and his columns, which had attempted to pass into the mountains, were kept in check. Finding, however, that General Kleist had fallen back into the main position, General Miloradovitch withdrew entirely from the river Spree and the town of Bautzen, and occupied the ground marked out for him in the general line.

Previous to entering into a description of the battle about to ensue, it may not be irrelevant to make a few short observations. Two great armies had now been three days in presence of each other. The allies determined to meet the attack in the position they had chosen ; having weighed the consequences likely to result from a retreat, even to a more favourable one at Gorlitz, against the advantages they now possessed: and they decided wisely, for every retrograde movement, in the present posture of affairs, prejudiced public opinion; and the soldiers had already begun to lose something of their *morale,* as the Russian troops were not fitted at this particular crisis to support a retreat in the immediate presence of an enemy, although vigorous, orderly, and careful to avoid needless exposure. The ground that had been selected for the battle was open, and adapted for cavalry in the centre. On the left flank, the mountains were not unlike those which flanked the left of the English army at the battle of Talavera; and some strong batteries added to the security of this part of the position. It then extended through some villages, which are strongly entrenched, and the plain to some commanding hills on the right, rising abruptly, and affording strong points of support. But the country beyond these was open, and intersected by roads in all directions; and there appeared no impediment to the enemy's moving round the flank of the allies, if their columns of infantry could cope with the masses of cavalry on the plain.

At this period, reports of the enemy's movements were very contradictory. Some affirmed that Buonaparte was in person at the camp opposite Bautzen; that Beauharnois' corps, Marmont's, and the troops of the Rhenish confederation, were with him; and that he meditated an immediate attack: others conjectured that not more than 30,000 men were immediately in our front. There appeared some difficulty in the interior arrangements of the Russian army, between the Emperor and his general-in-chief. The Prussians were in much the same relation to their allies, as the Portuguese in the Peninsula were to the British; and the King, depressed both from public and private misfortune, lived much secluded with his aides-de-camp and staff. At this period Count Stadion arrived ; and the ministers, it was understood, were busily employed in framing terms of mediation and pacification; so that it was generally believed that Austria would now come forward and join the alliance. Such were the actual circumstances of the armies on the eve of the battle of Bautzen.

At day-break, the position in advance of Wurzen and Hochkirch was attacked by the enemy, under the command of Buonaparte in person, who, in fact, had assembled all his forces for this effort, and had not detached largely, as was supposed, to other quarters.

The ground selected by the allies to resist the enemy's approach on the great roads to Silesia and the Oder, was bounded, as I have before stated, on the left by the range of mountains which separate Lusatia from Bohemia, over which Marshal Daun marched to the battle and victory of Hochkirch. Some strong commanding heights, on which batteries had been constructed near the village of Teukowitz (separated from the chain of mountains by streams and marshy ground), formed the defence to the left of the position; and beyond and in front of it, many batteries, defended by infantry and cavalry, were stationed, on a ridge that projected into the low-ground near the river Spree. It then extended to the right, through villages which were strongly entrenched across the great, roads leading from Bautzen to Hochkirch and Gorlitz; thence in front of the village of Burschwitz, to three or four very commanding hills which rise abruptly in a conical shape: these, with the high ridge of Kreckwitz, were strengthened by batteries, and were considered to form the right point of the line.

The ground in the centre was favourable for cavalry, except in some marshy and uneven parts, where their .operations were impeded. *Flèches* were constructed, and entrenchments thrown up at advantageous distances on the plain: in front of which ran a deep rivulet, which extended round the right of the position. On the extreme right the country was flat and woody, and intersected by the roads above-mentioned, bearing towards the Bober and the Oder. General Barclay de Tolly's force was stationed here as a manoeuvring corps, especially to guard against the enemy's attempts on the right and rear of the allies, and it was not immediately in position.

The extent of the whole line was from three to four English miles. The different corps occupying it were as follows: Generals Kleist's and D'Yorck's corps in echelon, and in reserve on the right; General Blucher's, Count Wittgenstein's (commanded by General Riefski), and General Miloradovitch's, formed on the left; and the guards and grenadiers, with all the Russian cavalry, were stationed in reserve in the centre.

The enemy evinced early in the action a determination to press the flanks of the allies: a very strong corps had been stationed in the mountains on our left, which favoured their plan of warfare; but General Miloradovitch having anticipated this manoeuvre, had detached Prince Gorshicoff and Count Osterman with ten battalions of light troops, and a large corps of Cossacks, with their artillery under Colonel Davidoff, to occupy these hills. After a sharp skirmish in this quarter, and a distant cannonading on the right, which commenced the action, the enemy began to develop his forces, and move his different columns of attack to their respective stations.

The contest in the mountains gradually became warmer, and was supported on their side by a very powerful line of artillery. The Prince of Wirtemburg's and General St. Priest's divisions of General Miloradovitch's corps were here sharply engaged, and a successful charge of cavalry was made against some guns of the enemy.

Buonaparte was now visible, on a commanding spot, directing the battle. He deployed, in front of the town of Bautzen, bodies of his guards, cavalry, and lancers: displayed heavy columns of infantry on the esplanade before it; and brought up, in addition, a number of brigades of artillery, with which he occupied some advantageous heights between the position of the allies and Bautzen.

These demonstrations denoted an effort in this direction, and a disposition was accordingly made with General Blucher's corps and the allied cavalry to meet it; but an increasing and a more severe cannonade on the right, made it no longer doubtful where the chief attempt was directed.

Columns of attack, under cover of a heavy fire, were now in motion from the enemy's left, while others were filing to gain our right. General Barclay de Tolly was assailed by a very superior force, under Marshal Ney and General Lauriston, who, it was stated, directed the enemy's forces in this quarter; and, notwithstanding the most gallant efforts, was forced to abandon the villages of Klux and Cannewitz : having been outflanked by the enemy while they warmly engaged him in front, and occupied the heights surrounding the villages of Rackel and Barutt. He determined, in consequence of the enemy's efforts, to retreat to the heights and batteries on the right of Wurzen, where the imperial head-quarters had been established, which answered the purpose of covering the main roads through Wurzen and Hochkirch to the rear.

When it was perceived that General Barclay de Tolly was pressed by very superior numbers, General Blucher (afterwards supported by Generals Kleist and D'Yorck) was ordered to move to his right, and attack the enemy in flank, whom they thus succeeded in checking; and a most sanguinary contest now ensued. Too much cannot be said in praise of General Blucher's corps on this occasion ; and the Prussians in this eventful day, as at the battle of Lutzen, again evinced that ardour and prowess which never will fail them when headed by a king they love, and fighting for their country, their liberty, and independence.

A charge of 4000 of their cavalry on columns of the enemy's infantry, which had carried the village of Kreckwitz, succeeded completely; and the Prussians having again possessed themselves of it, displayed the greatest order and steadiness under a most galling fire. These gallant efforts, however, were arrested by the enemy's bringing up fresh troops; and although partial successes were obtained, the general issue was uncertain.

The enemy having gained an advantage by General Barclay de Tolly's movements, lost no time in making every exertion to turn it to account, by renewing the attack also on our left flank, and assaulting the batteries that covered the conical heights, as well as those of Kreckwitz on the right. Having made themselves masters of the latter, and also of one of our batteries, which from its situation commanded the low ground on the right and centre of it, they thus, as it were, gained the key of the position.

In every other part of the line, however, the allies firmly sustained the conflict; but it had now become apparent, that the enemy had not only superior forces to attack at all points, but had also the means of prolonging their flank movements on the right: thus obstructing our communications, and menacing our rear. Although it. would have been possible, by a general assault of the grenadiers and guards in reserve, to have recovered the heights of Kreckwitz, still the pressure round the flank on General Barclay de Tolly's corps would again have necessitated the abandonment of them; as, when these troops moved to their point of attack, the centre, where the enemy still exhibited a powerful force, would have been endangered.

It was only from such considerations that the allies were induced to change their position at five o'clock in the evening, having from daybreak admirably contested every part of the field of battle. The superiority of numbers was on the side of the enemy; but the firmness, ardour, and heroism displayed by the allies, must have excited admiration and respect even in their enemies.

The dauntless personal courage of the Emperor of Russia and the King of Prussia, who never quitted the field of battle, made the greatest impression on all around them; and had not reasons of prudence, united with the most important considerations, prompted them to relinquish their ground, the most ardent and anxious desire was evinced by them by renewed attacks to sustain the position.

It is very difficult, especially for an observer unacquainted with much of the detail, to do justice by description to this battle, and the extraordinary efforts made on the occasion. The determination having, however, been taken to place the army in a new position, the troops moved off about seven o'clock in the evening for the ground surrounding Weissenberg. The enemy immediately opened a tremendous fire from the heights of Kreckwitz and the village of Cannewitz on the retiring columns; but every gun was withdrawn from the batteries, and the troops moved off as at a field-day. The corps of Generals Barclay, D'Yorck, Blucher, and Kleist, marched off from their right to Weissenberg; those of Generals Wittgenstein and Miloradovitch from their left by Hochkirch. The retreat was made in echelon, covered by the cavalry, and was conducted with the most perfect order. General Kleist's corps formed the rear-guard of the corps moving on Weissenberg; and a battery of forty pieces of cannon, placed by Count Wittgenstein on the heights of Wurzen, impeded the enemy's advance. General Miloradovitch covered the retreat of the troops on the line of Hochkirch.

The allied army were in their new position at night. From the most authentic accounts, the force of the allies did not exceed 65,000 men: that of the enemy in the field was estimated at least 100,000. The loss on both sides was very considerable. The battle throughout was well contested: the troops performed their duty in the most intrepid manner; but there was unfortunately some deficiency in management, which motives of delicacy and diffidence prevent me from dwelling upon.

Count Wittgenstein, on all occasions, displayed great personal courage; but certainly he did not possess the general confidence of the Russian army, because perhaps he was not a Russian. They have most confidence in their own native good fortune and ability.

While Kutusoff was living, (said the military critics,) there was a great and scientific mind to guide the whole; but the talents of the new chief were not yet made manifest, and no implicit reliance, was placed in the great directing power. There were the usual difficulties amongst the Russians as to their numbers; and it was impossible to procure a correct estimate. Barclay de Tolly's corps was calculated and declared at 18,000 men, but it barely amounted to 13,000; and having lost near 4000 in the action of the 20th, he had not more than 9000 men under arms on the 21st, when two corps, if not three, of the French army poured down upon him. If other misstatements are averaged in the same ratio, it may be calculated that the allies had not more than 65,000 men in the battle. The enemy must have had from 110,000 to 120,000 men. They showed much more cavalry than was expected; upwards of 5000 were seen in front of Bautzen. Their artillery was most numerous; and their movements were made throughout with regularity and steadiness, not having the appearance of new troops.

I early conceived our right would be the enemy's real point of attack; and when the Emperor in the field was pleased to ask my opinion, as to renewing the combat and regaining our ground, I ventured to say to His Imperial Majesty, that I feared the position was gone the moment Barclay de Tolly moved; and unless he could carry his whole force there, which was now too late, recovering the heights immediately in our front could be of little avail.

The retreat had hitherto been conducted with great success; but the losses on the 20th and 21st (which could not have been less than from 15 to 18,000 men) were so heavy, that we were enabled only to bring our rear-guard into action. Barclay de Tolly's corps suffered most severely, and Blucher's was very much cut up. Miloradovitch, Kleist, and D'Yorck, all sustained, on the former day, considerable loss; but notwithstanding these circumstances, it is just to state that the spirit of the army was unbroken : its conduct and firmness continued unaltered and unabated; and more was done for the common cause by fighting the battle, than if the allies had retired from the presence of the enemy without awaiting his onset.

By its line of conduct the army was still pre-eminent for intrepidity and exertions, and respected by the enemy and the world: by a different course, the hopes excited would have been abandoned without an effort, and the Emperor of Russia might justly have fallen in public esteem. Many imagined, previous to the engagement, that Buonaparte would not venture upon a direct attack upon the position taken up by the allies; but his great mass of force accounts for his having done so.

It was now reported that Barclay de Tolly had been offered the command (Wittgenstein not being in favour), but that he declined it. Miloradovitch likewise desired to be relieved from the rearguard; and Count Pahlen, an excellent officer, was appointed to it.

The army continued to retreat on the 22nd, in two columns, on the great road to Buntzlau and Lowenberg. The enemy made an attempt to intercept the corps of General Miloradovitch, in which he completely failed. At Reichenbach the rear-guard took up a position, which was defended in the most obstinate manner against the enemy's advance, led by Buonaparte in person. The enemy showed a strong force of cavalry, and made several charges on that of the allies: one even into the town of Reichenbach, which was successfully repulsed, with the loss of some hundred killed, wounded, and prisoners; among whom were several officers. By bringing up a number of guns and a large force, and by outflanking our rearguard, he obliged us to leave Reichenbach; but the rear-guard fell back to Gorlitz in the best order. The conduct of the troops,. after their long service and unequal combat of the 21st, was beyond all praise. Throughout the late movements there was no loss, on the part of the allied army, of guns, tumbrils, or baggage of any importance.

General Bulow, whose corps had been joined by General Borstell's in the neighbourhood of Belitz and Trebbin, (finding that the enemy had withdrawn the corps of Marshal Victor in that quarter, for the purpose of his general operations against the allied army,) resumed the offensive, and pushed patrols to Baruth and towards Wittenberg. The enemy did not advance rapidly; and the army retired in perfect order on the 24th. The corps of Generals Barclay de Tolly, Blucher, D'Yorck, and Kleist, moved on Lignitz; those of Count Wittgenstein and General Miloradovitch in the direction of Jauer: but the latter had his advanced-posts on the river Bober, the enemy occupying Lowenberg. The allies moved in the direction of Schweidnitz: thus having communication by Czenstochau with the Vistula, and being enabled from its immediate position to take every favourable advantage.

Considerable reinforcements were arriving daily. Up to the 31st, the retreat was continued on Breslau and Schweidnitz. The imperial head-quarters moved from Jauer to Streigau on the 27th, and on the 28th to Schweidnitz. A new dislocation of the army having now been made, General Count Wittgenstein resigned the command of the combined forces (which he held after Marshal Kutusoff's death until definitive arrangements were made) to General Barclay de Tolly; and was himself appointed to the command of the Russians; General Blucher to the Prussians ; and General Miloradovitch, being indisposed, had given up his command for the present to General Count Pahlen. It was at this time that the corps under the orders of General. Blucher exhibited (against the division of General Maison, *debouchéing* from Hainau,) what may. be justly considered one of the most distinguished cavalry attacks against solid squares of infantry that has been recorded during this war. The Prussian cavalry were dexterously concealed behind ground highly favourable to the accomplishment of their object. The eagerness to attack was so great, that the signal was given before the enemy were sufficiently advanced, and the result was consequently not so decisive as it would otherwise have been; but notwithstanding the premature onset, twelve pieces of cannon and 1300 prisoners fell into the hands of the allies. Some other partial exertions were crowned with considerable success on the 27th.

It is due here to a distinguished officer, Sir Robert Wilson, who was attached to the allied armies by His Majesty's Government, to mention a marked distinction that was conferred upon him by His Imperial Majesty the Emperor of Russia, in the camp in front of Jauer. It is so grateful a task to witness the merits of a brother soldier justly rewarded, and there was so much in the manner in which this honour was conferred, that I shall stand excused for detailing such a signal testimonial of approbation, even at the expense of prolixity.

The Emperor ordered a grand review of the troops in camp near Jauer. His Imperial Majesty went along the line, and was received with enthusiasm by the soldiers. Observing a favourable moment, when he was surrounded by his general and staff officers, and in front of the troops, His Imperial Majesty called Sir Robert Wilson to him, and addressed him in the following gracious speech:

"Sir Robert Wilson, I have duly appreciated the services, gallantry, and zeal, which have distinguished you throughout the war: in testimony of which I have determined to confer on you the third class of the Order of St. George."

And then, as if desirous of doing it in the most gratifying manner, the Emperor directed General Augerausky to take his cross from his neck, and he delivered it to Sir Robert Wilson. The gracious mode, the well-chosen moment, and the pride experienced by a British officer in seeing one of his companions in arms thus decorated in front of the imperial army, justify me in recording this event in my narrative.

On the 27th, eight squadrons of Russian cavalry, half Cossacks attacked near Gottesberg twelve squadrons of the enemy's *cuirassiers de* Napoleon; and made 400 men and several officers prisoners: a partisan-corps also captured a large ammunition park, and several prisoners. General Blucher's *corps d'armée* retired on the 28th to Pruasnitz, on the Streigau river, while the main army took up a position near Schweidnitz.

The enemy, since the affair of Hainau, had not pressed General Blucher, nor had they attempted any thing in front of this part of the army; it was therefore conjectured they were moving in force on our right, to put themselves in communication with Glogau: their advance, it was said, had reached Neumarkt. A report was prevalent, that Grand-Marshal Duroc had been killed in the affair at Reichenbach. Buonaparte's head-quarters were, on the 31st, at Lignitz: the head-quarters of the Emperor of Russia and of the King of Prussia at Groditz.

There was much reason to apprehend, from reports received, that a reinforcement of several hundred men, with a battery of artillery, on march from the Oder to join the main army, had fallen into the hands of the enemy, who were now on their march on Breslau. Woronzoff's cavalry fell in with a body of the French in the neighbourhood of Dessau, and put them to the rout: they suffered considerably in killed and wounded; among the former was a general officer; and 500 prisoners were taken by the allies, with a colonel and twenty-two other officers.

General Bulow's active operations in the rear of the enemy deserved the highest commendation: he had pushed his partisan-corps in all directions, and had kept the enemy in continual alarm on their flank and rear. General Zastroff, who commanded the Prussian *landwehr* in this neighbourhood, made the greatest exertions; and a very considerable force of this description was collected to act in combination with the allied troops now in position.

The enemy having entered Breslau the evening of the 1st, the allied army could not remain in their position, and accordingly marched at night in the direction of Neisse. It subsequently continued in its new position in the neighbourhood of Schweidnitz until the 4th of June, when the armistice agreed on by the contending forces was made known. The Emperor of Russia and the King of Prussia fixed their head-quarters at a country-house near Reichenbach; General Count Wittgenstein's and General Blucher's *corps d'armée* remained at Schweidnitz, and its neighbourhood. General Barclay de Tolly had his head-quarters at Reichenbach.

It appeared the enemy had detached a corps, immediately preceding the armistice, against Generals Borstell and Bulow; and a sharp affair occurred with the former, who fell back some short distance, having been greatly overpowered by numbers. Operations in the rear of the enemy, on the other hand, still continued to alarm him, and to be attended with success.

Within the last few days, many prisoners had been brought in by various partisan-corps. A brilliant achievement of General Czernicheff's at Halberstadt, hereafter detailed, was also reported.

It is difficult to give an adequate idea of the anxiety that prevailed at this eventful crisis with respect to the decision of Austria. The allied armies had thrown themselves upon her frontier: they had abandoned their main line of communication by Kalisch; had placed themselves absolutely in a *cul de sac;* and had Austria not declared for them, it would be easy to calculate what the consequences might have been: on the other hand, if she declared in their favour, Buonaparte's position was equally critical. It was improbable he would have ventured so much as he did, if he had not been in his own mind quite sanguine as to the result. Austria, as a mediating power, was now in a commanding position Two attempts to treat separately with Russia, it is said, had been made and rejected: Buonaparte was doubtless engaged elsewhere.

The Austrian declaration, on the point of coming forth, was deferred from one day to another. It was first fixed for the 24th of May, then for the 1st of June, and was now postponed till the 10th. A review of the state of the army, at this moment, may not be altogether superfluous. The Russian force at the battle of Bautzen, including every thing, did not exceed 43,000 men. The Prussians amounted to about 25,000. Since the battle, the Russians, by Wittgenstein's return in camp on the 27th, only amounted to 35,000 effective men: it may be asked what had become of all the forces that were held to exist; and it is difficult to pronounce on the causes of the rapid reduction, independent of garrisons and besieging corps in the rear. Reinforcements were no doubt arriving, but many might be intercepted: and the enemy had taken 800 men, ten pieces of artillery, and a large number of tumbrils that were moving towards Lignitz, ignorant of present events. The great line of communication being abandoned, much exertion was necessary to turn off the reinforcements in time into the new direction.

With regard to reinforcements expected, there were 15,000 guards at Kalisch, and General Sachen's corps of 10,000 men: eight battalions arrived on the 28th from Labanoff's corps. General Tolstoy's corps was as follows: eighty-four battalions; twenty-five squadrons; seventeen regiments (Basquirs); six companies of artillery: total number, 70,000 men; of these 50,000 were effective. A fever prevailed among the troops, occasioned by fatigue and exhaustion; and their effective strength became more doubtful. The head-quarters of Labanoff's corps, which was stated at 40,000, were at Biadacz. It was said that its divisions would arrive in succession; but we prepared ourselves not to expect any large and sudden reinforcement. These were the principal great bodies of troops that were reckoned upon: of course there were other detachments, which would do little more than supply casualties. Prussia having withdrawn the blockading force from Glogau, was now rated at between 22,000 and 23,000 men ; and she required time before she could bring forward more troops. Good as were the materials, and great as was the spirit observable in this army, it was very much outnumbered by the enemy. The want of order just now was also visible in it: as far as the means of subsistence went, there was an improvident waste among the Russians; a French army husband what they procure, though their wants are more exorbitant. A deficiency of ammunition existed; and the army could ill afford the loss of the supplies that were coming up.

On retiring from Bautzen, there were two great lines of retreat open—to have proceeded to Breslau and Kalisch; or to adopt the resolution of throwing ourselves on Bohemia, keeping up our communications by Kosel and Czenstochau. The Emperor, with great magnanimity, decided on the latter, wishing to give the best chance of re-uniting ourselves nearer to Austria. Every thing on the Kalisch line was abandoned; and our new communication was now establishing by Oppeln, &c. The object, at present, was to gain time-; to delay the enemy, by making a demonstration of fighting, but still not to give him battle. A camp was taken up in front of Schweidnitz; but if the enemy showed a disposition to attack it, the intention was to have moved to the entrenched camp at Neisse, which had been some time preparing, and to have assembled all the landwehr and irregular force at Glatz, and there, if pressed, to have made a stand. In the mean time, the enemy appeared moving all their forces on our right. The reinforcements that actually arrived after the battle of Bautzen were as follows: six battalions of guards, 3000; three squadrons of cavalry, 900; garrison of Petersburgh, 3000; reserves of two divisions from Finland, twelve battalions, 6000; General Sachen, 7500: amounting, in all to about 15 or 20,000.

It may be difficult, perhaps, in a military narrative, and more especially when the writer professes not to enter into any details of the diplomatic transactions in which he had the honour to bear a part, to advert with propriety to the great political questions that were now in agitation. Nevertheless, as the armistice— he decision of Austria in favour of the alliance—and the combinations that resulted therefrom, bore immediately upon the military operations of the moment, they cannot be passed over entirely without allusion to them and to their effects. Of the policy of the allies in agreeing to the armistice, .at this juncture, different opinions were entertained.

Buonaparte, it was stated, could make greater efforts, during the period of the truce, than the allies; and the general conduct of Austria led to a supposition that she was more anxious to dictate a peace, than to incur all the dangers that might result from a protracted war in the centre of her own empire. On the other hand, the object of Great Britain was to preserve the allies from again entering into those separate treaties with revolutionized France, which had always proved fallacious in themselves, and injurious to the common cause of Europe.

The armistice was undoubtedly, at this moment, advantageous for the position of Prussia; while the councils of that monarchy had been for a long time wisely and naturally directed towards Austria: and it is worthy of remark, that there was considerable lenity shown, in the acts of Napoleon, towards Prussia, which may be accounted for by his anxiety to conciliate Austria. As a proof of French amity to Prussia, no contributions had been levied in Breslau; every thing was paid for in money in Silesia, and the people in the Prussian states were at this period universally well treated by the enemy. But there was not a shade of doubt as to the firmness of the King, and the perfect good faith and adherence of his Prussian Majesty to the system of the alliance. Various were the statements as to the terms of peace that Austria might attempt to negotiate with Napoleon. The allies were supposed to desire, first, aggrandizement for Austria and Prussia; secondly, the separation of the duchy of Warsaw from Saxony and France; thirdly, the cessation of the Rhenish confederacy; fourthly, the re-establishment of the old dynasty in Spain; and fifthly, the independence of Holland: while Austria, it was believed, would be satisfied with the three last stipulations.

The measures of aggrandizement Napoleon might possibly sanction; but the separation of the duchy of Warsaw, it was certain, he would never consent to. The disputants, on the actual posture of affairs, arranged themselves under two classes: those who doubted the part Austria would take, were pacificators; those who believed she would come forward as a belligerent, looked with eagerness and confidence to the renewal of hostilities.

The plenipotentiaries who had gone to the French headquarters to effect some military arrangement of detail, were earnestly pressed to enter into further and general negotiations; but they resolutely refused to treat on any other subjects, stating that every proposition must first be referred to Austria. In an article in the *Moniteur* of the 25th of May, it was stated that. Buonaparte intended to assemble a congress at Prague, and that Austria had assented to this arrangement. The heterogeneous mixture in the article was amusing; but it showed that Buonaparte was aiming at a continental peace. Austria had placed herself in a position in which she would have had *beau jeu* at a general negotiation; and however much Count Metternich was criticised, it must be allowed that, from the date of Buonaparte's having said in 1809— "The House of Lorraine has ceased to exist," he had done more in a short time to elevate his country, than perhaps any other individual had ever accomplished: strengthening her on the side of Galicia; making the Pruth the boundary with Russia; withdrawing the Austrian contingent from France; disarming the Poles; and ultimately superintending mainly the terms of negotiation for all the continental powers.

The present policy of Count Metternich appeared to be to play his game with the allies against France. The council of Vienna believed their plans would be rejected by Buonaparte; and that then being in full preparation, and having gained all the time they wanted, they could declare for the general cause. If, however, the terms settled by Austria were accepted by France, they would then be proposed to the allies; and if refused by them (from their adherence to the understanding with Great Britain and their first proposals), the war would continue, although it would, from diminished means, assume a more defensive shape. On the other hand, it was urged that Austria's project, amended by France, would be received, and form the basis of the future plans of the allies. Austria having brought Buonaparte, by a menacing attitude, to consent to her individual objects, and to establish her mediation; Russia and Prussia would struggle to the last for all they could obtain: while England would be brought forward, and be included in the negotiations, not only from recent treaties, but as being the only power that could make any restitution at the general arrangement of the affairs of Europe. The allies likewise saw that a continental peace, without a maritime one, would never continue; and the alliance with England thus become more cordial.

Every little circumstance that now occurred near the theatre of war was brought to bear, in one sense or other, upon the probability of Austrian co-operation, or the reverse: such, for instance, as the following.—Prince Schwartzenberg, on his arrival at Prague, called for a return of the number of 18-pounders mounted: as this is an enormous large field-piece, few of them had carriages ready prepared. These were to be got, and to be put in order, and extra horses procured for them. Difficulties were made: upon which he declared, that as the French had 24-pounders in order of battle in position, the Austrians must at least have 18-pounders. Fifty pieces were consequently put forthwith in a state of preparation, and 800 horses got for them. This fact, as soon as it became known, immediately created sanguine hopes. Another circumstance, of like character, was also spoken of; two battalions of every Austrian regiment had, in the first instance, marched to assemble in Bohemia; but on General Count Bubna's last return from Dresden, the third battalions of each regiment immediately received orders to follow. This looked like being in earnest.

In a contrary belief as to Austria, however, it was now declared that Prince Poniatowski's corps had arrived at Oglau, on the 2nd of June, from Zwickau; that he was continuing his march to Waldkirchen; that the Austrians did not impede his progress, and that he was even now directing his route so as to get into the French military line of operations.

Some account of these Poles may not here be uninteresting. Prince Poniatowski stopped at Teschen, and despatched General Moyenski to Vienna, to gain intelligence of what had taken place on the Elbe. The Polish corps marched in five columns: their fire-arms, during the march, were conveyed in wagons which accompanied each regiment, in order that at each halting-place the troops might have them in readiness. The non-commissioned officers retained their arms, the cavalry their swords and lances. Each column was composed of infantry, cavalry, and artillery. The whole amounted to 15,000 fine, robust, well-clothed men. The Austrians received them with military honours, and great demonstrations of friendship.

These troops would have proved a formidable addition to Buonaparte's force: indeed, had not Poland been wrested from French influence, a secure state of things could not have been enjoyed. Prussia was desirous that their King should have been declared Duke of Warsaw, and wished at once to have secured Poland. The Emperor dreaded Austria in this measure; and having also his own views, he remained passive.

The state of the allied army was now nearly as follows; guards (reserve), 6000; grenadiers 6000; and cavalry, 5400, under the Grand-Duke's command; Barclay's corps, 7500; Wittgenstein's, 12,000; Miloradovitch, 8000; Sachen, 7500; Prussians, 21,000; Prussian reinforcement at Breslau, 5000: total, 78,400. The Prussian *landwehr* at Glatz were averaged at 20,000, and daily increased. The above amount included convalescents and reinforcements, and was made at the highest calculation.

The army, with the cavalry and guards, had now taken up a position in echelon, with their front towards the Breslau and Brieg routes. The main body remained at Groditz, waiting the issue of events which were then pending.

The loss of the French army since the opening of the campaign was estimated at 60,000 men; but they had reinforcements arriving: and Buonaparte was now anxious to have it believed, that it only depended on him to make separate negotiations either with Austria or Russia. In the mean time, under the arrangements commanded by His Britannic Majesty, his diplomatic servants had finally concluded the subsidiary treaties between Great Britain, Russia, and Prussia; and thus ensured to the alliance a commanding and effective force constantly in the field.

Having now brought down our military details at head-quarters to the important epoch of the signature of the armistice, I proceed to give a rapid *coup-d'œil* of the operations more immediately in the north of Germany. The consequences of the battle of Lutzen, as affecting the affairs on the Lower Elbe, were very disastrous. General Lyon, in his communications, had expressed a confident hope that the defensive positions on the line of the river might be maintained; but when Marshal Davoust pressed forward with not less than 10,000 men, this expectation was disappointed. Tettenborn, Dornberg, and Czernicheff, all fell back on Hamburgh, where they were for some days united. The further movement of a French force under Sebastiani, induced Walmoden to take up a position at Danitz, and to leave Hamburgh to its own resources, and the uncertain aid of some of the new levies. On the 8th, Davoust, who was in force opposite Hamburgh, attacked and carried the island of Wilhelmsburg, and threatened Hamburgh itself with an immediate assault.

The fate of the city was for a short time suspended by the remonstrance and hostile demonstrations of a Danish force stationed at Altona, supported by some gun-boats. It was not, however, consistent with the policy of the Danish court to persist in this spirited resolution: their troops were withdrawn on the arrival of a detachment of Swedes, who undertook the defence of the place; but the diminution which this independent movement would have caused in the Swedish forces, made its propriety more than questionable; and the detachment was shortly recalled, having had only one opportunity of showing its military qualities, by taking part in the defence of the town against an attack made upon it on the 22nd.

On the 30th, General Tettenborn evacuated the city; and it was occupied by the French and Danes : the last of whom had now formally declared war against the allies, and taken part in the hostile operations. General Lyon had fortunately succeeded in withdrawing the stores and treasures entrusted to his superintendence, and had retired provisionally to Wismar. The importance of the Swedish co-operation, at this moment, was too generally acknowledged to leave room for any feelings but those of regret for the fate of Hamburgh. A great military error would have been committed, if the *rassemblement* at Stralsund and in its neighbourhood had been interrupted by any efforts to send detachments to the Lower Elbe; and it would moreover have exposed this part of the combined operations to certain failure, inasmuch as the Crown Prince of Sweden must, by partial actions in detail, have been disqualified from pursuing the great objects which an undivided force, under the guidance of his military reputation, might accomplish.

The same spirit, however, which had displayed itself in the offensive operations of the earlier movements, was fully maintained now that the war had assumed on our part a character almost wholly defensive. It was a system of defence ever watchful for opportunity; and though carried on in the face of a vigilant and powerful enemy, such opportunity was not wanting. Reports were made of several brilliant enterprises, which I proceed to notice in the order of their occurrence.

General Czernicheff left the Lower Elbe, and placed his corps in cantonments between Magdeburg and the junction of the Elbe and Havel. He learnt there that the Westphalian General Ochs would arrive at Halberstadt with a convoy of artillery: he therefore determined to surprise him; and crossing the river, marched with his cavalry thirteen German miles. He had with him the hussars of Isum and Riga, with several pulks of Cossacks, and two guns. He arrived before Halberstadt at five o'clock on the morning of the 30th of May, but found the enemy prepared to receive him: 1600 infantry and eighty *gens-d'armes* were placed behind ammunition wagons, supported by fourteen pieces of cannon. Notwithstanding this disparity of force, the Russians, after a desperate resistance, carried the strong position of the enemy: of whom 400 were killed, as many wounded, and 800 taken prisoners. General Ochs was among the latter; wounded, but not severely.

The Cossacks of Czernicheff on this occasion distinguished themselves, by displaying as much steadiness and firmness as regular cavalry: an advantage arising from the superior manner in which they were led on by that very gallant officer. Their loss was considerable: the French fought desperately, and would not accept of quarter. All the guns were taken; and the ammunition wagons of the convoy were either blown up during the action, or afterwards destroyed.

In respect to General Bulow's affair at Luckau on the 4th inst; it was stated that Marshal Oudinot's corps was equal in numbers to the whole of the Prussians, and that only three brigades of General Bulow's came into action. The French attacked General Bulow, who had posted himself in and behind the town; but they made no impression, and retreated at night, setting fire to the suburb which they had occupied during the engagement. Their loss was computed at about 3000 men; 500 of whom were prisoners: two guns and one howitzer were taken. The enemy retreated towards Tormeswalde, and were pursued by the cavalry.

After the action, General Bulow was joined by Generals Borstell, Borgen, and Harpe; and the armistice alone prevented this combined force from making a most powerful diversion in the rear of the enemy's army.

General Czernicheff, who had recrossed the Elbe after the affair at Halberstadt, having learnt that General Arrighi was at Leipsic with about 5000 men and considerable magazines, and that there were also a number of wounded French in the town, communicated with General Woronzoff, who commanded the Russian corps before Magdeburg; and they agreed to make a joint attack on the enemy: they were joined by the Prussian partisan-corps of Lutzow. General Czernicheff took up a position at Bernburg, and succeeded in drawing the attention of the enemy from the real point of attack.

In the mean time, the corps of Woronzoff and Lutzow were directed by rapid marches to the neighbourhood of Leipsic: when they had reached Dolitsch, General Czernicheff joined them, by a forced march of nine German miles in one day. The French had scarcely time to take a position before the town at the village of Zaucha: they had some cavalry, which opposed but a weak resistance, and were routed in a moment; their infantry then formed, but being attacked by the Russian cavalry, and that part of General Woronzoff's infantry which had come up, their columns were broken, and they retreated precipitately towards the town. As their cavalry was completely beaten and dispirited, there is no doubt the issue of the contest would have been as at Luneberg and Halberstadt, one half of the combined troops not having been brought into action before their opponents were actually discomfited; but unfortunately, just as they were coming up, General Arrighi sent forward two officers with a copy of the armistice. General Czernicheff, at first, refused to believe it, and referred them to General Woronzoff, as the senior officer; but upon examination of the document, the latter being convinced of its authenticity, the victorious troops were obliged to abandon their well-earned success. General Czernicheff had taken 400 prisoners, and General Woronzoff 150. The loss of the French in killed and wounded was considerable.

Captain Colon, a Prussian partisan, who remained in Saxony in rear of the French army when the allies retreated, employed himself in annoying the enemy in the remote parts of Saxony towards Franconia. Having heard of the expected arrival of a train of fourteen pieces of cannon, six howitzers, and a number of ammunition wagons, which were to advance by the road of Hoff, he formed an ambuscade, and attacked the convoy. The French, completely surprised, either fled or were made prisoners. The artillery was rendered useless, and the ammunition blown up: the guns were buried in the woods by the peasants. Captain Colon was afterwards joined by Major Lutzow with 600 cavalry and many volunteers. They established themselves in the mountains of the Vogtland; and their successful enterprises were only arrested by the conclusion of the armistice.

Conformably to the terms of the armistice, the line of demarcation was settled as follows:—The French line commenced at Travemunde on the Baltic, and followed the course of the Trave as far as Lubeck, including a circuit of one German mile round the town, thence extended to the frontier of Holstein, and passed by Bergedorf and Alten-Gamm to the Elbe. The Russian line commenced at Dessau, and was extended by Hollenbach to that river. The portion of territory included between these two lines was declared to be neutral, and was to remain in its actual military position until the termination of the armistice. The line of demarcation then followed the course of the Elbe to a little above Magdeburg; thence it passed along the frontier of Prussia and Saxony to the Oder, the course of which river it followed to the confluence of the Katsbach. Here a neutral space was again established: the French line passing by Dittersbach to the Bohemian frontier; our line attaining the same point by following the Oder to Althof, and thence passing by Landshut and Pfaffendorf.

The actual position of the troops of the grand army on the 15th was as follows:—The left wing occupied the villages on the left bank of the Neisse to the frontiers of Bohemia: the Emperor of Russia and the reserves at Peterswalde and the neighbouring villages: the King of Prussia at Neudorff, and his guards at Groditz, Emsdoff, and the adjacent villages: General Wittgenstein's corps at Waldenburg: Generals Blucher, D'Yorck, and Kleist's corps extended from Strehlin to Breslau: Generals Lachen and Schaulau at Ohlau: the cavalry were on the right bank of the Oder: General Barclay de Tolly and the head-quarters at Reichenbach.

CHAPTER 5

The Swedish Forces

No sooner had the conditions of the armistice been definitively adjusted, than the attention of the allied monarchs at head-quarters was turned to the negotiations about to be entered upon through the mediation of Austria. Of the prevailing impression of public opinion, some idea will have been formed from the sketch in the foregoing chapter: conjecture was still very busy, and had a wide field for action. It was known that much discussion was taking place as to the manner in which the conferences should be carried on; Russia and Prussia having positively declined to send plenipotentiaries to communicate directly with the French authorities. It was at length determined that negotiators should proceed to an appointed rendezvous, where, without being invested with full powers, they might enter into conferences with Count Metternich and the French authorities. The distinction was certainly a very nice one; but all things considered, it had its importance. Skilful and adroit as the French Emperor had ever shown himself in the arrangement and conduct of diplomatic discussion, he was on this occasion met with at least equal dexterity. The matter was conducted by the Austrian minister with so much address, that while the French Emperor was prevented from carrying his points in the cabinet, he was equally shut out from all opportunity of exercising a favourite political manoeuvre; namely, that of turning his discomfiture in negotiation into a means of making an impression on the public mind in France. These were the views with which the conferences were about to open: the rendezvous was fixed at Gitschin in Bohemia.

In the mean time, Prince Schwartzenberg's head-quarters were fixed at Braudeiss; and the Austrian force was drawn together in cantonments, extending from the line of the Moldau to the Reisengeberge mountains. My own position, at this period, bore no direct relation to the negotiations in progress. The treaties of concert and subsidy with Prussia had been completed, and signed; and I was now at liberty to give attention to the other objects of my mission. These were such as to render it desirable that I should set out, with as little delay as possible, for the north of Germany; and in consequence I left Reichenbach on the night of the 22nd, and reached Berlin on the 25th of June.

I found on my route the best spirit prevailing in the country, and indications in. every place that the Prussian army was rapidly becoming more effective. A circumstance had happened with respect to one of the, free corps which had raised the greatest indignation. This corps had been acting in the enemy's rear, when, on the news, of the armistice, they desired to have a free passage from the neighbourhood of Hoff to the right bank of the Elbe. The French general received them, and promised them safe conduct. He however, in their march, fell upon them with superior numbers: two-thirds only of the corps effected their escape, and this with great difficulty. The excuse pleaded was, that he had received instructions to exclude from the benefit of the armistice all those who carried on war, like marauders, in the rear of their opponents, and to treat the free corps especially with great severity.

This proceeding would have afforded sufficient ground for breaking the armistice, if the ruling powers had been so inclined. The people of Leipsic were so exasperated, that their town was declared in a state of siege. A burgher guard was formed, and placed under the orders of a French colonel; and it was expected they would immediately be marched to join the French army: a measure which wore the twofold character of punishment for past resistance, and a pledge taken to prevent the recurrence of new acts of hostility. This, however, was not deemed sufficient; as the *Leipsic Gazette* of the 24th contained a long article threatening that all who had been in communication with the allies, assisted them in any way, or who had spoken ill of the French, should be delivered over to a military commission.

Having been detained at Berlin by an accident, I endeavoured to turn the interval to account by making an accurate inspection of the fortress of Spandau. It is situated at the confluence of the Spree and Havel, two German miles from Berlin. The suburbs on the Berlin side can be inundated, so as to render the approach impracticable. The country around is flat, and cannot be commanded; nor would it be possible to attack the place on both sides simultaneously. The citadel is strong, and well placed: it consists of four large bastions with short curtains. There are in the different bastions embrasures for forty pieces of cannon.

When it was taken from the French, the attack was made from the right bank of the Spree, and was directed chiefly against the west, or Queen's bastion. This bastion during the siege was destroyed by an explosion of the French powder-magazine: an accident which, it will readily be admitted, was very fortunate for the besiegers, whatever the causes may have been to which it might be ascribed. I found the Prussian commandant, Colonel Blankhaus, a very distinguished officer, busily engaged in forwarding the repairs of the fortress. There were, however, only about 600 men within the walls, though the garrison ought not to be less than 3000: indeed, the casemates in the citadel alone, would hold 3000 men. There were, as I was assured, 2000 pieces of ordnance in the place; and my impressions on the whole were very favourable, with reference both to the diligence and skill exhibited in restoring this important fortress.

The state of public feeling in Berlin was most satisfactory. A strong entrenched camp had been formed at Charlottenburg; and works were thrown up round the town to secure it from surprise or military insult.

I delayed my departure from Berlin until the 3rd of July, to inspect (as I was told) near 20,000 *landsturm*, or local militia, when these were collected: however, they diminished to about 4000; among which were two brigades of guns, manned and appointed by the citizens of Berlin. These appeared to be the most efficient part of the military spectacle. The men, considering their little practice, worked the guns well: the horses belonging to them were remarkably good; and this artillery proved efficient. The *landsturm* were formed into six battalions: the generality of the men were fine, but there was a great proportion of boys amongst them. About 150 of each battalion were armed with rifles or muskets, the rest with pikes: they had been sufficiently drilled to march tolerably, and they were moved without confusion, which was as much as could be expected from them in so short a time after their formation.

General Bulow, who showed me these people, informed me they were only a fourth of the force in the neighbourhood of Berlin, but that it was not convenient to have them assembled at once. I believe from 20 to 25,000 of these citizens, the immediate population of the town, were counted upon with certainty to add to the *landwehr* and other troops that were employed in its immediate defence in case of need.

I proceeded from Berlin, on my way to Stralsund; and arrived on the 5th inst. at Greifswald, the head-quarters of the Prince Royal of Sweden, and found him on the point of setting out for Trachenberg, on a rendezvous to meet the allied Sovereigns. The following day, General Adlercreutz was so good as to propose to me to review the Swedish division of troops in camp near the town, consisting of 10,000 men. The appearance of the troops, collectively, was good; individually, they had not the air, gait, or dress of disciplined soldiers: neither the old troops or new levies were steady under arms: their clothes were ill made; and their appearance, after seeing the Russians and Prussians, was not prepossessing. However, I must do them the justice to admit, that their performance in the field exceeded my anticipations. Their guards and artillery were composed of the choice of their men; and throughout, the composition of the Swedish soldiery was respectable.

The regiments exercised and moved on the French system of tactics: they were generally loose in their formations, and had not then acquired that celerity which counterbalances the other fault. I saw four brigades of artillery—two were mounted, and two were called *artillerie assise*—carrying the cannoniers: this was formerly the practice in the Austrian service, but was abolished there, and should be every where, as it is disadvantageous when guns are to move rapidly on bad ground: these were of iron, and seemed to be particularly inefficient; the, carriages, and every thing relating to equipment, were very far behind those of the present day, and those in other armies.

I enquired for the artillery received from England; and was much surprised to find that they had parked it in the Isle of Rugen, and preferred bringing forward what was evidently so much inferior. I saw four regiments of cavalry: two of hussars, one of heavy cavalry, and one of chasseurs *à cheval* The Swedish horse is not a good animal, having a very short neck, and an immense thick cart hind-quarter: he may endure fatigue, but in point of appearance and movement he is a sorry exhibition. There were, however, some few tolerable foreign horses in their cavalry; but in their exercise they were infinitely below par: nor, indeed, is it to be wondered at, as I understand few regiments of cavalry in Sweden are ever kept together. Proprietors of certain estates were obliged to keep a man and horse for the government, equipped to serve in the cavalry, and to find them in every thing. They had little opportunity of exercise, or being assembled: so that this arm, which required the most constant practice and vigilant attention to bring it to perfection, was very much in arrear in Sweden.

It was not surprising, therefore, after contemplating Russian, Prussian, and English cavalry, that the Swedish regiments should have appeared to such disadvantage. However, I do not mean to assert that they were not fit to take the field; and if they could have been brought to act in conjunction with a better description of force, they would, I am sure, have been efficient. The squadrons were weak, about thirty-two file each: the regiments were of five or six squadrons when completed.

I believe the Crown Prince brought with him about 4500 cavalry, and 27 or 28,000 infantry; which certainly fulfilled this part of his engagements. The infantry were serviceable, without being parade troops. The division manoeuvred by changing its front to the right, where they supposed an enemy, formed two lines; sent forward their artillery, supported by cavalry and infantry; retired in *echequier*, second line supporting; charged with their cavalry as a finale; and, on the whole, performed the movements without confusion, although without precision; which, considering their little experience, is saying much. I doubted whether the generality of the regiments were well officered; but I was not well informed on this head. It appeared to me, from seeing these troops, that they were capable, in good hands, of great improvement; and a campaign or two with troops more *aguerris,* would bring them to a military state.

In the repetition of movements, the recapitulation of forces, and the ordinary details of a military narrative, much sameness must ensue; and there will be a great dearth in this narrative of the light anecdote and personal exploit which interest the unprofessional reader: but it must be considered that a British officer, in witnessing the operations of foreign armies, cannot possess that intimate knowledge of their interior, as he would have when acting with the troops of his own nation.

There is always, moreover, a considerable difficulty for a stranger in obtaining information of what is going forward on an immensely extended line of operation, and on those interesting incidents which the scene of a great assembled army produce.

A description of the course of life at the grand head-quarters of the army, which I had just left, may not be here entirely out of place, and serve to vary the monotonous military detail.

The quarters of the ambassadors and foreign general officers attached to the Sovereigns were always allotted by the staff in those towns or villages where the head-quarters were established. Marked attention, as to accommodation and convenience, was always shown to His Britannic Majesty's servants: indeed, the general respect and deference with which they were treated, strongly indicated how much value was attached to the powerful co-operation of the British government.

About ten o'clock every morning, the Sovereigns had a parade of the guards and troops in the cantonment. On these occasions, every effort was made to demonstrate the perfect union of the alliance. The Sovereigns wore the uniforms of the regiments they had been appointed to in each other's army: they headed those corps, of which they were the colonels, in the routine and forms of parade; and the staffs of the armies mingled together, as if they belonged to one directing head, and had but one impulse.

After the attendance at parade, a levée was usually held for business at the Sovereigns' quarters; and ministers, ambassadors, and officers, transacted such affairs as they were charged with. The dinner-hour was two; and the Sovereigns invariably invited one or more of the ambassadors, ministers, or military commissioners, to dine with them. Excellent supplies always existed; and nothing could be more agreeable than these repasts.

In the head-quarters of the Sovereigns, more especially at the period of the armistice, many of the Princes of Germany, and their courtiers and nobles of the first distinction belonging to the different potentates, were assembled; resorting, as they now did, to the seat of deliberation and war, for every thing that was valuable or important to them. Many were joined by their consorts; and the beauty and attractions of the Princess Pauline of Wirtemburg, Madame D'Alopæus, the Princesses of Courlande, and others, deserve to be eloquently described, and with other anecdotes might prove more interesting to many than my military narrative. But my duty is not to deviate from, but to adhere to the dry detail of the campaign. However, it will be seen from the above, that female society of the most perfect description was within our reach; and its allurements and dissipations often divided the mind of soldier and politician from their more severe duties.

Exercise after dinner, *des courses,* or parties of pleasure in the neighbourhood, and re-unions in the evening, filled up the period of each day when the army was stationary; and each ambassador or minister, of any calibre, kept his own table, and always received a certain number of guests.

As my immediate avocations divided my attention between the grand head-quarters and the Prince Royal of Sweden, I shall now revert to his army; and at a future moment give further accounts and anecdotes of the mode of life during the interesting period of the years 1813 and 1814.

I dined on the day of my arrival at Greifswald with the Prince Royal of Sweden, and had two long conferences with His Royal Highness. His engaging manners, spirited conversation, facility of expression, and the talent which displayed itself in all that he said, convinced me on my first interview that he was no ordinary man. It was, however, my duty not to permit myself to be dazzled by his brilliancy, but to ascertain if possible, through the glitter that surrounded him, what were his real views, and how far the warmth of his expressions and splendour of his designs would be borne out by the reality of his services to the general cause.

The cautious line he had adopted and maintained during the last campaign, had been of the most important consequence to the allies. Nothing had yet occurred in his demeanour which could be made a matter of reproach; but, it must be owned, there was nothing to justify confidence: it remained to be discovered whether the future would wear a more promising aspect. The unequivocal proof of his sincerity would have been, to have boldly and unreservedly committed his new subjects against his old friends: it was not possible to believe him fully in earnest, until we should see him fairly in action at the head of his Swedes, with French troops for their opponents.

He was on the eve of setting out to Trachenberg, at the moment of my arrival. The time, therefore, was too short to allow of systematic discussion; and our conversations, on both sides, assumed a very miscellaneous character. Of these conversations, and of all the points embraced in them, my position debars me from giving a complete account; but the impression left upon my mind will be conveyed exactly by a phrase of which I availed myself when recording what had passed—"He clothed himself in a *pelisse* of war, but his under garments were made of Swedish objects and peace;" and further to confirm me in my belief that these sentiments were not erroneous, a celebrated and distinguished general officer, who was at this period one of my colleagues at the Swedish head-quarters, emphatically assured me, "*Le zèle du Prince se montrera toujours plus à mesure qu'il se croira moins nécessaire.*" In the progress, however, of my detail, I shall bring forward circumstances and facts that will enable the impartial reader to form his own judgment.

In this part of the narrative, it is only necessary to state that there was, in truth, no natural link to connect him with the allies: policy had brought him forward; but both policy and affection restrained him from committing himself absolutely against that nation, the love of which was early engrafted in his breast. I must, however, beg to be understood in any observations I make, as not having adopted them from any official source: they will be confined solely to the sentiments I formed myself on the bare military subjects that came forward, and were then in agitation. My opinions may be incorrect; the data for my judgment deficient; the difficulties of the Prince Royal's position known better to himself than to others; but such as my sentiments are I give them, with honesty, and, I hope, becoming deference, while writing a military narrative.

It happened very fortunately, that the news of the debates on the Swedish treaty in the two Houses of Parliament, and of the very considerable majority in its favour, had preceded my arrival. At Stralsund this had a most satisfactory influence; and it was natural to ascribe much of the Prince Royal's cordiality to this cause. Of the individuals by whom His Royal

Highness was surrounded, the most prominent was a Colonel Camps, his foster-brother, a Frenchman: the Swedish generals were undoubtedly honest, upright, and sensible men; but there existed a secret ascendancy over some of the staff-officers, which it was difficult to develop. I must however do, thus early, full justice to Baron Wetterstedt, the secretary of state, General Adlercreutz (since dead), General Count Löwenhehn, and some others: never were more valuable officers than these, nor men more devoted to the common cause of their country and Europe. If reports were to be credited, at times there was a less direct and less respectable means of influence than these in operation. There was certainly nothing in the character or habits of some leading persons at the Prince's head-quarters, which made it impossible to believe the reports in circulation. A celebrated actress had lately taken her departure from Stralsund, and it was said had been conveyed to General Vandamme's outpost with an escort. As to the nature and extent of her communications, rumour was not idle. But I advert to the fact only, for the sake of reminding my reader that the manoeuvres resorted to by Napoleon were not always of a strictly military character.

For ten days or a fortnight after the Prince Royal's departure for Trachenberg, my attention was taken up in arranging matters of importance connected with the state of affairs at the anticipated renewal of hostilities. General Arentschildt, of the Russian German Legion, had arrived; and with him I settled the supply of arms and necessaries for his division. Major-General Dornberg had communications to make relative to the formation and organization of the Hanseatic legion. These troops had been newly taken into British pay, and the General had much to accomplish before they could be made effective.

On the 15th, intelligence reached us from the Prince Royal that the armistice was prolonged to the 10th of August. Speculation was busy as to the ulterior movements of the Swedish troops, should the suspension of arms be protracted until winter. The island of Rugen becoming then insecure as a point of retreat, my anxiety was to keep the attention of these Swedish officers, who spoke to me on the subject, alive to the real aim of the campaign, that they might give up the notion of partial retreat and all separate objects, and look to war on a grand scale. The Swedish troops, it was quite certain, could winter well in Germany and Colberg; and other points would offer means, of re-embarkation, if necessary: but to talk of Stralsund and Rugen as *places, d'armes* for retreat, was viewing things within narrow limits, and under a false light.

My intention of effecting a tour of military inspection, had been postponed in consequence of the Prince Royal's absence ; but on the 17th, Major-General Arentschildt, commanding the Russian German Legion, having arranged with me to see his corps, I had great satisfaction in being able to make a detailed report upon it.

The legion, as far as its numbers went, was not only perfectly fit for service in the field, but it was a matter of considerable surprise to find that, notwithstanding the short time they had been raised, and the very arduous marches they had made, they should have arrived at a state of field discipline creditable to any description of troops. I could not but attach the entire credit of this to, the general officer, and the officers commanding corps: and the two officers commanding the cavalry regiments, Colonel Count Goltz and Major Count Dossman, appeared to me to be remarkably intelligent, clever officers.

The commanding officers of the infantry battalions, as well as the corps of officers generally, were, to all appearance, admirably selected, and exactly what might have been desired. And here I should not omit observing, that so excellent an *esprit du corps* reigned amongst them, that one or two young officers who had not conducted themselves in a satisfactory manner, according to their brother officers' opinions, had been forced by them to leave their regiment. My inspection of the Hanoverian levies was yet to be completed; but I had already seen enough to satisfy me that we should soon have a considerable and efficient British force in this quarter, not less than 20,000 men. In what manner this force could be employed, and in what degree it would conduce prominently to the general issue of the campaign, remained to be decided. My own anticipations as a British officer were sanguine.

Early on the morning of the 16th we were gratified by the arrival of a British messenger, bearing the glorious news of the battle of Vittoria. The Prince Royal returned the same evening from Trachenberg; and it was easy to perceive that Lord Wellington's great achievements had produced as great a change in the political atmosphere of Dresden and the north, as it could have effected in southern Europe. On the Prince Royal's arrival, I had the honour of an interview: he declared very frankly his satisfaction at the favourable news, and held out brilliant hopes for the future. The maps were spread out; and we had the advantage of hearing much said by His Royal Highness that was very eloquent and scientific on the subject of the great combinations which were to be entered upon. Nothing was left to wish for, but that the troops should be put in motion; his dislocations being completed, and his masses assembled. This desirable event seemed likely now to take place.

On the 20th the Prince Royal began to put his troops in motion; taking up a line, with the right at the Lake Schwerin, the left at Demmin and Pau. The Swedish division of Lieutenant-General Laendel's, under Major-General Tettenborn, and a Prussian division of about 5000 men, were the forces destined for the corps of observation against the Danes and Hamburgh; to which was to be added the Hanseatic Legion, as not being quite in a fit state to go forward. This corps of observation remained in the neighbourhood of Wismar.

The Prince Royal proceeded himself to Berlin, along the line of demarcation, to see the troops; but despatches from General Barclay de Tolly, relative to the assembling of General Winzingerode's corps and the troops that were to be placed under his orders, obliged His Royal Highness to move rapidly; and I had the honour to accompany him, after seeing the Hanoverian levies in our way.

CHAPTER 6

Armistice

Mr. Thornton now received the details of the British force arriving under Major-General Gibbs. Colonel Cooke was ordered by me to afford them every assistance on their landing, and to communicate between them and the Swedish authorities.

The most important points at this moment for the deliberation of the British government were as follow:

1st. If the armistice should by any unforeseen occurrence be prolonged, what in such case was expected of the Prince Royal?

2nd. If the Prince Royal should determine on remaining in Germany during the winter (to which he did not in any event positively object), whether Great Britain would be disposed to give an increased subsidy next year? This arrangement was strongly urged by the Prince Royal.

3rd. In the event of France accepting any basis proposed by Austria, and acquiesced in by Russia and Prussia, whether it should be positively admitted that the corps of the Russian German Legion was to be considered as a corps at the disposal of Great Britain, and to follow the Swedish army, or such orders as it might receive from Great Britain?

In a detail of troops which was sent as Russian troops afforded by the Emperor to the Prince Royal, the Legion was included: this gave dissatisfaction to the Crown Prince.

The Hanoverian levies were also detailed by Russia in this paper; and it was left to His Royal Highness to appoint chiefs to these corps. All this was incorrect; for the whole of these troops, paid by Great Britain, should have been considered as a British force, furnished solely by the Prince Regent to Sweden.

The Prince Royal, to do him justice, was entirely of this opinion; and would neither appoint officers, nor make any arrangement not dictated by the British government. It was, however, now of importance that all these points should be finally determined.

With regard to the appointment of officers to the levies, it was mainly in the hands of Lieutenant-General Count Walmoden: but some check to the very great patronage this afforded seemed necessary; and the regency of Hanover, as well as the officer superintending the levies (Brigadier-General Lyon), obtained, at my instigation, proper control on this head. Baron Bremer, a very intelligent and zealous Hanoverian, was directed to reside at the head-quarters of these levies, to assist in their arrangements in the field.

Orders were at this time received for the incorporation of the Hanseatic Legion into the Hanoverian levies: the Legion would not agree to this arrangement; and declared it must be preserved, if at all, as a corps subject to be conceded to Hamburgh when required.

The same proceeding occurred with respect to the Dessau battalion; and it was. only afterwards that propositions and treaties were framed, by which their services were defined and secured.

Some abuses prevailed under the management of those whom Great Britain so largely and liberally supplied. At Stralsund, the English ordnance storekeeper was not only paying for store-houses, but actually for the disembarkation of every article of arms, whether for the Swedish or other services. It seemed so extraordinary, that the Prince Royal and the Swedes could not take upon themselves the landing of what was for their own use, that I immediately insisted on a complete and satisfactory arrangement with the Prince Royal on this subject. Other points might be mentioned; but at last every thing was landed free of expense: receipts were given for the use of any horses or wagons—whatever was for the Swedish army, they were to defray; and what went for the services of the other troops in British pay, the two governments were to settle hereafter, as might be agreed on.

Colonel Cooke was placed by my orders in charge of all the service and details before mentioned, and always went through them with indefatigable assiduity and attention. Lieutenant-General Count Walmoden and Brigadier-General Lyon communicated with me on every military exigency that arose; and measures were adopted to put the troops in an effective state to take the field. Major MacDonald, who was placed by Lord Bathurst under General Lyon, was stationed at Stralsund to assist Colonel Cooke until further orders.

The Prince Royal showed some uneasiness as to the intended regulations of command, on the arrival of Major-General Gibbs' corps, in the garrison of Stralsund. His Royal Highness was assured by me that General Gibbs would not interfere with the command of the place, so long as the Swedish general, Englebrecken, remained; and all that must be understood was, that General Gibbs was not to be interfered with in the command of his own people. The Prince Royal added, that Lieutenant-General Laendels would command the corps of observation; and that in the event of his falling back, or other accidents, General Gibbs would report to him. To this I did not conceive there would be any objection.

Having completed the inspection of the Hanoverian levies, considering the disadvantages under which they had laboured since their formation, they were in a better state than I had expected: but there was still much room for improvement. I must not forget to record here the strong interest, zeal and ability that were displayed by His Royal Highness the Duke of Cumberland, who was residing now at Strelitz, at his father-in-law's court, in aid of the military preparations in the north: he had been waiting for my arrival there, in order to accompany me both to Stralsund and on my way back to the grand head-quarters. I represented to His Royal Highness the uncertainty of the period of my stay at Stralsund: the knowledge I entertained of the Prince Royal's immediate departure for the interview of Trachenberg; and, finally, my belief that it would occasion him considerable inconvenience in travelling with me. He was therefore pleased to forego accompanying me to Stralsund, and waited for me at Strelitz, in order to proceed with me back to the grand army; where I shall hereafter have occasion to speak of His Royal Highness.

To return again to the military impressions of the Prince Royal. When I repeatedly persevered, previous to his departure, in speaking of the troops to be put under his orders, including General Winzingerode's corps, His Royal Highness seemed rather to think disparagingly of these forces, and gave me the idea that he felt events would counteract these arrangements. He said, if he had an army of 80,000 men, as stated in his letter to the Emperor of Russia, he must be independent of the grand army: to advance when he thought right; to retire when it was prudent; and that he would not commit his fate or operations to the direction of other men with other objects. In reply, I respectfully advanced that I concluded the Emperor and the King of Prussia would enter into a complete arrangement, and combine plans of operations with him, for which their meeting at Trachenberg had been concerted, than which nothing could be more advantageous to the common cause; and, if I were so fortunate as to see him on his return, I trusted to see all such arrangements completed to his satisfaction.

The Prince asked me about our treaties of concert and subsidy with Russia and Prussia. I communicated with him frankly the substance of them; and when he asked my opinion, if the armistice would be prolonged, I said I did not see how it could be so under our treaties, without the consent of England. He thought as I did on this subject. He denied that Sweden had accepted the late mediation of Austria; and while he was impressing on my mind the renewal of the war with vigour, I plainly perceived that he had no confidence in the issue of events proving fortunate for the allied cause; and if I could read into his secret thoughts, there was little desire that this should be the case.

I should not forget to mention, that the news had arrived of the division in the House of Commons on the Swedish treaty the day I conversed with the Prince Royal, as above detailed; and, notwithstanding the warmth with which I expressed my feelings, often differing entirely with His Royal Highness, he dismissed me at parting, as he received me on arriving, with two French embraces.

I feel a delicacy in adding much more here on the subject of the Prince Royal, which I should have done, if there had not been present about that period a most able English officer, *viz*. General Alexander Hope, whose mission did much to elucidate the British government on the state of affairs in this scene of action on which I was momentarily introduced. I had several conversations with the Crown Prince on his return from Trachenberg; and to judge of his intentions by his sentiments, and the manner in which he expressed himself satisfied with all that had passed, they were most favourable. The impression of Lord Wellington's success had been strong and universal; and produced ultimately, in my opinion, the recommencement of hostilities.

His Royal Highness produced as usual his map, and talked most eloquently and scientifically of the great combined operations we should be engaged in. This was all as it ought to be; but I wanted to see his army in motion; and in pressing this object, he passed me by, saying, it would not be prudent to collect his masses too early, as the enemy would be aware of their points of concentration: but he assured me that 10,000 men had marched.

Whenever the Prince Royal conversed, it was always with the greatest affability and cordiality. It is impossible to resist the fascination of his eloquent expressions, or be indifferent to his insinuating tone and manner; and when armed, as he always is, with a bottle of *Eau-de-Cologne* in one hand, and a white handkerchief in the other, inundating lavishly every thing around him with the perfume. It requires some hardihood to be quite collected, and insensible to beautiful phraseology, so as to discover the drift or solidity of the extraordinary man into whose presence you are at all times admitted, and accosted as "*Mon ami*."

To do His Royal Highness however justice, he was invariably kind and civil, particularly to me; and when I mentioned the probability of my being at his head-quarters during any interesting operations, he assured me I should always be *le bien-venu;* but at the same time distinctly told me, he never would agree in any convention or treaty to have British officers, especially general officers, placed near his person. Russia and Prussia might do so, but he had a different way of thinking on these points; thus evidently showing that he would be extremely jealous of the idea of any counsel or control. All this I took in as respectful a manner as possible.

I now determined to proceed from Strelitz to the imperial head-quarters: but before I take leave of affairs here, I shall state the cause of His Royal Highness the Duke of Cumberland's change of purpose, as to accompanying me thither. In the course of conversation with the Prince Royal, I intimated the Duke's desire to see the active operations that might take place; but that His Royal Highness's high rank and his general situation imposed difficulties in the way of arrangement. The Prince Royal listened with great interest to all I advanced; and then added, that although he should be most desirous of forwarding any views agreeable to any branch of our royal family, still that the nominations to the command of any troops in his army in British pay must entirely originate with the British government.

Owing to this communication, the Duke of Cumberland decided on repairing to the grand allied army; but to my surprise at Strelitz, after His Royal Highness had had a private audience with the Prince Royal, the former informed me that the latter had pressed on him the command of all the Hanoverian troops; saying, it was essential that one of the family should head them: that this offer opened to him a prospect of active employment; and that he was to meet the Prince Royal again at Potsdam on the 10th, when he was to hear more in detail what the Prince Royal's views were: that at present he had confined his answer to the Prince Royal, to an expression of his desire to do whatever was most consistent with the good of the common cause, and whatever the Prince Regent's government might decide upon. Now the conduct of the Prince Royal was certainly disingenuous. It arose either from a desire to remove General Walmoden, or from a wish to conciliate one of our princes, by an offer which the Prince Royal felt himself could not be arranged.

With regard to his desire of seeing General Walmoden removed, it was evident that he was not pleased with that distinguished general officer: however, I was inclined to consider that this feeling on the part of the Prince Royal was just the reason that ought. to induce me to wish the general to remain in his command; for I believed him to be an excellent, vigilant officer, and above all; devoted to the Prince Regent and to the British objects. I must remark, that the result of what passed between the two Princes was, that the Duke of Cumberland decided on remaining at Strelitz.

A singular and ludicrous anecdote occurred to me at that court, which I cannot forbear relating, as a testimonial of the hospitality and kindness of the late Duke of Mecklenburg Strelitz: a prince who was beloved and respected not only by his subjects, but by all who knew him; and who marked by a particular kindness all English visitors and residents in his states. I had ordered myself, on arriving very late at night in the town, to be driven to the inn; but being sound asleep in my carriage with my *aides-de-camp* on entering the gates, my chasseurs and orderly from the box showed my passports. I was not aware that orders had been sent from the palace to the guard-house to send my *cortège* to. the reigning Duke's brother's house in the town.

On alighting, I found myself shown into magnificent apartments, lighted up, with numerous servants, and with a grand *couvert* laid for supper. Congratulating myself with my companions on our capital inn, we proceeded to call about us, ordered and made free, precisely as if in the first Paris hotel. The wines were excellent; more and more were ordered up; a provision directed to be laid aside to carry forward on the next day's march: in short, we all went to bed in the sweetest delirium. But the consternation that followed the next morning was appalling: when awakening, I was informed that the Duke's brother was in the ante-room, waiting to know, "*Si son Excellence étoit content de sa reception.*" The ridicule attached to me for this anecdote, did not leave me during the few very happy days I spent at the delightful palace of the Duke of Mecklenburg at Strelitz, and in the most enchanting society that then embellished it.

During the stay of the Prince Royal at Mecklenburg, we had no little difficulty as to the etiquette of this small court with the two Princes. The Prince Royal, as heir to the throne of Sweden, considered that he should take the *pas*. The Duke of Cumberland most properly and rationally could not brook his blood should give way at his uncle's court to Bernadotte, much less did he incline to cede, the fair Princess who presided there. The old Duke of Mecklenburg, under these circumstances, entreated me to settle upon some plan for them to get from the saloon into the dining-room. After some reflection, I proposed that the two ladies of rank present, the Princess of Solms and the Landgravine of Darmstadt, should go out together, and that the royal Princes should follow hand in hand. This was adopted after considerable difficulty; but the Duke of Cumberland soon assumed his just rights, and took the first place by the Princess: which the Prince Royal not only perceived, but certainly resented it, by showing extreme ill-humour during the dinner.

From Strelitz the Prince Royal of Sweden repaired to Berlin, where he arrived on the night of the 24th of July, and immediately began to occupy himself with the general arrangements of the army placed under his orders. General Bulow's head-quarters were at Berlin, and Count Woronzow and some of the principal Russian general officers were also in that place. A report at this time arrived from the advanced-posts on the Elbe, which caused a considerable sensation: it stated that the enemy had collected considerable masses at Magdeburg and Wittemberg, and strengthened their advances on the Elbe; and on enquiry being made into the cause, the French general, Le

Marois, commanding at Magdeburg, and others, appeared to feign ignorance of the armistice being prolonged, and seemed by their demonstrations as if Buonaparte was preparing to strike some unexpected blow.

The fact of the enemy's concentration of 60,000 or 80,000 men being reported, orders were issued for General Bulow to assemble the greater part of his troops at Mittenwalde and Belitz to cover Berlin: the Swedish armies were to be further advanced, and the necessary measures taken to prevent any breach of treaty, if it should be attempted, on the part of the French.

The numerical forces in the neighbourhood consisted of Bulow's corps, said to be about 30,000 men, including *landwehr*; General Count Woronzow's corps, 9400 cavalry and 5000 infantry; and General Winzingerode with 12,000, chiefly infantry: to these may be added, the corps on the Lower Elbe.

The Prince Royal now received a letter from General Tauenstein before Stettin, pressing very strongly for the positive orders to assault that place, having no doubt of its immediate capture; observing also on the advantages of liberating his corps from its blockade. The Prince assured me that he should not delay sending him complete powers to act when the moment arrived; but it did not seem quite so clear when, in His Royal Highness's opinion, that would be. The accounts from Dresden now mentioned Buonaparte's extreme rage at the news from Spain. Every one was afraid to refer to the subject with him: at one instant he declared eternal war against England, and then more calmly he would revert to a pacific arrangement. The advice of his most confidential people, it is said, was for peace; and risings in the interior of France urged it.

The *état-major* of the Prince Royal of Sweden's army was at this period arranged; and it was settled that General Baron Adlercreutz should be chief of the staff; Baron Taverst to be employed for the business of the *chancellerie;* and Count Löwenhehn for more active duties with the Prince Royal. Officers from the different corps, selected by their chiefs, were to assist in the general arrangements under the above chiefs.

On the 27th, intelligence arrived from the grand head-quarters at Peterswalde, informing the Prince Royal that Austria was much satisfied with the consent given for the prolongation of the armistice. It then stated that Napoleon desired that the commissioners sent to his head-quarters should proceed with the arrangements that had been agreed upon; but Napoleon accompanied this communication, by requiring that French officers should be sent to the fortresses charged to superintend the supplies of provisions, and that a return should be furnished for 50,000 men and 6000 horses: numbers very considerably superior to the garrisons, and to what, had hitherto been provided under the stipulations of the armistice.

The Emperor of Russia thought himself peremptorily called upon to resist this demand; and the language held in reply by the French was, that Buonaparte would not ratify the prolongation of the armistice, but would recommence hostilities immediately if his demands were rejected. The Duke of Vicenza had not proceeded to Prague as was expected; and since Count Narbonne's arrival at that city, up to the 22nd, not the least step had been taken to enter upon the business of the negotiations. It was then calculated, that allowing for the time of His Imperial Majesty's answer to reach Dresden, and the rejoinder to be received, added to the six days necessary for the Denunciation of the truce, the 2nd of August would be the earliest period when hostilities could recommence.

Austria was extremely mortified at this new instance of unreasonable conduct on the part of France; and Count Metternich declared most positively, that any neglect of their mediation, or an attempt to infringe what had been agreed on, would be followed by an immediate declaration of war on their part. It was not very probable that Buonaparte would prematurely and injudiciously force Austria to decide against him; and indeed it was more likely that the French Ruler was merely trying how far he could, by manoeuvres and artful management, accomplish his objects. The Emperor of Russia, however, remained firm; and the Prince Royal was pressed to forward his arrangements, so that the allies might not be taken unprepared. The plan of the campaign had been settled at the meeting at Trachenberg; and the Emperor was already taking measures for the immediate movement of his troops. Meanwhile, Buonaparte proceeded himself to Luckau, and was there on the 22nd, where a very large force had been assembled, with the view, as was supposed, of striking an immediate blow against the Prince Royal; in which event the Emperor of Russia was immediately to move forward.

The arrangements of the Prince Royal, made in consequence of this communication from head-quarters, were to assemble General Bulow at Mittenwalde; the head of General Winzingerode's corps was to arrive also in the neighbourhood of that place on the 1st of August; General Woronzow was to assemble on the right; and General Czernicheff was to move forward towards Spandau and its vicinity. The Swedes were to advance, so that their head-quarters were to be established in the centre: the Russians and Prussians forming the flanks of this army; and orders had been sent to the officer commanding at the advanced-posts, to call upon the enemy to declare positively in what manner they regarded the armistice. The second Swedish divisions, from Rostock and Greifswald, were now marching forward; but the Wismar division had not yet been put in motion. The Swedes were wonderfully healthy. In the Rostock division of 9400 men, there were only thirty-one sick. The second division amounted to about 21,000 men. General Walmoden's corps was also now advancing. It was feared there would be difficulties here about provisions; but this evidently arose only from want of arrangement.

During the period of the suspension of hostilities, the belligerents on both sides occupied themselves in bringing forward all their resources to re-open the campaign with effect; but it became generally evident, that Napoleon only consented to the prolongation of the armistice with a view of detaching Austria, by manoeuvres and negotiation, from the common cause of Europe.

The Duke of Vicenza (Caulaincourt) arrived on the 28th of

July at Prague, but not invested with such full powers as could give any hopes of a favourable, issue to the affairs pending; and the 10th of August, the day of declaring the armistice at an end, now approached, without the parties having advanced a step in the principal objects of their negotiations.

The general *apperçû* of Napoleon's forces and dispositions at this crisis was as follows:—The first corps, under General Vandamme, was assembling at Dresden from Magdeburg; Marshal Augereau, collected in Saxony; Marshal Gouvion St. Cyr, at Freyberg: all these united composed a force of not less than 350,000 men in Silesia and Saxony. Murat arrived on the 14th of July at Dresden, to take the command of the cavalry, in the place of Marshal Bessières.

The disposition of the grand allied army may next be briefly sketched as follows: General Blucher commanded in chief his army of 70,000 men; composed of General D'Yorck's corps, and two Russian corps under Lieutenant-General Count Langeron. General Gniesenau was chief of the staff of this army: an officer whose distinguished military reputation and high fame in Europe are established on too firm a basis to require any eulogy from me. The remainder of the grand army was composed of, 1st. the corps of General Count Wittgenstein, under whom were Prince Gortchakoff, Prince Eugene of Wirtemburg, and Count Pahlen; 2nd. the Prussian corps; 3rd. the Russian reserves, and the Russian and Prussian guards, under the Grand-duke Constantine and General Miloradovitch, then forming 80,000, which now proceeded to join the Austrian army in Bohemia: making with them a total of about 200,000 men, under the command in chief of Prince Schwartzenberg. General Radezky was named chief of the staff to this army: the head-quarters of which were now stationed at Prague; and on the 18th of August the Emperor of Russia and King of Prussia arrived there.

In addition to the illustrious warriors who graced this vast theatre of action, particular mention must be made of the celebrated French General, Moreau, who now arrived from New

York, and. adopted the title of *aide-de-camp* to the Emperor Alexander, to oppose his former companions in arms, under the despot who now ruled them.

War was declared by Austria against France on the morning of the 11th of August, in conformity with the intentions announced in M. de Metternich's despatch to Count Stadion; and the French ministers received their passports, accompanied by a note, in which it was declared that, no answer having been returned to the Emperor's ultimatum, the congress was at an end; and that His Imperial Majesty joined his forces to those of the allies to extort peace. It appeared that the Austrian minister's ultimatum was made known to M. de Caulaincourt on the 8th; and that he was permitted to take a copy of it.

In a long conversation which ensued between them, General Caulaincourt told M. de Metternich that if he were Buonaparte, he would accept, without hesitation, the Austrian proposals (the nature of which I need not enter into); but that he was without full powers, and did not think that they would be accepted by the Emperor. A courier was despatched with them to Dresden the moment when the conference ended. Although hostilities were not to commence until six days after the 10th, as originally stipulated, nevertheless, from the latter period, Austria became a co-belligerent; and even if Napoleon had now changed his mind, his propositions must have been addressed to the allied powers, the mediation being at an end.

It is difficult to describe the enthusiasm generally created by the Austrian declaration of war. The spirit of the army also was at the highest pitch. When the three allied Sovereigns met at Prague, it excited a proud sensation in the breast of such British subjects as witnessed the event: for the persevering and energetic conduct of their own country, under the wise administration of the Prince Regent's government, and, above all, the glorious exploits of British arms in Spain, had ultimately, and I may say exclusively, brought into action a complete and efficient alliance against the ambition of France, and the tyranny of its chief; affording rational hopes of a glorious termination of the contest.

The recently dubious conduct of Austria having thus terminated, she nobly and magnanimously brought to bear her great and commanding advantages in point of numerical forces; and England, with her wonted generosity, was the first to acknowledge her sincerity, and restore to her her confidence.

The allied army now continued its march into Bohemia. The treaties of subsidy and concert between England and the allies having been signed and settled at Reichenbach, I will not further allude to them, nor to any separate or secret conventions made between any. of the powers: suffice it to say, that the alliance was preserved with that solid union, good faith, and complete understanding, which promised, and finally produced a successful result.

CHAPTER 7

Dresden

On the 15th of August I proceeded to Landeck, where His Prussian Majesty's head-quarters then were, for the ratification of the treaties before alluded to, when intelligence was received that the French had crossed the line of demarcation on the roads to Landshut, Jauer, and Neumarkt. General Blucher took up a position at Schweidnitz; and General Sachen had orders to occupy Breslau. It was stated to have been said by the French general, Girard, at Lowenberg, that a very large army was to move on Berlin. Davoust was advancing with the corps assembled round Magdeburg. The troops at Leipzic, Dessau, and throughout Lusatia, were now also in motion.

Private accounts gave the detail of the French army as divided into thirteen corps: the 4th, which was in cantonments near Sprottau, marched thence on the 12th of August towards Greseberg. It was supposed that this corps would pass the Oder, and proceed along the right bank of that river towards Kustrin. The corps of Ney, Lauriston, and Bertrand, were in the neighbourhood of Lignitz. The 5th corps had been encamped hitherto near Goldberg, but had marched on Lignitz. The 6th corps left Bunzlau on the 12th for the same destination. The 11th corps marched on the same day from Lowenberg towards Lignitz; which place had been strongly fortified. Another corps, encamped at Greiffenberg, was not yet put in motion. The French park of artillery at Bunzlau was sent to Lignitz. Sebastiani had arrived at Haynau. The 2nd corps consisted chiefly of nineteen regiments of cavalry, which were however weak, not having more than 300 or 400 in each regiment.

It was believed that the French troops assembled upon the Katzbach were not intended to act offensively against Silesia, but were to enter Bohemia through the Riesen-Gebürge, in concert with another French *corps d'armée,* to penetrate from Zittau: thus breaking in on the line of march of the Russians and Prussians on Prague, and turning the positions of the Austrians on the banks of the Elbe.

It was intimated that the Emperor of Russia was disposed to place the whole of the army of Barclay de Tolly under Prince Schwartzenberg; and General Moreau was to be requested by both Emperors to assist the Austrian field-marshal. His Royal Highness the Duke of Cumberland now arrived from Strelitz, having learnt that His Prussian Majesty was at Landeck, on his way to Prague, whither His Royal Highness determined to proceed.

When I found the head-quarters were moving to Prague, I immediately applied to Count Stadion for passports for His Royal Highness. The Count declined giving passports until he had communicated with his Emperor on his arrival at Prague, but promised to send his answer to Landeck. The King of Prussia left Landeck for Prague on the 16th; and as I received no answer from Count Stadion, I arranged with His Royal Highness that he should remain at Landeck, whilst I went forward and prepared for his reception at Prague.

I found, on my arrival there, that no point had been so much canvassed as that of the chief command. The Emperor Alexander nobly aspired to the title of a military captain: his personal intrepidity, perseverance, and firmness, entitled him to great consideration in this respect; and my impression is, had Austria consented to place the whole of the allied forces under his orders, there would have been a unity of design, productive of beneficial results. The King of Prussia was not disinclined to this opinion. I do not mean to advance that the Emperor did not reserve some advice and assistance in command, but with General Moreau and the council the chief direction might have been well placed in His Imperial Majesty's hands; and considering the temper of the Russians, if they became dissatisfied, it did not appear the least advisable arrangement.

Austria naturally wished, from the prominent part she had taken, to be the arbiter of an universal peace, and have the glory of her own work; and she was therefore desirous of an Austrian for the military command. A certain degree of jealousy of Russia on political points operated against her yielding to the Emperor's wishes; and, above all, the arrival of Moreau created discontent amongst the Austrians, and was perhaps the principal reason why the command in chief was not offered to the Emperor Alexander. At this period, Prince Schwartzenberg sent the orders of the day secretly to Barclay de Tolly; but they were promulgated to the Russians as if emanating from their own general. Generals Moreau and (afterwards) Jomenil, both at the head-quarters of the Emperor Alexander, pressed strongly for His Imperial Majesty's assuming the chief command. This was natural; as their own influence would be thereby more conspicuous in the eyes of Europe, in conducting the operations with an Emperor of Russia as commander-in-chief than an Austrian Prince, whose character was established as an excellent and experienced officer.

Next to the command in chief there was renewed contention regarding the Breslau central commission, and the occupation of the territories wrested from the enemy. This last point had become (owing perhaps to Baron Stein's presence and want of employment) a topic of much deliberation. Austria did not like to agree to such an arrangement as was formed at Breslau: it remained then to be seen whether a new one might not be concocted more agreeable to all parties.

There was incessant debate relative to the immediate offensive or defensive operations among the great military chiefs in the respective armies. Austria thinking her troops young, preferred waiting Buonaparte's attacks; but Russia and Prussia overruled this caution; and the campaign was pressed on the general plan, as laid down at Trachenberg: a reference to which, and to the map, with what I have described, will convey, I trust, a general idea of the operations.

It may not be wholly uninteresting to revert here to the general observations made at Prague upon the rupture of recent negotiations. Count Narbonne left Prague on the 14th; Caulaincourt remained till the 16th, and instead of answering direct the Austrian ultimatum, made some new propositions. It was however intimated to Caulaincourt that he could not with propriety remain in Prague, where the Emperor of Russia and King of Prussia were hourly expected; consequently he withdrew to a country-house in the neighbourhood, where he stayed until his overtures were rejected. He was very urgent to obtain an audience of the Emperor of Russia; but that was positively interdicted. The purport of those propositions was rumoured to be; 1st. Napoleon was willing to cede the duchy of Warsaw, provided the King of Saxony received elsewhere an indemnification of 500,000 souls for this cession; 2nd. Prussia receiving Poland, was there-out to provide for that indemnification. Buonaparte, also agreed to yield Dantzic and its territory after a certain period, with the express condition that the works were to be completely destroyed. He consented, likewise, to restore the Illyrian provinces, with the exception of Istria; and some added Fiume and Trieste. These were the outlines of the last offer.

Austria was reported to reply, in answer, that her powers had ceased as a mediator; but she consented to submit the proposals to the allies, by whom they were formally rejected, as wholly inadmissible. Caulaincourt then departed, but his conduct was very moderate; and if it had depended on him, the terms of Austria would probably have been accepted. Narbonne, in all his communications to his Emperor, before Caulaincourt's arrival, expressed his firm conviction that Austria would never act hostilely, but only threatened to accomplish her own objects. Caulaincourt suddenly arrived at Prague, and positively ascertained Count Metternich's determination to declare war after the 10th, and saw that Narbonne had been deceived. His consternation was then great; and courier upon courier was despatched to Buonaparte.

Buonaparte was much urged by the Empress and Senate at Mayence to make peace on any terms. His answer is reported to have been, "*Tout ou rien:*" meaning to preserve all his conquests, or try the chance of war. His language always indicated confidence in his own genius and physical strength. He had, according to the most accurate accounts, above 300,000 men on the right bank of the Rhine. The Austrian force was now computed at 160,000 men in Bohemia, 30,000 in the valley of the Danube, and 50,000 on the banks of the Saave.

The command was at length confided to Prince Schwartzenberg. The two Emperors were to remain at or near the head-quarters of their respective armies, and the King of Prussia with those of the Emperor Alexander. Little was hitherto positively known of Buonaparte's intentions. He went from Dresden to Bautzen, and thence proceeded towards Gorlitz. Many augured that he would commence his operations against the Prince Royal of Sweden; whilst others said such a measure would be too hazardous, and conjectured that he would retire behind the Elbe, and enter Bohemia by the roads of Peterswalde and Sebastiansberg.

Prince Paul Esterhazy was now named by the Austrian government for the embassy to England; and intelligence arrived from home that the Earl of Aberdeen was appointed His Britannic Majesty's ambassador to the Emperor of Austria, and was on his way to the head-quarters of the army.

Previous to noticing the arrival of a British ambassador, I cannot help doing justice to the noble sentiments which were unofficially expressed to me by Count Metternich, at an interview I had with him at Prague, at this interesting epoch. He began by detailing the course he had pursued since he had taken the reins of government. He found the finances of the Austrian monarchy in a state of insolvency, and the despondency of its subjects at the lowest ebb. He arranged the marriage of the

Archduchess, to give his country the first ascending step from the abyss of misfortune into which it had fallen: never intending, when existence and power were again secured, that the marriage should direct or influence the politics of the cabinet of Vienna. He persevered in his course, he added; and deaf to the opinions and entreaties of all, he would not stir, notwithstanding the most urgent solicitations. When the Russians were on the Memel, he told them to come to the Oder and to the Elbe; and when Austria was ready, she should act. He was universally suspected; but he had only a single object in view—to raise his country, and through her reascendancy give peace to the world. He said he knew that the British cabinet had always doubted him: he did not wonder at it; but that he hoped he should at length stand justified in their opinion, and that of posterity. He wished for nothing so much as to establish the most cordial relations between the two courts, which he hoped would be effected without delay. And here I am bound to add, that from this period to the death of that statesman who then presided over our foreign affairs, there never was any serious divergence of sentiment on any great European question. The last letter from Bassano to Metternich was received previous to the above conversation. This despatch began and ended in an offensive tone, stating that Austria *avoit prostitué* the character of a mediator, for that to Bassano's knowledge she had been long united with the allies. Nevertheless, the extreme and urgent desire of the Emperor for peace, prompted him to make another offer; that some neutral point should be fixed for negotiators to assemble even during the progress of hostilities. The deliberate answer returned by Metternich was, that the allies would never refuse to listen to negotiations for peace, provided England and Sweden consented, and assisted at the negotiations, of which the propositions of the 16th of May were to form the basis.

The Austrian army was reviewed by the three Sovereigns near Schlan, six miles from Prague; on the 19th of August. It was a most sublime military spectacle; ninety-one battalions of infantry and fifty squadrons of cavalry defiled before their Majesties. The battalions were about 800 strong; and the infantry amounted to something more than 70,000 men. The cavalry present did not exceed 7000: the remainder of it and light troops formed the advanced-guard, consisting of three divisions, about 30,000 men; these were in advance, and not inspected.

The composition of this army was magnificent, although I perceived a great many recruits: still the system that reigned throughout, and the military air that marked the soldier, especially the Hungarian, must ever fix it in my recollection as the finest army of the continent. The Russians may possess a more powerful soldiery, of greater physical strength and hardihood, but they cannot equal the Austrians in discipline or military *maintien*. The general officers of the latter are of a superior class; and the army has a fine *ton* in all its departments. To see one Austrian and one Hungarian regiment, is to see the army: for a complete equality and uniformity reign throughout; and they have no constant changes of uniform and equipment: their movement was beautifully correct, and the troops seemed formed in the most perfect order. Twenty-four squadrons of cuirassiers and sixteen of hussars deserved to be particularly noticed. Among the former were the cuirassiers of the Emperor, who were presented with new standards; and the three Sovereigns nailed in unison their standards to the pole in front of the army, as a token of their firm alliance. This was a most exhilarating moment. The hussars are peculiar to this army in their style and appearance: in vain do others imitate them; and it is but strict justice to admit, that they are incomparable, I may say matchless.

The artillery seemed less well appointed; and the ammunition-wagons and horses for their guns and train were of an inferior description to those of the Russians (whose artillery horses are perfect); but the officers and men are scientific and expert, and the artillery is not to be judged of by its appearance.

From the military reports now current, it appeared that the grand allied and French armies were making two conversions, as it were— the allied armies wheeling from Bohemia into Saxony, by the passes of Peterswalde and Komotau; and the French forces withdrawing from Silesia were turning towards Bohemia, and collecting on the right bank of the Elbe. These demonstrations denoted the approach of a serious conflict; and it was argued that if it should occur, the allies would probably engage with their front towards the Elbe; and the enemy having it in their rear, would offer a tremendous resistance; and that if Napoleon acted upon military principles, he would retire to the left bank of the Elbe, and rather give battle on that side.

The French forces having commenced their retreat on the 15th from Grünberg and Freystadt in Silesia, abandoning the line of demarcation, the allies immediately moved forwards. General Blucher's corps, as has been before observed, from its position at Schweidnitz, occupied successively the points evacuated by the enemy. General Sacken's corps entered Breslau; and on the 18th the greater part of Silesia, and particularly the towns of Parchwitz, Lignitz, and Goldberg, were abandoned. General Blucher had his advanced-posts at Lowenberg.

From these movements, it was expected that the interesting intelligence would soon arrive of the French having wholly retired into Saxony; but while the retreat was continued here, an effort was preparing in another quarter. By the reports up to the 17th from Berlin all seemed quiet in that direction, the Prince Royal having his head-quarters at Potsdam: thus it was apparent that the grand armies, on the frontiers of Bohemia and Saxony, would first Come in contact.

The enemy's great assemblage of troops was at Zittau, Grossenhayn, and Chemnitz. From the former place they moved a corps on the 17th against the Austrian general, Neuperg, who was at Friedland with about 25,000 men. General Regnier and Poniatowski's corps made this movement. The Austrian general, as the enemy's approach was sudden and unexpected, retired. The great operations of the allied armies were now in activity on the principal roads to Leipsic, by the passes of Peterswalde and Komotau. The Russian and Prussian armies were proceeding by the former, namely, the corps under Count Wittgenstein and General Miloradovitch, with the reserve of the guards and cavalry; General Kleist being on the right, and the Austrian army occupying the left. The advances approached near St. Sebastiansberg and Lobositz, thus pressing on the enemy's flank; and as he had delayed his retreat so long, according to all reasonable calculation he must have severely suffered from it.

Buonaparte reviewed his guards at Leipsic on the 10th (called 30,000. men); and his having withdrawn them from Dresden, indicated that he meditated his great concentration near the former place. The Emperor of Russia moved his head-quarters on the 21st to Walditz; the Emperor of Austria to Lahn; and the King of Prussia followed on the 22nd.

Mention has been made of the French general, Jomenil: he had come over from the enemy, and was an officer celebrated for his military writings. He was appointed (I believe) a lieutenant-general in His Imperial Majesty's service; and his experience and knowledge were no doubt of the highest importance in the approaching crisis. In a conversation I had with this officer, he stated Napoleon's force to be very strong; and, above all, that the exertions he made in France to re-equip and re-organize a great mass of artillery were quite astonishing. He added, that his contemptuous conduct had deprived him of every sincere friend he ever had; and that he lived in the army only from the fear entertained of him, and the ability he possessed, which his most inveterate enemy was compelled to admit. This opinion of his talents, from such a source, was at any rate interesting.

It was no ordinary satisfaction, at this juncture, that intelligence reached the allied army from Paris, dated the 12th, stating that Lord Wellington had completely defeated Soult, near Roncesvalles, on the 28th of July. The French General had retired first on St. Jean de Luz, and afterwards to St. Jean Pied de Port, near Bayonne; and Lord Wellington was following him, up to the 31st, when the accounts came away. All Soult's baggage, artillery, and 15,000 prisoners, were said to be taken. St. Sebastian's, and it was believed also Pampeluna, had both fallen. On the Mediterranean side, Suchet was retiring from Barcelona towards Perpignan; and was so annoyed by the British fleet, added to his general position, that the greatest apprehensions were entertained at Paris for the safety of his army. It was added, from the best authority, that Soult had written, that unless Buonaparte could send him 50,000 fresh troops that had never been in Spain, it would be quite impossible to maintain any footing in the Peninsula. Intelligence arrived also from Toulon and other quarters of French disasters; and the greatest panic prevailed in the south of France, and families were flying in all directions. Such were the gratifying details circulated through the allied army; and the glory of the above achievements could be equalled only by their opportune occurrence.

To return to the military operations before us. While the main Russian army under General Barclay de Tolly, including the corps of Wittgenstein and Miloradovitch, and the Prussian corps of General Kleist, together with the whole of the Austrian army, were to act offensively from Bohemia, under the chief command of Prince Schwartzenberg,—General Blucher's *corps d'armée,* composed of a division of Prussians under D'Yorck, Generals Sachen's and Langeron's Russian divisions were to move from Silesia on Lusatia, and threaten the enemy in front. General Blucher was directed to avoid any general action, especially against superior numbers.

In conformity with these instructions, General Blucher advanced, on the 20th, in three columns, from Lignitz, Goldberg, and Jauer, on Bunzlau and Lowenberg; General Sachen's corps moved to the right on Bunzlau; D'Yorck's in the centre, and Langeron's on the left. The enemy abandoned Bunzlau, destroying their works and magazines. General Blucher's force advanced to the Bober, where they were attacked, on the 21st, by the enemy under Marshal Ney, and by the 6th corps under Marmont. These moved in great force on Bunzlau, Lowenberg, and Lahn; and a very serious affair took place. It was reported that Buonaparte also was in person in the field, and that he opposed 100,000 men to the force of Blucher.

The allied troops contested the ground with great bravery; but as General Blucher had received orders to avoid a general engagement, he withdrew in the best order to Haynau, Siegendort, Horschberg, and behind the Katzbach. The loss of General Blucher in this affair was reported to be 3000 men: he took, however, several prisoners. The enemy suffered considerably; but General Blucher deemed it expedient to fall back with his army on Jauer.

Having now detailed the first movements of the army of Silesia, I return to the grand armies on the side of Bohemia, which, on the 20th and 21st, commenced passing the frontiers. Count Wittgenstein's and General Kleist's columns proceeded by the pass of Peterswalde, and the Austrians by Komotau. On the 22nd, Count Wittgenstein's corps fell in with the enemy, and had a very serious affair with them near Timscht.

The enemy encountered the allies on the frontiers; but, although they endeavoured to defend every inch of ground, they were beaten back from all their positions towards Dresden. The different columns of the allied armies *débouchéd* from the mountains, and passed at such concerted points as would probably have operated fatally on the enemy, if the arrangements, as planned, had been completely, carried into effect. But the eagerness of the troops to push on and engage, brought, on the morning of the 22nd, the right corps into action before the other columns were up.

The French were commanded by Gouvion St. Cyr, and their force consisted of upwards of 15,000 men: they were supported by their troops from Koningstein, and by the camp of Lillienstein, which amounted to at least 6000 men, under General Bonnet. After a very sharp action, Count Wittgenstein drove the enemy before him, and took 3 or 400 prisoners. The French had also a vast number killed and wounded: the loss of the allies was not severe.

After this action, the enemy retired into Koningstein and his entrenched camp, and also into the various works he had thrown up round Dresden. The allies pressed forwards on every side; and the grand army now manoeuvred to encircle Dresden.

On the 26th, the hussar regiment of Grodno, belonging

to Wittgenstein's corps, had a very brisk engagement close to Dresden, in which they took four guns and some howitzers. The advanced-guards of the Russians, Prussians, and Austrians, encamped that night on the heights above Dresden.

On the morning of the 26th, the French abandoned the ground which they had occupied, in advance of Dresden, called the Grossen-Garten, and withdrew into the suburbs and their different redoubts. As no official reports were made out, every hour being fraught with events, details may in many points be imperfect; but certainly the history of war no where offers any period like the one before us, in which two such immense armies stood committed to such bold operations. If Buonaparte maintained his positions in advance, it was evidently with an intention of forcing a passage into Bohemia, and adopting that plan of campaign against the allies which they so successfully foiled and imitated. The possession of Koningstein afforded him a facility of passing the Elbe at that place, moving into the mountains of Bohemia, and acting against the pivot of the force with which he was contending: on the other hand, such an attempt was sure to be hazardous, and if it failed destructive.

Napoleon felt at this period the absolute necessity of his presence on the Elbe, in front of the grand army. He arrived, therefore, on the 23rd, with Marshal Ney, leaving Marshal MacDonald in command of the army opposed to Blucher in Silesia, consisting of the 3rd, 5th, and 11th corps; and on the 24th, Marmont's corps, the 6th, and General Latour Maubourg's cavalry, also received orders to return to Dresden.

Two Westphalian regiments of hussars, commanded by Colonel Hammerstein, now came over from the enemy, and were eager to be incorporated with the allies, and take their revenge for the misery the French had inflicted upon their country.

The enemy having on the morning of the 27th abandoned the ground surrounding Dresden, called the Grossen-Garten, and having withdrawn into their works and into the suburbs of the town, it was deemed expedient, as its possession had become of considerable importance, to make an attack with a large force upon the place. During the morning of the 26th, in the attack of the gardens, Count Wittgenstein's and General Kleist's light corps, on the right of the town, experienced some loss; and indeed the enemy had so much improved by art the defences around it, that the capture by assault was evidently an enterprise of considerable difficulty. The most important of the fortifications of the city, were three strong redoubts on the left bank of the Elbe; one before the Freyberg, and the others before the Plauen and Dippoldiswald gates. The troops moved to the attack at three o'clock in the afternoon: Count Wittgenstein's corps, in three columns, on the right of the Grossen-Garten; while General Kleist's moved one column through these gardens, and two on the left. The left column was headed by Prince Augustus of Prussia.

Three divisions of Austrians, at the same time, on the left of the town, under the immediate direction of Count Colloredo and Prince Maurice of Lichtenstein, joined the Prussians; these formed the centre attack, the Russians being on their left. A tremendous cannonade commenced this grand operation: the batteries being planted in a circular form round the town. The effect was magnificent. The fine buildings of Dresden were soon enveloped in smoke and flame; and the troops moved forward in the most perfect order to the assault. They approached on all sides close to the town; and the Austrians took an advanced redoubt, with eight guns, in the most undaunted and gallant style. The work was of the strongest, description, situated about sixty yards from the main wall; and nothing could surpass the gallantry with which it was stormed.

The enemy fled from it only to shelter themselves behind new defences, manning the thick walls of the town, in which it was impossible, without a long and continued fire of heavy artillery, to make a breach. The French, with the aid of the means of resistance which a strong town affords, now held in check the troops which had so gallantly carried and entered the outworks. The night was fast approaching; and the enemy now attempted to make a sortie with all his guards, amounting at least to 30,000 men, in order to separate the allied troops, and take each wing in flank and rear. This was immediately perceived; and as it appeared evident that it was not practicable to carry the place that night, orders were sent to draw off the troops, which returned to their several encampments. Prince Maurice of Lichtenstein adopted an admirable disposition on the side where the enemy made their sortie, and by which all disorder was avoided. This enterprise, in proportion to its importance, was one of great difficulty.

No troops could have signalised themselves more than those of the allies engaged in this day's combat; and if it had been physically possible to have carried the place under the circumstances, they would have accomplished it. Unfortunately, there were no breaches practicable for the troops to enter; and the artillery, although brought up at the close of the evening to within one hundred paces of the wall, was unable to batter it, or make any material impression. From the best calculation, the loss of the allies was under 5000 men; and in this attack the Austrians chiefly suffered. The sortie of the enemy was a prelude to a more general engagement, which took place the following morning, on the 27th. Buonaparte having a strong force in Dresden, at least 130,000 men, determined on attacking the allies, who occupied a very extended position on the surrounding heights. The enemy had great advantages in their disposition for attack. Dresden, bristled with guns, was in their rear; while their communications were not intersected. If they made an impression, they could follow it up; and in case of failure, could withdraw in security. The allied troops, if victorious, could not pursue under the guns of the fortress. One of the worst days ever seen added materially to the embarrassment of the allies, who had arrived at their positions by rapid marches, through bad roads and defiles; and their supplies of every kind it was difficult, if not impossible, to bring up.

Availing himself of the advantages above stated, Napoleon displayed an immense number of field-pieces on the morning of the 27th; and heavy cannonading on both sides formed the chief feature of the battle. Charges in various parts were made, as well with Russian and Prussian, as Austrian cavalry, and they distinguished themselves highly; but the main bodies of the infantry in both armies did not come into contact. The weather was hazy; the rain incessant. The action was sustained at all points under the heaviest disadvantages; and towards the middle of the day a catastrophe occurred, which awakened more than ordinary sensibility and regret throughout the allied army.

General Moreau, while in earnest conversation with the Emperor of Russia on the progress of operations, had both his legs carried off by a cannon-shot (the ball piercing the body of his horse). Thus the good cause and the profession of arms sustained a heavy loss. It was impossible not deeply to lament the hard fate of an amiable man and gallant soldier, whose talents, patriotism, and courage were doubted and decried, and his life cut short by his own countrymen. The enemy continued his efforts on the position of the allies till the evening, when finding he could make no impression, the action ceased.

The battle cost the allies 6000 or 7000 men; the enemy must have suffered more. In one charge of Russian cavalry against infantry and a battery, a great number of prisoners were taken, though the guns were not brought off.

CHAPTER 8

Battle at Toplitz & Kulm

The general difficulties which the allied army had to encounter, owing to their failure on Dresden (by no means anticipated), now became apparent; not only from the large force opposed to them, but from the opinion that Napoleon would pass a considerable body of troops across the Elbe at Koningstein and Pirna, to possess himself of the passes in the rear of the Abur: these and other considerations operated in forming the resolution to withdraw the allied armies behind the Eger. Orders for this purpose were issued on the evening of the 28th; and the army commenced its retrograde movement in different columns. The enemy did not follow vigorously; but the roads through the passes were extremely bad, and the difficulty of getting the artillery and baggage through them was extreme.

It was impossible not to regret that so fine and numerous an army, perfectly entire in all its parts, should have been reduced to the necessity of making any retreat; as miscalculations might be made on the event, and the enemy might suppose he had gained essential advantage. But it was certain the allied army was as eager as ever to meet the enemy; the same determined spirit existed: though a partial change of operations might be deemed necessary, the general result of the campaign was in no degree doubted. The enemy's force was not diminished on the side of Lusatia, from his efforts on the Elbe up to the 23rd, as he again attacked General Blucher on that day in great force, who retired upon Jauer; of,which I shall speak elsewhere. During these events, the Austrian corps of General Neuberg had also advanced in the direction of Zittau for some days past. In the bold game both armies were now playing, Buonaparte had this great advantage—there was one mind directing one force; whereas the allies, with national jealousies ever arising, had to encounter great impediments. In these first operations, Wittgenstein was much censured for having engaged his columns too soon, and advanced too rapidly, before the other corps *debouchéing* from the mountains had got more into the rear of the enemy, advancing on the frontiers. The attack on the town of Dresden was boldly attempted: yet I could not but feel surprised that the Austrians, so well versed in war, should have moved their columns of attack up to the glacis of a town in which no breach had been previously made, and without scaling-ladders, or means of accomplishing any lodgement when the troops should arrive at the fosse.

The bravery of the troops was unquestionable: but the previous plan was ill-digested; and the necessary preparations for ensuring success were, I conclude, confided to some unskilful subordinates. The assault was certainly commenced at too late an hour in the evening, as it became twilight the moment the troops arrived at the ramparts; whilst the enemy had perfect light to observe the directions in which the different columns approached. Now the desideratum in similar attacks is to arrive concealed at the points where the troops are to mount, and to wait for light to begin the work. When the Austrians carried the advanced works, they were tediously exposed to a galling fire from the enemy, owing, to the want of their pioneers to destroy the palisades, through which they could not penetrate. However, nothing ever surpassed their gallantry. When the sortie was made as it was growing dark, there was some disorder; and I was fortunate enough, with Prince John of Lichtenstein and my *aide-de-camp*, to gallop through a French column; and we were in rear of their batteries before we were aware of our danger. In this extremity, our only chance was to dash through, trusting to our being undiscovered in the *mêlée*, which, in the obscurity of the evening, occurred. The brunt of this attack chiefly fell upon the Austrian army. The most that can be said of this battle is, that the rain was intense and the mist general; the positions were remote, and the intervals between the corps of the army so extensive, that at one position little or nothing could be distinguished of what was going on at another. Buonaparte, on its immediate flank, below the extensive heights that surrounded Dresden, with his army collected, moved it with facility, and preserved it compact. His cavalry, under Murat and Latour Maubourg, was always available, and of the highest service. The allies extended, and occupying the larger circle, distant from their supplies, having bad roads in their rear, and sadly oppressed by the weather, laboured under every disadvantage.

The failure of the attack on the city was the first misfortune. Why it was not bombarded by all the mortars in the army, and why such insufficient measures were taken to ascertain the real state and improved strength of it before any attempt was made, remains for others to explain. If one asked the reason why Dresden was attacked under such circumstances, the answer received was, that being before the town, it was necessary to do something. Much of the great evil resulted from the difficult and perplexing state in which the command still seemed to lay. Schwartzenberg nominally issued orders, and was undoubtedly chief; but the Emperor, all along eager for the glory of generalship, acted as a man who still aimed at and desired to obtain his favourite object. His own partisans and officers depreciated Schwartzenberg's military abilities. The latter was called upon for explanations of all orders he gave, when he should have been thinking of future directions. Possibly only half his own plans, with half those of the Emperor's, who was aided by Moreau until his wound disabled him, were adopted; while Jomenil, who was also in council, filled up the measure of embarrassments.

No one would own the project that had just failed; and each diverted the storm of blame from himself. The error was in grasping at the object too precipitately, and passing the defiles before means were collected to ensure the subsistence of the army; and before it was perfectly determined what the army was to accomplish when it came before Dresden, already entrenched and made a respectable fortress. Buonaparte could never have annoyed our movements, by acting on our right flank, if we had not been too far and two heedlessly committed. The strong fortress of Theresienstadt, the works on the frontiers, and the Austrian corps of General Neuperg, who had been left to guard the defiles, gave ample security for the right; and the most feasible movement, as I conceive, was for all the corps *debouchéing* from the left to have made a detour, so as to have appeared before Dresden previous to our right flank having forced the enemy from his forward positions near the passes. By thus proceeding, our right would have been always secure and respected; our pivot, as it were, unmolested; and the force that arrived before Dresden would have compassed all we had in view, until we could see further into the intentions of the enemy.

The allies should never have lost sight of the five very strong and important fortresses (no doubt fully supplied with every article of war) which Buonaparte had on the Elbe—Hamburgh, Magdeburg, Wittemberg, Torgau, and Dresden—which gave him the facility of being *à cheval* on that river in every point. Like a snake, he could twist and turn himself, making front every way; having his fortresses, his depots, and his means at his back. The numbers he possessed enabled him to meet the allies in any quarter; and, above all, he had advantages that existed in the unity of action of his single word and undivided command.

Both the movements beyond the passes and the attack on Dresden were undertaken against the advice of General Moreau. His conduct and demeanour, since his arrival at the army, had been generally spoken of in the highest terms; and he was the greatest loss the army could then have sustained. His heroism was truly great: after the fatal shot he spoke to the Emperor with the most perfect self-possession, never uttered a groan, and smoked a cigar the moment after the shot had struck him.

Prince Schwartzenberg, with whom I had much conversation after the retreat, mentioned that Barclay de Tolly, to whom he sent orders on the day of the general action to advance and attack, declared that it was impossible, as the enemy were too superior. It was undeniable that the retreat was attended with some disaster and confusion: the corps were mixed, retiring through the different defiles; ammunition, stores, and supplies, were every where deficient. A great quantity of baggage was taken: the stragglers and wounded were left behind; and we lost at least 2000 men, up to the 28th, by the retreat. But Schwartzenberg excused himself by the observation, that there was no commanding with Emperors and Kings on the spot; and he certainly had a difficult card to play.

From the general complexion of affairs, it appeared that if Buonaparte persevered in making propositions, there was great probability they would be listened to. The conferences, political as well as military, became frequent. The Emperor of Russia, from the disappointment of not having the command, was less eager to share in the contest; and Prince Schwartzenberg informed me, he deemed it judicious, at that moment, to avoid general actions, unless he were forced into them, and to act wholly on the defensive.

I must now revert to General Blucher's army of Silesia, in position on the 24th at Jauer, and to that part of the French army which was before him upon the Katzbach. On the 25th, Marshal Blucher advanced, and took up the position of Hennersdorf; and on the 26th he made a general attack on the enemy. His three corps, of Sachen, D'Yorck, and Langeron, were to pass the Katzbach, between Goldberg and Lignitz. The enemy deployed between the villages of Weinberg and Eichholz. After an obstinate combat, General Sachen's corps took possession of Eichholz, which turned the enemy's position; and among the Russians, the Generals Wassiltsihakoff, Navorossky, and Lieven, greatly distinguished themselves. The rain fell in torrents during the action, which was both bloody and decisive; and the French were in full retreat, when a reserve arrived from Lignitz, with sixteen pieces of artillery, and attacked the right flank of Blucher's army, in the hope of saving

Lauriston's corps from entire annihilation. Generals Lieven and Navorossky, however, again repulsed the enemy, and took the train of artillery; maintaining their success until night closed on this brilliant action.

On the 28th, the Silesian army, passing the Katzbach, continued its pursuit of the enemy, who was forced to retire by the only passage over the Bober at Bunzlau. The division of the French general, Pacthod, which had been detached towards Jauer to operate on Blucher's rear, was now cut off; and a corps under Prince Scherbatoff, and cavalry under General Korff, forced the surrender of his division, after a gallant resistance. This division consisted of many officers, 400 men, and two standards.

On the 1st of September, Blucher's head-quarters were established at Lowenberg; and he announced to his army that since the 26th he had taken 100 pieces of cannon, 250 tumbrils, three generals, many colonels, and near 20,000 prisoners. We must now return to Bohemia. Napoleon, greatly elated by the retreat of the allies, considered them as substantially broken, and took immediate measures for a vigorous pursuit of their different columns. The cavalry, with the 1st corps under General Vandamme, and the 6th and 14th, were immediately put in motion. Murat and Victor advanced to Freyberg; Marmont to Dippoldiswald; St. Cyr and Vandamme towards Nollendorff. Mortier took post at Pirna with part of the guards. On the 29th, Murat was at Leuchtenberg with the 2nd corps; the 6th at Falkenhein; and the 14th at Reinhartsgrimma.

General Vandamme followed the corps of the Russian general, Osterman-Tolstoy, from Nollendorff towards Toplitz: the latter disputed every inch of ground with the enemy. A very brilliant action now took place on the road from Toplitz towards Peterswalde, about two German miles from the former place. The Russian column under Count Osterman, retiring by the pass of Peterswalde, found the enemy, who had eventually crossed the Elbe at Pirna and Koningstein, in possession of the pass in the mountains; and Osterman's corps were to force their way through with the bayonet.. They there remained in action with the enemy till late in the evening; and having been reinforced by the reserve of the Russian guards, cavalry, and infantry, the former under the orders of the Grand-Duke Constantine, who were sent rapidly to their support, this body of troops, consisting of about 8000, held in check during the day two corps and one division of the French army, under Generals Vandamme and Bertrand, amounting to at least 30,000 men. As to the dauntless conduct of His Imperial Majesty's guards, were I to describe here the admiration I felt at witnessing their reckless bravery, I should fail for language to express it.

The light cavalry of the guards, consisting of the Polonese and dragoon regiments, charged columns of infantry, regardless of every disadvantage or rule of modern warfare. General Diebitsch, an officer of great merit, and now commander-in-chief of the Russian army in the East, particularly distinguished himself: Prince Demeter Gallitzin in like manner, and he was wounded in the attack. Count Osterman, towards the close of the day, had his arm carried off by a cannon-shot. The general commanding the cuirassiers of St. George was also wounded.

The importance of the firmness and audacity displayed by these troops is highly augmented, when it is considered that had they not held their ground, the columns of the army and the artillery retiring by Altenburg, which were delayed by the bad roads, would have been *aux abois*.

His Prussian Majesty was in Toplitz when the enemy pushed on by Peterswalde; and he made the most able dispositions to reinforce; Count Osterman. By his coolness and personal exertions, he preserved order and regularity; which even the momentary idea of the enemy *aux reins* is apt to destroy. The admirable conduct of this Sovereign, on every occasion, was the theme of invariable praise in the armies. The corps of Count Osterman lost 3200 men in this day's action, *hors de combat*. The French loss may be averaged at double. General Vandamme's corps suffered very severely. The cavalry of the Russian guard took two standards, and 300 or 400 prisoners. The enemy followed the rear-guard during the day, on the Dippoldiswald road; and they met with considerable check from the rear-guard, commanded by the Austrian general, Count Hardegg.

His Royal Highness the Duke of Cumberland arrived at Toplitz on the 28th, at the moment the enemy were making their impression in that quarter. His Royal Highness ran considerable risk of being taken; but repaired immediately to the field of battle, and assisted in the operations through this and the following days, with all that ardour, true personal courage, and ability, that are proverbially the attributes of the royal family of England.

The brilliant action of the 29th, in which the Russian guards covered themselves with glory, was followed up by a very general and decisive victory over that part of the enemy's force which had advanced from Koningstein and Pirna, on the great *chaussée* leading from Peterswalde to Toplitz. It became of the utmost importance to make this attack; not only to give time for those columns of the army to fall back, which were still retiring upon the Altenburg and Dippoldiswald roads, but at the same time to extricate the corps of General Kleist, which had not disengaged itself from the mountains. The enemy had the advantage, in pushing rapidly forward upon our right flank, of a good line of road; whereas the columns of the allied army, although retiring by shorter lines, were impeded as well by the unfavourable state of the weather as by almost impassable roads. A great proportion of the artillery-train and baggage of the allied army had not got clear of the mountains, when the enemy had arrived at Nollendorff and Kulm, about three German miles distant from Toplitz, the scene where the action took place.

The attack being determined upon, the following arrangement of the troops destined for that purpose was immediately made. Prince Schwartzenberg charged General Barclay de Tolly with the chief direction of the attack, and placed the divisions of Colloredo, Bianchi, and Philipe de Hesse Homburg, with the Russian corps, at his disposition.

Six thousand of the grenadiers of the latter, 2000 infantry and 4000 cavalry, under the immediate orders of General Miloradovitch, together with 12,000 of the Austrians under Count Colloredo and General Bianchi, commenced the attack: the remainder of the troops collected for this enterprise being formed in columns of reserve upon the adjacent plain. The village of Kulm is situated at the bottom of a range of mountains, which forms an almost impregnable barrier between Saxony and Bohemia: from this point branch off two distinct ranges, east and west, between which the ground is generally flat, affording however, in some places, good defensible positions. Upon this ground, immediately fronting the Tillage of Kulm, the enemy collected a strong force of infantry, with a considerable train of artillery. A galling fire was maintained incessantly from this point upon the Russians, under General Miloradovitch.

Such was the strength of the adjacent heights of Kulm; and so ably had the enemy disposed of their force for their defence, that it was judged more expedient to make the principal attack by the right: in consequence of which, the Austrian infantry were directed to move along the high ground upon the right, while the Russian guards and infantry were to commence their attack upon the left, as soon as the Austrians were sufficiently advanced. While these movements were executing, the corps of General Kleist, which had not been disengaged from the mountains, appeared in the enemy's rear, descending the road by which the latter expected to retire in case of need.

On all sides the attack was commenced in the most vigorous and decisive manner. The enemy's left was turned by the skill and bravery of the Austrians, under Count Colloredo; the cavalry charging repeatedly: while upon the other flank, General Miloradovitch, with the hussar imperial guards and grenadiers, forced every position, which the enemy in vain attempted to defend. Upon this point, above forty pieces of artillery and sixty tumbrils, much baggage, and the whole equipage of General Vandamme, fell into the hands of the Russians. Completely beaten in front at all points, and intercepted in their rear by General Kleist, nothing was left for the enemy, but a desperate and precipitate dispersion. Five hundred French horse immediately dashed through the Prussian *landwehr*, and actually took possession, for a few minutes, of the whole of General Kleist's artillery: it was, however, immediately recovered, by the rapid advance of the Russian and Austrian cavalry.

The rout now became general; the enemy throwing down their arms in every direction, and ceasing all resistance, abandoned their guns and standards to seek for shelter in the forests. The fruits of this victory were considerable: no less than the general commanding, Vandamme, six other general officers, among whom were Generals Giott, Heinberg, and Prince Reass, sixty pieces of artillery, and about 6000 prisoners, with six standards. The whole of General Vandamme's staff, and many officers of rank, were also numbered among the prisoners. The enemy continued their retreat, closely pursued by the Cossacks and allied cavalry.

Having received a severe wound in the thigh, by the explosion of a shell, shortly after the commencement of the action, I was under the necessity of quitting the field of battle late in the evening; and my details must necessarily be more imperfect. It may be fairly stated, however, that the enemy's force in this battle was annihilated, except a small body of cavalry that escaped under General Dumonceau, with other officers. This signal action amply compensated for the failure before Dresden; and with Blucher's brilliant victory of the Katzbach, renewed all the former enthusiastic hopes of the allied armies. After the battle, the grand army encamped in the neighbourhood of Toplitz, where the head-quarters of the three Sovereigns were established.

The Prince Regent of England now sent the Order of the Garter to the Emperor of Russia, as a mark of his high esteem and personal consideration. It was conveyed to His Imperial Majesty by Sir T. Tyrwhitt, who suffered not a little difficulty and embarrassment in his heavy equipages, traversing the bad roads, and mixing in the columns of march in the mountains; and at this time the Emperor of Austria also conferred the Order of Maria Theresa on the Emperor of Russia and the King of Prussia.

Leaving their Imperial Majesties in the delightful environs and luxurious residence of this far-famed and delicious watering-place, where there is a magnificent palace of the Austrian prince, Clari, we must turn our eyes for a short time to the events in the north, under the Prince Royal of Sweden. Here, however, I can give only a cursory detail, as the care of my wound at Toplitz, with other circumstances, deprived me of that information, which otherwise I was likely to have obtained.

The Prince Royal, on the 17th of August, assembled his army between Berlin and Spandau, with his head-quarters at Charlottenburg. Marshal Oudinot now received orders to attack him with the 4th, 7th, and 12th corps, and a mass of cavalry, under the Duke of Padua. On the 21st, the Prince Royal moved his head-quarters to Potsdam. On the same day, the French attacked the line destined to cover Berlin; and on the 22nd, the Crown Prince took up the following positions:

The Swedish army was stationed at Potsdam; the Russians were at Juterbock; the Prussian corps at Wittstock; and General Winzingerode and his Cossacks at Belitz. On the 23rd, General Bertrand attacked the Prussians, under Bulow, Borstell, and Tauenstein, at Gross-beeren; but was repulsed, with the loss of twenty-six guns, sixty tumbrils, and 2000 prisoners. Partial actions continued to take place in this quarter during many of the following days; and the Prince Royal transferred his head-quarters to Saarmund, and then to Buchholz, on the 30th. On the 4th of September he was at Rabenstein, where His Royal Highness projected passing the Elbe at Rosslau to move on Leipsic.

In the mean time, Napoleon was unwilling to abandon his enterprise of taking Berlin; he reinforced his troops in this quarter, and on the 4th entrusted to Marshal Ney the chief command. That general moved on the 6th on Neundorff, Juterbock, and Roterbeck. General Bulow met the advancing columns with the brigades of Borstell, Thümen, Kraft, and Hesse Homburg, and the corps of General Tauenstein. These, for some time, arrested the whole of Ney's force, amounting to 80,000 men, till the Prince Royal, with seventy battalions of Russians and Swedes, 10,000 cavalry, and 150 pieces of cannon, advanced, and obtained a complete and signal victory.

After the battle of Roterbeck and Juterbock, the enemy retired: their loss amounted to 14,000 or 15,000 men, eighty pieces of cannon, and 10,000 prisoners. The Russians, on the part of the allies, suffered most, having 8000 men killed and wounded. In the mean time, General Blucher, with the Silesian army, passed the Neisse; and was following up his victory, when Napoleon, now liberated by the retreat of the grand army through Bohemia, turned all his remaining force from Dresden against Blucher, who took up a position behind the Lobauer-Wasser.

Napoleon attacked the army of Silesia on the 5th before Reichenbach, and obliged Blucher to retire across the Neisse and the Queis; but he was unable to follow the Prussians, as the victory of Kulm, and the advantages gained by the grand army, made him aware they would soon resume the offensive: he returned, therefore, to Dresden on the 6th. The delay that now occurred in the operations afforded the main army some repose, and placed them in a more efficient state: supplies of all kinds, particularly shoes, arrived. Count Wittgenstein proceeded to Peterswalde; and Prince Eugene of Wirtemburg's division advanced to Dippoldiswald. The enemy took up strong positions in rear of the above places on the different roads. General Gouvion St. Cyr commanded their advance; and the ground on the Peterswalde side was formidable, in case it were to be attacked.

The intelligence from Dresden, that Napoleon had gone with all his guards towards Bautzen with a view of acting on Blucher, hastened the movement of a large corps on Zittau to gain communication with the Silesian army. It had been finally determined that 50,000 Austrians should make this movement; Prince Schwartzenberg taking the command of them; and they were to arrive at Zittau on the 13th. The divisions of Meerveldt, and all the reserve under the Prince of Hesse Homburg, composed this force.

Prince Maurice of Lichtenstein's light division proceeded, in the direction of Altenburg, to observe Freyberg; and General Kleinau's division marched upon Chemnitz, to support the light corps of General Thielman: which last was to continue its demonstrations towards Leipsic. The movement to the right bank of the Elbe with so large a support to General Blucher, both from the intelligence received and the general complexion of affairs, was certainly the most prudent and judicious operation.

By advices received, General Bennigsen's army of reserve had its advance already at Lignitz, where that general himself now was in person: it was stated at 80,000 men. The losses since the opening of the campaign to the grand army were not less than 35,000 men. The attempt to pass the range of mountains in front of the grand army having already been attended with so little solid advantage, it was not likely, to be again resorted to; nor indeed would it have been wise or judicious, when we considered that the season of the year was too far advanced to reckon with certainty upon favourable weather.

The late success against Vandamme appeared to ensure some offensive operations, which otherwise would have been avoided; although no positive decision was yet arrived at as to what these offensive operations should be. I am apt to believe it was the intention immediately to reinforce the Austrian general, Neuperg's, corps, which hitherto consisted only of 6000 or 8000 men: this had been stationed between the main army and that in Silesia and Lusatia. The allies seemed disposed, while they acted offensively, to do it at the least possible hazard: they reinforced their troops upon the right bank of the Elbe, while they made demonstrations of meditating another formidable movement against Dresden and Leipsic. With this object, a corps had already been detached of 4000 horse on the Chemnitz road to Leipsic; and it was to be followed by a larger flying corps, as soon as the troops had taken a few days' repose. The French troops in Lusatia had been filing towards the Elbe, appearing to retire to the left bank of that river; but hitherto their intentions were by no means known.

However great and formidable the alliance against France now appeared—however cordial and zealous were the allied powers for the common cause, still it was impossible the great leaders of the different armies should not have their military opinions in some degree governed by the immediate interests of the powers they represented. It was Russia's interest to act in Saxony, inasmuch as she might be looking to that feeble duchy as a future prize. It was Austria's to rouse the Tyrolese, to recover their own freedom and Italy. The movements chalked out for Bavaria upon the Danube were more congenial to her objects, and made her feel more secure. It was the interest of Prussia to remove the war from Silesia, and regain her strong holds. All these objects would be accomplished by the overthrow of the enemy: but it always has been, and will continue to be, the essential defect of great coalitions, both military and, I believe, political, that the several powers concerned will not divest themselves of the bias of their own immediate interests, or consent to forego the chances of attaining and securing their own objects during the progress of the operations they carry forward.

CHAPTER 9

The Armies Manoeuvre

On the 8th of August, the corps of Count Wittgenstein, and part of General Kleist's, under the orders of General Zeithen, which had advanced through the mountains beyond Peterswalde and on the road towards Dresden, were attacked by a very superior force of the enemy, and a sharp affair took place. Count Wittgenstein had his head-quarters at Pirna when the enemy began their advance. The chief contest during the day was for the village of Dohna, which was defended with much steadiness and bravery by the allies; but the enemy bringing up increasing numbers towards the evening, Count Wittgenstein determined to fall back, and evacuate Dohna. General Zeithen's corps, therefore, was ordered to occupy Pirna in the evening, and Count Wittgenstein's corps fell back towards Peterswalde.

The loss of the allies in this day's action may be estimated at about 1000 killed and wounded: that of the enemy was much more considerable. His Royal Highness the Duke of Cumberland was in the field, and assisted throughout the engagement. General Kleinau, with a corps, had been detached towards Freyberg and Chemnitz, on the left; while the Austrians had moved to Aussig and Leutmeritz, on the Elbe. On the 9th the enemy continued their advance; and the allies retired, fighting every inch of ground in the mountains. Buonaparte arrived from Dresden; and a very large force was advancing, either with a determination to make a general attack, or for the purpose of a great demonstration to cover a retrograde movement, and the removal of a large magazine of powder from Koningstein to Dresden.

On the advance of the enemy, orders were immediately sent for the Austrians to counter-march; and the allies immediately began to collect all their forces in the now victorious fields of Kulm and Toplitz. On the 10th, the enemy pressed, apparently with greater force, from the mountains, on Kulm and towards Toplitz. They had advanced not only with the columns that followed Count Wittgenstein's rear, but also with another very considerable corps by Kraupen. At this time the Austrian columns had not come into close communication from Aussig and Leutmeritz; and it was known the Russian and Prussian force in front of Toplitz was greatly outnumbered by the enemy. It was however determined to give him battle in the event of his advancing, and the disposition was accordingly made. The enemy continued, upon the 11th, to make such demonstrations as indicated a general attack; and on the 12th they advanced, and took possession of the village of Nollendorff, approaching close to Kulm. Above half the Austrian corps had now rejoined the army, and come into position: they had been marching in very bad weather and worse roads, without intermission, from the 10th instant; but arrived in excellent order. Buonaparte could at length perceive the allied army of upwards of 100,000 men in position, with 800 pieces of cannon, ready to give him battle. It seems, however, that he began his retreat about midday from Nollendorff: the allies began immediately to clear their front, and to send out strong reconnoitering parties; and General Kleinau's corps was again detached to the left, and reinforced by two divisions under Prince Lichtenstein. Up to mid-day on the 13th the enemy still continued his retreat, breaking up and destroying the roads in every direction towards Dresden. This rather delayed the pursuit of the allies, and made even any lateral movement more difficult. Accounts were now received of General Blucher's having entered Bautzen on the 10th; and on the 9th, the Russian colonel, Prince Modatoff, of Alexandroski guards, had executed a brilliant *coup de main* between Bautzen and Dresden. He blew up 200 ammunition wagons, took a part of the baggage of Napoleon, and made 1200 prisoners. On the 13th, General Count Bubna, who now commanded the Austrian corps, lately under General Neuperg, which had been much reinforced, entered Neustadt and Neukirchen; and came into close communication with General Blucher, who had his head-quarters at Hermshutt, with his advanced-posts beyond Bautzen: the enemy having retired to Bischoffswerde. On the 14th, in the morning, the advanced-posts of the grand army advanced again to the frontiers by the Peterswalde road. The rear-guard of the enemy, consisting of two battalions of infantry and a regiment of cavalry, and some guns, were forced from Nollendorff by Count

Pahlen, commanding Count Wittgenstein's advance: the artillery of the allies, and more force, was in readiness to follow, as soon as the roads could be made practicable. The Prussians, under General Kleist and Prince Augustus, moved to Ettersdorf.

Buonaparte assisted personally at the grand *reconnoissance* made on the 10th; He had his head-quarters at Liebstadt on the 11th; and moved forward on the left of the allies to Barenstein, near Altenburg, on the 12th. The plan of the enemy appeared to have been to attack the allies, if he could do so with an evident advantage; if not, to impede their advance, and by menaces gain time, either to extricate himself from the dangerous predicament in which he stood, or to manoeuvre the allies out of their position. On the 15th, in the morning, the enemy continued to retire; and Prince Schwartzenberg ordered a general *reconnoissance* to be made on all sides. Count Wittgenstein and Count Pahlen's corps fell in with the enemy near Peterswalde. Four squadrons of Russian cavalry very gallantly charged a French column, and cut down several hundred men. To give some idea of these attacks, from a French return which was found of the loss of the 7th Regiment of infantry, when the Russian cavalry in Count Osterman's action charged, they had 825 wounded and 730 killed: the residue of fugitives remaining were 600. The enemy's corps in advance, opposed to Count Pahlen, consisted of 12,000 men, under General Bonnet. They made a good stand near Gotleibe: six Russian light guns did great execution, and forced this column to leave their ground. The main position of the enemy was not attacked. An Austrian corps of 17,000 men, under Count Colloredo, equally reconnoitred the enemy on the side of Berenstein and Breitenau.

The head-quarters of the enemy were now moved to Dippoldiswald. General Thielman's partisan-corps met with considerable success. He took possession of the town of Weissenfels, which was occupied by infantry and artillery; and made a general, forty officers, and near 1300 men prisoners: these partisans were very useful. The Austrian colonel, Mensdorff, took a French courier between Leipsic and Dresden, charged with despatches and letters from the French army for Paris, at least 5000 in number: these letters gave the most doleful details of the French army, and of their defeats. Of the whole corps engaged under Marshal Ney, only 16,000 men had escaped: 10,000 had arrived at Dresden under Marshal Oudinot; the rest, according to these letters, were left at Wittemberg and Torgau. Reinforcements, amounting to 15,000 men, had reached Erfurth; but they were troops of an inferior description. It was also stated in these letters, that the new guards, and particularly the artillery, suffered dreadfully in the battle near Dresden: Generals Vachot and Leibu were killed, and Generals Dentail, Zios, Boisildieu, Maison, Ween, and Aubert, severely wounded. On the 15th, in the evening, the enemy brought up more troops against Count Pahlen; and as it was not the intention of the allies to engage in a general affair in the mountains and defiles of Saxony, the advanced-corps moved back to Nollendorff. The French had two *corps d'armée* supporting their advanced-corps of 12,000 men. General Blucher's last accounts were from Bautzen, with his advanced-posts within a German mile of Dresden; and he was, at this period, in communication with the Prince Royal's army.

Active preparations were made at the allied head-quarters for movements in advance by our left. General Kleinau's corps was at Marienburg. A considerable body of the enemy were at Freyberg, and a corps of their cavalry between that and Rossen. It was reported, on the 16th, that Buonaparte had retreated back to Dresden, clearing it of all non-combatants, and that he was concentrating to cover the recent movements, to which the late successes of the allies had reduced him. Accounts from Klagenfurt, dated the 6th, stated that the Viceroy of Italy had been engaged on the Drave, in a general battle with General Hiller, near Rossuk, and had forced him from his position: later accounts, however, brought the satisfactory intelligence, that the latter had gained advantages over the Viceroy.

The enemy, on the 16th, still occupied the mountains and heights in front of Nollendorff in considerable force: they made in the evening an attempt to turn the right of the allied position before Kulm, while they also assailed the centre and left. Buonaparte appears to have assisted in person at this affair: 15,000 men were detached to turn the right; 8000 advanced in front and on the left: about 30,000 infantry and 8000 cavalry in reserve formed the attack on the part of the enemy.

On the 17th, the corps moving on our right being concealed by an intense fog, and advancing through dense woods, had succeeded in gaining our flank before its movement was perceived; while the enemy, in very superior force, drove the Russians and Prussians from the village of Nollendorff; but they were kept in check on the left. General Colloredo now, with a corps of Austrians, fell on the enemy's advanced column, which had gained our right; and with an intrepidity, steadiness, and order, that gained universal admiration, completely defeated his flank, took between 2000 and 3000 prisoners, among whom were the general of division, Kreitzer, and many officers, with ten guns. Our loss was about 1000 killed and wounded. At the time the enemy made their attack on the centre, the Prussians were about to be relieved by the Russians, which occasioned some momentary disorder. A very fine young man, a son of General Blucher, who was distinguishing himself very gallantly in re-establishing order, was killed. The enemy, repulsed at all points, retired at night into their former position on the mountains, occupying, however, Nollendorff. The allies took up their old ground, extending across the plain in a semicircular position. It was determined, from these frequent demonstrations and partial attacks of the enemy, and from the numbers he had assembled, that any movements on the left by the allies, as before resolved upon, should be deferred; it not being prudent to detach largely while the enemy was collected in force. The continued affairs and skirmishes during the last fortnight cost many men on both sides; but there was no doubt of the enemy having suffered in at least a double proportion. It was stated that Buonaparte had his horse shot under him, while reconnoitring on the hill on that day. The Austrian troops that formed the advance of General Kleinau's corps, under the immediate command of General Scheüther, had entered Freyberg, where they surprised and made prisoners 400 of the enemy, with their general. It was a singular and pleasing circumstance, that two of the remaining squadrons of the Westphalian hussars, which did not come over from the enemy with their two regiments (being on detachment), formed a part of the prisoners taken. An Austrian corps also advanced towards Chemnitz.

On the 19th, the enemy remained in position at Peterswalde. Buonaparte slept at Pirna. On the 20th, they retired still further towards Dresden, and withdrew also from Nollendorff. The Prussian corps under General Zeithen immediately followed them. An order was intercepted from Marshal Berthier to General Lobau, commanding the advanced troops of the enemy, directing him to make all his dispositions for retreat on Dresden. All accounts agreed in stating the extreme distress of the French army in the mountains: they were losing numbers of their horses daily, and their troops were in the greatest want of provisions. It seemed probable that Buonaparte would remain *à cheval* on the Elbe as long as possible.

General Bennigsen's army was expected to arrive in five or six days by the pass of Zittau, when more extended movements were contemplated. According to the general report and information, Buonaparte arrived at Bischoffswerde on the 23rd, and he meditated some attempt on General Blucher; but finding that officer not only prepared for him, but actually making preparations to act offensively, Buonaparte retired again on Dresden. The old guards were still stationed there with various depôts of regiments. The enemy were working at the place. The redoubts at Pirna gate were demolished; but new ones were erected at those of Falken, Freyberg, and some other. Provisions were very scarce in the city; one loaf was divided amongst eight men. To add to these distresses, two magazines were burnt down, containing hay and oats; one to the value of 30,000, and the other 40,000 rix-dollars. It was believed the enemy was retiring gradually to the left bank of the river: 4000 men and sixteen guns had lately returned from Bischoffswerde to the heights of Potshafel. Marshal Lefebvre, according to the French account, had 30,000 men at Leipsic. In Magdeburg there were 9000 men, and the artillery was very complete. Marshal Augereau set out for Branberg on the 23rd, 11,500 strong.

Great exertions were now making in the different fortresses on the Rhine. Ehrenbreitstein was to be repaired, and rendered as strong as possible. All the troops that had measured back their steps across the Elbe were in a miserable condition: Count Bubna attacked the enemy's troops near Holpen: the Austrians suffered some loss. The enemy's movements, on the whole, seemed very wavering; and it was difficult, with certainty, to determine their immediate intention, though of their ultimate attempt to retreat no doubt was entertained.

The whole of General Bennigsen's corps was not expected in their positions until the 3rd or 4th of October; but the following movements were determined on. Prince Maurice of Lichtenstein was to march with 5000 Austrians to Gera, to *donner la main* to all the partisans, Platoff, Thielman, &c. who communicated quite round the enemy's positions with the Prince Royal's light corps from the army of the north. General Kleinau's corps, upwards of 25,000, were to move to Chemnitz; General Count Wittgenstein's and Kleist's corps, above 30,000, to Marienburg; the Austrian corps of Giulay to Zwickau; the 1st and 2nd corps of the Austrian army to Komotau; and General Barclay de Tolly, with the Russian head-quarters, to Brüx. General-Bennigsen was to have his head-quarters at Toplitz. This flank movement was to be prolonged in the direction of Erfurth; and an attempt was to be made to destroy the enemy's corps and magazines, &c. in that place.

In the mean time, it was presumed that the favourable appearances from the side of Bavaria would shortly put in motion a combined force, in the direction of Wurtzburg, which would complete the enemy's embarrassments in every quarter of Germany. A report was received on the 30th, that a joint attack was made by Platoff and Thielman on the enemy at Altenburg, near Leipsic, in which 2000 prisoners were made. One regiment of hussars escaped, but it was supposed it would still be taken.

The affair near Altenburg proved of-more importance than was at first supposed; and the Hettman, Platoff, with his usual ability. and gallantry, performed a brilliant exploit against a considerable corps of the enemy's cavalry. This corps was under the orders of General Lefebvre-Desnouettes, and consisted of the French light cavalry, the Polish *uhlans* of the guard, and a brigade of light dragoons under the orders of General Pivot. The force consisted of 8000 cavalry and 700 infantry, one squadron of Mamelukes, and a small party of Tartars of the guard, under a Colonel Mucol. The whole were attacked by Platoff, and completely put to the rout. A general was reported by the prisoners to have been killed: 1500 prisoners, five guns, and forty officers, including three officers of the staff, were the fruits of this enterprise.

The army broke up from Toplitz on the 1st of October, and was in movement to the left. On the 30th of September, the corps of General Count Wittgenstein was at Komotau, and that of General Kleist near Brüx. The Austrians marched upon Chemnitz. A report from the enemy stated that Napoleon, attended by the King of Saxony and family, had departed upon the 28th instant for Leipsic, whither his head-quarters were about to be removed; and a French corps, under Marshal Augereau, had marched upon Coburg. The Russian and Prussian army now exceeded 80,000 men; and it was to assemble on the Chemnitz and Freyberg line. To this may be added the corps of Kleinau of 10,000 men, together with all the Austrians. General Bennigsen's corps was reviewed this day, and was found in a very efficient state; and a reinforcement of 7000 men for the Prussian corps of General Kleist was upon the road from Prague.

After the late actions, Prince Schwartzenberg, with the grand army, confined his offensive system to constant skirmishing of light troops and affairs of out-posts, under General Thielman, Colonel Mensdorff, and others. The various successes, however, of the general-in-chief in the main operations, afforded to the armies of Silesia and the north the advantage of coming into close communication.

Being anxious now to carry into execution the measures with which I was charged, I set out again for the head-quarters of the Prince Royal of Sweden. Previous, however, to my leaving the grand army, I ought to record that owing to their late splendid successes, and also to the victories of Lord Wellington in Spain, astute means of opening negotiations, in the specious form of a general congress, had been adopted by Napoleon. This was done by letters addressed from himself through the Duke of Bassano on that subject direct to the Emperor of Austria.

It was a glorious and exalting era for Great Britain; at the present moment she saw herself rewarded for her unexampled perseverance and generosity, by the whole continent of Europe relying upon the wisdom of her councils and the exploits of her arms, which were about to. decide the destinies of Europe. Nobly were her labours repaid; gloriously were her efforts crowned, by the bright and cheering prospect that now beamed upon the civilised world. It is in vain, however, to conceal that, owing to a concurrence of circumstances, the great powers of the continent appeared to think, if they could obtain a peace upon fair terms, it would be preferable to protracting the present sanguinary contest. The length of its duration, the little jealousies of individual commanders in the allied armies, the peculiar objects of each power (demonstrated in various quarters), with the consideration of the family alliance between the Emperor of Austria and Buonaparte, which certainly influenced in some small degree the Austrian minister, *au fond* the commander-in-chief, as well as the prime minister: All conspired to accomplish a peace by the shortest and safest way possible, father than to continue the struggle. It. was difficult to point out how the congress proposed was to proceed, if assented to by all parties; but Count Metternich always had his eyes open, and saw at once the cessions Buonaparte might make, and how the general interests of Europe might be poised: he was not so young in politics as, in contemplating a particular measure, not to divine, the result.

The world will not, I trust, accuse me of vanity, but give me credit for an honest pride, if, before I take leave of the very interesting details of the battles of Dresden and Kulm, I venture to annex an indulgent, though unmerited autograph letter I received from that brave and virtuous monarch, the Emperor of Russia, at that period.

Toplitz
September 27, 1813
Monsieur le General Stewart,
J'ai été témoin comme toute l'armée du zèle infatigable que vous avez déployé dans cette campagne, où toujdurs présent, aux champs de l'honneur, vous vous êtes fait remarquer dans les endroits les plus exposés, par le sang-froid, et la plus belle valeur.
Il est de mon devoir d'honorer d'aussi brillantes qualités, et je crois vous donner une preuve de la justice que je leur rends, en vous envoyant les marques de l'ordre de St. George de la quatrième classe.
Vous savez qu'elles. ne s'accordent qu'à la vertu militaire. Elles vous rappelleront la mémorable journée de Kulm, où votre sang

a coulé, et tous les braves qui y ont combattu vous verront avec plaisir porter une décoration, qui atteste que vous avez partagé, et leur gloire et leurs dangers.
Recevez avec ces témoignages particulières de mon estime, l'assurance de mes sentimens.
Alexandre

I received at the same time a letter from the Prussian Chancellor of State, conferring on me, by the King's command, all the Prussian orders, including the very highest, that of the Black Eagle. All these testimonies of the feelings of the allied courts towards the British nation in my person, His Royal Highness the Prince Regent was graciously pleased to permit me to accept and wear.

The army of Silesia now moved forward from the Pleisse along its whole line, to circumscribe the enemy in their position round Dresden; while the army of the Prince Royal, profiting by their late victory, crossed the Elbe, the French corps opposed to them retired towards Torgau. I joined the head-quarters of the Crown Prince of Sweden at Zorbig on the 8th. After the brilliant passage of the Elbe by General Blucher at Elster, in which both decision and judgment were pre-eminently displayed, and the consequent crossing of the same river by the Prince Royal's army at the points of Rosslau and Acken, His Royal Highness conceived that a movement of the whole allied force to the left bank of the Saale would either force the enemy to a general battle, or effectually embarrass and impede his retreat, if he should determine upon a measure which the combined movements of the armies of Bohemia, Silesia, and the north of Germany, on his flanks and on his communications, seemed to render so indispensably necessary.

Buonaparte, it seems, had, according to reports, manoeuvred from Dresden with a large corps of cavalry on the right, and all his infantry on the left bank of the Elbe, as far down as Strehlau. A strong demonstration, from 25,000 to 30,000 men, was made from Torgau towards the point of the Elster on the 8th, where General Blucher passed, probably with a design of menacing him, and forcing him to repass the river. The bold determination of the allies was not, however, to be arrested; and the whole army of General Blucher being now in close communication with that of the Prince Royal, the former marched from Duben on Jasnitz on the 9th, and passed the Mulda, while the Prince Royal concentrated his forces near Zorbig. The enemy, according to accounts, appeared to be collected about Eulenburg and Oschatz, between the Mulda and the Elbe. On the 10th, General Blucher moved from Jasnitz to Zorbig; and the armies of Silesia and the north of Germany were here assembled.

The determination being taken to pass the Saale, orders were issued in the night; and General Blucher moved with the Silesian army: bridges being constructed for that purpose. General Bulow, with his *corps d'armée,* was in like manner to pass at Wettin; General Winzingerode, with the Russians, at Rothenberg; and the Prince Royal, with the Swedes, at Alsleben and Bernburg. The whole allied force was then to place itself in order of battle on the left of the Saale, waiting the further development of the enemy's movements. General Woronzoff, who formed General Winzingerode's advanced-guard at Halle, was to refuse battle, and fall back on the forces passing at Wettin, if he should be attacked by superior numbers; but otherwise, to retain Halle as long as possible. By these decided movements, the points of passage on the Elbe, by which the armies had passed, were to be abandoned, and destroyed, if necessary; while other bridges were prepared below Magdeburg, in case of need.

The corps of observation, under General Thümen, before Wittemberg, of about 6000 men, in the event of the enemy forcing a passage there, (for the purpose of *allongéing* the right bank of the Elbe, and returning by Magdeburg, in the extremity in which he was placed, or in another improbable, but possible event of his pushing with all his forces to Berlin,) had orders to retire on General Tauenstein, who with 10,000 men was to remain at Dessau; and, according to circumstances, either to manoeuvre on the right bank against any possible effort of the enemy's, or by forced marches strengthen, if necessary, the armies assembled on the Saale. General Tauenstein was to be assisted by all the landsturm, and some smaller detached corps were also to join him.

Information now arrived that General Platoff, with his Cossacks, was at Pegau; Generals Kleist and Wittgenstein, with the advance of the grand army of Bohemia, were approaching Altenburg; and communications seemed to be established in the rear of the French army by our light troops. Information of the movements of the enemy was vague; but accounts were brought in, on the evenings of the 11th and 12th, that he was moving troops from the different points of Lutzen and Wurzen towards Leipsic; and it was added, that Buonaparte was expected to arrive there. His force between Dresden and Leipsic, exclusive of garrisons, was estimated, at the highest calculation, at 180,000 men: that of the Silesian army at 65,000; that of the Prince Royal at 60,000 men, with 100 pieces of artillery; and it was impossible to see finer troops, or more fully equipped in all essentials.

General Platoff, with his Cossacks, had arrived at Lutzen, having taken some hundreds of prisoners at Weissenfels; and he was in complete communication with the advance of General Woronzoff's Cossacks from Halle. Platoff reported the assembling of the enemy round Leipsic. The army of Bohemia was between Altenburg and Chemnitz; and General Bennigsen, with the Austrian division of Colloredo which Had been joined to him, was meditating a demonstration towards Dresden. Such were, at this period, the general outlines of the positions of the respective forces; and it was impossible, on looking at the map, not to be sanguine as to the result. Buonaparte seemed to have the advantage of concentration: that he might carry his whole force against the grand army, or the Prusso-Swedish army, was evident; but in either case the army, unattacked, was close in his rear. The Cossacks and light troops were hovering on all his communications; they even passed through his army in different directions, and his position seemed similar to that in which he was placed on the Beresina.

Chapter 10

Contest at Mockern

The bold and offensive system now so gallantly commenced by General Blucher, gave a new tone to the operations of the allies. The glorious career of the Silesian army, daily engaged in action since the opening of the campaign, and hourly covering itself with laurels, merits the historian's loftiest eulogy: it stood pre-eminent in the advance next the foe, with its venerable and gallant leader eagerly availing himself of every opportunity to augment his heroic reputation, rescue his country, and avenge her sufferings. General Blucher was not enabled—the bridge being incomplete—to traverse the Saale at Wettin; but proceeded to Halle, where he passed. General Bulow had not got over on the 11th of October; but the rest of the allied army crossed to the left bank of the Saale on that day. On the 12th, the Prince Royal's head-quarters were at Seyda. General Winzingerode's cavalry occupied Dessau and Köthen.

On the 14th, the Prince Royal moved to Coswick; on the 15th, to Zerbst. Various affairs of advanced-posts now took place: the details of which, however deserving of praise, would hardly fall within the extent and object of the present narrative. The army of Silesia and that of the Prince Royal continued *à cheval* on the Saale, up to the 11th instant. On the 12th, it appeared that the enemy had collected considerably on the right bank of the Mulda, between Duben and Eulenburg; while at the same time, it was believed, he remained in force against the grand army. But his chief strength seemed concentrated between the Mulda, Leipsic, and Torgau.

The grand army, on the 12th, was posted as follows:

The main body was at Altenburg; General Wittgenstein's corps at Borne, where it appears he had a successful affair with the enemy; General Kleinau at Freyberg; Generals Giulay and Thielman at Zeitz; Prince Maurice of Lichtenstein at Pegau; General Bennigsen's had advanced from Peterswalde and Dohna to Waldheim; and General Bubna had a very brilliant affair before Dresden on the 10th; he also succeeded in carrying the *tête du pont* at Pirna, destroyed the boats, and took some cannon and prisoners. The enemy had left about 12,000 men in garrison at Dresden. To this general information was added, that of the enemy having *debouchéd* from Wittemberg on the right bank of the Elbe, and succeeded in forcing the corps of General Thümen to retire on the 11th.

It became now of the greatest importance to ascertain the amount of the enemy's force passing at Wittemberg. That Buonaparte should adopt the measure of crossing with his army at Wittemberg and Torgau, by which he abandoned all his communications, and allow the whole allied armies to be united and placed between him and France, seemed so desperate, and so little in accordance with military calculation, that until the existence of the step was beyond a doubt, it was impossible to act upon its adoption. The Crown Prince, in the present state of affairs, recrossed the Saale on the 13th, and marched to Köthen, where he took up a position; being thus within march of General Blucher at Halle. Each army would reciprocally support the other, and combine their movements, while the grand army was expected every hour at Leipsic. Six divisions of the enemy, with the guards, had passed at Wittemberg, and were directing their march on Berlin. Our communications across the Elbe at Rosslau and Acken were attacked; and the former were given up by General Tauenstein, who had passed at Wittemberg, joined General Thümen, and then fallen back on Zerbst, and towards Potsdam.

The momentary loss of the communications across the Elbe, except below Magdeburg, was a temporary inconvenience; but the annihilation, if possible, of the French army being the grand object, the Crown Prince resolved to march to Halle, and join the corps of General Blucher and the grand army. When the allied forces should thus be united, the fate of Napoleon might be decided. The intelligence of the treaty being signed between the allies and Bavaria arrived on the 15th; and at this period also news was received that the King of Wirtemburg had joined the common cause, and that his forces, which were assembling under the orders of General Baron Wrede, would immediately join the grand army. General Walmoden's corps in the north, and the other forces, were to act according to circumstances.

The accounts received of the six divisions of the *jeune garde* of the enemy having *debouchéd* from Wittemberg, as also troops from Torgau on the right bank of the Elbe, likewise of his having taken possession of Dessau, caused a momentary anxiety; but later intelligence stated that he was recalling his forces from the direction of Wittemberg to the Lower Mulda, and seemed to be assembling them in the neighbourhood of Leipsic, Tamhu, and Eulenburg. This report was in part derived from a lieutenant-colonel of the French *état major,* who had been taken prisoner; on whom was found a letter addressed to Marshal Marmont, enjoining him to put himself in march for Leipsic, and place himself under the orders of Murat.

The enemy's force employed in manoeuvring on the right bank of the Mulda, and which had crossed the Elbe, was commanded by Marshals Ney and Marmont; and they had so studiously concealed their movements by marches and counter-marches, and the country was so enclosed and difficult near the conflux of those rivers, that the information was not precise.

The enemy's assemblage in the neighbourhood of Leipsic was now positive. On the 14th he retired from Zerbst, and withdrew from Acken, where he had shown himself. Having destroyed our *tête du pont* at Rosslau, he abandoned it; and the Cossacks of General Winzingerode's corps of the Prince Royal's army drove him from Dessau, which was re-occupied. These different events confirmed the other intelligence; and appearances denoted the movement from Wittemberg to have been undertaken with a view of alluring the northern army to repass the Elbe. Upon general and military principles, for the allies to have crossed that river without possessing the *appui* of Wittemberg, might be considered by many a doubtful, if not an injurious, undertaking; but on the other hand must be balanced the advantages derived from the union of above 300,000 men surrounding the enemy on all points, the state of demoralization in his army, their distress for provisions, which, hemmed in as they were, necessarily increased daily; and, lastly, the advantage of being able to undertake vigorous and offensive operations in all quarters.

The Prince Royal of Sweden detached on the 14th a division of his army, under the orders of the Prince of Hesse Homburg, to re-establish his communications at Acken, and to ensure the passage of the river and the town, which is strong, by fortifying it still further, if possible. The garrison of Magdeburg made attempts upon the post of Bernburg on the Saale—a point of infinite importance for the passage of that river, in case of necessity. They were here, however, again checked by a detachment of Cossacks of General Winzingerode's corps; and two battalions and some guns were placed to reinforce the garrison. The Prince Royal's army, on this day, extended its right in the direction of the mountain called St. Peterberg—a point which forms a principal feature in this country, from its abrupt rise; its left towards Köthen and Elsdorf; while his advanced-guard was pushed into the villages on the left bank of the Mulda.

The Silesian army was in position near Halle, with its advanced-guards at Merseburg and Skenditz.

By despatches from the grand army, Count Wittgenstein made a general *reconnoissance* on the 13th, and marching to his left, occupied Pegau with the greatest part of his corps. On the 14th, establishing his communication on the left with the Austrian corps of Count Giulay and Prince Maurice of Lichtenstein posted at Weissenfels and Naumburg, he joined with Thielman and Platoff towards Lutzen; and on the right with the corps of Count Kleinau, who marched to Borne, and was to detach to Grimma and Colditz. The Russian grenadiers and cuirassiers were at Altenburg. The main body of the grand army, namely, the corps of Meerveldt, the Austrian army of reserve, the Russian and Prussian guards, took post at Zeitz; the corps of Colloredo at Chemnitz and Penig, and detached towards Rochlitz. General Bennigsen had orders to make himself master of the roads leading on Nossen and Meissen, and to push on with all possible expedition. In this general position, the armies were to press on, closing in the enemy till they were enabled to make simultaneous attacks.

Under these circumstances, if the enemy forced his passage against any one of the corps, the others united would be able to fall on the point attacked. This operation became the more easy, in proportion as the communications between the different armies became established; and the circle which the allied troops occupied round the enemy narrowed. In the event of a retreat, the left bank of the Saale afforded a very strong line on the one side, and the position of Lutzen, Weissenfels, and Altenburg, on the other. The Bavarian corps of Count Wrede, and the Austrian corps of Prince Reuss, were ordered to advance, by forced marches; and every effort was made to take possession of Wurtzburg, and to fortify the line of the Maine. All the corps of the grand army had moved forward on the 15th; General Blucher to Gross-Kügel and Skenditz, with his advance pushed towards Leipsic; while the Prince Royal had his right in front of the St. Peterberg, the left at Zorbig, with the Swedes near Wettin.

The glorious army of Silesia now added another victory to its list; and the brow of its valiant leader was again decorated with a fresh laurel. Forty pieces of cannon, 12,000 killed, wounded, and prisoners, one eagle, and many caissons, were the fruits of the victory of Radefeld and Lindenthal. To give the clearest idea in my power of this battle, I must revert to the positions of the armies of Silesia and the north of Germany, on the 14th instant, when certain intelligence was received that the enemy was withdrawing from the right bank of the Elbe to collect on Leipsic.

At this time the Prince Royal was at Köthen, and General Blucher at Halle: the former in possession, with his advanced-guards, of the left bank of the Mulda; and the latter, of Merseburg and Skenditz. General Blucher moved his head-quarters on the 10th to Gross-Kügel, pushing his advance on the great road to Leipsic, and occupying the villages on each side of it. The enemy were in force in his front; still holding Debitz and Radefeld with some troops along the Mulda. The Crown Prince of Sweden issued orders to march to Halle on the night of the 14th; but when his troops were *en route,* he took up his head-quarters at Sylbitz, and placed the Swedish army with its right at Wettin, and the left near to St. Peterberg. General Bulow occupied the centre of his line, between Peterberg and Oppin; and the corps of Winzingerode was on the left at Zorbig. His Royal Highness seemed to have apprehended, either that the enemy were not clear of the Elbe, or that we might be attacked from the Mulda: the bridges, however, had been broken. His advanced-guard was on it; and a direct march on Zorbig, and towards Debitz and Radefeld, would, without question, have brought the army of the north into action on the 16th, which would have rendered the victory much more decisive.

General Blucher found the enemy's forces, consisting of the 4th, 6th, and 7th corps of the French army, and great part of the guard under Marshals Ney and Marmont and General Bertrand, occupying a line with their right at Freyroda, and their left at Lindenthal. The country around these villages is open, and very favourable for cavalry; but the enemy was strongly posted in front of a wood of some extent near Radefeld, and behind it the ground is more intersected: generally speaking, however, it is adapted to all arms. The disposition of attack of the Silesian army, was as follows:—the corps of General Count Langeron was to attack and carry Freyroda, and then Radefeld, having the corps of General Sachen in reserve: the *corps d'armée* of General D'Yorck was directed to move on the great *chaussée* leading to Leipsic, until it reached the village of Lutschen, when turning to its left it was to force the enemy at Lindenthal: the Russian guards and the advanced-guard were to press on the main road to Leipsic: the corps of General St. Priest, arriving from Merseburg, was to follow the corps of Count Langeron: the cavalry and the different reserves were formed in the open ground between the villages.

It was nearly midday before the troops were at their stations; and hopes were entertained, which proved fallacious, that the cavalry and flying artillery of the Prince Royal's army would be in line. The enemy soon after the first onset gave up the advanced villages, and retired some distance; but tenaciously held the woody ground on their right, and the villages of Gross and Klein, Wetteritz, as also the villages of Mockau and Mockern, on their left. At Mockern a most bloody contest ensued; it was taken and retaken by the corps of D'Yorck five times: the musketry fire was most galling; and this was the hottest part of the field. Many of the superior officers were either killed or wounded. At length the victorious Silesians carried all before them, and drove the enemy beyond the Partha.

In the plain there were several brilliant charges of cavalry. The Brandenburg regiment of hussars distinguished itself in a particular manner, and supported by infantry, charged and carried a battery of eight pieces. The enemy made an obstinate resistance also on his right, in the villages of Great and Little Wetteritz, and in the surrounding wood; and when he perceived we had forced his left, he brought an additional number of troops on Count Langeron, who was chiefly engaged with Marshal Ney's corps, from the neighbourhood of Duben. The Russians, however, equally with their brave allies in arms, made the most gallant efforts, and they were fully successful; night only putting an end to the action.

The Russian cavalry acted in a very conspicuous manner. General Korff's cavalry took a battery of thirteen guns; and the Cossacks of General Emanuel, five. The enemy now drew off towards Siegeritz and Pfosen, and passed the river Partha, retreating from all points. General Sachen's corps, which supported General Langeron, very much distinguished itself in the presence of Napoleon, who, it seems (according to the information of the prisoners), arrived from the other wing of his army at five o'clock in the evening. The corps of D'Yorck, which displayed the utmost coolness and courage, had many of its most gallant leaders killed or wounded. Among the latter were, Colonels Heihmetz, Kubzler, Bouch, Hiller, Lowenthal, Laurentz, and Majors Schon and Bismark. The momentary loss of these officers was seriously felt, as they nearly all commanded brigades from the reduced list of general officers in the Prussian army; and we had to lament that His Serene Highness the Prince of Mecklenburg Strelitz, who was distinguishing himself in a particular manner, having had two horses shot under him, and whose gallant corps took 500 prisoners and an eagle, received a severe, though happily not mortal, wound. Among the Russians, General Chinchin and several officers of distinction were killed or wounded; and I average General Blucher's total loss at near 6000 or 7000 men, *hors de combat.*

Let me here own my anxiety to perpetuate the renown so deservedly acquired by this brave army, in endeavouring feebly, but I declare faithfully, to detail its proceedings. Liberated Europe will, I am confident, justly appreciate the enthusiasm and heroism with which its operations were conceived and effected. It had measured its strength in twenty-one combats, several times with the best troops of France, including the guards. I attached that excellent and able officer, Colonel, afterwards Brigadier-General, Hudson Lowe, to General Blucher in the field the early part of the day, being myself with the Prince Royal; and it is due to the talent and zeal of that officer to record, that I derived great assistance from the activity evinced in all his reports.

To turn to the operations of the grand army up to the 16th, and the disposition for the attack to be made on the 17th. The corps of Generals Giulay, Prince Maurice of Lichtenstein, Thielman, and Platoff, were collected in the neighbourhood of Mark Ranstedt, and were to move forward on Leipsic, keeping up the communication with General Blucher's army and the other, corps to their right. General Nostitz's cavalry were to form also on their right; and in case of retreat, these corps were to retire towards Zeitz. The reserves of Russian and Prussian guards were to move on Rötha, where they were to pass the Pleisse, and form in columns on its right bank. The reserves of the Prince of Hesse Homburg, Generals Meerveldt and Wittgenstein, were also to take. post at this station. General Barclay de Tolly commanded all the columns on the right bank of the Pleisse. Generals Wittgenstein, Kleist, and Kleinau, advanced from their respective positions on Leipsic: the Russian guard formed their reserve; and General Colloredo moved from Borne as reserve to General Kleinau. The retreat of these corps was to be on Chemnitz. Generals - Wittgenstein's, Kleist's, and Kleinau's, on Altenburg and Penig.

The army of General Bennigsen was to push on from Colditz towards Grimma and Weingen. The corps of Count Bubna had been relieved before Leipsic by General Tolstoy's. A very heavy firing continued all the day of the 16th. from the grand army. Late at night a report reached General Blucher, that Buonaparte had attacked in person the whole line of the allies, and forming his cavalry in the centre, succeeded in making an opening in the combined army before all its cavalry could come up. He was, however, not able to profit by this grand *coup de main;* he retired in the evening, and the allies occupied their position as before.

On the 17th, the combined corps were ready to renew the attack. The Prince Royal, who had his head-quarters at Landsberg and his army behind it, marched at two o'clock in the morning, and arrived at Radefeld towards midday. Generals Winzingerode's and Bulow's corps had moved forward in the night near the heights of Taucha. No cannonade being heard on the side of the grand army (though General Blucher's corps was under arms), and as it was also understood that General Bennigsen would not arrive until this day at Grimma, and part of the Prince Royal's army being still in the rear, it was deemed expedient to wait till the following day to renew the general attack. The enemy showed himself in great force in a good position on the left of the Partha, on a ridge of some extent parallel to the river. There was some cannonading in the morning: the enemy made demonstrations; and the hussars charged on advanced parties into the suburbs of Leipsic, and took some cannon and prisoners.

The state of affairs was now so changed, that the most sanguine expectations were justly entertained that the glorious cause in which Europe was engaged would immediately triumph.

I shall now offer some personal observations relating to the Prince Royal's position at Köthen on the 14th, when General Blucher was at Halle. No sooner was information received, and ascertained to be correct, that the enemy's corps beyond the Elbe were returning towards Leipsic, than I conceived that a forced march of the army of the north to concentrate at Zorbig (having its advance towards Dolitsch and Duben) was indispensably necessary, in support of the plan of taking a forward position. I expressed this opinion to the Prince Royal of Sweden; and stated, that according to the reports of the dispositions of the allies from the grand army, and of General Blucher's operations, if His Royal Highness did not cover that general's left, it seemed to me he might be deprived of his share in the anticipated struggle. The Prince Royal replied, that I was urging him to make a march with his flank to the enemy as at the battle of Eylau, which could not fail of being disastrous. I answered His Royal Highness, that as all the bridges on the Mulda were destroyed, and as its passage was so difficult, that His Royal Highness had told me he could not pass it to attack: the enemy, I was certain, if they were present in force, could not attempt its passage to attack him, especially with General Blucher before them, and the grand army so close. Besides, I told him he had 60,000 men, with a river to protect his flank during his march, on which he might, if necessary, throw an additional corps to his advanced-guard during this movement: and, above all, as we knew the enemy was filing towards Leipsic, there could be no possible risk. After more conversation, in which I blended the respect I had for his military renown with an honest disclosure of my sentiments, I expressed my gratitude for his condescension in listening to me, where he had an undoubted right to consider himself as best qualified to judge. His Royal Highness at length determined to march to Halle: I urged, with deferential earnestness, that Halle was in rear of General Blucher, and if the General should engage, His Royal Highness would never be able to support him during the conflict. His Royal Highness answered, he would be in second line, and able to support if necessary: and in his orders on the following day, he directed his army to prepare to follow the enemy if they were beaten, and to do them all possible mischief in their retreat, evidently showing he did not intend to assist in the action. I left the Prince Royal, however, in the evening, with a promise, on his part, that he would change the direction of the march from Halle to the left on Zorbig, when the troops should be in route in the morning. Here I must observe, my urgent proposition was to reach Zorbig on the 14th, which could easily have been achieved, as we remained two days at Köthen; still it was something to approximate the army towards the former place. On the 14th, I left Köthen, and rode with the Prince on the morning of the 15th; but my surprise and chagrin were equal when, instead of directing his troops to the left on Zorbig, as he had promised, or even to Halle, he marched the Swedes by Gropzig, in the rear of the Peterberg, towards Wettin; the Prussians to the Peterberg and Oppin; while the Russian corps had their left at Zorbig.

 The army collected at Köthen on the 14th: their obvious march, to support General Blucher and to meet the enemy, was to the left and forward; but His Royal Highness directed them to the right, in rear of General Blucher, and backward, making at the same time an angle to the rear, which nearly doubled their distance. At Sylbitz, where the Prince Royal stopped to issue orders to the troops, I respectfully but urgently requested it might be weighed whether the other armies would not complain of this movement, especially General Blucher, when it was intimated that any one who recommended a march to the left of Zorbig was *un sot:* after some time, however, I had the satisfaction of finding the Russian corps ordered to Zorbig. Baron Witterstedt, still minister of Sweden, and General Adlercreutz, also, were present, but took no part in this discussion.

I must here observe, that the orders intentionally (for they could not be ignorantly) issued on this day by the Prince Royal were for the different corps to have brigades formed towards the Elbe, evidently to give the impression that the enemy were to be looked for in that quarter. On the 16th, in the morning, being personally much chagrined at the Prince Royal's resolutions, I repaired to General Blucher. All I had been able to accomplish by dint of persuasion, was to get the Russians to Zorbig; and General Blucher fairly and naturally sympathised with my painful sensations on this result.

The Prince Royal however assured me, that in case General Blucher should make an attack the following day, I might give the General his word that he would be on the ground in the direction of Dolitsch and Eulenburg, with 8000 or 10,000 cavalry and light artillery to support him, even if his infantry could not arrive. This pledge I stated *totidem verbis* to General Blucher when I joined him. I there wrote and despatched by my own *aide-de-camp* from the ground, while the dispositions for General Blucher's attack were making, the following letter to His Royal Highness:

> *Le 16ème Octobre, 9¼ heures a.m.*
> *Monseigneur,*
> *D'après le rapport de M. le Général Blücher, l'ennemi a quitté Dolitsch. Il est de la première importance, selon ses idées, que l'armée de V. A. R. se porte à la gauche, derrière Dolitsch: les marais et les défilés la mettent absolument hors de risque; et V.A. R. sera en état de prendre part au combat, qui sera plus décisif avec votre armée et vos talens militaires. Comme toute la force de l'ennemi est dans les environs de Leipsic, permettez-moi de vous observer que les momens sont précieux. La nation Anglaise vous regarde; il est de mon devoir de vous parler avec franchise. L'Angleterre ne croira jamais que vous êtes indifférent, pourvu*

que l'ennemi soit battu, si vous y prendrez part ou non. J'ose supplier V. A. R., si vous restez en seconde ligne, d'envoyer le Capitaine Bogue avec sa brigade de Roquetiers, pour agir avec la cavalerie, au Général Blücher.
J'ai l'honneur d'être, &c. &c.
Charles Stewart
Lieut-Général

General Blucher now urged me strongly to hasten to the Prince Royal in person, that the object of this letter might be insured. I proceeded immediately, and met an *aide-de-camp* of the Crown Prince's on the road, bearing a letter from General Adlercreutz, acquainting me that, in consequence of my pressing solicitations, His Royal Highness had consented to move with his advance (the Russians) to the left of Landsberg on that day. The Prussians were a march behind the Russians, and the Swedes one more behind the Prussians.

In vain I sought the Prince Royal; and despairing of an interview, I stated to General Adlercreutz, at Landsberg, how imperiously necessary it was for the Russian cavalry and light artillery to advance immediately in the direction of Taucha; and that the Prince's word had been pledged to it. The general replied, if I could arrange that step with General Winzingerode, he would answer for the concurrence of the Prince. I hurried to this general, who stated that his orders were positive from the Emperor of Russia not to act but by the express commands of the Crown Prince; that he dared not move in person, but he would send 3000 horse forthwith, and 8000 on the following morning, if I could procure such order. I returned to General Blucher greatly disappointed; but was happy to learn, in the sequel, that 3000 horse were actually pushed forward that evening, on General Adlercreutz seeing the Prince, and they appeared on General Blucher's left in the morning. After seeing General Blucher's action, and being uncertain where to find the Prince Royal, I rode late at night to Halle, where I found Baron Witterstedt; I prevailed upon him to send an express to His Royal Highness with the following letter:

Halle
Le 16ème Octobre, à 9 heures du soir.
Monseigneur,
Je viens du champ de bataille du Général. J'ai l'honneur de vous envoyer les détails de cette affaire.
J'ose supplier V.A. R. de vous mettre en marche le moment que vous recevez cette lettre, et de vous porter sur Taucha.
Il n'y a pas un instant à perdre. V.A. R. me l'a promis. C'est vous parler en ami. Je parle actuellement comme soldat; et si vous ne commencez pas votre marche, vous vous en repentirez toujours.
Jai l'honneur d'être,
de V.A. R., Monseigneur,
Le très-obéissant Serviteur,
Charles Stewart

The answer from Baron Witterstedt afforded me the satisfaction of knowing, that by repeated and strenuous efforts the head of the northern army would have been in their place at twelve on the 17th, if an attack had been made.

I think I have said enough to show that, if the Prince had exerted all his faculties, and the mental and physical energy he possessed, the corps of Marmont, Ney, and Bertrand, would have been more completely overthrown, and the serious losses of D'Yorck's corps of Prussians spared, by the timely arrival of the Prince Royal's army. A moment's reference to the map, and the detail of the positions, will convince the world of this fact. If the northern army had marched to Zorbig on the 14th, or even on the 15th, with its advance towards Dolitsch, evacuated by the enemy on that day, the Prince Royal would have been enabled to have acted upon Ney's force, which, on General Langeron's attack, filed from the neighbourhood of Duben and Dolitsch, and protected Marmont's right; and if an impression had been made and followed up to the Partha, simultaneously with General Blucher's attacks, the whole force of the enemy must have been destroyed.

Bold as these remarks are, I have no solid motive for disguising them: as a soldier devoted to his country and his profession, fearing neither the frowns nor courting the favours of any man, I publish my own observations and sentiments as they arose in my mind out of the circumstances which passed within my own knowledge. Of these facts others may judge; and form their own, and perhaps different conclusions, influenced as they may be by conflicting accounts, or the knowledge of latent motives, operating upon the chief actor in these very interesting proceedings. I have at least one consolation, that if these details give dissatisfaction in any quarter, the King and country I served were, at all events, satisfied with my humble exertions.

I have merely to mention, before closing the present chapter, that in the battle of the 16th, a most brilliant charge was made by the Adjutant-General Orloff with the Cossacks of the guard, directed in person by the Emperor Alexander, when they took twenty-four pieces of cannon. There were also various exploits in every part of these bloody fields to which I much lament my pen is unable to do justice; for such was the hurry and confusion of the moment, and the rapidity with which event followed event, and victory battle, that it was totally impossible to collect all details.

CHAPTER 11

Leipzig: the Battle of the Nations

Before describing the great operations connected with the battle of Leipsic, by which the fate of Napoleon, in my opinion, was entirely and irrevocably decided, I wish to direct the reader's attention to the corps in the north. The Prince Royal left General Walmoden with his corps, and those of General Tettenborn, Dornberg, &c. to keep Marshal Davoust in check; and on the 18th of August, in a well-contested action at Vella,. 2000 cavalry under Walmoden held in check 15,000 French, commanded by Davoust. That general, in consequence of the successes of the Prince Royal, evacuated Schwerin, where he had his head-quarters; the Danes, however, now separated themselves from the French, and took post behind the Stecknitz river.

A very brilliant action took place on the 15th near Dömitz. General Walmoden left General Vegesack to observe Davoust, and marched to join General Tettenborn, who found the enemy placed between the villages of Ollendorf and Euchdorf with 10,000 men and eight pieces of artillery. The disposition being made, General Walmoden succeeded on every side, destroyed the entire division of Pécheux, and took thirty officers and 1500 men. After the action, Walmoden placed his head-quarters at Dennewitz, and Davoust retreated behind the Stecknitz. Many brilliant skirmishes were reported in that direction; amongst which a Prussian colonel, Marwitz, greatly distinguished himself.

The great crisis now approached, by Napoleon concentrating

all his force in the environs of Leipsic. Why he decided upon this measure, and did not rather determine on taking his first position behind the Saale, or carrying his army in the direction of Magdeburg, was a point often and much debated on.

The allied army being at length assembled, the Field-Marshal Prince Schwartzenberg issued the following order:

> Braves guerriers! L'époque la plus importante de la sainte lutte est arrivée; l'heure décisive vient de sonner; préparez-vous au combat. Le lien qui réunit les plus puissantes nations pour un et même but, va se resserrer encore sur le champ de bataille : Russes, Prusses, Autrichiens, vous combattrez pour la même cause, pour la liberté de l'Europe, pour l'indépendance, pour 1'immortalité. Tous pour un, un pour tous, que ce soit votre cri de guerre dans ce saint combat: restez-lui fidele dans le moment décisif, et la victoire est à vous.
>
> Charles P. Schwartzenberg

Such was the order issued to the grand army by its commander. Europe now approached her deliverance; and England might fairly and triumphantly look forward to reap that harvest of glory her steady and unexampled efforts in the common cause so justly entitled her to receive. I can only regret the absence of an abler pen in the individual commissioned to make known to the British government the events of the 16th, 17th, and 18th of October, but such was the task imposed on the writer of this narrative; and in endeavouring rapidly to describe the prominent features of these memorable days, pregnant with the fate of so many millions, with any thing like military connexion and precision, he conceived he best fulfilled his duty as a soldier.

The battle of General Blucher on the 16th was followed by a complete and signal victory on the 18th, by the combined forces, over Buonaparte, at the head of his army, in the neighbourhood of Leipsic. The collective loss of above 100 pieces of cannon, 60,000 men, an immense number of prisoners—the desertion of the Saxon army, and also of the Bavarian and Wirtemburg troops still remaining in the French ranks, consisting in all of artillery, cavalry, and infantry—many generals killed, wound-

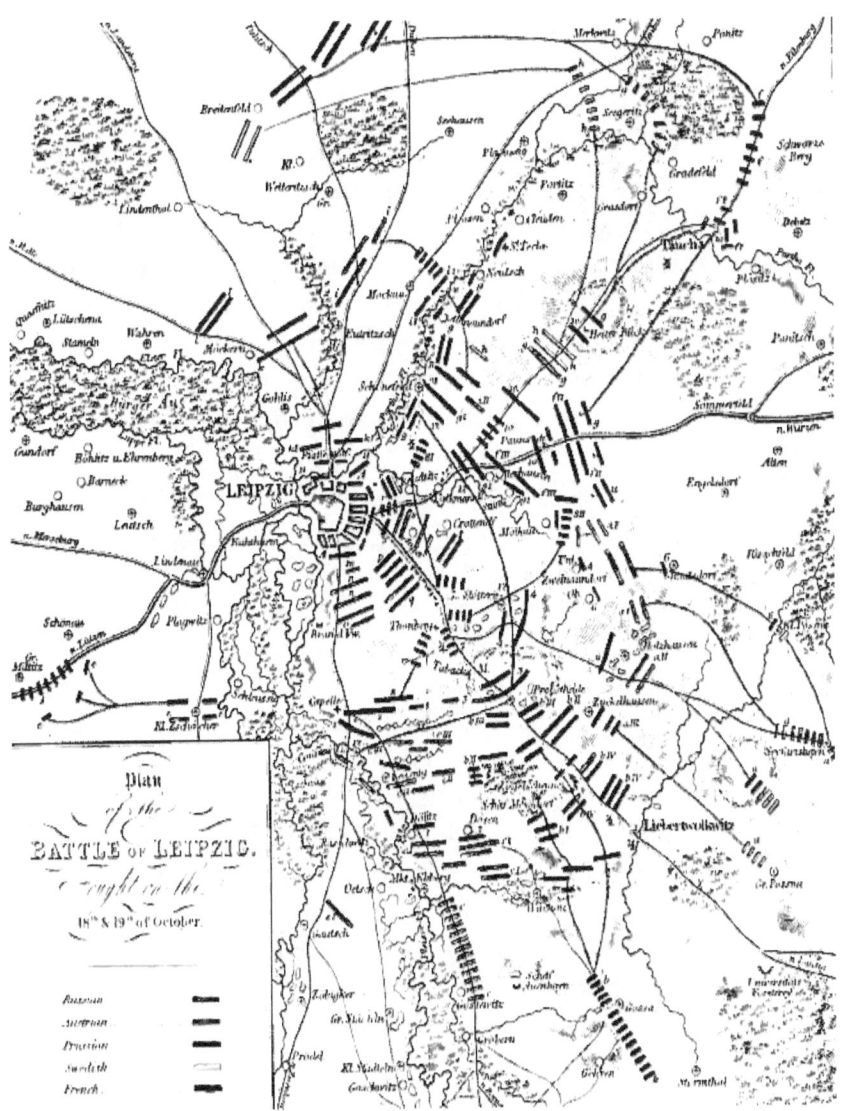

ed, and taken prisoners, among whom were Regnier, Valberg, Brune, Bertrand, and Lauriston, were some of the first fruits of the glorious day of the 18th of October. These were followed by the capture by assault of the town of Leipsic; the magazines, the artillery, stores of the place, with the King of Saxony, all his court, the garrison, and the rear-guard of the French army; the whole of the enemy's wounded, the number of whom exceeded 30,000, with the complete *déroute* of the French army, it being entirely surrounded, and endeavouring to escape in all directions: such were the prominent subjects of exultation. Buonaparte was fortunate enough to escape by rapid flight two hours before the entry into Leipsic of the allied forces. The further results may be obtained from a statement of the day's military manoeuvres and positions, which it will here be my endeavour to give as succinctly as possible: firstly, of the general and combined operations determined upon by the imperial and royal generals; and secondly, a description of what immediately came under my own observation, namely, the movements of General Blucher and the Prince Royal.

The positions of the, allied armies, up to the 16th, have been already detailed. It being announced by Prince Schwartzenberg that it was the intention of their majesties, the allied Sovereigns, to renew the attack upon the enemy on the 18th, and the order above detailed for the army having been issued, the armies of the north and Silesia were directed to co-operate. Napoleon's army was situated on the 18th nearly as follows:

The 8th, 2nd, and 5th corps, under Murat, at Cannewitz; the right was commanded by Prince Poniatowski; Victor formed the centre at Probstheide; the left, under Lauriston, occupied Homburg; the guards occupied Thornberg, where Buonaparte was in person; Ney was with Napoleon; Oudinot supported Poniatowski with the *jeune garde,* and Mortier was charged with the defence of Leipsic. The dispositions and orders of the grand army were as follows:—the 1st column, under Barclay de Tolly, composed of Wittgenstein's corps and the Russian and Prussian guards, were to advance to the heights of Wachan; the

2nd column, under the Hereditary Prince of Hesse Homburg, a most gallant and skilful officer (since married to our English Princess Elizabeth, but unfortunately now no more), was composed of the divisions of Bianchi, Maurice Lichtenstein, and Weissenwolf, with the reserve, marched on Dolitsch, with Colloredo's corps as a further reserve; the 3rd column, under Bennigsen, with the corps of Kleinau and Guthin, marched on Holzhausen.

Whilst the grand army was to commence the attack from the different points of assembly, on the principal villages situated upon the great roads leading to Leipsic, the armies of the north and Silesia were jointly to attack the line of the Saale, and the enemy's position along the Partha river. General Blucher entrusted to the Prince Royal of Sweden 30,000 infantry, cavalry, and artillery; and with this formidable reinforcement, the northern army was to attack from, the heights of Taucha; while General Blucher was to retain his position before Leipsic, and use his utmost efforts to gain possession of the place. In the event of the whole of the enemy's forces being carried against either of the armies, they were reciprocally to support each other, and concert further movements.

That part of the enemy's force which for some time had been opposed to the Prince Royal of Sweden and General Blucher, had taken up a very good position upon the left bank of the Partha, having its right at the strong point of Taucha, and its left towards Leipsic. To force the enemy's right, and obtain possession of the heights of Taucha, was the first operation of the Prince Royal's army. The corps of Russians under General Winzingerode, and the Prussians under General Bulow, were destined for this purpose rand the Swedish army was directed to force the passage of the river near Plosen and Mockau. The passage was effected without much opposition: General Winzingerode took about 3000 prisoners at Taucha, and some guns; and General Blucher put his army in motion, as soon as he found the grand army engaged very hotly in the neighbourhood of the villages of Stetteritz and Probstheide. The infantry of the Prince Royal's army had not sufficient time to make their flank movement before the enemy's infantry had abandoned the line of the river, and retired over the plain, in line and column, towards Leipsic, occupying Pounsdorf, and Schönefel in strength, so as to protect their retreat. A very heavy cannonading, and some brilliant performances of General Winzingerode's cavalry, marked chiefly the events of the early part of the day; towards the close, when General Count Langeron, who had crossed the river and attacked the village of Schönefel, he met a determined resistance, and at first was unable to force his way: he however possessed himself of the villages, but was driven back; when the most positive orders were sent him by General Blucher to reoccupy it at the point of the bayonet, which he accomplished before sunset.

Some Prussian battalions of General Bulow's corps were warmly engaged also at Pounsdorf, and the enemy were retiring from it, when the Prince Royal directed the rocket brigade, under Captain Bogue, to form on the left of a Russian battery, and open upon the retiring columns. Congreve's formidable weapon had scarcely accomplished the object of paralysing a solid square of infantry, which, after our fire, delivered themselves up, as if panic struck, when that estimable man and gallant officer, Captain Bogue, of the British royal artillery, received a mortal wound in the head, which at once deprived society of a noble character, and this country of his valuable services. Lieutenant Strangeways, who succeeded in the command of the brigade, received the Prince Royal's thanks, conveyed through me, for the important assistance they had rendered. I felt great satisfaction at witnessing, during this day, a species of improved warfare, the effects of which were truly astonishing; and produced an impression upon the enemy of something supernatural. During the action, twenty-two guns of Saxon artillery, with two Westphalian regiments of hussars, and two battalions of Saxons, joined us from the enemy: the former were instantly led again into the field, our artillery and ammunition not being all brought forward. The close communication was fully established between the grand army and those of Blucher and the north. The Grand-Duke Constantine, Generals Platoff, Miloradovitch, and other officers of distinction, joined the Prince Royal, to communicate the events carrying on in the several quarters of this great field of battle.

The most desperate resistance was made by the enemy at Probstheide, Stetteritz, and Cannewitz. But the different columns bearing on those points, as above detailed, carried every thing before them; General Bennigsen taking the villages on the right bank, and General Giulay manoeuvring 25,000 Austrians on the left bank of the Elster. General Thielman's and Prince Maurice Lichtenstein's corps moved upon the same river; and the grand result of the day was, that the enemy lost above 40,000 men in killed and wounded, sixty-five pieces of artillery, and seventeen battalions of German infantry, with all their staff and generals, who came over in a mass during the action. The armies remained, during the night, upon the ground which they had so bravely conquered. The Prince Royal had his bivouac at Pounsdorf; General Blucher remained at Wellens; and the Emperors and King at Roda.

About the close of the day, it being reported that the enemy were retiring by Weissenfels and Naumberg, General Blucher received an order from the King of Prussia to detach in that direction. The movement of the Prince Royal's army completely precluded the retreat on Wittemberg; that upon Erfurth had long since been lost to them, and the line of the Saale appeared alone to remain. As both the flanks and rear would be operated upon during their march, it was difficult to say with what portion of his army the enemy could get to the Rhine.

On the 19th the town of Leipsic was attacked, and carried, after a short resistance, by the armies of Blucher, the Prince Royal, Bennigsen, and the grand army. Marmont and Mac-Donald commanded in the town: these, with Augereau and Victor, narrowly escaped with a small escort. Their majesties, the Emperor of Russia and King of Prussia, and the Crown Prince of Sweden, each heading their respective troops, entered the town at different points, and met in the great square. The acclamations and rejoicings of the people are not to be described: handkerchiefs waving from the windows, hands clamorous in applause, and lastly, but most eloquently, tears rolling from the eyes, announced the delightful era of the liberation of the world from the tyranny of the despot to be at hand. The moment was too enthusiastically felt to be described in adequate terms, and I confess myself unequal to it. The multiplicity of brilliant achievements, the impossibility of doing full justice to the talent and prowess shown in the series of enterprises arising from the boldness of conception in our commander, Prince Field-Marshal Schwartzenberg, and the other intrepid and experienced captains, will be admitted by every one, and plead an excuse for a sketch which scarcely merits the name of a description.

I sent the account of this battle to England by my *aide-de-camp,* and cousin, Mr. James, who most gallantly was every where in the hottest of the action, and had been distinguished for his ardour in the service since he had been with this army. In order also to take every measure to accomplish the transmission home of this vitally important intelligence as speedily as possible, I was induced to avail myself of the services of Mr. Solly, a Prussian gentleman, largely connected in England; who with indefatigable zeal, and at great personal risk and inconvenience, undertook to carry a copy of my communication direct to the English government through the midst of the French armies. He embarked in an open boat, and arrived in London with this glorious intelligence in an incredibly short space of time. One palliating circumstance connected with my imperfect detail of this combat is, that I wrote it nearly as I have given it above on a stone in the field of battle, when the fire had ceased, without correction or amendment. I ought here to record the gallantry displayed, and the efficient assistance I received from my *aides-de-camp*, Captain Charles, now Major, Wood, and Lieutenant-colonel Noel Harris: the latter brave officer lost his arm, in the following year, at Waterloo.

An officer arrived on the 19th from General Tettenborn, bringing the intelligence of the surrender of Bremen to the corps under his orders; and the keys of that town were presented by the Prince Royal to the Emperor of Russia in the square at Leipsic.

The losses sustained in the last four days' combats could not with precision be stated; but they were averaged, on the part of the enemy, at 15,000 prisoners, without reckoning 23,000 sick and wounded found in the hospitals at Leipsic, 250 pieces of cannon, and 900 tumbrils. Prince Poniatowski, Generals Vial, Rochambeau, Dumoutier, Campans, and Latour Maubourg, were killed; and Ney, Marmont, and Souham, wounded. Fifteen generals were made prisoners. The loss of the allies was equally serious. The Prussian corps of D'Yorck lost 5000 men: the Austrians enumerated no less than sixty officers of distinction killed in this sanguinary contest.

I have now to record an ingenious device of the enemy to excite delay and discussion amongst the allies. General Meerveldt, who had been taken on the 16th, was liberated on his parole by Buonaparte, charged with propositions of peace to the Emperor of Russia. Buonaparte saw General Meerveldt in the village of Lutschen: he spoke very earnestly on the subject of a general pacification; but first declared. that he had 200,000 men in line, and a much more considerable cavalry than the allies had expected. He offered, on condition of an armistice during the negotiation, to evacuate Dantzic, Modelin, Stettin, Custrin, Glogau, Dresden, Torgau, and even, in case of necessity, Wittemberg. He promised to retire behind the Saale; and he said, as to terms of peace, that England could receive Hanover; the neutrality of the flag of Hamburgh and Lubeck might be ensured, as well as the independence of Holland; and Italy be united with an independent monarchy. He hesitated as to the restitution of Mantua to Austria; and repeated, that Italy should be kept entire. Meerveldt observed, that the allies might object to Murat as the sovereign of Naples. The answer was, that it was not necessary to anticipate that arrangement; and Napoleon again and again declared he did not believe

England would make peace; and never without a condition to which he could never submit, *viz.* limitation of the number of French ships of war.

General Meerveldt then inquired, whether he would resign Erfurth, as well as the other fortresses? Napoleon hesitated: the General then said, the resignation of the protectorship of the Rhine was necessary. Buonaparte replied, it was impossible; but on being told that Bavaria had withdrawn from his protection, the courier from Munich having been taken, and that other treaties were negotiating, he exclaimed, Then the protectorship of the confederation ceases of itself. As to Spain, it was a question of dynasty, *je n'y suis plus*—therefore, that question is decided. These were the principal topics of conversation, as given by General Meerveldt. His impression also was, from Napoleon's manner and all he said, that he would fall back upon the Rhine: he looked jaded and ill at this period, and was very much depressed.

This interview, it must be understood, took place before the last battles; and there was certainly amongst the allies a disposition to accept of Buonaparte's terms, and open a negotiation.

In further reference to my correspondence with the Prince Royal of Sweden, already detailed, it is right for me to state, that returning to the head-quarters of His Royal Highness on the morning of the 18th from General Blucher at Breitenfeld, when dispositions were making for the attack, the general officers being present, the *aide-de-camp* in waiting desired me to walk in.

On entering, I was no less surprised than hurt, when the Prince approached with a look bordering upon suppressed anger, and withdrawing towards the window, he addressed me nearly as follows, but in a purposely low tone, that others might not overhear:

> *Comment! Général Stewart; quel droit avez-vous de m'écrire ? Ne rappelez-vous pas que je suis le Prince de Suède, un des plus grands Généraux de l'âge? et si vous étiez à ma place, que penseriez-vous si quelqu'un vous écrivoit comme vous m'avez écrit? Vous n'êtez pas accrédité près de moi: c'est par mon amitié que vous êtes ici; et vous m'avez donne beaucoup de peine.*

I answered in the most respectful tone:—It was possible my zeal had carried me too far; but, according to my own conception of my duty, I could not repent one step I had taken. I had urged the march to Zorbig: His Royal Highness had reluctantly, and in part only, consented to that measure. I had entreated the movement forward to Landsberg; and His Royal Highness had adopted that idea. After General Blucher's victory, my letter and entreaty induced His Royal Highness to break up at two o'clock in the morning from Landsberg, and bring the head of his columns at that critical moment into position. His Royal Highness could then see whether I had mistaken the views of the enemy. The whole circumstances were known to his staff, his ministers, and the principal officers of his army. I desired to be judged by Baron Wetterstedt and General Adlercreutz whether the result had not been attained by my individual, but humble, importunity and exertions. I had never been intentionally deficient in respect towards His Royal Highness's exalted position; but it was a little hard, instead of receiving thanks for my services, to be visited with displeasure: it is true, I was not formally accredited as British minister to the court of Sweden, but I was charged generally with the military interest of Great Britain in the north of Europe. England paid the Swedish army; and my reports whether that army did what I considered its duty to the common cause, actively or passively, must operate seriously upon the alliance. I was incapable of the vanity of placing the value of my military opinions on a par with those of so great a general; but it required very little discrimination to perceive that His Royal Highness had been literally pressed into the recent transactions—that his original orders were evidently a departure from the system of combination, and foreign to the dispositions of the grand armies. But independently of these demonstrations of isolated objects, certain expressions of his own were most explicit, and this was not a moment for diplomatic concealment. I spoke my opinion openly and firmly, but respectfully. I never should shrink from my duty in the most painful situation; which I fairly confessed, after listening to His Royal Highness, the one I was then placed in appeared to me to be.

The expression of his countenance during my discourse varied considerably, and at length had become calm; and he replied with *bon-hommie:*

> *Eh bien! voulez-vous que nous soyons amis ? Vous savez, mon ami, l'amitié que je vous porte; pourquoi ne pas causer ensemble des dispositions militaires? Dites-moi vos pensées ; mais ne m'écrivez plus, je vous en prie de grâce.*

I assured His Royal Highness I felt honoured by his friendship, when I considered he was acting as became the Crown Prince of Sweden: that if he was displeased with my correspondence, I should write in future to General Adlercreutz; although his own invitation, on my first arrival, had led me rather to address my letters to the *Generalissimo* in person. My anxious efforts were to assist the Swedish nation; but I could never see their chief depart from what I knew were the true interests of his situation, without remonstrating boldly. The Prince upon this took my hand, assuring me of his friendship. We discussed the principal features of what had passed, and I felt myself restored to favour; so much so, that he invited me at dinner to meet the Emperor and King, I being the only minister present.

However distressing this scene was to my feelings, I relate it to show the difficulties of the duties imposed upon me; and I experience a sensible pleasure in stating, that those able, experienced, and highly-talented general officers, who were placed by the allied powers near the person of His Royal Highness, amongst whom General Pozzo di Borgo stood pre-eminently conspicuous for his high abilities and acute discernment, aided me in my most difficult task. If the time should ever arrive to allow of the correspondence of those general officers, Generals Baron Vincent, Krusemark, and Pozzo di Borgo, with their courts (much of which I have in my possession), to be made public, I shall have no hesitation in giving them to history, as more than corroborative of my candid statements. Posterity will then do justice to the extreme difficulties we had to surmount in the execution of our duties. General Pozzo di Borgo had made himself very unpalatable to the Prince Royal, through his ardent zeal for the common cause, heightened by his personal knowledge of the dangerous character of Buonaparte; and every effort was made at Leipsic by His Royal Highness, to remove him from the head-quarters of the Swedish army. I was the fortunate medium, however, of arresting that measure; and the Emperor of Russia ordered no change to take place: and by making my own government privy to General Pozzo di Borgo's able reports, I confirmed the confidence the English government had in his capacity. After the battles above detailed, His Royal Highness presented me with the Swedish military Order of the Sword, which the Prince Regent graciously permitted me to accept.

CHAPTER 12

Retreat & Pursuit

The pursuit of the enemy continued along the whole line; and prisoners, baggage, and all the *attirail* of a flying army were hourly sent in by the Cossacks and light troops. I felt most anxious about the fate of Buonaparte, conceiving that his ultimate destiny could not be doubtful or remote. He reached Lutzen on the 19th; and I concluded he would either direct his march across the Saale, and make for Nordhausen and the Hartz, in order to place himself behind the Weser, calling Marshal Davoust's army from the north to his aid, or attempt to move on the *chaussée* towards Erfurth, after passing the Saale at Weissenfels. It was almost impossible he should escape, except with the wreck of an army; but it was easy to imagine that the remnant of his masses, directed on one line, might force their way through smaller corps.

The following disposition of the allied armies was now concerted, with immediate preparations to carry it into effect. The grand army of Bohemia marched on the enemy's right in the direction of Frankfort on the Maine; taking the rout of Pegau, Zeitz, and Eisenberg. The army of General Bennigsen, united to that of the army of the north, and under the orders of the Crown Prince, followed the enemy's centre, in the direction of Lutzen and Naumburg. The triumphant army of Silesia, when near Leipsic, diverged still further to the right, and was to *cotoyer* the enemy's left by Merseburg; and its cannon was soon heard reverberating in that direction. If the enemy passed the

Saale at Weissenfels, the army of the Prince Royal was to move on Freyberg. The Saxon troops were joined to the Swedish army; but 2000 Baden troops were considered prisoners of war. The captures continued to be still greater than those hitherto detailed; fifty more pieces of cannon were discovered, besides those buried by the enemy. Prince Poniatowski, who received two wounds in attempting to pass the Elster, urged by what the French call *un beau désespoir*, was drowned in that river; decked, it was said, with brilliants, and too heavily charged with coin for a retreat *à la nage*.

Several battalions of Poles joined the allied army. The Emperor's head-quarters moved on the 31st towards Eisenberg. The Prince Royal preferred a change in his line of march, and moved to Merseburg the same day. His Prussian Majesty nominated General Blucher to the rank of Field-Marshal, as a fit recompense for his pre-eminent services; and their majesties, the Emperor of Russia and the Emperor of Austria, conferred on Prince Schwartzenberg the First Class of their respective military Orders of St. George and Maria Theresa, and the King of Prussia that of the Black Eagle.

By intelligence received from Count Tolstoy's corps, which was left to watch the force under General Gouvion St. Cyr, in garrison at Dresden, the enemy, finding the grand army had moved away, commenced an offensive operation on Count Tolstoy, which they followed up with some success, as he was much outnumbered. He lost 4000 or 5000 men; but took up a defensive position at Peterswalde.

The allied armies continued their pursuit of the enemy; and no day passed, since the memorable battle of Leipsic, without cannon, prisoners, baggage, and carriages of all sorts, falling into their hands. Marshal Blucher's pursuit was the closest, from the position in which he occupied on the 19th, as he followed the enemy on the Lutzen road. Marshal Blucher thus formed the centre army: the Prince Royal the right, and the grand army the left of the allied forces.

I am unable, from my own personal observation, to afford the details of the advantages obtained at this epoch in pursuit by the armies of Silesia, Bohemia, and the north; and to recapitulate the information obtained from different sources would require volumes. The Crown Prince put his army in march on the 20th, and had his head-quarters at Merseburg on the 22nd; at Querfurt the 23rd; and at Artern on the 24th.

By advices received, General Gouvion St. Cyr, after his action with General Tolstoy, evacuated Dresden, taking with him the garrison, and directed himself on Torgau and Wittemberg. It was computed that he could collect between 30,000 and 40,000 men: which force, it was presumed, would march upon Magdeburg, and probably attempt to form a junction with Marshal Davoust's corps. As this army's movement might occasion a momentary alarm, General Bennigsen, with a corps of 10,000 men, exclusive of cavalry, was directed to put himself in march immediately; and he was ordered to assume the command of all the allied corps on the Elbe, under Generals Tolstoy, Tauenstein, &c, amounting to between 60 and 70,000 men. This army was first to find out General Gouvion St. Cyr, wherever he might be, and fall upon him *en masse*. They were then to undertake the sieges of Torgau and Wittemberg, should they still hold out.

Lieutenant-General Count Walmoden's movements were to be guided by those of Marshal Davoust, and in combination with those of General Bennigsen. The other two divisions of General Bennigsen's army were added to the Russians under General Winzingerode. The Saxon troops were detached to join General Count Tolstoy.

According to further advices, the enemy were collecting about Erfurth on the 27th of October. The following was nearly the position of the different armies:

The grand army was at Weimar; Marshal Blucher at, or about, Eisenach; General Langeron at Wisbach; General D'Yorck at Sommerda; General Bulow at Colleda; the Crown Prince at Artern; and General Winzingerode at Kindelbrück. By the above arrangement, if the enemy, stood his ground, the wings could all fall back upon the grand army, and inflict the *coup de grace* upon that hydra of demoralization and destruction still lingering in Germany. Some thousand French, surrounded and succourless, now laid down their arms near Weissenfels.

The enemy's columns continued their retreat with so much rapidity, that however difficult to keep *l'épée aux reins,* yet increased harasses and further discomfiture daily ensued. General Count Wrede had arrived with his army of 58,000 Bavarians and Austrians. On the 24th he was to surround Wurtzburg, to summon the fortress, and bombard both that and the city in case of refusal to surrender. General Wrede next proposed to place himself *à cheval* on the Maine, and to occupy and break up the roads to Mayence, in order to impede the enemy's retreat, and attempt to take possession of the *tête du pont* of Cassel.

The Grand Army moved on by its left, in two columns, from Weimar towards Erfurth. The first column, composed of the 1st, 2nd, and 3rd Austrian divisions, and the advanced-guard, pressed forward on Erfurth and Gotha: Generals Wittgenstein's and Kleist's corps observed Erfurth; and in the event of the enemy having left only a small garrison, they were to blockade the place with a corps, and move on in pursuit. The second column, composed wholly of Russian and Prussian guards and reserves, marched from Weimar by Berka and Kranichfeld, where the head-quarters were to be established on the 28th. The enemy evacuated Erfurth, leaving a garrison in it. In the centre, the army of Silesia never allowed itself a moment's repose, or ceased from those extraordinary efforts by which its whole progress had been characterised. The Russian advanced-guard, under General Wassilchikoff, made 2000 prisoners near Lutzen: after which, General D'Yorck came up on the 22nd, reached the enemy near Freyberg, took 1500 more prisoners, liberated 4000 Russians and Austrians, captured eighteen pieces of cannon, and compelled the enemy to destroy 500 ammunition wagons.

Marshal Blucher's march, through defiles and bad roads, was most difficult and appalling: added to which, the soldiers had to contend at this unfavourable season with almost total destitution of necessaries; but he proceeded through Weissensee and Langencalza, always on the enemy's flank, who kept the great *chaussée* to Erfurth and Gotha.

On the 26th, the field-marshal again came up with the enemy near Eisenach; they appeared in a column of about 20,000 men, in tolerable order: the ground was unfavourable for the Marshal's cavalry, being between the Thuringian mountains and the Hortelberg and Kahlenberg; and as the greater part of his infantry had been directed on Gross-Leipnitz, more on the enemy's flank, it was late before the struggle commenced. General D'Yorck's corps, however, when it arrived from Gross-Leipnitz, attacked the enemy entering the town of Eisenach, and he was thrown into complete disorder. General Langeron coming up made 2000 prisoners; and the enemy abandoned here, as elsewhere, a whole train of caissons, most of which were blown up. Night closed this brilliant and decisive affair. On the 27th, the enemy retired from Eisenach, pursued by Marshal Blucher. It was believed General Bertrand's division was completely separated, and cut off from the grand route of Frankfort, and forced to take the mountain roads in the direction of Schweinfurth: General D'Yorck was sent after this corps. Buonaparte left Eisenach at five o'clock on the morning of this action. Marshal Blucher moved on the high road to Frankfort; and it was conjectured that this would be Buonaparte's great line of retreat.

Marshal Blucher's successes since the battles of Leipsic might be fairly averaged at 6000 prisoners, 4000 Russians liberated, forty pieces of cannon, and 100 caissons taken, exclusive of those blown up. Of the corps of Marmont, which was composed of the best French troops, only 3000 now remained: in short, the disasters of the enemy were hourly, and of every description.

Colonel Hudson Lowe being at this period attached by me to Marshal Blucher, I can confide in the authenticity of the information which I give, as received from that able and intelligent officer. Marshal Blucher's army, since leaving Leipsic on the 27th of October, had out-marched the grand army even in its own line of march, and now formed in the van. The colonel conceived that the 26th might have been a most fatal day for Buonaparte, had the Silesian army put itself in movement at an earlier hour, or had there been officers of greater activity and combination at the head of the Russian cavalry. A prompt march upon Eisenach, which lies in the very centre of defiles, would have rendered all further retreat on that line impassable.

It would have cost some lives, however; and the infantry had already suffered so much, and were so exceedingly harassed, that it would have been unreasonable to expect much more could have been done by them. The extraordinary effort must have been made by the cavalry, with such artillery and infantry as could follow.

Notwithstanding, sufficient was done, as it was, to establish a fair claim to public approbation. Even Napoleon, who by the rapidity of his march, had placed himself at a very secure distance from the grand army, must not have been a little surprised and alarmed at finding his Silesian opponents close upon his flanks, and arriving at Eisenach at almost the same moment as himself. The colonel continues to write as follows:

> I had mentioned to General Gniesenau what you desired me to say. He is of opinion, as every other person must be, that the Prince Royal could not do less[1] than he has done to meet the extraordinary services you have rendered to the cause and to him.
> General Gniesenau has had the cross of a commander of Maria Theresa conferred on him. I wish sincerely that our country had some method also of distinguishing the services of officers known to it, who deserve so well for their exertions in the public cause. There is nothing which appears to afford Marshal Blucher so much gratification, as the idea that his name and exploits will be well considered in England: any testimony of approbation, either from the Sovereign or the country, would, I am sure, delight him.
> I hope, sir, you will do me the justice to believe that I am

---

1. This alludes to the Prince Royal of Sweden having conferred the Swedish military Order of the Sword on General Sir Charles Stewart.

incapable of abusing your indulgence, so far as even to express a desire of remaining with General Blucher's army, whilst there are duties of a more indispensable nature for me to perform in any other quarter. If there can be any situation more enviable than another, it is that of being attached to such an army; and the longer I remain with it, the more agreeable I feel I should find it: but the business I have in the other quarter I know must be terminated, and I shall be therefore ready prepared at your first call to proceed, and join you wherever you appoint me to receive your further directions. Perhaps one of the columns may come to a halt in two, three, or four days, which may appear to you the most suitable time.

The interest of the present moment is so very great, Napoleon so near, and the Bavarian army marching across his supposed line of retreat, that not many days can elapse before some crisis ensues. However, I beg to say I am entirely at your orders for an immediate move, wherever you judge my services most necessary. In the mean time, whether it may be my good fortune to be attached to Marshal Blucher on any future occasion or not, I shall always feel a most lively sense of the high favour you have conferred on me, by placing me near him at the present important crisis.

I must now inform you, that General Blucher, at the suggestion of the King of Prussia, detached General D'Yorck's corps, and a body of cavalry under General Wassilchikoff, to harass the enemy in his retreat. General Wassilchikoff came up with the enemy near Lutzen, and made near 2000 prisoners. General D'Yorck, who moved with his infantry by a wider route, did not come up with the enemy till the 22nd, near Freyberg, where he attacked a column that had marched by that road, took eighteen pieces of cannon, 1500 prisoners, liberated nearly 4000 Austrians and Russians, whom the enemy was conducting as prisoners into France, and compelled him to burn upwards of 400 ammunition wagons.

Before daylight on the morning of the 27th of October, the enemy had quitted the town of Eisenach, which was immediately after entered by Marshal Blucher's army; an advanced corps of which had been sent directly in pursuit, and came up with the rear of the enemy at the entrance of the defiles in the mountains, within about a German mile from the town. The blowing up of the several ammunition wagons, the destruction or abandonment of baggage, and the capture of several stragglers, was the immediate consequence; but the enemy had penetrated far into the defiles, where the ground was not favourable for the advance of the cavalry; and it was only by following his march for the three subsequent days, that the precipitancy and disasters of his flight became obvious.

For an extent of nearly fifty English miles, from Eisenach to Fulda, carcasses of dead and dying horses, without number, dead bodies of men, who had been either killed or perished through hunger, sickness, or fatigue, lying on the roads or in the ditches; parties of prisoners and stragglers, brought in by the Cossacks; blown up or destroyed ammunition and baggage wagons, in such numbers as absolutely to obstruct the road, sufficiently attested the sufferings of the enemy; whilst pillaged and burning towns and villages marked at the same time the ferocity with which he had conducted himself.

The number of dead bodies on the road had been considerably augmented, from a resolution that had been taken to carry off all the sick and wounded; not resulting surely from any principle of humanity, but probably as matter of boast, in the relations that might be given to the world of the event, as several of these men were found abandoned on the road in the last gasp of hunger and disease: the dead and the dying were frequently mixed together, lying in groups of six or eight, by half-extinguished fires on the roadside. Several of these men must have been compelled to move on foot, as their bodies were found on the road with the sticks with which they had endeavoured to support their march lying by their sides. The dead might have been counted by hundreds; and in the space from Eisenach to Fulda could certainly not have amounted to much less than a thousand.

The enemy continued to be closely pursued during the three days' march from Eisenach to Vach Hünefeld and Fulda, and frequently cannonading ensued at the head of the advanced-guard; but the nature of the country not permitting the cavalry to act, the enemy escaped with only such losses as have been enumerated.

On arriving at Fulda, it was ascertained that Buonaparte had fled in the direction of Frankfort; but a subsequent relation assured us that General Count Wrede had taken Hanau, with his Bavarian troops, by assault, on the 28th: Napoleon would be therefore compelled to turn towards Coblentz, and Marshal Blucher had made his dispositions for following him in that direction. General Count St. Priest, of General Baron Sachen's division, had in the mean time entered Cassel. General Baron Sachen, who had not found it necessary to pursue him in that direction, halted this day at Lantubach; General Count Langeron at Luder, and General D'Yorck at Neuchoff. The whole were to move forward on the Lahn.

It had been the original intention of Field-Marshal Blucher to keep the high road to Frankfort, on which he was already the foremost in advance; but the columns of the grand combined army following close on the same route, the solicitations of the Prince Marshal commanding it, who represented the difficulties of subsistence, and the advance of General Wrede on Hanau, induced him to turn off to the right, so as effectually to provide against the enemy's effecting his retreat by the way of Coblentz.

The first day's march was to Ulrickstein, an old town with a castle, on the highest pinnacle of the Vorelberg mountains. The roads to it were full of every obstacle that hills, woods, ravines, morasses, and roads that had never been destined for wheel conveyances, could present; and were, in fact, such as, according to any usual military calculation, would have been considered as impracticable for the movements of a large army: infantry, cavalry, artillery, and baggage, every thing, however, were pushed over them. The Russian twelve-pounders frequently stuck in the road; but where six horses were not sufficient, twelve were tackled; and finally, every thing was made to yield to the perseverance and determined resolution which had distinguished all the operations of this army.

The troops after their long march were cantoned in several of the small mountain villages; and corps of 3000 men were allotted to some, whose usual population would not amount to as many hundreds. The inhabitants supplied their wants with cheerfulness in every thing: the soldiers were delighted; and they had equal reason to be satisfied with each other. The soldiers from Caucasus and the Volga, forgot all the fatigues of their long marches in the hospitable reception the peasants had afforded them.

On arrival at Ulrickstein, accounts were received by Field-Marshal Blucher that General Wrede had fallen in with the enemy, during their retreat on the 29th, and taken 4000 prisoners, many of them of the guards. On the 30th, he was himself attacked by Napoleon, but enabled to keep his position. On the 31st, another affair was reported to have taken place; the result not known. At or near Gelnhausen, General Platoff also fell in with the enemy; and, as reported to the field-marshal, had taken 3000 prisoners. The field-marshal marched this day to Giessen.

It was here reported that Napoleon was still in Frankfort, and had concentred his army between and round Hanau, Frankfort, and the Rhine; that General Wrede, who had possessed himself of both Hanau and Frankfort, found it, necessary to draw in his force to resist the attacks of Napoleon, who, after his first affairs, returned from the Frankfort road to attack the General; and that he was now in position about these towns, both of which he occupied. There were further reports of another battle, in which General Wrede had been successful; but no accounts to be relied on had been received.

General Blucher did not commence his march until after the assault of Leipsic. After six days' rapid marches, by cross-roads, through Freyberg, Colleda, Weissensee, and Langencalza, in a thick clayey country, where preceding rains had rendered the defiles almost impracticable, whilst the enemy, followed by the grand combined army, was moving his columns along the great *chaussée* that leads from Leipsic to Erfurth and Gotha, General, now Field-Marshal, Blucher found himself on the enemy's flank, in his line of retreat from Gotha to Eisenach. He appeared to be in a strong column of from 15,000 to 20,000 men, the main body marching in tolerably good order; but a considerable number of stragglers, many without arms, on their flanks and in the rear.

The field-marshal made the following dispositions: the whole army had marched on that morning, the 26th of October, from Langencalza. He ordered the corps of General Count Langeron to move on Frederichsworth, and that of Generals D'Yorck and Sachen on Gross-Leipnitz, to reconnoitre the heights and villages on their front, and to attack where circumstances admitted. The *chaussée* on which the enemy was proceeding runs in a valley; bounded on one side by the great chain of the Thuringian mountains, and on the other by a range of minor heights, called the Hurthberg, Horselberg, and Kahlenberg. The river Horsel runs closely parallel to the *chaussée:* the ground was not, in consequence, favourable for the operation of cavalry, or for bringing artillery speedily up to the attack; and the enemy had occupied all the ravines and lower eminences bordering on the road with his *tirailleurs*. The main body of the field-marshal's infantry had been directed upon Gross-Leipnitz, considerably in advance towards Eisenach.

It was not, therefore, until late in the evening that the attack commenced. General D'Yorck's corps advanced from Gross-Leipnitz, and threw itself upon the enemy as he was entering the town of Eisenach. A heavy cannonading and musketry ensued on both sides: the enemy was thrown into confusion; and General Count Langeron, who had pushed on at the same time with his corps in the rear, and gained the great *chaussée,* made 2000 prisoners, and compelled the enemy to blow up several of his powder-wagons. General D'Yorck suffered a loss of nearly 300 killed and wounded: the enemy must have suffered in a greater proportion; and in regard to prisoners, his entire loss was not ascertained, as several stragglers were every moment hurrying in.

On the 27th of October the enemy quitted Eisenach, pursued by the field-marshal's advanced-guard. It was ascertained that General Bertrand's division of the French army had taken the direction of Schweinfurth. General D'Yorck had received orders to march across that line. General Baron Sachen's corps was to move towards Cassel.

Field-Marshal Blucher, accompanied by the chief of his staff, General Gniesenau, followed him with the corps of General Count Langeron on the high road to Frankfort, which the marshal conjectured would be his line of retreat. Thus was the army of Silesia, after taking the most circuitous marches, again the first in its pursuit and attack of the enemy. The number of prisoners taken by it, since the retreat from Leipsic, cannot be estimated at a less number than 6000 men; whilst nearly 4000 had been gained for the cause, *viz*. the liberation of the prisoners that had been taken by the enemy.

Information was now received that Lieutenant-General Count Wrede, at the head of an army of 58,000 Austrians and Bavarians, had advanced as far as Wurtzburg, and was pursuing his march on Frankfort, so that sanguine hopes were entertained of his arriving there before the enemy could reach that point. On the 20th the Prince Royal moved his army to Sondershausen, and the 28th to Mulhausen; having his advance, under Lieutenant-General Woronzoff, on the great roads leading towards Cassel, to which point His Royal Highness's immediate attention now seemed directed.

Lieutenant-General Czernicheff, who joined General Winzingerode's command, with his usual activity, was alive in all directions in the enemy's rear and on its flanks; and he never gave them breathing time. He had a brilliant affair at Enterode, near Eisenach attacking with 200 horse the division Fournier, 800 strong: he made 200 prisoners, and killed many more. The general then resolved to march on Fulda, to head the enemy's columns in that direction.

Buonaparte generally remained with his rear-guard, which was composed of his guards. Marshal Kellerman, it was believed, had not more than 4000 or 5000 men at Frankfort. General Czernicheff marched without guns for greater rapidity, and generally advanced eight or ten German miles a day. General Tauenstein reported all quiet in the quarter of Wittemberg, and the right bank of the Elbe; and it was now said that General Gouvion St. Cyr was directing himself on Chemnitz. General Bennigsen's corps continued its march by Leipsic. The *ci-devant* King of Westphalia had fled from Cassel, forcing the inhabitants to buy all the valuables he had and could not carry off with him: he decamped with a good booty.

While successes crowned the efforts of the allies on all sides, the firm and cheerful behaviour of the troops, amidst all their fatigues and deprivations, was remarkable: yet it became necessary before long to give the armies repose, in order to recruit their ranks, to re-equip the soldiers, and carefully to superintend the hospitals. Numbers of men had been left behind, worn down by suffering and exertions almost superhuman. But while this measure appeared so necessary, it was still a secondary consideration with the allied Sovereigns, so long as the enemy remained on the right bank of the Rhine.

A successful *coup de main* by a partisan, Colonel Chrapowitski, who entered Gotha on the 22nd, took the French minister, Baron St. Aignau, seventy-three officers, 900 men, prisoners, and blew up fifty ammunition wagons, terminated this campaign. Many interesting letters were intercepted by the capture of the above-named *diplomate* who was now about to play a prominent part on this great scene of action.

CHAPTER 13

Hanau

To return to the movements of the grand army; on the 23rd of October, Napoleon seemed to be concentrating and reorganizing his army at Erfurth. On the 25th, the two Emperors, the King of Prussia, and Prince Schwartzenberg, established their head-quarters at Weimar; while the Silesian army, anticipating the probability of a future combat at Erfurth, proceeded to Langencalza: a movement which, threatening Napoleon's rear, compelled him to abandon his position at Erfurth. Marshal Blucher then marched on Eisenach, as has been already recorded. The enemy continued their rapid retreat by Fulda and Frankfort, harassed by the cavalry and Cossacks, under Platoff, Sloweiski, and Czernicheff.

In the mean time, General Wrede, with the Bavarian army, made rapid marches towards Mayence, in the hope of arriving at Frankfort before them, and of cutting off the major part of the retreating army. The grand allied army marched in two columns: one by Fulda, and the other by Aschaffenburg, on Frankfort. The Silesian army continued its route by Wetzlar. The Prince Royal of Sweden, up to this period, moved in the direction of Cassel: but changes took place here, which shall be presently detailed. General Count Wrede, with the Bavarian army, having very gallantly assaulted three different times the strong capital of Wurtzburg, ultimately succeeded in forcing its capitulation on the 26th of October, and pressed on his march as has been before mentioned. On the 27th he arrived at Aschaffenburg, and on the

28th entered Hanau. The Bavarian General now learned that the main French army was before him: he was obliged, therefore, to evacuate the place until all his troops came up; and he took up a position in the rear of it, and on the following days had various skirmishes with the enemy. At length he collected about 36,000 men; and taking a position with his right to Reineck, and his left to Gelnhausen, he determined to attack the enemy, however superior in numbers.

Napoleon, however, had upwards of 60,000 men and 120 pieces of cannon, and only wanted to disengage the line of march for his retreat. His generals, Nansouty, Sebastiani, and Davoust, ably and skilfully fulfilled the orders that were given; and a great portion of the French army filed off during the night towards Frankfort. But on the following day, General Wrede made a most gallant and desperate attack on Hanau, which he took by assault, receiving a severe wound in the action, while leading on his troops with dauntless intrepidity.

Napoleon, meantime, continued his march by Stockstadt, on the right of the great road near Hanau, leaving Marshal Mortier, with a rear-guard of 14,000 men, to cover his retreat. On the 31st, the light cavalry of the French passed the Maine, and entered Frankfort; and at twelve on that day, Napoleon established his head-quarters there. The result of the battle of Hanau was stated to be 15,000 killed and wounded, 10,000 prisoners, and nine generals.

On the 1st of November, Napoleon continued his retreat from all points. The Emperors of Russia and Austria, and the King of Prussia, accompanied by Prince Schwartzenberg, Generals Barclay de Tolly and Wittgenstein, surrounded also by their other generals and suite, made their magnificent and solemn entry into Frankfort on the 4th; and the main French army was now effectually driven from the right bank of the Rhine.

I now return to the Prince Royal's army. The intended movement of the main body of the army of the north on Cassel was arrested; and the Prince Royal was induced to direct his operations towards Hanover and the north, for the following substantial reasons:—Marshal Davoust was still in position on the right bank of the Elbe, and seemed very unwilling to separate from the Danes, so long as he could maintain his positions. The corps of Lieutenant-General Count Walmoden was not of sufficient force to act offensively, without considerable aid. The extermination of the enemy in the north of Germany; the possession of Bremen; the mouths of the Weser and the Elbe; the speedy reduction of Hamburgh; the advantage of opening an immediate communication with England during the winter; the liberation of His Majesty's electoral dominions, and the organization of its civil and military power; the facility that would be afforded to the future operations of the northern army, either in Holland or on the Rhine, when their rear should be entirely secure; and, lastly, the hope of cutting off Marshal Davoust completely from Holland, were the united considerations which determined His Royal Highness to alter his proposed movement.

The army of the north was consequently put in march, towards the end of October, for Bremen and Hanover; from whence it was to be directed against the remaining forces of the enemy in the north of Germany. The Prince Royal transferred his headquarters from Mulhausen to Dinglestadt on the 29th; on the 30th to Heligenstadt, and the 1st of November to Gottingen.

The advanced-guard of Woronzoff, and the Russians under General Winzingerode, entered Cassel on the 30th. The Swedes and Prussians were in the neighbourhood of Heligenstadt on that day, when His Royal Highness determined on a change in his line of movements. Reports received from General Czernicheff, dated from Newens, on the 27th, detailed, that having joined General Sloweiski with another partisan-corps of the grand army, he proceeded to Fulda, which town he occupied, making 500 prisoners; he then destroyed the enemy's magazines, and proceeded to break down the bridges, and render the roads as impracticable as possible, having contrived to post himself between the enemy's main body and their advance. The manner in which General Czernicheff harassed them was not to. be described. While in his position at Fulda, he perceived the advance of their collected force, consisting of some squadrons of *gendarmes,* moving towards the town: he immediately advanced with his Cossacks, charged, and overthrew them, and then returned to follow the advanced-guard on the great road towards Frankfort, carrying destruction before him, and depriving the enemy of all their means before their arrival.

General Czernicheff, moreover, stated, that Buonaparte went from. Eisenach to Vach; and that he had the intention of going to the Weser, but the march of the Prince Royal and Marshal Blucher prevented him, and he supposed his line would be Frankfort. He added, his army was reduced to 60,000 strong, armed and collected; many of the enemy, however, were retiring in different directions, even without arms: the retreat forcibly resembled that from Russia. All accounts agreed that the greatest consternation reigned in France, and that interior discontent was very generally manifesting itself.

From the. intrepid and dexterous, exploits of the partisans, we now turn, with equal cause for exultation, to the movements of the armies. Marshal Blucher, with the Silesian army, reported from Philipstadt and Hunefeldt, on the 29th, that such was the disorder of the enemy's flight, he could not for a moment desist from the pursuit, however harassed his troops might be: His Excellency was daily making prisoners. General Bennigsen reached Halle on the 29th. It seemed that the corps of General Gouvion St. Cyr, originally stated to have left Dresden for Torgau or Wittemberg, and latterly supposed to be moving to Chemnitz, had, nevertheless, remained at Dresden. A part of General Regnier's corps, probably separated from the French army by the operations of the allies and the battle of Leipsic, had been mistaken for that of General Gouvion St. Cyr. This corps was now encamped near Torgau, on the. right bank of the Elbe; and General Bennigsen was moving towards the Elbe, to act with all the different corps under his orders there in the most vigorous manner.

There was now a report of a corps of the enemy, about 12,000 men, under General Mollitor, moving from Holland; but it had not advanced further than Bonstanger. General Cara St. Cyr re-occupied the town of Bremen with a part of his force, after General Tettenborn had evacuated it: it was, however, soon again free. The movements of the Prince Royal's columns in march were as follow:—the Russians proceeded from Cassel by Paderborn to Bremen and Oldenburg; the Prussians, under General Bulow, to Minden; and the Swedes, to Hanover.

On the 28th of November, I witnessed, with inexpressible pleasure, the entrance of the allied troops into the Electoral dominions. The enthusiastic loyalty and unbounded joy of the people is not to be described; and although ten years had elapsed since that country had been governed by its legitimate sovereign, it was obvious that he still reigned in their hearts with the same deep-rooted affection. The reception of the Prince Royal must have been highly gratifying. The few English present were greeted with joyous acclamations.

It is a remarkable and pleasing anecdote, that during the existence of the new *régime,* and the studied obliteration of every memorial of the ancient dynasty, the bust of our revered Monarch, which I believe was a present of Her Majesty's to the professors and students, retained its place in the university: no sacrilegious hand had ever presumed to remove it.

Active measures were taken, under the authority of the regency, for the re-establishment of all the civil authorities; and His Royal Highness the Prince of Sweden, with the utmost attention and care in providing for his troops by requisitions, made arrangements for payment; and in every thing considered the country and its inhabitants the most favoured soil.

So soon as His Royal Highness the Prince of Sweden changed his plan of operations, on the 30th, His Royal Highness the Duke of Cumberland joined the corps of Lieutenant-General Walmoden; but the Crown Prince expressed fears that if the Duke of Cumberland entered Hanover under existing circumstances, embarrassment would arise.

General Walmoden now became discontented with his situation and position. This was the more to be lamented, considering the extraordinary favour that had been shown him by His Royal

Highness the Prince Regent. The frequent representations he made to the Prince Royal of his critical and forlorn predicament, operated as an argument, which His Royal Highness did not fail to make use of, to lead his forces to that quarter, where the Prince Royal's inclinations had been so long leaning. As it appeared now of the greatest importance to open the communication, without loss of time, from the Weser with Heligoland, in order that packets might go from thence with our communications, I addressed a letter to the Governor of Heligoland by a confidential person for this object.

On the 4th of November, the Prince Royal, in a conference, was pleased to communicate to me that he had despatched the Count Lowenheilm, one of the officers of his staff, to His Imperial Majesty, to propose the following disposition for consideration:—That the grand army of Bohemia should place its left on the Maine, stretching with its right to the conflux of the Sieg with the Rhine : the army of Silesia, or the army of the centre, to have the *appui* of its left on the right bank of the Sieg, and to post its right towards Dusseldorf: the army of the Prince Royal, after disposing of the enemy's forces in the north, was to undertake the siege of Wesel, directing itself from thence upon Holland; of which country His Royal Highness proposed to undertake the liberation: the armies in the several positions on the right bank of the Rhine were, in the first instance, to reorganize themselves as far as possible; the recruiting of them was to be carried to the highest possible pitch; and, at the earliest moment, operations were to commence on the left bank of that river: the troops employed in the blockades of the different fortresses on the Elbe were, as soon as possible, to undertake the sieges of them, as well as of those on the Oder.

The Crown Prince expected that Torgau and Stettin would fall in the course of fifteen days: these appeared the general outlines of His Royal Highness's ideas; which I deem interesting, in a military point of view, to record. No official account was yet promulgated, from whence a judgment could be formed of the manner in which Buonaparte, with the remnant of his army, had extricated himself after the sanguinary and hard-fought actions with General Wrede, who merited, unquestionably, the highest encomiums. The force of Buonaparte, as he retired on the great line of his communications, was probably augmented by troops at Erfurth, and other places on its march. In his battles with General Wrede, he brought forward 60,000 or 70,000 men: a force much beyond what we estimated him to possess after his various losses. It was quite clear, however, he did not think himself secure with this number, as, during the last battle, he appeared to seek his safety with an escort of 10,000 cavalry; which General Czernicheff very gallantly attacked, and roughly handled.

Marshal Blucher's army being directed out of the great line of road on Frankfort, on which they were following the enemy, were marched, as I have before stated, on Wetzlar and Coblentz. I certainly considered, when General Wrede occupied Hanau and Frankfort, that Buonaparte would march on Coblentz; but it was to be regretted that our numerous cavalry ever lost sight of the enemy, so as to have made the question of his march for a moment doubtful. By Marshal Blucher being turned into another direction, it appeared that no part of the grand army did or could arrive in time to take part in the actions with General Wrede, which was much to be lamented, as the final escape of Buonaparte, and his passage of the Rhine, became the object of much discussion; and I am sorry I have it not in my power to afford ample and complete information on so interesting a matter.

The Prussians, under Bulow, were now at Minden; and General Winzingerode was to arrive in a day or two at Bremen: the Swedes were marching towards Harburg; the corps of General Bennigsen descended the Elbe, and arrived at Lutzen. This General, with Count Walmoden, had orders to operate on the right bank, against Marshal Davoust's position on the Stecknitz.

The Prince Royal's plan at this moment seemed to be, to proceed to Strasburg with part of his army, in order to be ready to cooperate in the attacks upon Marshal Davoust; as also to possess himself of Hamburgh, and, if possible, secure an *appui* on the Elbe, before he pushed forward with the whole of his forces into

Stralsund. Generals Winzingerode and Bulow, however, were not to be delayed in commencing their marches. General Bennigsen brought ample force with him; while General Bulow recruited his army, in His Prussian Majesty's ancient states, to the number it amounted to before the opening of the campaign. The generous and liberal aid of the Prince Regent, in arms and clothing, was of invaluable importance to these brave Prussians at this moment: they were the means of re-equipping and arming the *corps d'armée* forthwith, nearly on their original establishment. It must be as gratifying to the English nation as creditable to its government, to see how opportunely their aid was forthcoming. The gratitude of Marshal Blucher and General Bulow, as expressed to me, was most satisfactory to the country I served.

On the return of Count Lowenheilm from the imperial head-quarters with the plan from the Prince Royal of Sweden (the outline of which I have before stated), he brought a counter-project, or rather a plan of operations, which it seems had been there decided upon. The Prince Royal, on its receipt, expressed himself much hurt at being so little considered: he said that it was by his plan at Trachenberg the allies had obtained so much success—that he was not in a position to be directed by any one—that if the plan fixed was that of the Emperor of Russia, or of any military man of great character, he would, bad as he thought it, be disposed to acquiesce; but that he knew it was either the offspring of the ideas of those *Faircuis,* alluding, I apprehend, to the Russian *état major,* who had yet to be as much instructed in war as he was; or else a plan which Austria was anxious to grasp at to cover her hereditary states in Italy, to liberate that country, and to forward her own objects rather than the common cause, or it would not have been adopted.

His Royal Highness then called my attention to the situation in which he stood; the Swedes looked up to him for something. Of all the powers, he was the only individual who had not recovered some valuable possession: his rear must be made secure, and Hamburgh occupied. He further told me his determination was taken to write observations on the Emperor's plan, detailing fully his opinions; it appeared to the Prince, that the projectors at the grand head-quarters had founded their present reasoning and project pretty much on the general ideas the Prince had laid down at Trachenberg, without ever adverting, as His Royal Highness observed, to the wide change and difference that existed as to the relative situation of our general political affairs and the armies. To expose this difference—to elucidate his own ideas—to make himself heard, if not heeded, the Prince determined to draw up a military paper of observations.

In discussing these important subjects, I could not refrain from admitting, that in my opinion there was much weight in many of the opinions of His Royal Highness; but I put it to His Royal Highness fairly, to consider whether a plan even with some objections, acted on in perfect concert, was not better than for each army to pursue its own objects without a perfect understanding. The Prince, in reply, assured me, that after he had made his representations to the Emperor, after he had done himself justice, and after he had felt himself somewhat more secured as to Davoust's operations, and the line the Danes would adopt, he would, however unfavourably he thought of the plan, do his utmost to act his part, and carry it into effect; that he was anxious however, during the interval of concentration, to go in person to Minden and Bremen, and from thence to Stralsund, with his Swedes, in addition to General Woronzoff already there, and General Walmoden on the right bank of the Elbe; that he hoped this movement would bring something to a conclusion with Davoust. If, however, matters were protracted, he could at all events make new dispositions. His Royal Highness expressed himself much discontented at the idea of ordering his Swedes to be so much divided, and complained generally of the little consideration shown him in this instance. He appeared to entertain great horror at the idea of the Cossacks entering France; he was more than ever anxious to rouse that nation, which he loved, against their ruler, whom he abhorred: he wrote a proclamation, perfect in most respects, except where he dwelt on himself and his own exploits.

However eager I was, when a military plan of operations had come from the head source, to support it, without any reference whatever to my own ideas, still the Prince, in two or three conversations, seemed so fixed in the line he had adopted, and reiterated his reasons so strongly, that I perceived I could do no good by contending with him; and under all the bearings of the circumstances, I thought it prudent to desist until further advices should arrive from the grand head-quarters.

I must here remark, that the Prince was very anxious for a public declaration, by way of appeal to France, of the terms on which we would make peace: much of his reasoning and argument was formed on the injury we should do the common cause, if such a proceeding did not take place. His Royal Highness, it seemed, had not been informed, until I now made it known to him, that M. de St. Aignau had been charged by Prince Metternich with communications to Napoleon; of the purport of which, more hereafter.

When the Prince Royal became acquainted with this fact, he appeared delighted, but he thought the diplomatic mode not sufficiently public; and, indeed, if it were an object to urge the Prince Royal, in his military capacity, to do what the allies required, it was surely impolitic to put him so little *au fait,* in the first instance, upon so important a *demarche:* he had a right to expect his due share in these discussions. Finding himself thus excluded, he argued he was no longer considered; and his feelings operated accordingly. In proportion as the difficulty of managing the Prince Royal increased, the disposition to attempt so delicate a task diminished, his aid having become less essential.

The army of the north continued its march on Munster and Bremen; and that part of it under the immediate orders of the Prince Royal of Sweden moved on Haarburg, for the purpose of a combined movement with the forces on the right bank of the Elbe, directed against Marshal Davoust. The army did not make these movements with rapidity, as the troops needed re-equipment in the principal towns through which they passed; and as measures for the recruiting and re-establishing the proper authorities in the different districts required time during the progress of the march.

The Prince Royal of Sweden moved on the 16th to Minden and Bremen, to inspect and give the necessary orders in those towns. His head-quarters were to move to Celle; from thence he proceeded to Luneberg and Harburg. His Royal Highness joined his head-quarters again before they passed Luneberg; and he adopted the necessary measures to render himself master of the Lower Elbe. During this interval, His Royal Highness's operations towards the Rhine and Holland were not to be neglected. A report arrived that Marshal Davoust had broken up from Ratzeburg and his positions on the Stecknitz, and retired; but it was as yet uncertain whether he meant to throw himself into Hamburgh, or to withdraw into Holstein and the fortresses of Lubeck and Rendsburg: the latter was most probable, especially from his seizure of the bank of Hamburgh, and sending it to Altona. There were so. many accounts of the misunderstandings between the French and the Danes, and this last subject of the bank had so much added to the dissatisfaction, that some favourable issue was anticipated.

It appeared that Buonaparte was himself at Mentz. This seemed a central point, from which he could transport himself to the point most threatened. By a report from Lieutenant-General Woronzoff, at Luneberg, dated the 14th instant, at night, his advanced parties sent intelligence that Marshal Davoust had arrived with from 9000 to 12,000 men at Harburg, and it was thought with a view of directing his march on Bremen. This intelligence seemed too good to be true: in such an event, Marshal Davoust was infallibly lost, as our army would surround his force on all sides; and Lieutenant-General Walmoden's corps, disposable, would follow him across the Elbe, and march on his rear. This report was possibly circulated to cover his real movement into Hamburgh, or the fortresses in Holstein.

A report was now received at the head-quarters of the army of the north, that a capitulation was demanded and acceded to by General Thielman before Dresden; by which the garrison was to return into France, and be exchanged, man for man. This was ratified by the commander-in-chief.

Notwithstanding the formal protest I made to His Royal Highness the Crown Prince of Sweden against the impolicy and dishonour of entering into capitulation with Marshal Davoust, by which he should be permitted to return to France with his force; and notwithstanding His Royal Highness assured me that if I entertained such serious objections to it he would not attempt such a measure, the moment after my departure from Hanover to return to Frankfort, as I was informed by both Generals Vincent and Krusemark, instructions were sent to Lieutenant-General Count Walmoden to do his utmost to bring about a capitulation by Marshal Davoust of the nature alluded to. Having received the Prince Royal's assurance to the contrary only the preceding evening, I was surprised by this intelligence; and as His Royal Highness had left Hanover for Bremen, I had no alternative but to write to him the annexed letter, containing my sentiments on the subject.

> *Hanovre*
> *Ce 16ème Novembre, 1813*
> *Monseigneur,*
> *Permettez-moi de vous adresser deux lignes, au moment même de mon départ: le sujet est, selon moi, d'une grande importance; et j'ose croire que Votre Altesse Royale, avec votre bonté ordinaire, me permettra d'exprimer les sentimens de la Grande-Bretagne sur une considération militaire, dans laquelle elle doit prendre le plus grand intérêt. Selon toutes les probabilités le Dannemarc sera avec nous, et le Maréchal Davoust perdu: s'il retournoit en France par aucune capitulation, je prévois la tache la plus funeste à la gloire militaire de l'armée du nord; ce seroit de transporter ce corps de Davoust d'un endroit fatal où il sera perdu, et de le mettre encore en bataille contre les alliés. Mon Prince, vous m'avez comblé de bontés; soyez bien persuadé c'est à votre gloire, à vos intérêts personels que je pense. Je répondrai de l'opinion de mon pays. C'est avec une peine sensible que je viens d'entendre,*

d'après la manière que Votre Altesse Royale s'est exprimée envers moi, hier au soir, que le Général Walmoden à reçu de nouveaux ordres à cet effet.

Pardonnez-moi, je vous en supplie, Monseigneur, si je me suis porté trop loin. Je n'ai fait que mon devoir en réitérant les opinions de mon gouvernement, et désormais je laisse tout avec confiance à votre sage et digne décision.

Jai l'honneur d'être de Votre Altesse Royale le plus dévoué des serviteurs,
Charles Stewart
Lieut.-Général

I was fortified in my view of this act, by the intelligence that a capitulation of a similar kind at Dresden had not been ratified at the imperial head-quarters. In consequence of a communication I received while at Gottingen, the then head-quarters of the Crown Prince of Sweden, from His Majesty's ambassador at the court of Russia (Earl Cathcart), leaving me at liberty to open myself to the Prussian government on the subject of the important diplomatic instructions alluded to as being enforced just before the battle of Leipsic, I lost no time in proceeding to Frankfort.

On my arrival, I had frequent discussions with His Excellency Prince Hardenberg respecting my object; and had great satisfaction in finding him enter entirely into the views of His Majesty's government. He repeatedly assured me, that he was convinced the policy of Prussia was to cultivate the strictest union with Great Britain, and fully sensible both of the wisdom and justice of the proposals I was charged to make; being entirely of opinion that the instructions forwarded to me were preferable to any alterations that were projected by the ministers of either of the imperial powers, I felt it a duty I owed to this, government and myself to state to my court the determination of His Prussian Majesty. Union between the great powers was to be collected by inference and a sense of necessity, rather than to be found embodied in any ostensible and defined treaties: there were no grounds for departing from the great measure of consolidating the union of the allies by one general and complete understanding.

CHAPTER 14

Holland & Denmark

Napoleon, when forced across the Rhine, was obliged to employ the greater part of his disposable force in the garrisons upon that river, the Moselle, and the Meuse. At the close of 1813 he returned to Paris, and ordered the levy of 120,000 men of the conscription of 1814: by a *senatus-consultum* it was also decreed, that 160,000 men of the conscription of 1815 were to be called out; and by a further decree, he directed the assembling of 300,000 conscripts from the arrears of the years 1811 to 1814. These preparations produced the conviction that a longer delay on the part of the allied Sovereigns in following up their advantages, could only be prejudicial to their ultimate object—that of conquering France.

Besides the above efforts on the part of Napoleon, he ordered 30,000 citizens of Paris to form a national guard for its internal protection. These stupendous exertions induced the allied Sovereigns to issue a declaration of their principles, and the grounds on which they continued hostilities, dated the 1st of December, from Frankfort.

The allies equally resorted to gigantic efforts. A new confederation of the Rhenish states was formed, divided into eight principal *corps d'armée;* and the additional force which Germany was to bring into the field amounted on paper, according to the arrangements, to 280,000 men. Certain plans were concerted for the arrangement of the forces of the German states belonging to the Rhenish league; and a financial system was also adopted, not necessary to detail.

The general idea of reopening the campaign, which had been in some manner laid down by the supreme powers at the grand head-quarters, was, as usual, criticised by the Prince Royal of Sweden; and he made representations thereon to the allied Sovereigns.

On my arrival at Frankfort, no definitive resolution appeared to have been taken; and although the army was in march, much change was contemplated before the plan developed itself. A deviation of no trifling nature already occurred; it was said that the grand army, instead of going into Switzerland and Italy, which was at first proposed, would pass the Rhine near Basle and Huningen, and march direct on Befort, occupying the country in its neighbourhood.

At the same time a strong corps was to traverse Switzerland, and to come into communication by Milan with Marshal Bellegarde's army, advancing from Vicenza; and when the Italian army should be more closely united with that acting from the Rhine, the operations were to be combined, and they could mutually support each other. On the other hand, the proposed plans for Marshal Blucher seemed to be, that he should remain in the centre of the very extended line, opposite the fortresses, thirteen in number, which present themselves when we pass the Rhine at Mayence. This was confiding to the army of Silesia to play the same game that they had hitherto pursued—that of retiring, if the enemy advanced upon them, while they could pass the Rhine and make demonstrations, should the enemy move all his force against the grand army.

The army of the north was to have orders to enter Holland, as already projected, and pursue its operations independently. The same system appeared in this outline as in the plan hitherto acted upon. Switzerland was to become another Bohemia; Blucher acting in the centre, and the Prince Royal in the north. The difference in the execution, however, was the immense extent to be acted upon, and to preserve the road of communication between the armies, the occupation of Switzerland seemed essential. It presented an *appui* for the flank, in undertaking any operation; and it was argued, that by possessing the line of the Danube, behind the grand army, great resources in Bavaria, and the means for supplying-ammunition, would be secured.

These were the prevailing motives that determined the great feature of future operations; and it was now promulgated, that the head of the grand allied army was to arrive at Friburg about the 25th instant. About the 5th of December, it was supposed a corps might arrive at Befort; but, in the mean time, no order for movement of the head-quarters was positively given; and discussions still prevailed. I ought here to record, for the honour of his country, the eminent services rendered in the grand allied *état major,* and in all their councils and grand military combinations, by that highly-gifted Prussian officer, General Knese. He was constantly attached to the King's person throughout the war; but his genius, commanding talents, and experience, made him the most prominent adviser in every arrangement, and his ardour and skill in execution contributed towards every good result. I never can forget his personal kindness to me; and this eulogy is a very inefficient mark of the respect and affection to which his virtues entitle him; and which I sincerely feel towards him.

The Prussian general, Gniesenau, always remarkable for his activity, was much chagrined at the existing delays. Measures being still protracted from day to day, he framed and submitted to the Emperor a new plan, materially varying from the outline detailed; but his views appeared too vast, considering the then state of the allied forces. Amongst other points, he proposed to carry Marshal Blucher's army forward into Holland, instead of that of the Prince Royal.

No great progress was made in the organization of the German forces, while the allied army remained on the Rhine. The different interests, the various authorities, the confusion incident to new measures, and the means necessary, precluded the carrying into effect the intended arrangements: still the collecting, consolidating, and arming the German states was of so much importance, that it became an object to make such a disposition of the great armies, as would not impede the formation of those which would be so powerful as auxiliaries. This was another disadvantage of the delays that occurred in determining the line of operation. It was now given out that Marshal Bellegarde's arrival at Frankfort was anxiously waited for, in order to consult his opinions, and combine the movements of the army of Italy with that of the Rhine.

On this ground, fresh delay was excused. With respect to the army of the north of Germany, they came to the resolution at the grand head-quarters, that in the event of continued operations against the Danes being necessary, and of the Prince Royal still manifesting a disposition to engage in this warfare in preference to that of Holland, they would leave under orders of that Prince 50,000 men, including his Swedes, and consider him as quite independent of the combined operations into France; and place in the hands of another general the army destined to enter Holland.

It was however to be presumed from the accounts received, that the Prince Royal intended to direct his own march from Bremen to Holland, his Prussian corps having already entered it at various points; and General Baron Adlercreutz was to have the direction of the forces against the Danes. The affair of the capitulation of Dresden created great discussion, and awakened lively interest. Had the capitulation been ratified, Napoleon would have received 1700 officers, an important acquisition, in addition to the whole of Gouvion St. Cyr's garrison, as a nucleus to the new armies he was organizing. It was formally annulled; and General St. Cyr was offered permission to return and resume the command, which he refused.

I am about to touch upon a subject which I find myself precluded by my diplomatic position from so discussing in all its bearings, as under other circumstances I should most anxiously have desired; I mean that celebrated interview which the Austrian minister had with M. de St. Aignau at Frankfort. It took place in the presence of a British ambassador; and ended in a sort of minute of conference, productive of negotiations and correspondence, which became the cause of much complication and misunderstanding in the councils of the allies at this juncture. The archives of our Foreign Office contain, for the information of future statesmen, the course pursued by the diplomatic servants of the different governments at this interesting crisis. I shall only state that, having had the misfortune to differ from my colleagues in the principal features of that negotiation, I had the satisfaction, nevertheless, of receiving the approbation of His Majesty's government for the whole of my conduct and proceedings.

The alliance between the powers was placed on so clear a basis, that no proceeding should have been taken but in complete concert; and it never should have been imagined that when the allied armies were victorious on the Rhine, the Prince Regent's government should depart from those great principles of negotiation which were proclaimed when they were on the Oder, with the armies of France still unbroken before them.

The points in negotiation, from which it was known the British government would under no circumstances relax, were Spain, Portugal, Sicily, and the fulfilment of the existing engagements with Sweden. With regard to maritime rights, it was a question in which the mediation of any ally with Great Britain could not be accepted; and it was still less a question which Great Britain would ever discuss at a general congress.

How far these great points were compromised, or attempted to be compromised, perhaps undesignedly, in M. de St. Aignau's most extraordinary negotiation, time and future historians will develop. It was well understood, however, that Great Britain deprecated the assembling of a congress until a basis should be positively agreed to: and this basis, as regarded England, was distinctly established by diplomatic notes, in date of the 16th of May, as well as by subsequent instructions to her diplomatic servants.

At the moment the communications for peace were opened with Buonaparte through M. de St. Aignau at Frankfort, it may be well to remark, that the allied forces, if vigorous and proper measures were adopted, would arrive at an army of the following magnitude, arrayed for the cause of Europe, and able to bid defiance to all the efforts that could be made against it:

German army		291,120
Russian army	by treaty	150,000
Austrian army	by treaty	150,000
Prussian army	by treaty	150,000
Swedish army	by treaty	30,000
	Total	771,120

besides what it was conjectured would be obtained from Holland, and from the armies of the Duke of Wellington; and Holland now began to show a determined spirit to liberate herself from French dominion.

A revolutionary spirit broke out at Amsterdam on the 15th of November, which was quickly communicated to the far greater part of North Holland, and followed by the termination of the French power in that country.

I received immediate intelligence from the Earl of Clancarty, appointed His Britannic Majesty's ambassador to the provincial government of the Prince of Orange at the Hague, that a deputation was sent to His Serene Highness the Prince of Orange to invite him to his sovereignty, and to solicit arms and succours from the British government. The deputies arrived in London on Sunday the 21st of November; and having communicated with His Majesty's ministers, immediate orders were given for the despatch of 25,000 stand of arms, which had been previously embarked, in anticipation of this movement. A body of troops, composed of every description of force, to the amount of between 5000 or 6000 men, were ordered for embarkation, under the command of Lieutenant-General Sir Thomas Graham. A deputation also arrived from the Hague at the grand head-quarters: in consequence of which, His Majesty the King of Prussia immediately despatched the young Prince Frederick of Orange to the corps of General Bulow, in order that one of the Orange family might be present at the re-establishment of their dynasty.

The fortress of Stettin surrendered on the 5th of December to the troops of His Prussian Majesty. The garrison became prisoners of war, and were to be conducted to the Prussian territories on the right bank of the Vistula: Zamose, also, was taken by capitulation; and it was confidently expected that Dantzic would immediately fall.

General Bulow's successes in Holland were next announced: he had carried Dorsberg and Zutphen on the Issel by assault; both of these places were fortified, but had been stripped of their artillery, although they had strong garrisons. The enemy had inundated Deventer, and it presented more difficulty. Arnheim was carried in a very gallant manner. The utmost exertions were making to pursue the great advantages so gloriously opening in Holland. The allies having lost the opportunity of following up the enemy in the moment of panic, after concentrating at Frankfort, extended their flanks, and were disposed at length to operate simultaneously on the sides of Switzerland and Holland; while Marshal Blucher passed the Rhine near Mayence, and by drawing the attention of the enemy, to afford the armies on the flanks more liberty to act.

The army in Holland was to push to Utrecht, Rotterdam, and the Hague. Prince Schwartzenberg, with the grand army of nearly 180,000 men, was to pass the Rhine near Basle and Brisach, and assemble in the neighbourhood of Befort and Besançon; detaching a strong corps through central Switzerland, by Neufchatel, to Geneva. The three places of Huningen, Befort, and Besançon, would, it was thought, not require a greater force to observe them than Mayence. The main army was to endeavour to penetrate towards Lyons and Dijon, to cut off the enemy's communication with Italy; General Kleinau to march to reinforce the army of Italy, which was to be augmented to 100,000 men; and Marshal Bellegarde, who had now arrived at Frankfort, was to proceed to take the command of the whole. With respect to Switzerland, although deputies had arrived to concert and proclaim its neutrality, and to arrange a route into France without infringing its territory; and although there was a doubt on the part of the Emperor of Russia as to the precise mode to be pursued, still it was evidently too important a military feature, both for the safety of

Germany and Italy, not to secure it against any attempt from France. Every forbearance was to be shown to this small, but highly respectable republic, while the body of the main army was to cross the Rhine at Basle.

On the 9th of December, I was privately informed that an answer had been received from the Duke of Vicenza (Caulaincourt), in consequence of the overtures through M. de St. Aignau, by which France accepted the basis of negotiation proposed; and in order to explain the whole course of this proceeding, that ingenious and dexterous, as well as profound diplomatist, General Pozzo di Borgo, was, sent as a check against any English accounts, or as a joint expounder of circumstances, from the allied ministers at Frankfort to the cabinet of St. James's.

As I found, by despatches from the Earl of Clancarty, that he was extremely desirous of every information from the grand head-quarters to regulate matters at the Hague, I determined to send off immediately my secretary of legation, Mr. Jackson, with full details to his lordship, in order to put him completely in possession of the *carte du pays*. This subsequently procured for me the double advantage of having all my proceedings on M. de St. Aignau's mission thoroughly explained to my government: for Lord Clancarty, acting in that spirit of confidence and friendship which uniformly characterised his relations with me, when he found General Pozzo di Borgo waiting for a passage from the Hague to England, charged with a special mission, ordered Mr. Jackson to be accommodated on board the same packet.

In remarking on the state in which political affairs then stood, I could not but feel that the Prince Regent's ministers, with all their caution and all the detailed instructions they had sent, were placed, by an unfortunate train of circumstances, in a most embarrassing predicament. They were obliged, by the invitation now transmitted to them, either to send a plenipotentiary to open a negotiation *préliminaire* with a French authority (and in conjunction with the other three powers) on an undefined basis,—their resolutions having been previously clearly promulgated; or by declining such an insidious proposition, to incur the imputation of resisting a measure seemingly tending to a general pacification.

No negotiator could be sent from England without buoying up that nation with the prospect of immediate peace. And was England, in her present commanding attitude, to lend herself to a premature communication for a congress, if she did not discover a sincere intention on the part of France, evinced by decisive acts, or by declarations of such restricted views, as might tend to a probably favourable issue to the negotiation? Would it not be more fatal to enter into discussions, and encourage hopes of peace, if all were to end as at Prague, than to adhere to that wise policy which had marked the proceedings of the Prince Regent's ministers in all their previous measures? There was no temptation, in my humble opinion, and under all the suspicious circumstances by which this affair was accompanied, to send a plenipotentiary at a moment when we stood in such a proud position: on one side planting our standards in France; upholding the nations of the continent on the other: almost unanimous in our parliament; and one voice and one impulse directing the sound part of the British empire.

I should before have stated, that the military councils and the political proceedings which passed at Frankfort were largely and fully detailed to the British government, by the appointment of more English officers to the different corps of the allied armies. In addition to Sir Robert Wilson, who had been from the campaign of Moscow acting with the Russian, and subsequently with the Austrian, armies in the field, which gave him great insight into all that was planned, rejected, or adopted by the allied Sovereigns, Lord Burghersh also arrived, accredited to the Austrian army as military commissioner; and was immediately placed near Prince Schwartzenberg's person. The high favour he soon obtained amongst the Austrians, the friendship of their commander, with his own talents and energy, soon placed him in a position to render solid services to his government and the common cause. In short, so ample was the information from the central theatre of war, that, acting upon that discretionary power with which I was entrusted, I returned to the army of the north of Germany.

The outline of the plans for actively commencing the campaign remained generally fixed, as I have before pointed out. The grand army, passing the Rhine at Basle and Huningen, was to respect, as far as possible, the neutrality of Switzerland. General Blucher, with his Silesian army, was to cross the river at Mayence and Manheim, and push forward, in like manner, into France with all the forces on his right; while the Prince Royal was engaged on the side of Holland.

Dantzic fell on the 8th of December, by capitulation, to the Duke of Wirtemburg; but as it was a similar arrangement to that at Dresden, it was not ratified by the Emperor, and Dantzic was taken possession of by the allies upon their own terms.

During my absence from the head-quarters of the Crown Prince of Sweden, various affairs and skirmishes between the forces in that quarter took place, but none of very material moment. The Prince Royal and General Walmoden hemmed in Marshal Davoust in Hamburgh. Colonel Cooke, who was stationed there, gave me regular and able reports of all that occurred. I am bound, as a candid writer, to afford some account of those troops, in which the British government felt a peculiar interest. I subjoin the Colonel's report of the 14th of December from Eidestadt, near Kiel; although it does not give a flattering prospect of the new levies, judging from their first efforts.

> There has been a very serious affair in this neighbourhood with a part of Walmoden's corps, under the immediate command of General Arenscheldt, and the Danish troops, under the direction of the French general, L'Allemande. It was known that the Danish division, consisting of good men, intended marching upon Rents-burg; although they were aware that part of Count Walmoden's army was at hand to oppose them. The Prince Royal directed General Walmoden to meet them; adding, that General Vegesack's corps should be at hand to support him.

In consequence of this order, the Russian German Legion, the Dessau battalion, Lauenbourg, and Brigade Halkett, marched with the greater portion of the cavalry. In the neighbourhood of Kleswick the two armies came in contact. The Danes immediately withdrew into position, and were followed and attacked by the allied troops. No sooner, however, were the allies brought under fire, than they were broken, in spite of an enclosed country, stone walls, haystacks, peasants' houses, and steep banks: some Danish cavalry, who, it is true, fought most nobly, got among them, and continued the pursuit: two British guns were taken.

At this time General Lyon, from whom I have this account, not having reached this place from head-quarters until the ensuing day, received an order to advance with his division to support the troops engaged. The narrow road by which he advanced impeded his progress; and the broken troops of all description pressing upon his front, almost precluded the possibility of the best disposed troops getting forward.

Meantime, the Danish dragoons were employing themselves in routing the remains of the infantry named to you, without receiving any check. The conduct of the allied troops was far from creditable. At length the corps of General Lyon disengaged itself, and remained firm, drove back the cavalry, and covered the retreating troops. Disposition was immediately made for covering the bridge of Ulneiah: fortunately, the Danes, content with the advantages they had gained, moved away upon their right, and gained Rendsburg.

I have avoided entering into any minute detail of the outline of this operation, or giving my opinion upon it; but you will not fail to observe two very strong features—bad information of the enemy's strength, and an army not well disciplined.

The enemy had possession of Schested before we knew it:

some cavalry and light troops were sent against the place. The officer commanding requested succour: soon after he reported the retreat of the Danes; but upon the approach of the battalion sent to his support, the whole Danish army turned about, and drove them into the river directly in their rear upon a single bridge. Dornberg was at Eckersdorff; too distant to be of use in case of a battle.

We knew the enemy were at Kiel, and marching on Rendsburg. That fact established, what more simple than to collect the army between Schested and the Wittensee in position? By this means Rendsburg was always covered, our original object completed, and the Danish army must have capitulated.

It is believed, however, that the plan of advance and attack was the Prince Royal's; and although Walmoden did in some particulars object to the distribution, he was directed to adhere to the original order. Vegesack's division was in the rear at Nordorff. Had the enemy forced the bridge of Kluvesik, none of the troops engaged would even have got away. The enemy carried away about 400 prisoners and two British guns. General Lyon attributed the whole of the misconduct in the affair to some of the raw, inexperienced levies. The Dessau battalion had only forty men left, although few were killed; the Russian German Legion appear to have acted ill; and Colonel Halkett's report, in an official form, is of such a nature, as to attach a distinct charge of cowardice. Officers are what the levies stand in great need of, and a regular system of discipline, without which they will again be subject to a recurrence of a similar nature.

It appears now there is some negotiations going on. The Prince of Hesse sent a flag of truce to Walmoden, expressing surprise that operations in the field should still exist, when it was known that peace had been signed at Copenhagen. To this communication no reply was made by the Prince Royal. His Royal Highness is at Kiel; and has issued an order for all leading men of property to attend him there, in order to assist in the formation of a government for Holstein. His interest appears to lead him in every point of view to render this country the scene of his operations: he will linger here; and although no operation be effected, he will feed his Swedes on the country and the villages by requisition.

It was impossible, from this and various other similar reports, to blind myself as to the real motives influencing the restless spirit of the Crown Prince: all his movements were directed towards securing his own particular objects. The whole of his proceedings relative to a protectorship for the Hanse Towns, followed up by an attempt for the immediate annexation of Holstein to the crown of Sweden, denoted a conduct which required close observation. The system to be adopted by me towards the Prince Royal became a subject of very serious and anxious consideration.

By some communications which arrived from the Prince of Orange, it appeared that the Prince Royal was now persuading the Prussians so to reinforce General Bulow that there might be no necessity for Russians or Swedes in Holland; and as the command in the Prince of Orange's hands was a point now working to the exclusion of the Prince Royal, a desire was expressed by Russia that he should remain in Holstein.

Difficulties arose about the chief command in the Low Countries. Captain Perponcher arrived from the Hague to procure for the military questions in that quarter a proper discussion and arrangement—the plans of campaign on the Upper Rhine; the employment of Marshal Blucher in that direction, which engrossed the other force that might have been disposable for Holland; and, lastly, the necessity and importance of keeping the alliance together on its first principles, were all points that were canvassed and debated: for my own part, it was my intention to urge the Prince Royal in the strongest manner to advance into Holland, and commit himself honestly in the great contest with France.

I left Frankfort on the 14th of December, and arrived at Hanover on. the 17th, on my way to the Prince Royal. I understood at Hanover that His Royal Highness the Duke of Cambridge was immediately expected. I met. the secretary of legation of Count Bombelles on the road, who put me in possession of the late events in Holstein, and in some degree acquainted me with what had occurred at Copenhagen. He also stated, that an armistice was on the point of being concluded between the Prince Royal of Sweden and the Prince of Hesse on the part of the Danes. Being certain from these accounts that no further military operations would immediately occur in the Prince Royal's army, and being equally persuaded that he would wait in Holstein at least for the return of M. de Bombelles' secretary, and advices from the imperial head-quarters, I considered that I could not more usefully employ my time than, in the interval of the reorganization of the electoral dominions, awaiting the Duke of Cambridge's arrival at Hanover; and by a personal communication with His Royal Highness and Count Munster, deliver up, in the most satisfactory manner in my power, all those concerns relative to Hanover with which I had hitherto been charged.

His Royal Highness the Duke of Cambridge made his public entry into Hanover on the 20th of December, 1813. It was my good fortune to have witnessed, of late, many happy events; but the scene of the 20th pre-eminently surpassed them all, in the touching and. affecting demonstrations of joy exhibited by all classes at the return of this beloved descendant of their ancient race of sovereigns—a language that spoke from the heart, and which my pen cannot adequately convey: a loyalty and devotion displayed, which would have done honour to Britons, and which British dominion, so nearly resembling patriarchal sway, so universally inspires. In the necessary absence of military ceremony, from the Electoral troops being in the field, the citizens formed themselves into bands to honour the entrance of His Royal Highness into their capital: their wives and daughters, dressed in white, strewed his path with flowers;

and the voices of their innocent children, tutored to chant in one peal our national hymn, gave the whole of this spectacle a character as peculiar as it was interesting and affecting. Illuminations and other demonstrations of joy at night closed this first day of relief from anxiety and alarm, the harbinger of the subsequent prosperity and happiness of the Hanoverians under their natural protectors.

CHAPTER 15

Switzerland

I shall now shortly advert to the state of affairs in the north, and to the position of Marshal Davoust. He remained stationary in his entrenchments upon the Stecknitz; where he was assailed repeatedly by Generals Walmoden. Tettenborn, Vegesack, and Dornberg, in several affairs between the 6th and 12th of October. On the 13th, a corps of this army, under General Tettenborn, attacked Bremen; which was taken, as well as Nienburg, after a short resistance. This last success reduced Marshal Davoust to his communications with Denmark alone. On the 18th, Davoust made a general *reconnoissance;* attacked, but was defeated at all points. The glorious successes of the allies now insured the reconquest of Holland.

The whole of the military operations in Holstein appeared to me of an unpleasant character; and confidence in the Prince Royal's adherence was hourly diminishing. It seemed to me inauspicious, that he should now continue with all his force on the right bank of the Elbe, leaving Marshal Davoust by Haarburg, an open road into Holland. Without imputing any bad intention, still, after the desire shown to let Marshal Davoust return to France, if he should have escaped into Holland and created confusion, although he might ultimately have been destroyed, I should not have acquitted the Prince Royal, now that a Swedish division was marching on Schleswig and Gluckstadt for the immediate security of Drontheim. The Prince Royal was most anxious to retain the whole of Holstein and the fortresses. His

Royal Highness demanded that the Polish troops (cavalry), serving with the Danes, should be given up to him as prisoners of war. This would have been treachery as regarded the Danes, and should never have been required.

I had now very satisfactory communications with His Royal Highness the Duke of Cambridge and Count Munster, on their arrival at Hanover: they notified to me, that 15,000 men was the contingent which Hanover and Brunswick would furnish to the common cause.

I had much communication at this period with His Serene Highness the Duke of Brunswick, who arrived at Hanover. His mind was very unsettled: he expressed a wish to serve, yet declared he would serve neither under Walmoden nor the Prince of Sweden: he was likewise very uneasy about the arrangements for Brunswick. I endeavoured to convince His Serene Highness how much it was his interest lo subscribe completely to the Prince Regent's decision in all these points: to communicate with the government here as to his quota, the means of arming it, the assistance to be derived from Great. Britain, and his own personal situation as to the command of his own contingent, under such a leader as the Prince Regent might select; and His Serene Highness appeared at length satisfied with the line of conduct I urged him to pursue.

Since my departure from Frankfort the King of Prussia had written to the Crown Prince to say, that the corps of Putlitz and Marwitz (*landwehr*) were placed under his orders; and that His Majesty hoped he would have arranged with the Danes, and defeated Davoust; and that he would hasten to gather laurels in the Netherlands, as it was of the utmost importance not only to secure what was already gained in Holland, but also to push the advantages obtained there. His Majesty proposed that General Borstell should join General Bulow, and be replaced by part of General Winzingerode's corps; and that the Saxon corps, and the remainder of that of Winzingerode, should be ordered to advance to the Meuse, and support the left wing of General Bulow on his advance.

From Hanover I proceeded to Kiel, in Holstein, and arrived there on the 29th of December. On my arrival I found, to my great regret, that a prolongation of the armistice with the Danes, to the 6th of January, had been concluded between the Prince Royal and the plenipotentiary sent from Copenhagen. It was useless to complain, the thing was irretrievable; but from all the observations I could make, and the conversation I heard, it was evident Denmark was anxious to gain time by the prolongation of the armistice. Letters from the King of Denmark and Prince Royal of Sweden show the main grounds upon which the negotiation was accomplished, which gained Denmark to the cause of the alliance.

With regard to the military points, when I conversed with the Prince Royal on the absolute expediency of making every effort immediately for Holland, I found him so determined on taking no further steps whatever until the expiration of the armistice on the 6th, that it was a vain attempt to use persuasion; indeed, he sealed my lips by an entreaty to that effect. I think it right to mention another circumstance, on which His Royal Highness and I had some discussion, and which occurred to me as very singular. The Prince Royal ordered from Stralsund a number of French officers of all ranks, to the amount of 150 prisoners of war, to be marched back to France on their parole. I met them on their march through Hanover. General Borstell very properly wrote, that he could not permit them to pass by Wesel without the most positive orders. I inquired from the Prince an explanation of this circumstance, and suggested the serious mischief such a number of officers returning would create. His Royal Highness said, where he sent back a thousand officers, he gained a million of friends; that he had a right to do as he pleased with his own prisoners of war; and that he had settled this on an agreement with the Emperor Alexander: which last declaration, of course, silenced any further remonstrance.

After the 6th, when the armistice with the Danes expired, a momentary return to hostilities occurred; but Rendsburg and Schleswig being taken by the Swedes and Woronzoff's corps, peace was concluded on the 15th at Kiel, on the following basis:

1st. Denmark joined the common cause, declared war against France, and furnished a corps of troops to the army of the north.

2nd. Denmark yielded Norway to Sweden.

3rd. Sweden yielded to Denmark Swedish Pomerania and the Isle of Rugen.

4th. The troops were to evacuate Holstein, except those who formed the blockade of Hamburgh; in which fortress Marshal Davoust's corps still remain.

The siege of this place was now confided to General Bennigsen; and the Prince Royal intimated his intention of passing the Rhine, and engaging in the hostile operations in France. How far any subsequent service, however, was derived from these expressed intentions, will be seen in the sequel.

To return to the Upper Rhine, and the operations of the grand army. The neutrality of Switzerland having been respected in consequence of different negotiations, and its future integrity secured at a general peace by the sovereigns of the alliance, Prince Schwartzenberg moved his head-quarters on the 20th December to Lorrach; and on that day, his army commenced crossing the Rhine in different columns at Basle, Lauffenberg, and Shaffhausen.

It may be interesting to point out what was expected by the sovereigns of the alliance from Switzerland, and to give a sketch of its strength and situation.

The military force of this independent state might be raised to 25,000 or 30,000 men: the militia were immediately to be established to guard the towns on the frontier: the town of Biel made an offer to form two companies of guides who knew all the avenues and mountains of the Swiss confines.

Arberg is one of the most advantageous points in the centre of the line of defence of Switzerland. Nature itself has formed it a fortress against France; for the Aar surrounds it, and is only accessible by a bridge. It stands upon a hill of considerable magnitude, without being commanded by a higher point, as is the case with all the positions behind the Aar. By this circumstance the transports of cattle from the upper land of Bern could always be secured and facilitated.

Biel is an open place, surrounded by mountains; but the lake of Biel is connected with that of Neufchatel, by which the transports by water is managed, and the town may be protected against a *coup de main* by light troops stationed in the passes of Biel; but Arberg remains the most advantageous point as a basis for a line of operation: this line forms an angle which extends itself from Arberg on both sides to the extreme fortified points of Switzerland, Geneva and Basil, and forms with her mountains and defiles, which are easily secured and defended, the surest basis for all the operations against France.

The establishment of troops to be raised was to protect this line; and should Switzerland not join the offensive operations of the allies, this position protected her basis, her provisions, her transports, and her hospitals. At the frontier of Brantruth, on the French boundary, the following inscription had, been placed:

Malheur à celui qui franehira cette limite à main armée.

Threats and sentences of this tenor were generally the arms of all French generals on the frontier, which intimidate none but the timid of the country. This war of words was made use of in lieu of real forces, of which they now stood greatly in need. All the reports agreed that Buonaparte assembled his chief force round Paris: the means to form this force were of the most oppressive kind: the *gendarmerie* were to deliver up the greatest part of their horses, as the cavalry was not yet mounted. Napoleon, however, by this measure, got no more than 4,600 horses fit for service. These horses belonged to the *gendarmes* themselves, and this corps thereby was unable to perform its services; and the desertion in the army, that is, of the soldiers who returned to their homes, was so considerable, that the 10th regiment of line, which arrived from Lyons, consisted of but 500 men; and of a battalion of the national guards, which was expected in Befort, only the commander with 113 men arrived. Nobody belonging to the conscription ordered now appeared at his regiment: no taxes were raised; and the emptiness of the coffers may be conceived by the forced loan of 120 millions from the merchants; and the weakness of the regiments by the defence of the towns being entrusted to citizens, as belonging to the national guard. Whether the proprietor of a house would see it burnt down with the same indifference as the soldier, who had no property in it, remained to be seen. The poverty of the military chest in every state and canton was so great, that the officers in all the districts of the frontiers were reduced to half-pay. The struggle in France was now calculated to bring all classes of society, whatsoever were their opinions, to moderate principles. The present municipality of Besançon, Befort, and Bourg-en-Bresse, was composed of married priests, who planted the tree of liberty in those places: but this tree, which twenty years ago had no roots, frightened now even the adherents of Buonaparte; and the adherents of the red cap and of the imperial crown formed every where two parties, who endeavoured to aggrandise themselves by every means. This difference of opinion arrested all measures and things, in a country where formerly reigned only one will, which formed every thing according to its fancy.

Many passages over the Upper Rhine, in Switzerland, were practicable, and might be undertaken wherever it was thought proper; and from this side of France, (except a small part of Franche Comté, of Lothringen, and particularly Colmar,) the greatest part of the inhabitants being supported by a foreign power, it was supposed would show themselves active for the good cause.

The town of Basle lies without the line of defence of Switzerland, which line begins, at the mountain chain which rises behind Liechstall. The fortress of Huninguen is extremely strong, and seemed capable of resisting any attack. The fortifications of Geneva could also be increased; and another strong point on the declivity of the Jura, near the passes of Biel, perhaps Biel itself, would tend to make the line of Switzerland secure against France, and all transports to the allied army could with safety be forwarded through this country.

Yverdun is the next strongest position in Switzerland. There are three great lines leading to it; *viz.* by Yverdun, Moudon, and

Lausanne. These lines of march may bring corps stationed there by one march to the frontiers of Switzerland to any threatened point. The right wing of this position is covered by the lake of Neuburg; the left by a morass, which is only dry in the hottest summer season; and the front by the Orbe river, over which there are three wooden bridges constructed, that can be removed in a few hours.

Next to the general defences of Switzerland, the state of a Swiss soldier may be worthy of remark: he receives every day fifteen *kreutzers*, one pound and a half of bread, and half a pound of meat. The proprietor of the house where he is billeted is obliged to furnish him with salt, vegetables, wood and candles, which are paid for by the cantons, and cost a considerable sum, owing to the dearness of articles, especially in the small cantons. Of the troops themselves I must speak with approbation: they may be ranged in loyalty to the cause they fight in, and in appearance, with the best troops of Europe; and their chasseurs are very pre-eminent in enduring hardships, and as excellent marksmen.

The above detail may afford a general notion of the state of Switzerland at this crisis. The object of the allies was to place the country in a situation to refuse nothing, and to aid in every respect the common cause; and every step they could oblige or urge Switzerland to take against France placed her more in this situation.

To return to what relates to Marshal Blucher's passage of the Rhine, it will be as memorable in military annals for its rapidity and decision, as his passage of the Elbe; and I regretted that absence in Holstein prevented my being a personal witness of a military event remarkable for its brilliant execution.

The Marshal passed with his army at three points: Lieutenant-general Count St. Priest, of Count Langeron's *corps d'armée*, crossed opposite Coblentz on the nights of the 1st and 2nd instant: he occupied that town, took seven pieces of cannon, and made 500 prisoners. Generals Count Langeron and D'Yorck passed at Kaub; where Marshal Blucher assisted in person, without much resistance on the part of the enemy. On the 3rd instant, Count Langeron attacked and forced Bingen, which is considered very strong in point of situation; and was defended by a general of brigade, with cannon and infantry. Count Langeron made some prisoners, and his loss was trifling. He had already his advanced-posts established as far as the Salzback, opposite Ingelheim.

Marshal Blucher advanced, notwithstanding every difficulty of roads and season, to Kreugreach; and General D'Yorck's advanced-posts were directed upon the Lauter. General Baron Sachen's corps forced the enemy's entrenchments near Manheim, after passing the Rhine, and was directed on Allzey. The King of Prussia was(present at Manheim at the passage of the Rhine, and inspired all around him, as heretofore, with admiration of those military attributes that are so conspicuously his own.

Dantzic surrendered on the 2nd of January: the first capitulation was not ratified, but the garrison finally surrendered prisoners of war. It would be tedious to give a detail of those marches and combinations which brought the allied armies again into motion in the beginning of 1814: I shall confine myself, therefore, to the actual position of the combined forces early in the month of January, adding such observations as occur on the re-commencement of active hostilities.

The head-quarters of Prince Schwartzenberg remained at Lorrach on the 20th of December. Count Bubna had moved to Dole. The other Austrian corps between Dole and Montbelliard, in the valley of the Dauve. Detachments occupied Vesoul, Espinal, &c.: in the former place 200 prisoners were taken. Parties were also in possession of the valley of Martigny, the Semplon, and St. Bernard. The first division of the Austrian army moved on Aney; the second was at Montarlot, near Besançon; the third at Villersexelle; the division Greenfeld at Mollars; the division Bianchi at Befort; two divisions of Austrian grenadiers, and two of *cuirassiers* were in march for Besançon; the fourth division was at St. Amber; the fifth, composed of the Bavarians, formed the blockade of Huningen and Breisach, and extended to Schletstadt. Count Wittgenstein was before Kehl, and occupied also

Fort Louis, pushing his parties, very far advanced on the other side of the Rhine, in the direction of Nancy.

The Russian grenadiers were in march to relieve Bianchi's division in the blockade of Befort, in order that the latter might then be enabled to move forward. The Russian and Prussian guards and reserves were still at Altkirk and Lorrach, but were forthwith to march forward. The main body of the Cossacks, under their daring Hetman, Platoff, had advanced, on the 7th of January, as far as Corrimont, Vesoul, and Langres; and they might already be said to be threatening Napoleon's "good city of Paris." The enemy, under Marshal Marmont, had already been overtaken by Marshal Blucher. This French force was estimated at between 16,000 and 17,000 men: it occupied Kaiserslautern, which is the Hollendorff pass, as it were, of the country. The environs are so intricate and mountainous, that every step Marmont took, posted as the Silesian army would soon be, rendered his situation precarious. General D'Yorck and General Sachen were on the 5th of January between Frankenstein and Neustadt; and General St. Priest at Coblentz.

From the advanced position of General D'Yorck on Marshal Marmont's flank, and the march of the corps moving up in all directions, we flattered ourselves that if he delayed much longer at Kaiserslautern, Marshal Blucher would be able to force him to an action. The auspicious aspect of affairs that every day brightened to the view of the allies, the march of events as rapid as they were glorious, the success that seemed to attend upon the most trifling movement, military or political, produced a strong sentiment of religious gratitude in the public mind. The progress of the campaign hitherto seemed to promise even more brilliant consequences than its projectors could have anticipated.

Buonaparte for some time collected at Metz: for, by the march of General Bulow towards Holland, he possibly thought the allies were carrying their forces in that direction; and sent his guards, by rapid conveyances, towards Breda, about the 18th instant. However, when Prince Schwartzenberg crossed the Upper Rhine, on the 20th, the enemy's troops were as rapidly countermarched, being thrown into uncertainty as to the plans of the combined armies. Buonaparte seemed to have separated the remnant of his force, and they were dispersed in corps: there was no mass collected anywhere, and it must have been a large one indeed which could arrest in any manner the formidable legions of the conquerors.

The importance of the possession of Huninguen, on the Upper Rhine, to Prince Schwartzenberg, was considerable; but it did not seem that it could be easily taken. The capture of Befort was also of great moment; for, from such a base, the grand army might march immediately on Paris with perfect security against any possible contingency. The converging march of the different columns all bearing to the central point, so that on an emergency a large force might be collected, without unnecessarily risking any separate corps, with vigilant communications, and a due regard always to the main points of *appui,* formed the system on which the invasion of France was conducted: and if this principle had not been unfortunately departed from, many of the failures and disasters which intervened would never have occurred. After the battle of Leipsic, it was no way chimerical to predict that Europe approached her deliverance; and I now waited with the calmness of perfect confidence for the arrival of that happy moment, for my country and the whole civilised world, when it would fall to my lot to announce to the British government that the individual whose elevation had caused so many calamities had ceased to reign.

I think I may without presumption or indiscretion attempt here a very general view of the important negotiations on the tapis. The questions were of so extensive a nature, the arguments to be adduced so various, and, above all, the information I individually possessed so limited, that I look with some apprehension to the task of introducing into my narrative even such prominent diplomatic features as may be essential to the better understanding of the military combinations: still, where a point is to be gained, and a mass is to be digested, little hints may serve to throw some light upon the subject. Supposing, in the first place, it was expedient to enter into negotiations with Buonaparte, on the basis proposed by the allies through M. de St. Aignau, which M. de Caulaincourt's arrival at the advanced-posts, and the last communications, brought to a decision in the affirmative, the following were some, of the leading points to consider.

That Prince Metternich wished to accomplish a peace could not be doubted, and that the arrangements for Germany were, to be made as he planned, was pretty evident: that "he had also his own game nearer at heart than any other was not surprising; but it was not to be permitted that, in order to play this as he fancied, the other powers of Europe were to be confined in their natural views and objects, which the downfall of Napoleon and increased successes might in some degree alter. When Buonaparte subdued Austria did he not dictate peace? did he not insist on heavy pecuniary contributions to indemnify the people of France? At Tilsit, did he not, in like manner, drain Prussia of her last *kreutzer* to support his army, and alleviate the burdens of the French nation? Would not a just principle of retaliation direct, that if the allies now made peace with France, and confined her to her ancient limits, the amount of past robberies should be refunded? And yet, when we had the game in our own hands, we appeared, by a secret and extraordinary mission at Frankfort, and a demi-official declaration, referring to propositions which the world were unacquainted with, and which seemed now to be as binding in the minds of some as the best authenticated state document, to have lost the commanding position in which we stood.

It was argued that the propositions sent in embraced the twofold objects of accomplishing a general peace, and a more humbled state of the political and military government of France. How much more humble she would have been at this period, and how much less embarrassing our predicament, had those propositions not been made, can be best appreciated by remarking the effects produced by M. de St. Aignau's mission, with all the explanations and defences and shifts which followed it. If we negotiated now, it was determined, first, to make a peace with Buonaparte himself, in preference to holding out and attempting to obtain the legitimate government for France by his downfall. Secondly, we were content with obtaining the basis proposed, in the most extended sense and latitude, attached to it. Thirdly, this peace, such as we dictated, signed at Basle, seemed to be considered by some more advisable, than by undertaking a march to the capital of France incur the hazard of another revolution, which might bring all the horrors of the former to be acted over again.

It really seemed impossible, but yet it was given out that the great powers coincided in this general idea; and I must suppose, if so, that it arose from a difference of opinion amongst them as to what, if Buonaparte were set aside, would be the best and wisest government for France. Austria might prefer the King of Rome under a regency; which the spirit of her present minister, in a great degree, could direct or control: England, the Bourbons: the Emperor of Russia, possibly, as was said, his friend Bernadotte. In short, there seemed a dread of anarchy in France; and a disunion in the coalition, if a bold choice were made, which might produce a more convulsed state of Europe than that existing before the reign of Buonaparte.

If Napoleon were forced from the throne of France, it was to be considered whether the sentiments of the allies could be brought to the same decision on the great question of a successor. Should this be the case, a totally different line might be taken from what was then under contemplation. This view I founded on the certainty that the re-establishment of the Bourbons would be more acceptable to England than any other arrangement. If, however, as some maintained, England wished to see France reduced to as humble a position as possible, it might be policy to keep Buonaparte on his throne, with his wings clipped to the utmost, in preference to restoring the hereditary princes, who might again resume a sway similar to the times of Louis XIV., and become formidable alike to England and to the continent.

The difficulty of negotiation at this crisis appeared in fixing upon the fundamental principles to be adopted and the points to be obtained; and it seemed indispensable that the government of England should send their minister of foreign affairs to the then theatre of action, as no one could act with the same advantages. There were other considerations of a minor nature—which, however, were not to be overlooked—such as the trifling jealousies among powers and personages that might arise; and which made me firmly of opinion, that the British cabinet could delegate this duty to none but the Secretary for Foreign Affairs. He could see, in the progress of discussion, to what points it was possible that the political machine could be wound up: an object, under the then predicament of the allies, that seemed to be the general wish; although some had neither the boldness nor the will to avow it.

Having taken a hasty view of the probable train of negotiation, founded on the principle of treating with Buonaparte under the projected basis, before I proceed to enter at large into what the allies would have to contend for, or rather dictate, as their decision, I shall just advert to what might, in my judgment, have been the best policy, in case of deciding to await the expression of public feeling in France, in order to secure the overthrow of the existing dynasty, and the re-establishment of the Bourbons. Every delay in negotiation with Caulaincourt, in such case, should have been made. It might fairly have been stated that, so long as the King of Spain and the Pope were in captivity, the allies would not send their propositions: meanwhile, the armies might have continued their march; and six weeks, or two months, might have given rise to a general impulse throughout the nation expressive of their wish, without positively departing from the first proposals.

It was thus to be considered whether a plan of procrastination, under existing circumstances, might not make events lean to the great object of a lasting peace for the world, even more rapidly than they were actually advancing. Great Britain's decision expressed, might change Austria, and persuade Russia and Prussia. But the policy of these courts, I must say, was so anxiously, so impatiently bent upon insuring the blessings of peace, so long withheld from them, that they thought and dreamed of nothing else. Austria desired it on even reasonable terms with France; and the Emperor wished it, for the sake of a daughter he very much loved. Russia so eagerly longed for it, that no man but the Emperor, who stood alone as a sheet-anchor of perseverance and devotion to the common cause, could have kept his generals, officers, and troops, so long tranquil. Prussia sought for it after her sufferings, and the King after his misfortunes, public and private, in preference to any war that would insure her aggrandisement. The amiable domestic habits of that monarch led him rather to seek a mournful consolation, near the tomb of his departed queen, in Charlottenburg. In justice, however, to his revered, lamented, and incomparable minister, the Chancellor Hardenberg, I must declare that his firmness and conviction of the policy of a vigorous prosecution of the contest, greatly tended to press forward the power of Prussia.

Still the wish nearest the hearts of all became every day more and more evident; there was a general cry for no delay in its accomplishment. The project of continuing the war for the Bourbons was liable, in case of a reverse, to cause disunion among the powers, if they were not agreed in the principle of proceeding; and it was argued, at this period, that a march to Paris, in order that the Emperors might enter at the head of their guards to sign the same peace with Buonaparte as they could conclude at Basle, would be mere vainglory and parade; and a movement on Paris should only be undertaken for a specific and agreed object—the re-establishment of the Bourbons. No lasting peace with France could be made, in my mind, so long as Buonaparte was at the head of the government.

In the north of Germany still greater difficulties than those already described arose. Prussia had not only a right, after her treaties, to be placed in the state in which she was in 1805, but, independently of this, all powers were of opinion that Prussia should be placed on such a respectable footing as, combined with Austria, to oppose a barrier to Russia on one side, and to France on the other. Austria, it was said, desired this: they would assign to Prussia ten millions of souls; the latter had at that time not more than between four and a half and five millions. If they were to restore to Prussia all she had lost in Poland, it would give her two millions and a half of what was required; but Russia was only willing to give that part which joins Russia with Silesia, and wanted to carry her own frontier to the Vistula: hence arose to Prussia a deficit of two millions and a half.

The question of Poland likewise came under discussion; but as it is of immense importance, and cannot be treated at length, I shall not touch on it: I shall equally avoid alluding here more at large to the state of Switzerland. Russia desired to draw a line, from Johansberg by the Pilicia to the corner of Silesia; and she would not consent to give up this plan for any consideration. Prussia might be permitted to possess, as she desired, Saxony; and there seemed no objection, except as to a part which the Emperor of Russia wished to reserve for the Duke of Weimar. By this plan Prussia would acquire one million and a half of subjects. After this there would be wanting an indemnity for Hildesheim. There belonged to Prussia all her Westphalian provinces, Anspach, Bayreuth, and Neufchatel; yet, if she repossessed all these, she would not obtain near the extent of possession she had just pretensions to claim. If Prussia obtained Saxony, Anspach and Bayreuth would not-be too far separated, and she might be glad to recover them; but, even in this case, more indemnity must be found for Bavaria. Prussia, however, was not desirous of having these detached possessions, provided she could be remunerated in a collected body; but the difficulty to find this was the evil.

Nothing appeared to be more impolitic than the designs imputed now to Austria, of requiring, in case of a general arrangement, the possession of certain districts she formerly held in the Brisgau, on the confines of France. This policy was viewed as an attempt to remove a controlling power over the states which separate Austria from France; such as Bavaria, Wirtemburg, and Baden, and to secure them in her interests. It was argued that the result would be totally adverse to the designs of Austria; for the control would not be effectual for the purpose of influence and power over those states, and it would breed in them a perpetual jealousy, and lead them to consider the power of France as necessary to balance any design which might be conceived against them by Austria, and to dispose them to alliances with the former power. This policy was placing within the reach of France possessions which would give a pretence, in any war with Austria, for France passing the Rhine into Germany. She would have always a distinction in her favour that she was not going to attack the German league, but Austria only; and if France quarrelled with Austria only, exclusive of Germany, she would have a right to use this argument. But if we consider another course, and suppose Austria, from a principle of confidence in the German powers, to give up the idea of control, and to act upon the principles of sincere confidence, Austria could never be attacked but by the desertion of the three intermediate powers named from the cause of Germany and their own. It is against every principle of calculation that Baden, Wirtemburg and Bavaria would ever suffer a French army to pass the Rhine, except from jealousy of Austria; and so long as they are really united with her, they will form to her an impregnable barrier. Jealousy and suspicion of Austrian designs and pretensions can alone divide or unite them against her.

The divisions amongst the members of the German body have been the sources of all the wars which have desolated Germany. It should be the great object of Austria, therefore, to keep them united, which could alone be accomplished by renouncing all old claims of every kind, and making herself the protector of Germany, by resolving never to take an interested part in the quarrels in which Germany might engage, even if Austria, in consequence of her powerful interference and victories, had fair and just claims of aggrandisement. She would by this means secure herself against France, and be enabled to have her resources concentrated, in case of need, against Russia; whom, on every account, in looking over the vale of years, Austria has most to dread.

Nothing can be more disadvantageous to a nation than to have paltry distant posts and interests, which invite the attack of enemies, and prevent the whole of a nation's resources from being applied to the point of real danger.

If France and Russia showed themselves really friendly to the designs of Austria, now promulgated, in her desire to re-establish herself in the Brisgau, no clearer proof could be assigned that they were anxious for the downfall of that power.

Another question of some moment that agitated the great negotiation for a general arrangement of Europe, was the fate of Saxony. So long as this power remained independent in the rear of Prussia, the latter could not become a sufficient barrier to the north against Russian invasion: and if once the Prussian armies should be defeated on the Oder, and Saxony awed into neutrality or confederacy with Russia, Berlin and Pomerania would immediately fall. But should Prussia be put in possession of Saxony, were she beat upon her first line of the Oder, she could form again with renewed force and strength on the Elbe, and be enabled to collect all her resources, and those of her allies, before Russia could master her fortresses, which would not be the case if Russia, by the means of the treachery or imbecility of Saxony were to lay hold on the Elbe.

It was upon this reasoning that, mixed up as I was with other political projectors, I formed, under existing circumstances, a strong opinion that the possession of Saxony by Prussia, at a general settlement of its affairs, was essential to the preservation of Europe, and that means ought to have been found to have induced the king of Saxony to resign his dominions with a view to some such arrangement, even if he had done, nothing to invalidate or forfeit his titles to them, and if they had not been at this time under French occupation. Add to this argument that Prussia ought not to have been looked to as a barrier against Russia, or to be prepared to place herself, conjointly with Austria, in that position, unless means were supplied to Prussia by the powers of Europe for playing that game with security and with effect.

Prussia, from her contiguity with Russia, and her comparative weakness, was at this period lending herself to the views of that colossal empire. The great personal friendship that existed between the monarchs aided this course of action; and Prussia acted in a degree of subordination to a bolder policy: she was forced to consider the mere view of her own safety. If she detached herself, unprepared, and without arrangements, from Russia, to place herself as the advanced-guard of Europe against her, what had she not to expect from Russian resentment? The first favourable moment would be seized by that aggressive colossus, when Europe might be distracted and Saxony tangible for Russian purposes, and Prussia might then be sacrificed, Europe having denied her those resources which were necessary for the part she ought and was destined to play in maintaining the balance of Europe. I therefore consider, on every principle of sound policy, Prussia ought neither to have been expected to engage in forming a barrier against Russia, nor should Europe allow her to attempt it, unless she should be supplied with adequate means, which she could never have without the accession of Saxony.

As the peace that the allied powers might make with France, at the present moment, was of more importance than any negotiations that had ever yet been entered upon, so it was necessary to consider how its stability could best be secured, as well as for diplomatic theorists to give their opinions on all parts of the arrangements, and on all the contingencies, sacrifices, or aggrandisements that might occur. Consequently the grand head-quarters became a constant scene of political disquisition. The idea of forming minor states on the frontiers of the French empire, which could impose such a resistance to the encroachments of France as would afford time for the more powerful nations in the rear to get their forces into the field and their preparations in forwardness, was a point which next required to be maturely considered.

The basis, perhaps, of a lasting and efficient peace depended, first, on gaining sufficient territory from France for the formation of states on the frontier; and, secondly, on strengthening and consolidating, as much as possible, the powers in the rear interested in supporting them.

Here it was certain that Austria and Prussia were the principal powers alluded to: to augment their forces, and to form intermediate powers between them and France, were the main objects. Every plan had to depend and be modified on the extent of those conquests which France might be willing to restore on a peace. To consider the terms upon which the allies ought to insist with the greatest firmness:—it was evident that if Alsace were not wrested from the enemy, all the fortresses on the Rhine, as low down as Landau; should be destroyed: Strasburg might become, as heretofore, a free city; and then the ancient frontier of France, from Landau to Dunkirk, would be the most perfect military line. It was to be considered whether, in uniting territories under pretence of a sufficient barrier for Holland, we did not leave to France a greater population and extent than under her kings: we might give her the frontier of the Rhine from Basle to Landau, and then take what we might consider an adequate security for Holland, or for the power that would be placed between France and the Rhine.

Supposing it would not be possible to bring France to consent to the surrender of the four departments, La Lys, Jemappe, L'Escaut, and La Dyle, it might then be proposed to leave in her possession Avignon and the maritime Alps, or some other indemnity in lieu of two of those departments: at all events, the departments of L'Escaut and La Dyle ought to be surrendered; and with these we secured the important points of Antwerp, Namur, Luxemburg, and Mentz. Of Antwerp there *could* be no question; of the other three places stated, there *should* have been none. Namur was essential for the command of the Meuse, Luxemburg for the Moselle, and Mentz for the Rhine. I believe Namur was of as much importance as either of them.

The next best military line to draw would have been from Namur to Dinant; from thence along the Somme towards Aslon; and from thence to the Rhine: thus including Trevis, which might be fortified and made a very strong place.

If any of these frontiers were obtained, especially the two former, a very considerable territory would be gained on the left bank of the Rhine, and the military barrier of Holland secured. If Prussia had a possession in this quarter, it should be a large one; at least containing three or four millions of inhabitants, in which she could hold an army of 100,000 men. If Prussia were brought thus close to France and Austria, by the annexation of the Brisgau, which, many believed she would always cling to, and part of Alsace, also close to the Rhine, it remained to be considered whether this might not be the most secure plan for the tranquillity of Germany.

An idea prevailed, that a temptation might be held out to Hanover to change the electorate for territories of nearly double the population, between the Rhine and the Meuse, connecting the possessions of the Prince Regent more with Holland, and thus making Hanover and Holland the outposts, while Prussia would receive the Hanoverian provinces. This notion, however, I always thought impracticable; but it was stated, that instead of a population of 800,000 souls, which Hanover then had, she would be offered one of two millions, and a much more valuable position.

It is not necessary to enter into all the details and calculations of extent, position, and population, that were now going on; but the outlines I have stated will satisfy my readers that every possible plan was now under discussion for peace, and the future settlement of Europe. With regard to the south, there were as many projects and speculations; but it would be superfluous to detail them.

The columns of the allied armies continued their advance on all sides towards the capital of France. The head-quarters of Marshal Prince Schwartzenberg were, on the 12th instant, at Vesoul. At Langres, on the advance of General Giulay's corps, the inhabitants fired on the troops; but this was the only instance where the allies had not been universally well received.

Prince Schwartzenberg's head-quarters were to be at Langres on the 15th or 16th. General Bubna's corps had a new direction given it, from Dole towards Lyons, and it was on its march. General Bianchi operated against Befort; and there was a report that it had surrendered. Besançon was invested by the corps of Prince Lichtenstein. The Bavarians, under General Wrede, had a very serious affair with the enemy, commanded by Marshal Victor, near St. Drey. In the commencement of the action the former were repulsed, and the French cavalry, commanded by General Mulhaud, had some success; but on the arrival of General De Roy's Bavarian brigade, the enemy were in their turn completely repulsed, and retired towards Luneville, with the loss of several officers and some hundred prisoners. The Cossacks continued very far in advance. We anxiously expected intelligence of important events from Marshal Blucher: it seemed, however, that Marshal Marmont retired with precipitation from Kaiserslautern, and passed the Saar. Marshal Blucher had his head-quarters on the 10th at Kessel; and it was said he had proceeded as far as Saarbruch, and that he would be at Mentz on the 15th or 16th.

By accounts from Paris, the enemy were collecting some force near Chalons: if so, they probably meant to retire on it from Nancy; for by the approach of the allied armies on all sides, any force that delayed falling back would have been surrounded.

The Russian and Prussian guards and reserves, to the amount of 30,000, crossed the Rhine at Basle on the 14th, and denied before the allied sovereigns. It is impossible by any description to give an exaggerated idea of the perfect state of these troops; their appearance and equipment were admirable; and when one considered what they had endured, and contemplated the Russians, some of whom had emerged from the steeps of Tartary bordering the Chinese empire, traversed their own regions, and marched, in a few short months, from Moscow across the Rhine, one was lost in wonder, and inspired with a political awe of that colossal power. The condition in which the Russian cavalry appeared, reflected the highest reputation on this branch of their service ; and their artillery was admirable. I could not help, on seeing these Russian guards on this day, recurring to serious impressions with regard to this overgrown empire; and I much apprehend the present tidings from the east of Europe bear out my predictions in 1814, when the Russians were passing the Rhine.

If we consider the power of Russia, unassailable as she is, in flank or rear, hovering over Europe with an immense front, mistress of the Caspian, the Euxine, and the Baltic, with forty millions of hardy, docile, brave, enthusiastic, and submissive inhabitants, with immense armies, highly disciplined, excellently appointed; her innumerable hordes of desolating cavalry; her adoption of the French maxims in war, of making the countries where her armies march, or are cantoned, feed and maintain them, what may we not fear from her? When we further consider this power flushed with success, and disposed to consider treaties and engagements with her as waste paper, if they stood in the way of any project of aggrandisement; and if we further contemplate her determined will to surmount every barrier which engagements have interposed, in order to advance herself into the heart of Germany, to supplant on one side the ancient dominion of Prussia; on the other, to turn the northern flank of Austria on the Vistula, as she has turned the southern on the Danube; and demanding, as it were, by the fortresses of Thorn and Cracow, the keys of Berlin and Vienna;—when we further reflect on the natural march of empires from north to south, from the regions of frost, and snow, and famine, to the climates of warmth, verdure, and fertility, and recollect the revolutions which have taken place in Europe, Asia, and Africa, from the desolating invasions of the northern hordes, what may we not fear and expect?

When, in addition to these circumstances, we further reflect upon the successive aggrandisements and incorporations Russia has made within the last one hundred and fifty years; the numerous Tartar tribes she has embraced within her military system; the provinces she has successively added to her empire from Persia, the Porte, Sweden, and Poland; that her whole system of government is a military despotism, and nothing known in it or regarded but military subjection on the one hand, and military property, military rank, and military honours, on the other, what may not be the results? If we consider all these circumstances in all their bearings and dependencies, Is there a serious and reasonable man in Europe that must not admit that the whole system of European politics ought, as its leading principle and feature, to maintain, as an axiom, the necessity of setting bounds to this formidable and encroaching power? Weighed against this superior and imperative duty,—a duty urged by all the motives of self-preservation, every minor and secondary consideration, resulting whether from ancient rights or claims, from family feelings and alliances, from views of future political combination and power, ought to be postponed and disregarded. There was no better physical or moral safeguard against the stupendous greatness with which the continent might, ere long, be menaced and overwhelmed by Russia, than in the personal character of the reigning Emperor Alexander; a mixture of benevolence and rectitude, a high sense of religion, and a generous view on all subjects. These afforded, in my mind, the only and best guarantee against the far too formidable legions that were then defiling over the Rhine; and that guarantee we have, alas! lost.

    The details from the advanced corps continued to be of the most encouraging description. Marshal Blucher had taken near 3000 prisoners, and twenty-five pieces of cannon, since his passage of the Rhine. By his last reports from St. Arol, of the 8th instant, detachments of his troops were occupying Treves; and in a few days Luxemburg was to be invested. Marshal Marmont had been under the necessity of making the most rapid forced marches, to prevent the Silesian army from getting in his rear by the Vosges mountains. In his retreat he broke down all the bridges over the Saare; but Marshal Blucher pursued him closely. Reports of the confusion and disorder throughout France were prevalent: the assembling of the conscripts was very slow; those that were brought together wanted arms and all kind of equipment. There seemed nothing now more certain than that the allied armies could effect a march to Paris whenever they thought proper. Two-thirds of the French old soldiers that had re-crossed the Rhine were either dead or gone into the hospitals; and all the general officers and men of experience declared that no effectual resistance could be made.

Prince Schwartzenberg however was still at Vesoul on the 15th. The enemy were collecting at Langres, and the Prince Marshal was preparing to attack them, if they should remain there: he had made his. dispositions for this purpose, and his forces amounted to about 165,000 men. The line he occupied was, nevertheless, a very extended one, if the enemy had force to take advantage of it with collected means in any one point. The main Russian army, under General Barclay de Tolly, was to be ready to support Prince Schwartzenberg's offensive movement. General Wittgenstein's corps occupied the country between General Barclay de Tolly and Marshal Blucher; and the Russian and Prussian reserves, accompanied by the Emperors of Russia and Austria, left Basle to march on Vesoul. The French garrison that had retired into Besançon amounted to 8000 men. Befort was still bombarded, and General Schöffer commanded the forces engaged there. General Bubna was at Bourg-en-Bresse, having left detachments at Geneva and Fort l'Ecluse, which had been taken, as well as the fortress of Stettin. The Semplon and St. Bernard were, occupied: the Prince of Wirtemburg advanced from Epinal; the enemy retiring, after their defeat by General de Roy, towards Charmes, and the Prince of Hesse Homburg from Dole. General Scheuther surrounded the fort of Solins; while General Platoff's Cossacks were heard of in every quarter.

The entry of the Emperor of Russia into Vesoul, with the Russian and Prussian reserves; the abandonment of Langres, and the position around it, by the enemy; the advance of the Prince Royal of Wirtemburg in the direction of Chaumont; all carried the grand army nearer the final accomplishment of its glorious labours. The movement of so powerful a force as the allies now possessed, in all directions, upon any central point, rendered the best position the enemy could take up wholly precarious. In my opinion they could not have effectually covered their capital by any disposition whatever, the allies being determined to enter it:—and at length that triumphant moment was at hand.

Marshal Blucher's reports of the 17th instant, from Nancy, were, that he had sent the keys of that town to the grand headquarters. The Emperor of Russia met the officer bearing them as he was on his march to Vesoul: he immediately sent two of the keys to the King of Prussia, with an appropriate message, reserving two for himself. This showed the mutual deference and consideration that existed between the allied sovereigns on every occasion. Marshal Blucher was in communication with General Wrede's corps, and thus with the grand army. The former energetic veteran wrote that he was determined to plant his banners on Napoleon's throne; and he gave a life and vigour to all proceedings that afforded an invaluable example to every professional man. Another brilliant achievement of the Prussian arms now occurred : the king became again master of Wittenberg, and by no other means but the desperate valour of his brave soldiers.

The siege was begun on the 28th of December, and the place was in his possession on the 12th of January. No impediment of the season had arrested the spirited exertions of the besiegers.

The enemy made a respectable resistance: a breach was effected on the 11th, and it was practicable on the 12th, when a proposal to surrender was made and refused. At midnight, the assault was determined on in four columns. The gallant Prussians overcame every obstacle, and in less than half an hour they were masters of the place. All the garrison that did not lay down their arms were put to the sword. The governor had entrenched the castle and the hotel *de ville*: the latter was carried by the troops; and the governor, who was in it, surrendered at discretion, with the rest of the garrison.

This capture alone would establish the fame of that distinguished officer General Tauenstein; but his former exploits in this war were too brilliant ever to be obliterated from the records of his country. The siege cost about 800 men, and the assault alone, about 107 officers in killed and wounded. The Prussians found ninety-six pieces of artillery here, and made 2000 prisoners.

In Torgau they had already obtained possession of 316 pieces.

In these fortresses the Prussians also found considerable magazines of corn and powder.

General Tauenstein was now to proceed to Magdeburg; and it is not to be overlooked here, that every fortress which now fell by the admirable dispositions that had been made, augmented very materially the force advancing against the enemy: we had thus reinforcements, and three lines of reserve as it were on the Oder, the Elbe, and the Rhine, from which we constantly derived aid.

The head-quarters of the Emperors of Austria, Russia, and the King of Prussia, were on the 23rd of January at Vesoul. In continuing my account of the various operations and movements of the different armies, divisions, and corps, I ought to state generally, that in proportion as the large masses of troops approached to one point, *viz.* the capital of the French empire, the respective corps necessarily passed and repassed each other in the same direction, but on a more confined theatre of war. On this account, to trace the exact progress of all lines of march, and keep each clear and distinct, would require much greater information than I had the means of obtaining, and occupy also much more time and space than it is the object of the present circumscribed narrative to afford. All I mean to attempt is limited to a general and connected view of the most important movements and actions, and I leave to more experienced and able writers of each nation the task of a more complete and detailed history.

General Bubna still continued his march, possessing himself of the whole of the department of the Jura. Having repaired the fortifications of Geneva, he next took Dole, and made himself master of the bridge over the Doubs. General Zeuchmeister with his division occupied Aix and Chamberry on the 2nd instant, without opposition. Had General Bubna at this period been reinforced, he might in conjunction with Zeuchmeister have moved rapidly forward on Lyons; but the opportunity was lost, and Marshal Augereau now received orders to repair thither, and, if possible, organise a large force. General Bubna in consequence took up a position behind the Arve, and ultimately fixed his head-quarters at Geneva.

With respect to the leading operations on the 17th, Marshal Mortier, who was immediately opposed to the main advance from Vesoul on Langres and Chaumont, finding it apparent that his left flank might be turned by the Austrian General Giulay's division, abandoned his position at Langres, retiring on Chaumont, and the grand head-quarters were now taken up in the former city. General Wrede's corps having left a division to blockade Huninguen, now advanced in the rear, keeping up communication with the troops that blockaded the fortresses of Befort and other places.

General Count Frimont's corps marched on from Colmar to Rixheim: General Count Wittgenstein's division had followed Marshal Victor's corps from the side of Strasburg, and had now also united in the main line of operations, while General Wrede had orders to advance still further from the Meurthe river towards the Meuse. By this junction, and bringing up General Wrede's division between the grand army and the army of Silesia, the forces of the allies became united in one formidable line of attack.

Prince Schwartzenberg now determined to carry his army immediately forward from the line of Chaumont to Chalons-sur-Marne, where it was reported that Buonaparte had assembled all his forces with a view of giving battle.

CHAPTER 16

Into France

I have already adverted to the number of British officers employed with the different corps of the allied armies; from all of whom minute accounts were given, at this period, of the dispositions, movements, and operations of the respective *corps d'armée*. But I must particularly refer my readers, in order thoroughly to understand every part of the great military manoeuvres now pending, to the able reports of Sir Robert Wilson, Colonel Lord Burghersh, (who has written an able and excellent memoir of this campaign,) Colonel (now Brigadier-General) Sir Hudson Lowe, Colonels Cooke, and others. These will fully and clearly exemplify the minutest military operations: my province is an attempt to exhibit to my readers a more general view of the great drama, of which France was now become the theatre.

The grand head-quarters were established on the 29th at Chaumont, after a brilliant action of the Prince Royal of Wirtemburg, who drove Mortier from his position, and followed him on the route to Troyes and Joinville; while Giulay's corps, at the same period, repulsed the enemy from Bar-sur-Aube, and followed up his rear closely towards Chatillon.

On the 16th and 18th the army of Silesia had accomplished its junction with the grand army, between the Moselle and the Marne; the enemy retiring behind the latter river. He still, however, occupied Toul, which Marshal Blucher ordered the corps of Sacken to carry by assault. This was gallantly performed by

General Count Lieven. General D'Yorck's *corps d'armée,* in the mean time, had proceeded from Metz to the Meuse, leaving corps to blockade Sarre-louis, Thionville, and Luxemburg.

The two grand armies of the allies being now in line on the Meuse, Napoleon had concentrated in their immediate front the corps of Mortier, Victor, and Marmont. He had been himself constantly at Paris since the passage of the Rhine by the allies, making efforts to rally the first ban, or third of the French population, and to collect reinforcements of all kinds for his armies; and he now issued orders that every inch of ground was to be in future disputed by his generals in command. He himself repaired to the army at Chalons-sur-Marne, where he arrived on the 26th of January.

Marshal Ney also had now joined Napoleon; and several fresh bodies of troops and conscripts had come forward from Paris. His cavalry likewise was reinforced by part of the imperial guard; and Generals Lefevre-Desnouettes, Milliard, and Grouchy, were assembled at Chalons with a force of near 100,000 men. Napoleon's first plan was stated to be, to march to Nancy, and operate on the rear of the allies; but finding the grand army superior to the force he had collected, and to what he had expected, he determined to fall on Marshal-Blucher, and annihilate him, if possible, before he could be supported by Prince Schwartzenberg.

On the 28th Napoleon marched his army on Vassy; and proceeded, by the way of Montierender and Somevoire, in two columns, to attack Marshal Blucher's corps, now posted in and about Brienne. Marshal Blucher had only the corps of Sacken and part of that of Langeron with him. General D'Yorck was still at Ligny, and the Prince Royal of Wirtemburg's corps (which was the nearest in support of the marshal) between Dienville and Trannes. The action was reported to have been very bloody, but entirely in favour of the allies. The town of Brienne, for some time, was in possession of the enemy; but they were ultimately driven from it with great slaughter, and lost some guns. The marshal resumed his position; and it was most animating to see a very inferior force resist at one point the enemy who had collected in such strength before him.

Marshal Blucher had moved from Joinville to Brienne, placing himself rather in advance: this had probably tempted Napoleon to engage; but from what occurred, and the manner of the attack, it was doubtful if Buonaparte's plan were to bring on a general action in the country about Chalons: it rather appeared that he would not risk so desperate a game.

Field-Marshal Prince Schwartzenberg now made his dispositions, and collected all his troops, in case the enemy should still hold his ground. The Prince Royal of Wirtemburg was ordered up to the support of Marshal Blucher. The divisions of Giulay and Colloredo arrived at Bar-sur-Aube. General Wittgenstein's corps in Joinville was ordered to Vassy; as also General Kleist, not far in his rear. General Winzingerode, from the northern army, was likewise in march to join the grand army: General D'Yorck moved on the 30th to St. Dizier: General Wrede, with the Bavarians, to St Urbain, ready to support the movements of General Wittgenstein: the Austrian grenadiers and reserves to Colombey: the Russian and Prussian guards and cavalry were at and near Chaumont.

If the enemy should threaten any one corps before the allies had all their force brought up, that corps was to retire; but as in two days all the corps were to be united, and ready to act, there could hardly be a doubt of another day such as Leipzig, if Buonaparte ventured to afford the opportunity. On my visiting Marshal Blucher on the 31st, at Trannes, I found him occupying a very advantageous position; his left resting on that village and the Aube river, and his right at Maison, which was occupied by the Prince Royal of Wirtemburg. The enemy showed themselves with their right at Dienville, their centre above Lacoutiere, and their left extending towards Loulaine. In the middle of the day they appeared to be collecting on their centre; and their first movements indicated an attempt on Trannes and Marshal Blucher's position. Afterwards, however, it became, evident, by an advance of a considerable body of cavalry and the filing of troops to their right, that they had another object, and that the demonstration made was to cover it.

The country being unfavourable for ascertaining with precision the enemy's movements, and the reports of the patrols and light corps not having come in, it was difficult to pronounce as to Napoleon's intentions. By an intercepted letter from Berthier, sent in by General Scherbatoff, it became still more evident that it had been Buonaparte's first plan to fall upon the right or rear of the allies, and to get round the flank, and act upon our communications. Another useful lesson, however, received by Buonaparte at Brienne, when the second determination was taken, added possibly to the report of General D'Yorck's corps at St. Dizier, and General Wittgenstein's moving from Joinville, induced him entirely to abandon his project. He certainly would have found himself between three corps; and the whole allied army would have been united, ready to fall upon him.

The road from Brienne towards Troyes was now broken up, and the bridge at Lesmont destroyed by General Scherbatoff's partisan corps. Count Pahlen with all his cavalry made a movement from Marshal Blucher's position on the 31st to the right, to join Count Wittgenstein. This probably operated to accelerate the enemy's withdrawing from their left. The corps of the allied army on the 31st, at night, were posted as follows:—General Sacken's, and a division of Count Langeron's under Generals Lauskoi, Otterfief, and Scherbatoff, with the Prince Royal of Wirtemburg, were in position near Trannes and Maison.

The marshal's force might now be averaged at above 35,000 men. General Wrede with the Bavarians, amounting to 28,000, arrived at Doulevant; General Giulay, with about 18,000, at Bar-sur-Aube. General Colloredo with 21,000 marched on the great road from thence towards Troyes. Count Wittgenstein's, at or near Vassy, was stated at 15,000. General D'Yorck at St. Dizier had 20,000 men.

The reserves of the Russian and Prussian grenadiers and guards consisted of about 35,000. Thus from 160 to 170,000 men might have been concentrated against the enemy, on the morning of the 1st of February. General Kleist's corps then arriving at St. Michael, and General Winzingerode's following it, were not included. The whole of the enemy's force engaged against Marshal Blucher on the 29th, belonged to the guard. The marshal averaged his loss at not more than 700 or 800 men. The enemy's was very heavy; his immense superiority in numbers showed the powerful resistance he had met with.

Buonaparte was seen to encourage his troops and expose his person fearlessly during the combat; and Marshal Blucher's movement of his cavalry, which he led on himself, was spoken of in the highest terms. Napoleon, who, at this period, scarcely acted, in any instance, on common military calculation, drew up his army on the 1st of February in two lines, on the great plain before La Rothiere, occupying the villages, and neglecting much stronger ground in his rear about Brienne, evidently showing that he meant to play a desperate game. He led on *la jeune garde* in person against Marshal Blucher's army, to wrest the village of La Rothiere from the gallant corps of Sacken; but three repeated efforts were ineffectual. All agreed that the enemy fought with great intrepidity. Buonaparte seemed to have set his political existence on a die, as he exposed himself every where: his horse was shot under him, and he had the mortification of witnessing the capture of a battery of guns in charge of *la jeune garde.*

Had Marshal Blucher not previously immortalised himself, this day would have crowned him in the annals of Fame; for whatever were the well-grounded apprehensions entertained by many for the result of the Prince of Wirtemburg's attack on the right, the marshal dauntlessly effected those combinations upon which the result of the day depended.

The Russian artillery were spoken of in the highest terms: the ground was covered with snow, and so deep, that they were obliged to leave one half of their guns in the rear. Yet by harnessing double teams to the other half, they contrived to bring those forward and get a sufficient number into action.

The allies brought about 70,000 or 80,000 men into this battle ; the other corps of the army were not yet in line: the enemy were supposed to have had about the same strength. The enemy's last attack on the village of La Rothiere was at two o'clock on the morning of the 2nd, immediately after which they commenced their retreat. Passing the Aube river, they took up a very strong rear-guard position in the neighbourhood of Lesmont.

Dispositions were made to attack this position with the corps of the Prince Royal of Wirtemburg, Generals Wrede and Giulay; and there was a sharp fire on this spot. But the day was unfavourable, and the fall of snow so excessive, that the troops could make no progress.

In the mean time the Field Marshal Prince Schwartzenberg made his arrangements for the pursuit of the enemy, who had retired on Vitry, Troyes and Arcis. The two former places were supposed to have garrisons and cannon, and Vitry was walled and protected by a ditch of some extent. It was now resolved that the grand army should march by Troyes on Paris, and the army of Silesia by Lesmont upon Vitry, forming their junction with the corps of General Wittgenstein coming from Vassy, and the corps of D'Yorck from St. Dizier, which last place was taken by General D'Yorck, with some loss on the part of the enemy.

This great combined force was thus to proceed on the shortest route to the capital; and Marshal Blucher sweeping round by the right, and forming a junction with the corps above stated, was to overpower every obstacle. It was calculated he probably would come in contact with the corps of Marshal MacDonald, which it was reported was marching to unite near Vitry. Prince Schwartzenberg's head-quarters were on the 3rd of February at Vendœuvres, and Marshal Blucher's at Breaux-le-Comte.

In the battle of La Rothiere eighty pieces of cannon and 4000 prisoners were taken by the allies; the latter of whom lost 6000 in killed and wounded. The Emperor of Russia and King of Prussia were present, and by their heroic conduct infused life and vigour into all the operations. After this battle Napoleon, on the 4th of February, retreated upon Troyes, where he established his head-quarters.

With regard to the fortresses which were left to be blockaded by forces in their rear, while the allies made their rapid and glorious advance on the capital of France, it may be sufficient here to state a fact applicable to them all; namely, that the different corps left before them were so nearly amounting in force to the garrisons of the places, that the latter confined themselves to insignificant sorties, while the former were only desirous of keeping the fortresses invested.

In the march of the army forward, the French nation appeared to me generally to favour the allies; they seemed wearied with the wars they were engaged in, and still more weary of their military ruler. The peasantry, however, were not allowed by the existing authorities to be passive; and finding measures had been taken to arm them, Prince Schwartzenberg was induced to issue a general order to treat all the natives as enemies who were found with arms in their possession.

Napoleon took great care, after the defeat at Brienne and La Rothiere, to publish his own accounts in Paris, with that dexterity for which he was so conspicuous; and thus, by his own bulletins at this period, as well as during the whole of the succeeding battles, the citizens of Paris were kept in profound ignorance of the real state of events. There is no doubt that the military science and manoeuvres displayed between the months of January and March, 1814, are the most interesting and important that distinguish this or any other war. Napoleon, although defeated again and again, seemed to rise superior to his difficulties; and after the battle of Brienne he displayed more strikingly all those resources and talents against his adversaries for which he has generally been so conspicuous; while great and grievous faults were, subsequently to the above battle, committed by the allies.

A too confident sentiment now prevailed; and because Napoleon had been defeated in an open battle, it was supposed he could no longer maintain an effective resistance: little calculation was placed on the considerable reinforcements that the French empire continued to pour forth on all sides, and each of the allied armies thought itself capable of meeting the enemy unaided by the other; whereas nothing but their union, and a joint operation of the whole collected force, would ever have ensured success. Both the grand army and the army of Silesia were eager to have the *éclat* of first entering Paris. To this absurd desire many of the misfortunes and losses of Marshal Blucher in his march forward were to be attributed: it led him to advance far too rashly, and separate himself too widely from the support of Prince Schwartzenberg; and when he experienced a check, it became more fatal, from the Silesian army having no succours. Prince Schwartzenberg's marches were more measured; but there was a want of concert, which nothing but being oversanguine as to the ultimate results could account for.

With regard to the Prince Royal and his army of the north, he took no part in the grand manoeuvres towards Paris. The greatest part of Holland was, during the month of January, delivered and restored to her rightful sovereign, with the exception of some of the strong places. The remnant of the French force collected at Antwerp, and retired into Belgium, of which Generals Bulow and Winzingerode endeavoured to make themselves masters. In order to effect this object, General Bulow took up a position near Utrecht, where he had his head-quarters; and early in the year he addressed a proclamation to the Belgians, in which he declared that he was arriving amongst them to deliver them from the odious tyranny under which they had so long groaned.

General Bulow next advanced and passed the Waal, driving back the French corps on Antwerp. They still occupied however Bergen-op-Zoom, with 4000 men, while Marshal MacDonald had his corps assembled between the Meuse and the Lower Rhine, and he threw garrisons and provisions into the different fortresses on the Wesel. Napoleon was known to take the deepest interest in the operations carrying on in this quarter; and when he heard that the fortress of Breda had been taken by the Russians of General Bulow's *corps d'armée,* he sent directions to the French general commanding at Antwerp to hazard every thing in retaking it. The French general Roguet, in compliance with this order, attacked the garrison of the fortress, commanded by General Beakendorff, with 10,000 men.

General Bulow and Sir T. Graham learning this event, immediately sent reinforcements; but the gallant conduct of General Beakendorff had forced the French general to retire into Antwerp before the succours had arrived. Great praise was due to General Beakendorff for his conduct in this gallant defence of Breda. A second attempt was in like manner made, and proved equally abortive; a column of English troops having meanwhile arrived in the neighbourhood, as well as General Bulow's reinforcement.

The troops of the expedition from England, under Sir T. Graham, now united with Bulow's corps, and Beakendorff's cavalry, forming a division of at least 20,000 men, in the neighbourhood of Breda, sufficiently strong to compel the French troops to enter an entrenched camp between West Wesel and Antwerp, with a view to cover the latter place. Napoleon, aware of the discomfiture of his forces in Belgium, determined now to send General Maison with all the forces he could spare to Lisle, in order to provision and prepare further defences in that city, and in the fortresses. The French troops still occupied the country between the Waal and the Meuse.

General Bulow, in pursuance of his instructions to make himself master of Belgium, attacked Marshal MacDonald in the middle of January, in his entrenched camp near Antwerp. The attack was formed in three columns, commanded by Generals Borstell, Thümen, and Oppen: the two former succeeded, but the latter failed in his attack; and notwithstanding this offensive operation was well supported in the following days by renewed efforts, aided by the English corps, Bulow was under the necessity, at the end of the month of January, of resuming his former positions near Breda; and. Sir Thomas Graham's English division returned to Bergen-op-Zoom, which place they invested.

In the mean time the corps of General Winzingerode, which had been joined by all Czernicheff's cavalry, passed the Rhine at Dusseldorf, and in the middle of January occupied Aix-la-Chapelle and Liege. In the latter place Czernicheff had a brilliant cavalry affair, in which he was completely victorious. Marshal MacDonald moved his head-quarters, on Winzingerode's passing the Rhine, to Namur, and from thence he fell back to

Mezieres, and ultimately to Dinant and Givet, followed by Czernicheff's cavalry. Winzingerode's head-quarters were established in the end of January at Namur. Although the rapid march of Winzingerode's corps, aided by General Bulow's operations, was not attended with the full success that had been expected, yet the fall of Bois le Due by assault, and the capture of Brussels at the end of January, gave a complete triumph to military events in this quarter.

I shall now briefly recall the reader to that part of my narrative which touched incidentally upon the great diplomatic transactions in progress at this period, and those negotiations which led to the conferences of Chatillon. The principal secretary of state for foreign affairs having received his Majesty's command to repair to the head-quarters of the allied sovereigns, arrived in the month of January, and immediately entered into the strictest communication with the state-ministers of the allied powers. And here I cannot, in natural feeling, refrain from inserting a paragraph of Lord Burghersh's *Memoirs*, which states as follows:

> The decision now taken in England, was to depute one of the cabinet ministers to represent Great Britain in the congress, which appeared now likely to be held for the final arrangement of a secure and lasting peace. Lord Harrowby is understood to have been first thought of for this mission: Lord Castlereagh, however, undertook the charge, and in the beginning of January joined the head-quarters of the sovereigns. No measure was ever wiser, or productive of greater benefits. Lord Castlereagh, by the manliness of his conduct, by the talent which he displayed under the most difficult circumstances, secured more solid advantages, not only to England, but to Europe, than perhaps will ever be generally known or acknowledged. In the various changes of fortune which attended the operations of the campaign of 1814, the steady course with which he pursued the general objects of the alliance, being never led aside from them either

by reverses or success, placed him in triumphant contrast with others, who, elated or depressed by the events of each succeeding period, would have ruined their cause, as much by overstrained pretensions in one alternative, as by a conduct totally the reverse in the other. Lord Castlereagh is understood to have left England with instructions to negotiate for peace upon conditions honourable to France, but differing from those proposed at Frankfort, which the change of circumstances had rendered totally inapplicable.

The consequence resulting from M. de St. Aignau's early mission from Frankfort was the appointment of the Duc de Vicenza, Caulaincourt, as French plenipotentiary to treat for a general peace with the allied plenipotentiaries assembled at Chatillon for this great object.

The ministers met in the middle of February; Lord Aberdeen, Lord Cathcart, and Sir Charles Stewart having been named plenipotentiaries on the part of Great Britain; Count Razumoffski on the part of Russia; Count Stadion for Austria; and Baron Von Humboldt for Prussia. These plenipotentiaries continued to assemble and hold repeated conferences until the middle of March; and during the whole of this period the military operations were carried on. I was prevented by my diplomatic duties from witnessing, and consequently detailing any personal observations on the military movements during the same interval; but the British government were accurately informed of the course of the operations by Colonel Lowe's and Lord Burghersh's very able communications.

The time may possibly arrive when I shall think myself justified in giving the history of the diplomatic transactions of this little congress at this period. I retain my own minutes of every minister's remarks on all the subjects of discussion, from which a summary might be drawn up not uninteresting to posterity. It may not here, however, be irrelevant to remark, that it was easy to perceive from the first discussions as to the terms of peace for Europe, that the most serious difficulties presented themselves;

and while the statesmanlike views of the ministers were influenced by the peculiar feelings of their sovereigns on the spot, it was hardly possible to predict how any ultimate good could be accomplished.

To prove more strongly the truth of what I have asserted, I shall now relate an unofficial conversation I had about this period with the Emperor Alexander. His Imperial Majesty's known condescension of character, and the marked kindness and good-nature he invariably showed me, penetrated me with sincere attachment and devotion to his person, and on various occasions he honoured me by communicating his observations and sentiments. At this period, one of the most difficult and interesting points for adjustment at a general peace, was the fate of the Polish nation, and this peace now began confidently to be looked for. In one of my interviews with the Emperor, his Imperial Majesty dwelt at great length on the immense sacrifices of Russia, and putting these foremost in his statement, he declared how doubly necessary it became him, on the eve of a settlement of Europe, to look to the permanent interests of his own empire. His Imperial Majesty stated, that his moral feelings, however, and every principle of justice and right called upon him to use all his power to restore such a constitution to Poland as would secure the happiness of so fine and so great a people. The abandonment of seven millions of his subjects, were he to relinquish his Polish provinces in any general arrangement, without a sufficient guarantee to his country for the great utility and advantage of the measure, would be more than his imperial crown was worth. But the consolidating these provinces with the Duchy of Warsaw, under such a king, and such a constitutional administration as Russia would name, would be productive of the happiest effects. His Imperial Majesty continued to observe that his character was well known, and ought to give full confidence to Europe. I remarked in reply, that Europe could not ensure herself at all times an Alexander on the throne. To which his Imperial Majesty rejoined, that the Grand-Duke Constantine partook entirely of his own sentiments, as well as his two brothers. He was happy also to believe that the proposition he had started, and the mode in which he viewed it, were seen by Austria in the same light. That he had had a very long conversation with Prince Metternich a day or two since, in which the whole of his Majesty's plan had been opened, and that the prince *n'avoit rien contre,* or words to this purpose.

I was considerably struck at the time with so extraordinary a declaration from his Majesty; and I ventured not only to express my surprise, but to assure his Majesty that Prince Metternich had held a very different language to me, and that I never could suppose he would leave to England the task of being the only power which would oppose itself to his Imperial Majesty's views in case they should not meet with general concurrence, when, they were of so much more vital interest to Austria and Prussia.

His Imperial Majesty next alluded, rather in a menacing manner, to his power of taking military occupation of Poland, and seemed to be certain of the facility with which he could obtain his end; and I doubted much, from the firm and positive manner in which he expressed himself, whether he would ever be diverted from the purpose he now declared. This *exposé* of a great monarch's mind was deeply interesting at the moment it was communicated; and later events showed, (notwithstanding the complex character of this question,) how sedulously the Emperor of Russia's efforts were thus early directed towards it.

Averse as I had ever been to the whole arrangements and negotiations with M. de St. Aignau, followed up as they were by the conferences at Chatillon, I sincerely rejoiced at their termination; and it was soon indeed perceptible that the Duc de Vicenza neither talked the language, nor was kept *au courant* of the projects of Napoleon; and that the only desire the latter had was to protract an idle negotiation to cover his own deeper designs and objects. The allies were too long trifled with; and to have permitted it to be spun out longer would have been unpardonable. I must do Caulaincourt the justice to record, that if it had depended upon him, he was sincerely desirous of obtaining a peace for his emperor, whose predicament he evidently saw became daily more perilous.

To the memory of these interesting days I must add, that the conviviality and harmony that reigned between the ministers made the society and intercourse at Chatillon most agreeable. The diplomatists dined alternately with each other; M. de Caulaincourt liberally passing for all the ministers, through the French advanced posts, convoys of all the good cheer, in epicurean wines, &c. that Paris could afford; nor was female society wanting to complete the charm, and banish *ennui* from the Chatillon congress, which I am sure will be long recollected with sensations of pleasure by all the plenipotentiaries there engaged.

CHAPTER 17

Genius at Bay

Napoleon, after the battles of Brienne and La Rothiere, displayed, by his masterly movements with an inferior against two superior armies, and by braving his accumulated difficulties, that undoubted science in war which his bitterest enemies must accord to his genius. In proportion as his embarrassments increased, he seemed to rise superior as an individual. During his adverse fortune on the Elbe he appeared fluctuating and irresolute; and his lengthened stay in untenable and .disadvantageous positions was the cause of his fatal overthrow at Leipsic, and of subsequent misfortunes. But now he appeared once more to have burst forth with all his talent, and all his energies and mental resources.

During the early days of February Napoleon's army was in position at Troyes, occupying the main routes of Lesmont, Bar-sur-Aube, and Bar-sur-Seine. Prince Schwartzenberg determined to attack Troyes, by turning it by the side of Bar-sur-Seine. The divisions of Bianchi and Lichtenstein were directed on this object while Wittgenstein's corps moved on Vassy and Montmirail. After some hard fighting at Troyes, and on Napoleon's perceiving .that (the army of Silesia was advancing to the Marne, and might take him in rear, he retired from Troyes on the 8th of February to Nogent, on the left bank of the Seine. The Prince Royal of Wirtemburg's corps now advanced and occupied Troyes; the whole of the grand army followed, and on the 9th had its advance at St. Libaud. Marshal Blucher next pressed forward between the Seine and Marne; and it was perceived that Napoleon from Nogent was transporting a part of, his army in the direction which indicated another determined attack on Blucher, with the hope of crushing him before he could be followed by the grand army, which the difficulties of passing the rivers rapidly made a hazardous undertaking. Blucher had his head-quarters at Vertus on the 8th, and D'Yorck was at *Château* Thierry. General Kleist's corps was in the rear, and not able to form in position so soon as was required for the formidable attack Napoleon meditated:, orders were therefore sent by the marshal for Kleist and Sacken to retire, on Montmirail.

At this period it was generally lamented that the Silesian army had too much dispersed .its corps; and probably to this cause Napoleon's latter success over them was to be attributed. On the 18th Napoleon, leaving Oudinot and Victor opposite the grand army on the Seine, marched with Marmont, Ney, Mortier, Grouchy, and all his cavalry, from Sezanne and Champaubert; leaving then a division before Blucher, he moved rapidly after Sacken and D'Yorck, and falling upon them with superior forces, Napoleon gained a partial but decided victory at Marchais, and the slaughter was immense. Marshal Blucher, not aware of the defeat of his and other corps, marched forward to attack Marmont at Champaubert; but Napoleon now arriving from Montmirail, a most bloody contest ensued; when towards the close of the day of the 14th Blucher saw his army entirely surrounded between Champaubert and Etoges: he nevertheless determined *de se faire jour*, and made good his retreat upon the latter place, not without the loss, however, of above 8000 men, and ten or twelve pieces of cannon.

These defeats of the Silesian army operated as a temporary check to the advance of the allies at this moment, and tended to make them prolong and encourage the conferences at Chatillon. Prince Schwartzenberg was not well informed of Napoleon's movements, and did not believe that he was marching all his forces against Blucher. This may account for his inactivity during this interval; but the too great dispersion of the Silesian army and Napoleon's masterly and rapid manoeuvring were the true causes of the success of the enemy. He accomplished a march of thirty leagues in the space of seven days, between the 9th and 16th of February, fought three battles, returned into position on the Seine, and rejoined Victor and Oudinot.

On the 16th Napoleon had his head-quarters at Guignes; and having beaten Blucher separately, having reunited his divisions, and received the reinforcements from Maine, which had arrived by forced marches from Paris, he resolved to fall upon Prince Schwartzenberg, and strike another and he hoped decisive blow against him. Wittgenstein's corps, however, on Napoleon's advance, had retired; and Napoleon pursued him to Nanges. General Victor's corps moved to Montereau, and the head-quarters of the sovereigns fell back to Trainel. Prince Schwartzenberg then determined, the 19th of February, to collect his whole army at Troyes, and Blucher was ordered to concentrate at Mery and Epernay. On the 20th Napoleon moved his head-quarters to Nogent.

It may be necessary to record here, that when both Schwartzenberg's and Blucher's armies were thus collected, the latter proposed to pass the Seine and give Napoleon battle. But the Austrian field marshal did not think the environs of Troyes favourable; he moved therefore to Colomiers, still having his army collected. Blucher was attacked at Mery on the 22nd, and fell back with some loss. On the 26th the allied sovereigns again took up their head-quarters at Chaumont, and Prince Schwartzenberg determined to attack the enemy in his position of Bar-sur-Aube, with the corps of Wrede, Prince Royal of Wirtemburg, and Wittgenstein, which happily was attended with complete success; so that on the 2nd of March the grand head-quarters were transferred to Bar-sur-Aube. The Austrian field marshal next determined on attacking the enemy at Troyes with four corps of his army; but Marshal Oudinot refused battle, and retired on Provins behind the Seine. The armies remained then stationary for some days in cantonments; and some overtures for an armistice being made, it was supposed they would be attended with success.

On the 9th of March Blucher concentrated his army about Laon, and was again attacked by Napoleon; but Blucher repulsed him vigorously, and General St; Priest's corps much distinguished itself. The enemy under Marmont, however, entered Rheims, and took 2000 prisoners. Marshal Blucher, after this action, sustained his array on the Aisne; and Kleist, Bulow and Sacken were assembled at Soissons ready to march forwards, elated as they were by their success at the battle of Laon. That was indeed a critical moment. If a victory had not been won, Blucher would have been forced to retire on the Low Countries, and all our plans might have been rendered abortive. But this brilliant and memorable battle encouraged Prince Schwartzenberg to resume the offensive; he instantly determined on attacking Oudinot and Victor, who had retired to Provins. The head-quarters of the monarchs were again transferred to Troyes on the 15th of March, and immediate dispositions were made for the attack.

Napoleon had his forces collected also at Château Thierry, Feré Champenoise and Arcis; and on the 20th he moved in great force to the latter place. A general battle now commenced: it was warmest at a village called Torcy; and the result of this day's combat was that Napoleon maintained himself in his positions near Arcis and Torcy. The following morning Prince Schwartzenberg gave orders for a still more concentrated and general attack, which was performed at all points with the most triumphant success ; and the enemy suffered a complete and signal defeat.

Napoleon now found that he could no longer maintain his positions, having failed in his attempt to debouch from Plancis and Arcis across the Aube: having, moreover, abandoned his idea of attacking Prince Schwartzenberg in his position at Mesnil la Comptesse (taken up after the battle of the 21st), he seems to have been guided in his next operations by the desire of preventing the union of the armies of Prince Schwartzenberg and Marshal Blucher. Should he not succeed to the utmost in this object, it was evidently his best policy to force their communication as far to the rear, and to make it as circuitous, as possible. It was further manifest, also, by intercepted letters, that Buonaparte was of opinion that the movement he contemplated, on the right of Prince Schwartzenberg, (no other than the extraordinary project of passing by Vitry and St. Dizier, and marching upon Nancy on the rear, and on the communications of the allies,) might induce Schwartzenberg to fall back towards the Rhine, for fear of losing the base of his operations; and that then Napoleon would be able to relieve his places, and be in a better situation to cover Paris.

It generally occurs that manoeuvres are made with the advance on the head of the opposing army; but Buonaparte, under his present project, seems to have forced measures so far, by the passage of the Aube with all his troops near Vitry, as to have left himself completely open to that bold and masterly decision which was immediately adopted. Buonaparte put his corps in motion on the evening of the 21st for Vitry; and that night he remained at Sommosuis. On the following day the advanced corps arrived at Vitry, and summoned the place. It had been placed by the Russian commandant in a very tolerable state of defence, and had a garrison of between 3000 and 4000 Prussians. Marshal Ney endeavoured, by every menace, to obtain a surrender; but the brave commandant resolutely refused, and held the town, which reduced the French commander to the necessity of crossing the Marne river by bridges constructed near Frigincour. Napoleon crossed here also with his whole army on the 23rd and 24th, and was immediately ascertained to have taken the direction of St. Dizier.

Three objects might now be in his view by this movement round the right flank of the allies; namely, to force them back; and if this failed,.either to operate upon their communications, and proceed to form a junction with Marshal Augereau; or finally, by moving to his fortresses of Metz, &c. prolong the war by resisting on a new line, while he placed the allies in the centre of France, having taken the best precautions in his power for the defence of his capital.

On the 22nd, the allies having crossed to the right of the Aube, lost no time in forming a junction of the two armies to the westward, placing themselves thus between the French army and Paris, and proceeding with a united force of at least 200,000 men towards the capital of the French empire.

In order the better to mask this movement, the march of the allied army was made from Pougy, Lesmont, and Arcis, on Vitry, and the Emperor of Russia by two extraordinary marches of eighteen and twelve leagues, established his head-quarters with those of the Austrian field marshal at Vitry on the 24th instant. A very brilliant capture of several pieces of cannon, 1500 prisoners, and a large number of caissons, was made on the 23rd instant by General Augeroffski, of the cavalry of the Russian guard; and on that day, and the preceding, several advanced-guard affairs took place between General Wrede's corps, the Prince Royal of Wirtemburg's and the enemy. At the passage of the Aube by the enemy, owing as it was said to the late arrival of orders, General Wrede with the Bavarians missed an opportunity of attacking Marshal Ney with advantage as he defiled under the heights where the general was in position, the French army having at the same moment the Prince Royal of Wirtemburg's corps close on their rear.

When the Prince Marshal had decided on the advance to Paris, he made his dispositions accordingly, by forming a corps on the Bar-sur-Aube line, which he committed to the care of General Ducca, to protect the head-quarters of the Emperor of Austria; and as it was replete with circumstances of delicacy at this moment, for the father of the Empress to be with the advance as the allies approached Paris, his Imperial Majesty, Prince Metternich, and the first ministers of all the allied courts, remained in the rear under the arrangement above alluded to, constant communication being kept up with them; while they held themselves prepared to move forward as soon as the Emperor of Russia took possession of the French capital. General Ducca received orders to attend to the numerous convoys, supplies, &c. and carry them if necessary towards the army of the south, and also to secure his rear, while he pursued the objects confided to his directions.

The combined army marched in three columns to La Feré Champenoise on the 25th: all the cavalry of the army formed the advance, and were to push forward to Sezanne; the sixth and fourth corps formed the advance of the centre column; the fifth was on the right; and the three corps and the reserves, with the guards, on the left. Marshal Blucher was reported to have arrived with a great part of his army at Chalons. General Winzingerode and General Czernicheff, with all their cavalry, entered Vitry on the 23rd, and were immediately detached to follow up Buonaparte's march on St. Dizier, and to threaten his rear. General Winzingerode's infantry had remained at Chalons with Marshal Blucher, together with General Woronzoff's and General Sacken's corps. General Bulow had marched to attack Soissons; and Generals D'Yorck and Kleist had moved in the line of Montmirail.

By these simultaneous movements, had Buonaparte even not crossed the Aube, and passed between the two allied armies, he probably would have found himself in a similar position to that at Leipsic, and the result to him would have been, I have no doubt, of the same disastrous nature. The army bivouacked on the 25th at La Feré Champenoise.

It appeared now that the corps of Marshals Marmont and Mortier, who had been retiring before Marshal Blucher, were moving down towards Vitry to connect themselves with Buonaparte's operations; ignorant perhaps of his strategic intentions, which may not have been fully formed until Napoleon found himself too far committed to retract with success. The above corps of his army were much perplexed on finding themselves close to Prince Schwartzenberg when they expected to reinforce their own army.

It is a singular, but an undoubted fact, that Marshal Marmont's advance was within a very short distance from Vitry on the night of the 24th, without the enemy's being aware that it was in the occupation of the allies.

On the morning of the 25th the sixth corps of the Austrians, under General Reifski, fell in with the advance above mentioned, and drove them back to Connandrey and through La Feré Champenoise: in the former place a large number of caissons, wagons, and baggage were taken. In the mean time, on the left the Russian cavalry of the reserves, under the Grand-Duke Constantine, was equally successful, charging the enemy, and taking eighteen cannon and many prisoners. But the most brilliant movement of this day occurred after the allied troops in advance had passed through La Feré Champenoise. A detached column of the enemy, of about 5,000 men, under the command, of General Ames, had been making its way, under the protection of Marmont's corps, from the neighbourhood of Montmirail to join Buonaparte: this corps had in charge an immense convoy of bread and ammunition, and was considered of great importance with the force attached to it, which had just quitted Paris to reinforce Buonaparte. The cavalry of Marshal Blucher's army was the first to discover this body on their march from Chalons: my *aide-de-camp*, Captain (now Colonel) Harris, who was, during the whole campaign, most active and intrepid in all his duties, was fortunate enough, looking out with a party of Cossacks, to give the first intelligence to Marshal Blucher of their position. The cavalry of Generals Korf and Wasiltchikoff's corps were immediately detached after them, and they were driven upon La Feré Champenoise as the cavalry of the grand army was advancing from that village. Some attacks of this cavalry were made on this French corps, which had formed itself into squares; and it is but justice to say, defended itself in the most gallant manner, notwithstanding it was composed of young troops and *garde nationale*. When completely surrounded by the cavalry of both armies, some officers were sent to demand their surrender; but they boldly resisted the summons, marching on and firing; and they refused to lay down their arms, until a battery of Russian artillery had opened, and repeated charges of cavalry had thrown them into confusion. This light battery was especially directed by the Emperor of Russia in person; and he momentarily gave the command and charge of the service to the Earl of Cathcart. Nothing could have been served with greater precision and ability than the guns; and after a sharp and continued fire and a most brilliant resistance, Generals Ames and Pacthod, generals of division, five brigadiers, 3,000 prisoners, and twelve cannon, with the convoy, fell into the hands of the allies.

I witnessed here a very interesting, but I fear unfortunately too usual an occurrence, that took place in the capture of the convoy and enemy's baggage, &c. at La Feré Champenoise. Being forward in the *mêlée,* I perceived that some of the Cossacks, most probably from Bashkir, had not only secured a French colonel's *calèche* and baggage, but one of them had seized his wife, whose cries rent the air, and with the aid of two other gallant Tartars was placing her behind him. I will not detail the frequent histories of lawless troops, nor add to these pages instances of barbarity which I fear have been too justly given of the conduct of the Russian predatory hordes in their march through France; but I reflect with satisfaction that it was my good fortune to rescue, even for a moment, a lovely and most interesting Frenchwoman from the hands of these wild soldiers. Being, however, unable to listen to her afflicting details, and not knowing in what manner better to place her in security, I ordered my own orderly hussar, of the King's German Legion, to place her for the moment *en croupe,* and carry her to my billet at the head-quarters. I was unwilling, and indeed could not at that moment leave the field; but consoled myself with the thought that when I returned at night to my quarters I should receive the gratitude of a beautiful creature, and pictured to myself romance connected with this occurrence. But, alas ! how little can we reckon on any future event, and how idly do we all build *des châteaus en Espagne!*

I fear that my precautions were not so great as I flattered myself they were: the distance between the *champ de bataille* and Feré Champenoise was inconsiderable: the town was in sight; and from the number of officers and troops moving about, I could not imagine my beautiful prisoner would be recaptured; but, sad to relate, either the same *cossacks* returned, or others more savage and determined, and perceiving my faithful orderly hussar and prize, fell upon him, and nearly annihilating him, reseized their victim; and although the strictest investigation was made throughout his whole army, by the Emperor of Russia, to whom I immediately repaired, and related the melancholy tale, (and who heard it with all that compassion and interest it could not fail to inspire,) the beautiful and interesting Frenchwoman never re-appeared again. I drop a veil over the horrible sequel which imagination might conjure up, and I took much blame for my neglect of a sufficient escort. My hussar crawled to me next morning, half dead from ill usage; and his pathetic tale placed me in a state of mind scarcely less deplorable.

Chapter 18
Paris Falls

After the last battle the rear-guards of Marmont's and Mortier's corps appeared to have drawn off in the direction of Sezanne, and it was now difficult to say whether they would be able to effect their escape, as every disposition was making to harass and surround them. The grand army marched to Mailleret: the headquarters were now at Treffaux; and the advance pushed as far as La Ferté Gauchere. Marshal Blucher was at Etages, and was to advance towards Montmirail.

Upon the retreat of Marmont and Mortier's corps before the several columns of the allied armies, whose junction had been effected between La Feré Champenoise and Chalons, above eighty-pieces of cannon and a great number of caissons fell into our hands, independent of the convoy before alluded to. The guns were abandoned in all directions by the enemy in their rapid retreat, and were captured, not only by the cavalry under the Grand-Duke Constantine and Count Pahlen, but also by the corps of Riefski, and of the Prince Royal of Wirtemburg.

Generals D'Yorck and Kleist, who moved from Montmirail on La Ferté Gauchere, where they arrived on the 26th, greatly augmented the enemy's discomfiture. General D'Yorck's corps was seriously engaged with the enemy at the latter place, and took 1500 prisoners. It may be fairly estimated that this part of Buonaparte's army had been so roughly handled as to have lost one-third of its efficient men, with nearly all its artillery. Nothing but continued forced marches could have enabled any part of these corps to elude their victorious pursuers ; and when I state that Marshal Blucher's army was at Nismes on the 24th, and was fighting at La Ferté Gauchere on the 26th, making a march of twenty-six leagues, it will be evident that no physical energies could exceed those that the present unexampled crisis brought into action.

The grand army was in position at Mailleret on the 26th. The march was continued in three columns from La Feré Champenoise. The head-quarters of the sovereigns and Prince Schwartzenberg were at Treffaux; the cavalry of Count Pahlen were pushed beyond La Ferté Gauchere, joining the corps of Generals D'Yorck and Kleist. The cavalry of the reserves were bivouacked at La Vicquiere, on the right of the great road; the sixth and fourth were in the centre, the fifth on the left, and the third remained in the rear to cover all the baggage, artillery, parks, and train, and to make the march of the whole complete. Generals Kaiseroff's and Leschavian's partisan corps occupied and observed the country about Arcis and Troyes, and between the Marne and the Seine rivers. Intelligence was received from General Winzingerode, who with General Czernicheff, and 10,000 cavalry, and forty pieces of artillery, continued following Buonaparte's rear, that the latter was marching by Brienne to Bar-sur-Aube and Troyes, hastening back to the capital with the utmost precipitation; a plain demonstration (if any were wanting) that superiority of manoeuvring, as well as of force, was in his adversaries' scale.

The Prince Marshal continued his march without interruption: his head-quarters were established at Colomiers; the sixth corps arrived at Moison: Count Pahlen's cavalry and the Prince Royal of Wirtemburg, who were sent to turn the enemy's right, followed one part of the corps before us, which seemed now to have separated, to Crecy; while Generals D'Yorck and Kleist pushed the other by advancing from La Ferté Gauchere to Meaux, where they secured the passage of the Marne for Marshal Blucher's army. The fifth corps took up its ground near Chailley; the third at Mercelon, and the cavalry of the guard, the guards, and reserves, at Colomiers.

Marshal Blucher's head-quarters were now at La Ferté Jouarre; and his army passed the Marne, which it was expected the grand army would do at Lagny; thus concentrating nearly their whole force on the right bank of the river, and taking position on the heights above Paris. I was ignorant of the motives that might have directed the corps of the enemy in our front: whether a part had fallen back to form a *noyau* to *les gardes nationales* at Paris, with which they might attempt to defend the passage of the Marne; or whether they were moving by Provins to join Buonaparte, remained yet to be seen.

Whatever the ultimate result of the operations in progress might be, however brilliant they might appear, the sovereigns who were present, and the Prince Marshal who led these armies, had the proud and consoling reflection, that by their intrepid manoeuvres, they pursued the true interests and glory of their countries, their people, and the great cause they had resolved to bring to an issue: that issue, after such a decision, rested with Providence.

On the 28th the grand allied army, and that of Silesia, continued their advance to Paris. The sixth corps, the Austrian grenadiers, the guards and reserves, and the cavalry of the Grand-Duke Constantine, took up their ground in the neighbourhood of Conilly and Manteriel. The third corps was this day at Moison, and the fifth remained at Chailley, with the advanced guard in the direction of La Ferté Gauchere, observing the routes of Sezanne and Provins: the head-quarters were established at Quincy. The passage of the Marne at Meaux was effected by the sixth corps with little resistance. Part of Marshal Mortier's corps, under the immediate command of General Vincent, who retired through that place, broke down the bridge in their retreat, and delayed the allies in their pursuit. About 10,000 of the national guards, mixed with some old soldiers, endeavoured to make a feeble stand before the army of Silesia, between La Ferté Jouarre and Meaux; but General Korf gallantly placing himself at the head of some squadrons of cavalry, attacked and pierced a mass of infantry, drove them from their position, and took the French commander prisoner. The passage of the river was also disputed at Tressort, where the army of the marshal passed; but notwithstanding the fire of the enemy, the bridge was soon repaired, and the whole of this army passed the Marne on the 29th. The French, on their retreat from Meaux, caused a magazine of powder, of an immense extent, to be blown up, without giving the slightest information to the inhabitants of the town, who expected instant destruction from the explosion. Not a window in the town but was shivered to atoms; and great damage was done to every house, and to the magnificent cathedral.

The corps of Generals D'Yorck and Kleist advanced on the 3rd to Claye: the corps of General Langeron was on their right, General Sacken's in reserve, and that of General Woronzoff in the rear, at Meaux. Various bridges were constructed on the Marne to enable the grand army to file over in different columns.

As soon as the passage was effected, the allied armies, which had abandoned their communications, immediately opened others, more advantageous, considering the exhausted state of the country which they had left.

It must always be distressing to great armies to be without direct communications, and to depart from the base of their operations; but the line of Brussels, the Low Countries, and along the coast, would now afford so many facilities, that from the moment of the passage of the river, I conceived the armies might be deemed in security. It was not improbable that Buonaparte would attempt, by an operation on the rear of the allies, by Château Thierry, or some other point, to act in the above direction; but it would have been hazardous in the face of the army of the Prince of Sweden, and of that in Holland. General Bulow's corps blockaded Soissons, and was in march towards the Marne. This movement afforded additional security. General Winzingerode, who had followed Buonaparte's rear towards St. Dizier, was assailed on the evening of the 526th, and the morning of the 27th, by a very preponderating force of the enemy, especially of infantry. The details of the affair are not of great moment, but it appeared that the general was obliged to retreat in the direction of Bar-le-Duc.

From the most recent reports, Buonaparte was himself at St. Dizier on the 27th, and it was said his advanced guard was at Vitry: it thus appeared that he was marching after the allies, or directing himself on the Marne.

Paris was now to be summoned, and the appeal was to be made, not as conquerors, but as deliverers, implying a determination to support the wish of the nation. The Emperor of Russia, without the ministers of England and Austria, who were left in the rear of the army, was of course supreme; and it is but justice to say, that the determination and boldness of the enterprise of the march on Paris was mainly his own. When he decided on the advance the Emperor of Austria and allied ministers remained behind, as before stated, and there was no prospect of communication with them until the crisis was over. Paris was to be occupied as under a secret treaty, which it was said had been made. A report was prevalent that Buonaparte had left his own army, and by a-rapid movement had reached Paris in person; but this did not turn out to be correct.

The allies were very anxious for a disembarkation of troops, however small, in Normandy, from Jersey. All the prisoners in that quarter, near 200,000, would, it was supposed, join them.

Reports of Sir R. Hill being at Bourdeaux, and the white cockade having been hoisted, were now prevalent, but there was no official news of it.

A very interesting intercepted letter from the Empress to Buonaparte was at this period shown to me, in which, after expressing great affection, she states the effect which his late victories had produced at Paris; and ends by relating an anecdote of the king of Rome having a dream, in which he cried most bitterly, calling frequently on his papa; and when he awoke and was questioned as to the cause, no entreaty or threat would induce him to give the smallest explanation, or reveal the nature of his dream. This made the child very melancholy, and the Empress partook of it, though she rode daily in the Bois de Boulogne. It is quite certain that no princess ever performed the various conflicting duties of her situation so admirably as the Empress

Maria Louisa. Whatever sacrifices she made to what was considered her country's welfare at the period of her alliance with Napoleon, from that period during the remainder of her reign she acquitted herself in the most trying circumstances as Empress of France, as a wife, and as a mother, in a manner that must hand her name down to posterity as a character of the first order.

On the 28th, in the evening, a very sharp affair occurred at Claye, between General D'Yorck's corps and the enemy's rear. The ground the latter were posted on was very favourable for defence, and in a very severe *tiraillade* the Prussians lost some hundreds of men; but the enemy were driven back at all points.

On the 29th, the army of Silesia, leaving a corps on the Marne, was directed with its right to advance on the great road from Soissons to Paris. General Langeron was on the right near the village of Villapanto, Generals D'Yorck and Kleist were on the left, and Generals Sacken and Woronzoff in their rear. The sixth corps passed at Triport, and reached Bondy and the heights of Pantin at night. The fourth corps crossed at Meaux, with the guards, the reserves, and the cavalry. The former were immediately directed to gain the high road from Lagny to the capital, and to take post on the heights of Chelles; the third corps was to support the fourth; the fifth moved to Meaux, and remained on the left of the Marne, having its cavalry at Crecy and Colomiers.

On the advance of the sixth corps to Villeparisis some resistance was made; and as it was necessary to relieve Generals D'Yorck and Kleist, to enable them to move to the right, a cessation of hostilities for four hours was agreed upon by mutual consent. This delay prevented the march forward being so rapid as it otherwise would have been. The army this night had their right in a position towards Montmartre and their left near the wood of Vincennes.

After a brilliant victory on the 30th, it pleased Providence to place the capital of the French empire in the hands of the allied sovereigns; a just retribution for the miseries inflicted on Moscow, Vienna, Madrid, Berlin, and Lisbon, by the desolator of Europe.

It would be injustice not to declare, that if the continent had so long borne the scourge of usurpation under the iron sway of Buonaparte, it was also crowned with the blessing of possessing amongst its legitimate sovereigns one who, by a firm and glorious conduct, richly deserved the appellation of the liberator of mankind. This sovereign I have no hesitation at this moment in denominating the Emperor Alexander; for it is impossible to estimate too highly his energies and noble conduct in the short campaign from the Rhine to Paris.

The enemy's army, under the command of Joseph Buonaparte, aided by Marshals Marmont and Mortier, occupied with their right the heights of Fontenay, Romainville, and Belleville; their left was on Montmartre, and they had several redoubts in the centre, and an immense artillery along the whole line.

In order to attack this position the army of Silesia was directed on St. Denis, Montmartre, and the villages of La Villette and Pantin, while the grand army attacked the enemy's right on the heights before mentioned. Marshal Blucher made his own dispositions for his attack: the sixth corps, under General Riefski, moved from Bondy in three columns, supported by the guards and reserves, and leaving the great road of Meaux, they attacked the heights of Romainville and Belleville. (These as well as Montmartre are strong positions: the ground between is uneven and covered with villages and country seats, and their possession commanded Paris and the country round.) Prince Eugene of Wirtemburg's division of the sixth corps commenced the attack, and with the greatest steadiness endured for a long period a very galling fire of artillery. The division was supported by the reserves of grenadiers; and after some loss the heights of Romainville were carried, the enemy retiring to those of Belleville. The fourth corps, under their gallant commander, the Prince Royal of Wirtemburg, were engaged in the attack more to the left, directed against the heights of Bourg and Charonne: the eighth corps was placed in echelon near Neuilly-sur-Marne in reserve, as well as the cavalry.

The attack of the grand army had commenced some short period before that of Silesia (delayed by some accident); but it was not long before Generals D'Yorck and Kleist *debouchéd* near St. Denis on Aubervilliers. Here and at Pantin a most obstinate resistance was made. His Royal Highness Prince William of Prussia with his brigade, together with some Prussian guards, much distinguished themselves. The enemy's cavalry attempted to charge, but were brilliantly repulsed by the Brandenburg and black hussar regiments.

A strong redoubt and battery of the enemy's in their centre kept General D'Yorck's corps in check for some part of the day.

The enemy's right flank having been gained by the heights of Belleville, their great loss in every part of the field, and their complete discomfiture on all sides, reduced them to the necessity of sending a flag of truce to demand a cessation of hostilities, they agreeing to give up all the ground without the barriers of Paris until further arrangements should be made.

The heights of Montmartre were to be placed by the stated generosity of a beaten enemy in our possession (Romainville and Belleville having been carried) at the very moment Count Langeron's corps was about to storm them, and had already got possession of the crest of the hill.

General Woronzoff's division also carried the village of La Villette, charging with two battalions of *chasseurs*: they took twelve pieces of cannon, and were only stopped at the barrier of Paris, which they had forced, by the flag of truce. However, the Emperor of Russia, the King of Prussia, and Prince Schwartzenberg, with that humanity which must excite the admiration of Europe, acceded to a proposition to prevent the city of Paris from being sacked and destroyed. Count Orloff, *aide-de-camp* to the Emperor, and Count Paar, *aide-de-camp* to Prince Schwartzenberg, were sent to arrange the cessation of hostilities; and Count Nesselrode, his Imperial Majesty's minister, went into Paris to hold a conference with the constituted authorities at five o'clock the same evening, as soon as the battle ceased.

The results of this victory could not yet be known: numerous pieces of artillery, and a large number of prisoners fell into our hands. Our loss was considerable; but we had the consolatory hope that the brave men who fell had shared in accomplishing the downfall of despotism, and had assisted in rearing the standard of renovated Europe, about to return to its just equilibrium, and the dominion of its legitimate sovereigns.

I feel it impossible to convey an accurate idea, or a just description of the scene that presented itself on the 31st in the capital of the French empire, when the Emperor of Russia, the King of Prussia, and Prince Schwartzenberg, made their entry at the head of the allied troops.

The enthusiasm and exultation generally exhibited must have very far exceeded what the most sanguine and devoted friend of the ancient dynasty of France could have ventured to hope; and those who were less personally interested, but equally ardent in that cause, could no longer hesitate in pronouncing that the restoration of their legitimate king, the downfall of Buonaparte, and the desire of peace, had become the. first and dearest wish of the Parisians, who had by the events of the last two days been emancipated from a system of terror and anarchy which it is impossible to describe, and from a state of ignorance of what was passing around them, in which they had been hitherto kept by the arts of falsehood and deceit, almost incredible to an enlightened people, and incomprehensible to the reflecting part of mankind.

The cavalry under his Imperial Highness the Grand-Duke Constantine, and the guards of all the allied forces, were formed into columns early in the morning on the road from Bondy to Paris. The Emperor of Russia, with all his staff, his generals, and the suites present, proceeded to Pantin, where the King of Prussia joined him with a similar *cortége*. The sovereigns, surrounded by all the princes and generals in the army, together with the Prince Field Marshal and the Austrian *état-major,* passed through the barrier of Paris, and entered the Fauxbourg St. Martin about eleven o'clock, the cossacks of the guard forming the' advance of the march. The crowd was already so great, and the acclamations were so general, that it was difficult to move forward; but before the monarchs reached the Porte St. Martin to turn on the boulevards, it was next to impossible to proceed. All Paris seemed to be assembled and concentrated on one spot; one mind and one spring evidently directed their movements. They thronged in such masses around the Emperor and the King, that notwithstanding their condescending and gracious familiarity shown by extending their hands on all sides, it was in vain to attempt to satisfy the populace, who made the air resound with the cries of "*Vive l'Empereur Alexandre! Vive le Roi de Prusse! Vivent nos Liberateurs!*"

Nor were these cries alone heard; for with louder acclamations, if possible, they were mingled with those of "*Vive le Roi! Vive Louis XVIII! Vivent les Bourbons! À bas le tyran!*"

The white cockade appeared very generally, and many of the national guards whom I saw wore them.

This clamorous applause of the multitude was seconded by a similar demonstration from the higher classes, who occupied the windows and terraces of the houses along the line to the Champs Elysées. In short, to form an idea of such a manifestation of public feeling as the city of Paris displayed, it must have been witnessed, for no description can convey any conception of it.

The sovereigns halted in the Champs Elysées, where the troops passed before them in the most admirable order; and the head-quarters were now established at Paris.

I ought here, perhaps, to close this narrative: the objects of the war were established; the standards of the allies were planted on the walls of Paris; and Napoleon's political existence, at the same moment, was terminated. In my further short *résumé* I shall therefore merely add a few general observations that may be interesting, by way of explanation. Buonaparte moved his army from Troyes by Sons towards Fontainebleau, where the *débris* of Marshals Marmont's and Mortier's corps joined him. He arrived in person at Fromenteau (three quarters of a post from Paris) on the 30th, and would have been there that evening had not the capitulation secured it to the allies. On learning what had occurred, he retired to Corbeil, collecting his army in the neighbourhood of Fontainebleau; and it could not amount to more than 50,000 men. That he might make a desperate attempt was still possible, provided the army stood by him; but the senate and the nation now declared against him. The allied armies, with the exception of the guards and reserves, who remained at Paris, marched towards Fontainebleau, and were to be regulated by the movements of Buonaparte.

The Emperor of Russia and his minister, Count Nesselrode, together with M. d'Arnstedt, and General Pozzo di Borgo, now formed a cabinet, in whose hands the great arrangements of negotiation seemed chiefly to lie; and I must do them justice in finding fault with nothing but the preponderance which this state of things made visible. Prince Schwartzenberg, by nature easy and complying, had, to all outward appearance, given up the command of the army, except indeed nominally; and as Prince Metternich did not arrive in the commencement, to supply in ability and talents what the other wanted in firmness and management, I am not sure whether things did not turn out altogether for the best. It seemed, indeed, almost like a merciful dispensation, that the Emperor of Austria should have been separated from the head-quarters at such a moment, and thus prevented from witnessing the humiliation of a daughter, a son-in-law, and a grandson.

The Emperor of Russia and the King of Prussia dined on the 31st *incognito* with M. de Talleyrand. The latter was some time before he took his decision; but he did it in the end in a most decided manner. The proclamation directing the formation of a provisional government was hardly sufficiently known at this juncture to judge of its effects. M. de Talleyrand was to be at the head of this government. M. Barthelemy, the Duc d'Alberg, and some others were to be members. M. de Caulaincourt was at Paris during the battle of the 30th. The following morning he came out certainly in a most unaccountable manner to the Emperor of Russia at Bondy, with the deputation from the municipality, who presented themselves to make arrangements for the. occupation of the town. I was sorry that the Emperor thought proper to receive M. de Caulaincourt. At the interview, I learnt that he declared he would sign the Chatillon project, or any other immediately, No answer was given to this offer. He then stated that he did not come in the character of minister of foreign affairs, but as one of the municipality of Paris. Prince Schwartzenberg afterwards saw him. It seemed that M. de Talleyrand, who was personally a friend of M. de Caulaincourt's, had been endeavouring to keep him with the party of the new government, and to make him remain at Paris, as he was considered a man of considerable influence and interest, and amiable, and well meaning, in regard to promoting a peace.

CHAPTER 19
Aftermath

Paris was now quite tranquil; and notwithstanding several of Buonaparte's emissaries were in the city endeavouring to work on the people with money and promises to rise on the allies, no instance of disorder occurred.

So much did M. Caulaincourt at length despair of the possibility of Buonaparte's return, that he sounded M. de Talleyrand and the Due d'Alberg as to the intention of the allies with regard to his Emperor's future lot, as he considered him a lost man. The senate met to deliberate and to pronounce their decision; but since the declaration of the Emperor Alexander in the name of the allies, they had but one course to adopt, which was to declare Buonaparte *hors de la loi*.

The national guards, who had been commanded by Marshal Moncey, were without a leader, he having fled. Count Montmorenci remained, and what part he would take was yet uncertain. The brother-in-law to the late General Moreau was mentioned as likely to be placed at the head of the national guards; but hitherto every arrangement was necessarily incomplete.

A report now arrived by a letter from Toulouse, of a great battle having been fought on the 23rd *ult.* between Lord Wellington and Marshal Soult, in which the latter had been completely defeated, and driven into Toulouse, with only one piece of artillery left.

The decision of the senate, who met on the 1st of April, declared, that as Napoleon Buonaparte had deserted the government of France, they felt themselves called upon to choose another chief; and that they were unanimous in calling to the throne their legitimate sovereign, Louis XVIII.

The management of every new measure undoubtedly lay with the Emperor of Russia and the confidential cabinet which he had formed. Count Nesselrode, at no time very independent, fell somewhat into the hands of M. de Talleyrand, as well as General Pozzo di Borgo: the latter was now the person accredited by his Imperial Majesty to the provisional government of France; a man of consummate ability, but not yet of sufficient weight in Paris to afford any check to the mode of proceeding of the new French ministers.

It was to be lamented that the English secretary of state for foreign affairs by accidental occurrences had been thrown out of the way of affording that invaluable benefit which his presence at this crisis could not have failed to produce. The provisional government were now endeavouring, and straining every nerve to consolidate their power; in which they succeeded so effectually, that on the arrival of Louis XVIII, or his representative, it seemed as if he would find himself only the shadow of a king, dependent on these people, and mixed up with their proceedings. Every office in the government was filling up; the constitution was to be formed precisely as the provisional government pointed out; and the senate and *corps legislatif* were to declare it, the new government to approve it, and it was to be presented to the King for his acceptance. Buonaparte had managed every thing by his immense military power and the satellites appertaining to it, and M. de Talleyrand was no doubt endeavouring to become as absolute as a minister as the circumstances of the times enabled him.

It was now of the first importance that Monsieur, or some one of the royal family, should arrive in the capital with the least possible delay; as a surveillance over the measures of the new government and some immediate control, became essentially necessary for the satisfaction of the great majority of the people of France, and the successful issue of the cause of the Bourbons.

It became the more essential, because it was evident that the Emperor of Russia's policy was that of ingratiating himself with the nation, rather than making any public or manifest declaration of any wishes relative to Louis the XVIII. Of this there occurred a remarkable instance, which was subsequently much discussed. When the Emperor of Russia received the deputation of the senate, his declaration relative to the release of the French prisoners was made to them alone, and at their instance, when it afforded so favourable an opportunity to have done this popular act in the name of their legitimate monarch.

This anecdote coupled with others, gave rise to conjectures as to whether the Emperor had not some secret designs ; and his conduct since his arrival at Paris had been carried on with so much address, that it was incalculable what influence he had obtained over the Parisian character. The allies, and Great Britain in particular, had little more to hope for from the actual provisional government than the commencement of a new order of things; whereas, if the ancient government of the Bourbons had been at first re-established, they would have had every thing to expect, and there would have been less of that intrigue, ambition, and personal animosity, which so much governed the present proceedings of the capital.

It was universally known that the persons whom M. de Talleyrand protected could now be employed in any situations they pointed out. In the provisional government every man, except the *Abbé* de Montesquiou, was devoted to M. de Talleyrand. M. Caulaincourt would have been included by M. de Talleyrand in his arrangement if he could have prevailed on him to desert Napoleon; but after a good deal of negotiation, Caulaincourt remained firm. M. de Jaucourt was no doubt a sensible man, but M. de Talleyrand's interest made him a senator, and afterwards a chamberlain; he was therefore entirely under his control, as was also General Bournonville, who was a man of less consequence. M. de Barthelemy was equally devoted to M. de Talleyrand: and the *Abbé* Louis, another dependent of his, was appointed a minister of finance.

Three senators, who were Dutchmen, three Italians, and one or two Germans, who were introduced when Holland, Italy, and part of Germany were provinces of France, still remained, taking part in the deliberations. This gave offence; and there was much observation on the subject of their being now permitted to remain.

Two articles appeared in the *Moniteur*, and other papers, at this time, which afforded much discussion, and tended to create suspicions injurious to the allies: one was the account of the rupture of the negotiations at Chatillon of the 18th of March, by which it appeared that if Buonaparte had accepted the *projet* of the allies, we should have treated with him: the other was Lord Wellington's proclamation, dated February 2nd, relative to the Bourbons. It was asked, and justly, how such different measures were to be reconciled.

The revolution certainly appeared to be carrying forward with a degree of tranquillity very unaccountable; and the different appointments in the government, those of General Dessolles to be governor-general of Paris, and commandant of the national guard, and of General Dupont to be minister of war, were very highly approved: M. de Malhouet, minister of the marine, was also a good appointment.

In an accidental conversation I had with M. de Talleyrand at this period he told me that steps were taking to communicate with all the armies and the fortresses. He believed strongly in a movement among the troops favourable to the new order of things. Marmont and Le Fevre were the marshals who it was thought would declare first. On the other hand, it was said Buonaparte had an immense number of emissaries in Paris. M. Girardin, Marshal Berthier's *aide-de-camp*, was in the city with large sums of money at his disposal: some hundreds of the old guard had been introduced into Paris to head an insurrection, and Buonaparte was determined, at any risk, *de se faire jour dans Paris.*

These various histories amused the alarmists of the day; but an excessive tranquillity, and even indifference, reigned around. Much of this, it appeared to me, would have ceased if there had been on the spot some individuals who were free from all the guilt and suspicion which twenty-five years of revolution had more or less fixed on all those who were now carrying on the government.

Upon a communication which was now made to Marshal Marmont, he consented to pass over with his whole *corps d'armée*, amounting to between 9,000 and 10,000 men, and enrol himself and his followers in the cause of their legitimate sovereign. He stipulated two principal conditions: the one, that Buonaparte's person, if taken, should not be sacrificed: the other, that if in his march he should be attacked, the allied troops were to support him. This very favourable event, so decidedly denoting the downfall of the last hopes of Buonaparte, proclaimed the peace of the world to be accomplished. Marshals Victor, Nansouty, Kellermann, and several other officers of note in Paris, then declared themselves in favour of the good cause. The allied army remained in position at Chevilly.

The army of Silesia experienced at this juncture, by the illness of its gallant and veteran leader, an irreparable loss; but it was hoped that he would speedily be restored to such a state of health as would enable him to enjoy the laurels which encircled his brow.

General Barclay de Tolly was placed at the head of the army of Silesia, with General Diebitsch as chief of his staff. General Guisenau succeeded to General Kuesebeck's situation near the King of Prussia, the latter officer having been left sick at Chaumont.

Marshals Ney and MacDonald, and M. de Caulaincourt next arrived in Paris, for the purpose of endeavouring to treat for some sort of terms regarding the future fate and existence of Buonaparte. Great efforts were made to place Buonaparte's son on the throne of France, with a council of regency; but this was most peremptorily rejected. Negotiations for a peace were carrying on with the army on the base of assuring to Buonaparte specific terms, and also providing for many others.

The conferences which the French marshals now had, both collectively and separately with the Emperor of Russia, led to the determination to offer Buonaparte the island of Elba, as a retreat, with an income of six millions of francs, three millions for himself and Maria Louisa, and three to be divided between his brothers and sisters.

M. de Caulaincourt and Marshal Ney were very urgent and persevering in their endeavours to obtain a regency, Buonaparte having abdicated with that view. The Emperor of Russia was, however, firm, and gained over Marshal MacDonald (Marmont having been before secured). His Imperial Majesty declared that the allies had already announced they would not negotiate with Napoleon Buonaparte or any of his family, and that they were determined by the voice of the nation to proclaim the restoration of Louis XVIII.

Napoleon Buonaparte at length accepted the terms offered by the allies for his future existence and that of his family.

The exit of this individual from the stage where he had so long exhibited was marked by a degradation which his career had in some measure deservedly entailed upon him. Providence seemed to have taught the nations of the world a lesson which future ages would do well to record; and the events of the French revolution, connected with that of 1814, will hand down to posterity an awful and an instructive example. Marshal Ney announced that Buonaparte accepted the island of Elba, and the pensions granted by the bounty of the allies: that he was ready to proceed to such place as might be indicated; and requested that his family might be sent to him without delay.

The French army was to move to the environs of Paris. Every individual officer, even Berthier, left Buonaparte, whose present predicament could only deserve that pity which is extended by Christians to the most atrocious as well as to the most unfortunate of their fellow creatures.

I now deemed it right to send Colonel Lowe, who had been attached to me during the campaign, by Calais to England, furnishing him with copies of every official document of the provisional government, as well as an abstract of the act of the new constitution, which I received from the Prince de Benevento.

So much had been done, so various were the important objects to consider, and so multiplied were the reasonings that might be brought forward on every proceeding, that I deem it most prudent on all these points to say little. I also despatched Colonel Cooke, at the request of M. de Talleyrand, with a French officer of equal rank to the Marquess of Wellington and Marshal Soult.

Very considerable apprehension arose, after the Emperor of Russia made the offer of the island of Elba to Napoleon Buonaparte, as to the mischief and ultimate danger that might accrue if he were put in possession of it. Its extreme proximity to the shores of Italy, the power and influence Buonaparte still had there, the popularity of Eugene Beauharnais, the possible tergiversation of Murat, and finally, the number of discontented French who might follow Buonaparte's fortunes to that quarter, were adduced, together with many other reasons, to throw great doubt on the policy of this arrangement. If Napoleon could have possessed himself of Italy by any future manoeuvres, which certainly would rather live under his sole dominion than be parcelled out as it was likely to be; if he could have carried French soldiers and followers into that country; if his large pension was paid him; and if the other dangers I have above alluded to were to have been apprehended, it would no doubt have been wiser to have considered further before the act was irretrievable, whether a far less dangerous retreat might not have been found, and whether Buonaparte might not bring the powder to the iron mines, for which the island of Elba was so famed. It was of the greatest moment that all this should have been duly weighed. The offer of such an arrangement was made by the Emperor Alexander to M. de Caulaincourt. M. de Talleyrand and the French government I heard at the time much disapproved of it, as well as other powers; and the more so, the more it was brought under consideration; still it was ultimately arranged.

Having stated above how much the Emperor of Russia seemed to assume and direct the general march of affairs at this juncture, and having often expressed my great personal respect and attachment to that monarch, I have less difficulty in entering a little at large into my own views of the various causes and different grounds which directed his actions at this eventful epoch.

The Emperor undoubtedly began to presume on his success and popularity, and the decided influence he had gained over the King of Prussia, and he adopted a tone of superiority in the alliance, evincing a determination to make the arrangements connected with Russian policy no longer a matter of fair and amicable negotiation, but one of authority and dictation.

In order to soften this tone of assumption Austria and Prussia, with a view to their own objects, went so far in concession to Russia in confidential communication with the Emperor (as I was given to understand) as to admit the advance of his frontier as far as *Kalisch* at the general congress; not meaning, however, the one to cede Thorn, or the other to cede. Cracow or Zamoski, and not conceiving that the kingdom of Poland was to be revived under the Russian dynasty.

These great overtures of concession, however, did not satisfy the Emperor, who soon announced his intentions as to reviving the kingdom of Poland, and of retaining Thorn, Cracow, and Zamoski. He privately intimated that he had an army of 480,000 men ready for action; that he must have Thorn; and that he would not give a single village to Austria.

This tone of authority and this resolution to detain the frontier fortifications commanding the roads to Berlin and Vienna, gave natural and just alarm to the two courts; at the same time the concessions they had prepared themselves to make seemed to reduce the grounds for a new war in Europe, from the great question of a preponderance displayed by Russia unsafe to other states, to the narrow question whether Russia should or should not possess two or three districts and two or three towns, more or less; and it seemed that a new war originating upon so narrow a question would not be understood by Europe, and would be easily misinterpreted in Great Britain.

This view of the argument had also, as I believe, particular weight in directing the King of Prussia's feelings. The manner of dictating on the Polish question by Russia, the danger to be apprehended from re-embodying the Poles under a dynasty nominally national, though really Russian, the advancing the Russian frontier, protected by flanking fortresses and a great river, almost into the heart of Germany, discovered such dangerous designs, and afforded such efficient means for realising them, that when the settlement of the Polish system and limits came into real discussion, I believe that the two powers began to recoil at the dangers which threatened them. These two powers were at the time disunited in several of their other views. Russia to gain Prussia had promised Saxony to her, which Austria wished to restore to her natural sovereign as a frontier to Bohemia; and Austria had made private engagements to Bavaria respecting Mayence; whilst Prussia was resolved that it should never be given to that power, but at least be a confederate city.

Austria had been so alarmed by Russia, coupled with the subserviency of Prussia, and her views in Saxony, that at an early period she put forward the language of resistance; but when she was fairly questioned on the subject, and obliged to compare her powers with the joint forces of Russia and Prussia, she soon abandoned her warlike tone. It was evident she could not hope for a successful issue by arms without inviting and accepting the assistance of France;and the dread of bringing again a French army across the Rhine to fight German battles, appeared pregnant with more fatal consequences than a submission to Russia. At the same time it was ascertained that regenerated France was willing to support Austria on the Polish and Saxon question, in return for a compromise on the Neapolitan.

In this state of things, let me next consider what was the part, in my humble opinion, of the British minister. He must have felt the danger which threatened the adjustment of any equilibrium in Europe, if the Russian designs, aided by Prussia, were to be carried into effect contrary to the consent of Austria. It was evident, or at least feared, that the two powers who could dictate such arrangements must command in all others. He felt also equal danger, I should suppose, in case Austria, by similar management, should be induced to join in the plan, and lest it should lead to the complete subjection of Europe to a triple alliance. He felt equally the inexpediency of a new war, upon grounds which could be stated to be of very limited import, and which might not be generally felt or understood; and he was sensible of the danger of bringing France forward in the scene. The last objection also made him naturally averse to any public appeal, because such a measure would give open grounds to France for interference and action. His object therefore was naturally to effect the abandonment of her designs by Russia through a similar kind of management; to dissuade the Emperor of Russia from perseverance in his projects by statement and argument; and by showing the dangers which threatened the two courts, to endeavour to separate Prussia from Russia, and to induce the former to join Austria in closer alliance; under which, aided by Great Britain, and the German powers, they would be enabled to form a complete barrier against Russia on one side, and France on the other. I have reason to think the efforts of British councils with Prussia had an early appearance of being attended with complete success. The Prussian minister seemed cordial and decided; but when this progress towards the alliance had shown advances to maturity, the influence of the Emperor of Russia over the mind of the King of Prussia induced him to overthrow the scheme.

The statements made to the Emperor of Russia had the effect of obliging him to lower his pretensions, and accede, in appearance at least, to the principle of negotiation; but from the security the Emperor felt in the King of Prussia's personal adherence to him, the advantages to be hoped by negotiation soon vanished; for the Emperor considered himself as secure of carrying his plans by negotiation as by mere authority.

If the Prussian minister, whose sincerity was believed, had been cordially supported by his monarch, there was every reason to conclude that such a plan as I have detailed, if aided by a British minister, would have succeeded. Had Austria and Prussia reconciled their points of difference to the great consideration of limiting Russian encroachment, forming a barrier against her, and maintaining the balance of power in Europe, there can be little doubt but the plan above stated must, as has been affirmed, have completely succeeded. Russia could not have ventured singly to contend against Austria, Prussia, and Great Britain, Bavaria, Holland, Hanover, Hesse, &c, when united against her, aided by the general voice of Europe.

The Emperor of Russia still persevered in his designs; but with the pretence of satisfying the jealousies of his allies, he made a merit of offering that Thorn and its Rayon, Cracow and its Rayon, should be neutralised, Prussia getting the whole of Saxony; while Austria, from dread of war, felt a disposition to lend herself to the Polish point, provided she might restore the King of Saxony to his capital, and to that part of his dominions bordering on Austria.

It is obvious that this arrangement would not have substantially varied the state of things. Russia would have carried her frontier triumphantly near to the banks of the Oder; Prussia would have been proved to be a mere vassal; and Austria an intimidated power. The equilibrium of Europe would have been still lost, for a time at least, under Russian preponderance: it therefore occurred that a new effort ought to be made, and that the least objectionable mode of making such an effort was by an armed mediation of Great Britain, France, and Holland, possibly joined by other powers, for settling the points in discussion between Russia, Austria, and Prussia.

The advantages of this position were:

1st. It was a measure not of war, but preventive of war.

2nd. If war should ensue, it made the ground of it intelligible and popular to all Europe, by the open refusal of Russia to admit of fair arrangement.

3rd. It brought forward France in the best manner in which she could be brought forward as a mediating, not an invading power, for the accomplishment of a just settlement.

4th. It gave such immense accession of strength to Austria as would probably have intimidated Prussia by destroying all her hopes of getting the whole of Saxony, and of extending her possessions to the Rhine, and beyond it, by force; and it would also have induced her to abandon at once the cause of Russia, and join the cause of Europe.

When, however, this suggestion was opened to M. de Metternich, which I understood was the case, he recoiled at the very idea of bringing France into action, even as a mediator under the control of Great Britain; he felt still some hopes that a relaxation would be admitted on the Saxon point, so as to give an escape to Austria, without the entire loss of her respectability and dignity. He thought another tentative might be made, and of course the above proposal was dropped. It could only be successful if embraced with cordiality and spirit by Austria; and in a case, where Austrian interests and security were pressing and immediate, and those of Great Britain more problematical and distant, it was the duty of the British minister to show a readiness to act if required, but by no means to force a reluctant feeling, or obtrude an unacceptable line of policy.

A new tentative was accordingly now thought of by Prince Hardenberg upon a joint proposal of the two courts confined to the Polish question. Thorn, with the line to the Wartha, was demanded for Prussia; and Cracow and its districts to the Nidda and Zamoski, with its territory, for Austria. To this overture the Emperor of Russia signified that he was resolved not to recede from his pretensions as to the duchy of Warsaw: but that as Thorn and Cracow had been considered as aggressive points, he would consent that Thorn and its Rayon, Cracow and its Rayon, should be formed into independent cities, and be made like Hanseatic cities, with independent privileges; but upon these conditions, as a *sine qua non,* that in consideration of the concession made, as to Thorn and Cracow, the integrity of Saxony should be simultaneously confirmed to Prussia, and Mayence be made a city of the confederation of Germany, to be garrisoned by confederate troops.

In announcing this determination to Prince Metternich, Prince Hardenberg, whilst he expressed his acquiescence in it, and whilst he considered it as preferable not only to any quarrel, but even to any coldness with Russia, suggested the possibility that Cracow and Thorn might be possibly ceded, the one to Prussia, the other to Austria, on condition of their not being fortified; and he offered some small accessions to Austria in Silesia, in compensation for minor cessions to be made to Prussia in return; and further suggested the propriety of demanding from the Emperor of Russia the nature of the government and constitution he intended to give to the kingdom of Poland, in order that the arrangements as to the parts of Poland still remaining to the two powers might be modified. From all the above considerations and data, it became a most delicate question to examine, whether, if the great powers could not be brought to agree, it would be most politic to bring matters to a decision, which might lead to arms, to a public declaration of the opinion of Europe in a congress, or to keep matters in suspense, and negotiation open for a favourable moment, and finally to manage by delays.

The latter question depended much upon the principle of actual possession, or such possessions as might be privately contemplated and obtained. The great obstacle was, that Russia was not only in military possession of the duchy of Warsaw, but also of Holstein.

If she could be induced to retire from the latter, there would be little difficulty as to the rest. Prussia could be arranged, and she had Saxony in possession; and the longer her possession the better her title. Hanover was in British possession: Holland also enjoyed the same right. Hesse, too, was in possession; Baden and Wirtemburg nearly so; and arrangements might be made with Bavaria. Austria was similarly circumstanced. Sardinia might take Genoa; and France, Spain and Portugal.

In this state of things, and under all the great embarrassments and difficulties that presented themselves, the assembling of a general congress at Vienna appeared the most desirable arrangement.

CHAPTER 20

Poland

Before I dismiss the consideration of the policy of the Emperor of Russia, as to his fixed and determined projects upon Poland, I cannot avoid recording that many of the sincerest friends of His Imperial Majesty regarded with deep anxiety and sorrow the false system which he had unfortunately adopted. He now declared his determination of possessing himself irrevocably, in defiance of his allies, and the universal voice of Europe, of almost the whole duchy of Warsaw; while he meant to gratify, if possible, his friend the King of Prussia with the kingdom of Saxony. His design was to erect all the Polish provinces attached to the Russian empire into a new kingdom, to be called the kingdom of Poland, and to be governed by the Russian Emperor under a free constitution. This measure was viewed in two lights: first, as a mere project of Russian aggrandisement, giving her an accession of four millions of subjects, and in fact the keys of Berlin and Vienna; and secondly, as obtaining a complete command over Prussia, and a most dangerous influence in Germany, rendering also the former subservient to Russian views as a vassal power.

The King of Prussia, by the above measures, would be driven to compensate the loss of his frontiers by a measure extremely unpopular throughout Germany; and under this view, the idea of a free constitution for Poland was considered as a false pretext. It added weight to alleged projects of Russian ambition, by exposing the policy of the Emperor Alexander to the charge of duplicity, as regarded his Polish subjects, and of injustice to the King of Saxony. It was, moreover, taking unjust advantage of the King of Prussia, assuming a threatening attitude towards Austria, and undue influence over Germany; usurping, in short, a preponderance which might be fatal to Europe. This arrangement was viewed also on the principle that the Emperor of Russia's design, as to giving his new Polish kingdom a free constitution, was sincere; that he really intended, on the principles he proposed, to erect twelve millions of Poles into a distinct kingdom, and to separate all the Russian-Polish provinces from the Russian empire for that purpose; to govern that kingdom by a separate constitution exclusively Polish: *viz.* a Polish senate, Polish chambers of police and finance, and a Polish army; all his Russian governors, *employés* and troops, to be removed within the ancient limits of Russia.

In the event of this latter plan succeeding the danger to Europe was considered the same, if not greater at the moment; but it was compensated by the prospects it held out, that at no distant period Poland, having acquired at once freedom and consistency, might, when Alexander was no more, become impatient of subserviency to a Russian monarch. In its consequent struggle it might be supported by the neighbouring states in establishing its independence, by choosing a sovereign from among its own hereditary race of princes. This latter view of the subject caused, I believe, some alarm among His Imperial Majesty's Russian subjects, who were sensible of its more than possible danger, and who thought themselves bound in duty to resist in their monarch a project at once deemed dangerous and chimerical. It was, however, to promote this great event (as a measure of duty early imposed on his conscience, and according to his own creed) that the Emperor was determined to act. For this he was ready to resign all the reputation, character and glory he had acquired; to be no longer considered as the saviour, the pacificator of Europe, but to be looked on as a monarch who disregarded treaties and engagements for an object of ambition and caprice; and to incur, finally, the odium of many of his own subjects, and defy the sentiments of Europe.

Great Britain, from her unrelenting opposition to the plans of Buonaparte, had long been considered as the only remaining bulwark of the European continent; and the success of her resistance, added to her immense contribution to the general cause, had raised her to the highest elevation of character, commanding the admiration and applause of the nations of Europe.

The magnanimous efforts of the Emperor of Russia, his unparalleled firmness and constancy, his multiplied victories, and his unrelenting perseverance, crowned with ultimate generosity and moderation towards France, turned aside gradually the current of admiration from Great Britain, and directed the gratitude of the world as due to the Russian Emperor. When the settlement of France, and the treaty of Paris came under discussion, it may be affirmed, without exaggeration, that the Emperor of Russia stood upon the most elevated pinnacle of human grandeur that was ever attained by a monarch. The glory of Great Britain was eclipsed before him: but from the moment of his opening his Polish project his splendour began gradually to decrease, till it almost vanished, and the untarnished character of Great Britain rose again to its former superiority.

It was at this time generally known that the minister of Great Britain had submitted to the Emperor a most strongly reasoned argument against his Polish projects; but the sequel of the congress of Vienna demonstrated what Russian power originally planned, Russian means were enabled, in spite of all the efforts of Great Britain, in a great measure to accomplish.

The whole tenor of the correspondence above alluded to, should it ever come to light, is calculated, I will venture to say, to raise the character of the government of Great Britain as the real protectress of the true equilibrium of Europe, and to mark the Emperor of Russia's conduct as a mere attempt by the removal of French tyranny in the south to substitute Russian predominance in the north, and to characterise this spirit as founded upon the most dangerous of public principles.

It was evident, from the tenor of the diplomacy at this crisis that, from the good principles inculcated on the one side, and the mistaken ones vindicated on the other, the confidence of the continent in the British character rose in a considerable degree, so as to induce every nation to view, with diminished jealousy, her maritime preponderance, and to consider their own safety as combined in the policy of supporting it; whilst, on the other hand, Russia was held up to the jealousy and hatred of Europe; and every nation was induced to believe that it was necessary for their preservation to combine against Russian power. As Russia, moreover, from her conduct could no longer hope to effect a combination against the maritime power of Great Britain, she was sensible that her kingdom was so circumstanced, in regard to commerce, and that her interests were so intimately connected with the consumption of British produce, that she could not interdict her intercourse with England without serious internal danger to herself.

To revert to the state of affairs in the capital of the French empire: there remains little more for me to detail, as the public prints of the day, and the intercourse which was now established with England gave the full accounts of all transactions, military and political, from the moment when the allied armies entered Paris. Besides, ample particulars are afforded in an able memoir, which I have before alluded to, of Lord Burghersh. It winds up with accuracy and brevity the most important events of this period; and I would refer my readers especially to the plans of ground and battles which it presents, and which I have not been able to procure with so much precision.

The sovereigns of Russia and Prussia, attended by all the military heroes of the day, now prepared to embark for the shores of Great Britain, to gratify and render homage to the powerful and enlightened sovereign of that nation; who had never ceased, under every conflicting disadvantage, perseveringly to oppose alike the outrageous views of jacobinism and the designs of despotism.

The magnanimous efforts of the English people were at length justly rewarded by the interesting scenes of victory and triumph which the arrival of the sovereigns and warriors of Europe occasioned in London.

To recapitulate, in a few words, the close of the military events, as far as they came within my knowledge, is all that now remains for me to do to wind up this humble narrative.

It was on the 31st that Napoleon returned to Fontainebleau, when he was joined by Marshal Marmont, whom he ordered to take up a defensive line at Essonne and Corbeil, which position he inspected himself on the following days, with a view of making an offensive movement on Paris. For this purpose he gave the necessary orders, and formed his dispositions on the 5th of April.

Prince Schwartzenberg, in consequence of the intelligence of Buonaparte's movement, marched from Paris, and assembled his forces at Lanjunais. The whole of Marshal Blucher's and Prince Schwartzenberg's army were then collected, except the guards and reserves, which occupied Paris; and the marshals took up their head-quarters at Chevilly.

The negotiations and despatching of *employés* and couriers here commenced; and there was no end to the diplomacy, manoeuvring, and treachery that appeared to reign on all sides. But glorious as the moment was for the allies, and for Englishmen in particular, it was an awful lesson for ambition to see a mighty chief deserted, one by one, by all his great companions in arms, whom he had raised and called to their present glory; and to witness those troops, whom he had so often led to victory and triumph, under the animating cries of *Vive l'Empereur,* now turning from their colours, and demanding only *la paix et leur roi légitime!*

In the city every demonstration of joy, luxury, and gaiety was exhibited. The theatres and public places, the balls, and the entertainments, kept the conquering armies in a fever; and no soldier who witnessed the taking possession of Paris could. ever have pictured to himself such a scene, while it is impossible that it should ever be effaced from his memory.

Amongst the various anecdotes of the day, I cannot help here inserting an extraordinary adventure and escape, which happened one night to myself. I had been at the opera, and afterwards at a ball, and had returned late to the *hôtel de* Montesquieu, in *la rue de Monsieur,* where I was fortunate enough to be quartered; and here it may be observed, that on the entrance of the hostile armies into Paris the best hotels were taken possession of by the sovereigns and their suite, the ambassadors, general officers, and ministers belonging to, or at the respective head-quarters. In these magnificent palaces, for some time, the new inmates lived at free quarters, until regularity and order became established in the capital. I can never forget the kindness with which I was treated at the hotel above mentioned, nor the hospitality and friendship I received from its possessors. Returning home at two o'clock in the morning, as I before stated, I partook of my usual supper, which was always prepared for me, and taking off my hussar jacket and trappings, I threw them on my bed. On my pelisse I wore my stars and foreign orders (some of which I had set in diamonds). My bed-room and suite of apartments were on the *rez de chaussée,* and large French folding sashes opened into the garden, which communicated with the boulevards that surround Paris. These, owing to the heat of the night, were all open. On my tables in my room were my red dispatch boxes, containing interesting and valuable papers and documents, and every thing of real worth I had in the world.

Disembarrassing myself of my clothes, and overcome by fatigue and sleep, I got into bed, and my slumbers, fortunately, were profound, for when I awoke in the morning I found thieves (and no doubt assassins, if I had stirred from my heavy sleep) had entered in the night, and had cleared the room of every article belonging to me; my official boxes, uniforms, and clothes taken from my very bed; my swords and pistols; all my stars and orders; and in short every thing I possessed. I actually found myself without the means of getting up; for the commodes were also pillaged, and the whole clean carried off. This daring robbery made much noise at Paris at the moment, and every effort was tried by the police to lead to a discovery; but all proved vain. I had reason to believe afterwards that a French *valet de chambre* I engaged on entering Paris was an accomplice, if not the chief actor in this robbery, from the following circumstance.

It will be remembered that the Duke of Wellington closed his glorious career in the Peninsular war at the battle of Toulouse, after defeating Marshal Soult before that town on the 10th of April. After the arrangements were entirely completed, by the arrival of all the ministers in the city, and more especially by the presence of the English secretary of state for foreign affairs, one of the first acts of this ever-to-be lamented individual was to take the King's pleasure on appointing that warrior His Majesty's representative at Paris, who had, with the aid and means afforded him, conquered peace in the Peninsula. It was my Lot to receive my sovereign's commands through the principal secretary of state to proceed to Toulouse to offer the Duke of Wellington the post of His Majesty's ambassador to His Most Christian Majesty. I likewise was the individual who, on a former occasion, delivered to my commander the insignia of the Order of the Garter.

I arrived at Toulouse on the evening the Duke of Wellington was engaged at the hotel de ville at a magnificent ball, given by the inhabitants to the British army. It will not be easy for me to forget that moment of my life. The embassy was accepted by the Duke of Wellington; and I returned to Paris without rest, and (what opened my eyes to my robbery) without a *valet de chambre*. The rascal absconded at Toulouse, probably in the full possession of all my interesting valuables, and I never heard more of him.

But to return to more serious and important matters, and to wind up the concluding days of Napoleon's history at this period. It appears that after haranguing his army on the 5th of April, and promising them (as before mentioned) the pillage of Paris for forty-eight hours, amidst the cries of *Vive l'Empereur,* Marshal Ney and all the chief officers assembled round him; when the former stepping forward, at once announced to him that he was no longer Emperor, and presented him the act of his dethronement by the senate.

Buonaparte appeared thunderstruck, and with violent impetuosity at first seemed to resist the order of the senate. But no longer finding fealty among his troops, nor devotion in his officers, he was soon convinced of the absurdity and folly of resistance.

Referring himself therefore to the direction of Marshals Oudinot, Victor, and Caulaincourt, he sent them to Paris, to make the best terms for himself and his family, and to obtain what other objects they could for his advantage.

Marshal Marmont's *corps d'armée* had passed over to the allies on the 4th of April; and, as the first French general, he placed himself at the disposition of Louis XVIII.

On the 11th of April Napoleon signed the formal act of abdication, having failed in all attempts at gaining various conditions which he had attempted to negotiate.

Napoleon took his departure for the island of Elba, accompanied by four commissioners from each of the great powers, Great Britain, Russia, Austria, and Prussia.

On the 25th of April the plenipotentiaries of the allied forces and the Count d'Artois signed a formal armistice. The allied armies were to evacuate France; and, on the 30th of May, a definitive peace was concluded, and signed with Louis XVIII.

Such was the close of this eventful campaign, restoring the legitimate dynasty of the Bourbons to the throne of France, and rendering Germany, and indeed Europe, once more independent.

Little was it supposed at this moment, when the tyranny of Napoleon ceased, and every fair indulgence had been granted to France in the terms she had received from the allied powers, that the flame of war was shortly to be rekindled, and that the hero whose exit was believed to be eternal was shortly to reappear upon the same theatre, under more extraordinary circumstances, and seconded by a more powerful impulse of public feeling throughout France, and amongst his legions, than by any possible reasoning could either be accounted for or explained.

The details of the campaign of 1815, ending with the glorious battle of Waterloo, with all the various interesting circumstances and events at the first opening of the congress of Vienna, are points of too much magnitude to be treated of at the close of the narrative of 1813 and 1814, which I have endeavoured to relate. At some future period, if the present work, and its predecessor on the Peninsular War, should be approved, it may be my lot to offer to the public the whole account of the transactions of Vienna to which I was a witness, and in which I was engaged; as also to give all the military details and correspondence of the different officers employed under me, with the Austrian and Prussian armies, when they again took the field on Napoleon's escape from the island of Elba.

Declining for the present to enter into the great and important events that occurred in 1815, it remains for me merely to state generally to my readers, which I shall presently do, what the military position and forces of the allied powers appeared to be for meeting another new and unexpected campaign. Hereafter I may give a farther development of the whole of the proceedings of the year.

The allied sovereigns, except the Emperor of Austria, as it is well known, paid London a visit at the conclusion of the peace of Paris. Their brilliant reception, the enthusiasm which was demonstrated, especially in favour of the Silesian hero, the sumptuous and splendid entertainments that were exhibited by a British sovereign and his city of London, which in one single *fête* to Alexander expended 25,000*l*. sterling, are subjects so well known, and still so recently in the recollection of many, that it would be entirely superfluous to describe them. I constantly accompanied my friend Marshal Blucher to all the feasts and dinners given to him; and it was my pride and pleasure to translate his animated speeches, which were always given in German, to the public company.

Two other points, also, I wish to record, as deeply rooted in my memory. I was the only individual present, when I saw England's king clothe his august ally, the Emperor of Russia, with the robes of the garter.

The graceful manner and indescribable amiability with which the one performed his task, and the difficult and awkward mode in which the other ultimately managed to get into and put on the magnificent paraphernalia, cannot easily be forgotten; indeed the scene surpassed description.

Again; it was on the steps at the *fête* at Guildhall that I knelt down and kissed my sovereign's hand on his appointing me his ambassador to the court of Vienna, and at the same moment nominating me one of his lords of the bed-chamber; a circumstance entirely unlooked for and unexpected by me.

These appointments carried to my mind the grateful reflection that I had done my duty.

After the series of brilliant rejoicings in England, the sovereigns returned to Paris, preparatory to repairing to Vienna, and making arrangements for the European congress that was to be assembled.

It would be wrong in me, however, to overlook, without comment, the two great military reviews and manoeuvres that took place in France previous to the allied troops withdrawing from their cantonments within that country; namely, those of all the Russian forces at Vertu, and subsequently of the Austrians at Dijon.

The concentration of two such immense masses of foreign force in two very small *champs de parade,* in the midst of the French empire, will, it is hoped, remain a useful memento of the vicissitudes of war to French vanity, and a glorious record of European valour.

It was either on the 9th or 10th of September, 1815, that I left Paris, to witness the great review of the Russian, army, for which preparations had been making for nearly a month before. The number of the forces collected was so considerable, that it was not easy to bring them into a space sufficiently small for the parade movements of review; but it was at length effected; and they mustered, when we saw them, 28,000 cavalry, 132,000 infantry, and 540 pieces of cannon. This was made known from field returns, which were given to the sovereigns who were present. I was accompanied by my *aides-de-camp*, Sir Henry Brown, Colonel Harris, Captain Charles Wood; and I ought here to particularise especially the services of Mr. John Bidwell, of the foreign office, who was also with me. This gentleman had been attached to all my fortunes since the moment of my landing in the north of Germany. His constant and unremitting labour in carrying forward the various and voluminous correspondence with the foreign and war departments, I never can too highly appreciate; and it is always the most grateful task for my mind to acknowledge the merit, and to state what I feel I owe to the exertions and zeal of others. Sir Henry Hardinge also was of my party, having made his expedition *en courier* to Vertu in a manner that showed his active and tried zeal in the great cause, of gallantry, and his devotion to the service.

The day was exceedingly sultry, but tolerably clear; and the spot where the head-quarters first assembled to have a sort of bird's-eye view of the whole, was a small hill in the centre of a large plain, near the village of Vertu, a short distance from Chalons. Several English ladies, together with all the princesses, duchesses, and first persons of Paris, were assembled (having been invited), and made parties to proceed from the capital to witness this magnificent spectacle. Amongst our own countrywomen were Ladies Castlereagh, Combermere, Grantham, Mrs. Arbuthnot, Miss Fitzclarence, and others, whose names it would be tedious to enumerate, who graced this most brilliant and unparalleled sight.

In going through the field, several of the ladies rode in company with the gallant chiefs; and English beauty was signalised by the Emperor of Russia's presenting a beautiful black charger to one of our fair countrywomen, to carry her through the ceremonies of the day; but I never rightly understood the feeling that recalled this war-horse back to the imperial stables on the following morning. A flag-staff had been placed on the top of the hill, having an ensign ready to be hoisted on the arrival of the sovereigns at the spot. We were on horseback about seven o'clock; and at eight the King of Prussia, attended by the commanders-in-chief of the allied armies, the ambassadors of nearly all the powers of Europe, and many of their Prime ministers, with several of the French marshals,: and an immense staff of *aides-de-camp*, &c. &c. began to ascend the height.

On the arrival of the sovereigns at the spot fixed upon for them the ensign was unfurled, and a salvo of guns announced their presence; and the whole Russian army then assembled was seen drawn up in three lines, extending as far as the eye could reach. The sun glittered on their arms, and on the drawn sabres of the cavalry, to a distance that appeared almost imaginary. The eye had scarcely time to comprehend so vast a spectacle, when a single gun fired from the height where we stood was the signal for three hurrahs from the troops. Even at this distant day these hurrahs sound freshly in my ears: a second gun gave the time for a general salute. The cannon and musketry began at once, and the fire ran along the three extended lines, showing more distinctly than any thing else could have done the vast space they occupied, by the distant flashes and retiring sound of the. musketry. I forget exactly how long a time was necessary for three rounds from these saluting tens of thousands.

We rode down the hill, and the Russians broke from their lines into grand columns of regiments; and no one but a soldier can conceive the beauty of this great simultaneous change. A spot was then fixed upon for these masses to march by the sovereigns; and the Emperor of Russia putting himself at the head of the leading regiments, thus formed in column, marched past, and saluted the Emperor of Austria and King of Prussia ; then placing himself by their side to see the rest of the army go by. The whole of the day was only sufficient to give time for a reformation into line, and an opening of ranks, along which the cavalcade of monarchs and their immense suite rode.

The Emperor of Russia appeared greatly occupied with the Duke of Wellington (who was at this period our ambassador at Paris), as if anxious for his opinion of what was passing before them; and his whole attention was given to him when not taken up with his fair companions, who rode on both his flanks. Thus closed the first day, never to be forgotten by those who witnessed the grand military display it presented. Great dinners at different bivouacs were given on the ground; and my party of ladies and friends will make me long remember the day. The Duke of Wellington and Sir Lowry Cole, and various military friends, met together in the evening at my quarters, full of admiration of the movements they had seen; and I well remember the Duke of Wellington saying to me, "Well, Charles, you and I never saw such a sight before, and never shall again: the precision of the movements of those troops was more like the arrangements of a theatre than those of such an army.—I never saw any thing like it."

Much, however, as the duke was struck with the extraordinary perfection of the Russian formations, he was by no means satisfied with their slowness; and I remember a remark from him, "that his little army would move round them in any direction whilst they were effecting a single change;" an opinion which all who heard it re-echoed.

On the following morning this great army heard divine service in masses of 20,000 each; and the following day the Emperor selected from them 10,000 men, to be added to his guards.

Afterwards these forces broke up for the cantonments, from which they had been drawn for this review.

The impression given by this great military parade was certainly very favourable to the efficiency of the Russian army. The artillery was in beautiful order, and more particularly the horse artillery, every part of the equipment appearing perfect; and the wild-looking little horses, three abreast, galloped along with the well-polished nine-pounder as though they were scarcely sensible of its weight. These horses are Tartars, and are of excellent blood, and always keep their condition beautifully, as I have before stated. The clothing and appointments appeared excellent; and the horses of the hussars in perfect order.

On our return to Paris, it was said that the Emperor Alexander called the Duke of Wellington to fix some time for him to see the English army, and that the duke said they might be seen on the morrow if Alexander wished it. I believe they were reviewed on the day following, without preparation of any kind, under Montmartre, where they were put, through the movements of the battle of Salamanca.

It is not for me, however, to describe this army nor their exhibition.

The Austrians had assembled all their troops at Dijon; and here the sovereigns now repaired to review this army. The Emperor Francis had determined to visit his Italian states previous to his return to Vienna, and it was convenient to his route to take Dijon in his line to Vienna and Milan.

Their movements were confined to a simple *feu de joie,* and deploying before their majesties. The ground was neither so favourable nor so picturesque as at Vertu; neither were there any of those temptations at hand which always add zest to military spectacles. The inhabitants of the interior of France were now not well disposed to the Austrians. Few persons moved out of the town of Dijon: the day was not favourable, and the spectacle purely military. The Emperor of Austria gave a grand *couvert* dinner after the review, and proceeded on the following day on his route to Italy. The other sovereigns repaired to their different destinations.

CHAPTER 21

Opinions

Having now brought my military narrative to a conclusion as far as the year 1814, I shall not, as before stated, enter upon the last epoch of Buonaparte's career, nor into any of the critical details of the congress of Vienna. I am nevertheless disposed to gratify my military readers by adding to this work those recorded military opinions which formed the basis of the operations and movements of the allied forces in the campaign of 1815, previous to the battle of Waterloo.

These memoirs of some of the greatest military characters of the age must be invaluable for the study and perusal of every officer. It is on this account that I have annexed them to the present work; and I shall do so without further comment, reserving to myself, when I enter into the history of the year 1815, to show how far these sentiments were acted upon or departed from.

Protocol of a military conference held at Vienna on the 31st of March, 1815.

A une conférence tenue en présence de Sa Majesté l'Empereur de Russie par Son Altesse le Prince Royal de Wurtemberg, par Son Altesse M. le Prince de Schwartzenberg, Maréchal et Président du Conseil de Guerre de S. M. l'Empereur d'Autriche, et de M. le Maréchal Prince de Wrede, M. le Prince Wolkonsky, aide-de-camp de S. M. l'Empereur de Russie, Son Excellence Milord

Cathcart, Général-en-Chef de S. M. le Roi d'Angleterre, et M. le Baron de Knesebeck, Lieutenant-Général au service de S. M. le Roi de Prusse, on est convenu sur les points suivans :

Il se formera trois grandes armées sur le Rhin, savoir :

1. Armée sur le Haut Rhin, sous les ordres du Prince Schwartzenberg.

2. Armée sur le Bas Rhin, sous les ordres du Maréchal Blucher.

3. Armée dans les Pays Bas, sous les ordres du Maréchal le Duc de Wellington.

L'armée du Haut Rhin sera composée de—

Autrichiens	150,000
Bavarois	65,000
Wurtembergeois	25,000
Badois	16,000
Hessois de Darmstadt	8,000
Total	264,000

L'armée sur le Bas Rhin sera composée de 153,000 Prussiens. L'armée des Pays Bas par les troupes Angloises, Hollandoises, et Hanovriennes.

Le reste des troupes du nord de l'Allemagne, savoir,—Hesse-Cassel, Mecklenbourg, Nassau, Waldeck, Schwarzburg, Reuss, Lippe, Anhalt, Saxe Royale, Saxe Ducale, Oldenbourg, Brunswick, et des Villes Hanséatiques,—restent encore à distribuer dans les armées du Maréchal Wellington et du Maréchal Blucher.

On a été d'abord généralement de l'avis qu'il étoit évidemment nécessaire de renforcer autant que possible le Duc de Wellington.

On a remarqué alors sur les inconvéniens graves qui résulteroient militairement de toute mesure tendant à désorganiser un corps de 14 ou 15,000 hommes de bonnes troupes, à une époque où il est de la plus grande urgence à réunir sur les frontières menacées un nombre suffisant de troupes alliées.

On est convenu en suite sur les premiers cantonnemens à prendre par l'armée du Haut Rhin, savoir :

L'armée Bavaroise, sous les ordres du Maréchal Wrede, prendra les cantonnemens outre Mayence, Frankfort, et Manheim, et poussera une division sur la rive gauche du Rhin.

Le Maréchal Wrede se charge de la construction de deux têtes-de-ponts, une à Manheim, et une autre à Germersheim.

Le corps du Prince Royal de Wurtemberg cantonnera entre Bruchsal, Manheim, et Heidelberg, poussera une division sur la rive gauche du Rhin.

Le corps d'armée du Général Colloredo prendra ses cantonnemens entre Bruchsal, Offenbourg, et Pforzheim.

Le corps d'armée du Général Prince de Hohenzollern cantonnera entre Offenbourg, Freybourg, et Rothweil.

La réserve Autrichienne sera cantonnée entre Heilbrun, Halle, Ulm, et Eslingen.

L'armée Russe sous les ordres du Maréchal Barclay de Tolly sera cantonnée entre Würzbourg, Nurembourg et Bamberg.

Les chefs d'états-majors des différens corps se concerteront dans une autre conférence sur les détails de différens cantonnemens et routes militaires pour leurs corps d'armée.

La garnison de Mayence se formera par Autrichiens .	4000
Prussiens	4000
Bavarois	3000
De Frankfort, Isenbourg et Reuss	3000
De Nassau	1500
De Hesse-Cassel	4500

Mayence sera considérée comme une place d'armes pour les armées du Haut et Bas Rhin.

La forteresse aura un gouverneur Autrichien et un commandant Prussien. Les Cours Allemandes les plus rapprochées des frontières Françaises seront incessamment invitées à prendre des mesures de police générale, pour empêcher, autant que possible, l'espionnage de l'ennemi.

After these general heads of disposition and agreement were entered into on the 31st of March, 1815, the following interesting memoirs were handed in for the consideration of the grand military assembly :—

Opinions of Prince Schwartzenberg.

Vienne, ce 20 Avril, 1815.

A l'ouverture de cette campagne, l'Autriche part de certains principes généraux.

Le but de cette guerre est le repos et la sécurité de l'Europe, menacées par le caractère entreprenant et hardi d'un chef et d'une armée licencieuse.

Les forces qu'on a destinées à cette entreprise peuvent être au moins évaluées au double de celles qui leur sont opposées par le chef des Français. Elles ne peuvent donc se trouver en infériorité, que dans le cas—

Où, en se divisant trop, elles offriroient à l'ennemi une résistance trop faible sur de certains points, et l'occasion de réunir avantageusement ses moyens d'aggression.

Ou bien, en se resserrant trop elles formeroient un colosse immobile, qui n'auroit pas les moyens de se développer, et entraîneroit même l'impossibilité de pourvoir aux subsistances des armées.

Ou bien, si une partie des armées se portoit en avant avec trop de précipitation, et sans avoir suffisamment assuré ses communications contre les mouvemens qui seroient à redouter de la part des habitans du pays, s'ils étoient appuyés par les garnisons des forteresses qu'on seroit obligé de laisser en arrière.

Détruire l'armée et son chef est donc le premier but de cette guerre—éviter les dangers surmentionnés en est le second.

Il seroit dangereux de se laisser aller à des illusions flatteuses :—le tems qui pouvoit être favorable à un projet d'invasion est déjà passé, les armées des alliés étant généralement trop éloignées des frontières de la France. Les moyens de résistance des Français sont nombreux, et nous ne pourrons espérer de les combattre avec avantage, qu'en autant que nous nous attacherons à opposer un grand esprit d'ordre militaire et l'accord le plus parfait dans nos mesures, au principe du désordre et de brigandage, que Napoléon ne manquera pas de mettre en usage contre nous.

Ces considérations nous portent à établir les principes suivans :

1. Chacune des armées doit s'attacher à la base d'opération qui lui est la plus naturelle.

2. Toutes les armées doivent avoir un objet d'opération commun entr'elles, afin qu'elles puissent diriger tous leurs efforts vers le même point.

3. La route qui conduit de la base à ce point d'opération, doit être suffisamment assurée, soit par des retranchemens, soit par l'établissement de corps de réserve ;—en un mot, l'armée doit se trouver dans la plus parfaite sécurité, quant à ses derrières.

Il n'est pas probable que l'ennemi puisse opposer 400,000 aux 800,000 hommes, que nous mettons en mouvement contre la France : il sera donc forcé, ou de diviser ses forces en adoptant un système de lignes étendues, ce qui ne peut manquer de le conduire à sa perte ; ou bien, il réunira la majeure partie de ses forces pour nous attaquer avec supériorité sur un point.

4. Les armées qui avancent doivent donc être disposées de manière qu'elles puissent contraindre l'ennemi à découvrir entièrement une partie de ses possessions, s'il étoit tenté d'agir offensivement d'un autre côté.

5. Le moyen le plus efficace pour atteindre ce but seroit de menacer différens points assez distans les uns des autres pour pouvoir, dans le cas qu'une de nos armées essuyât des revers, rétablir les affaires en agissant avec vigueur d'un côté différent, l'empêcher de poursuivre ses avantages déjà acquis, et l'obliger peut-être à gagner avec rapidité un point opposé de sa monarchie.

Ce n'est qu'ainsi qu'une de nos armées battue gagneroit le tems nécessaire pour prendre l'offensive, et que même en admettant un second revers, l'ennemi finiroit par succomber à la continuité de ses efforts.

La base d'opération naturelle à l'Autriche n'est peut-être que celle qui favoriseroit, en la ligne la plus directe, la communication de son armée d'Italie avec celle de l'Allemagne, ainsi que le secours réciproque qu'elle pourroit se porter.

Son aile droite est appuyée par la place de Mayence ; sa gauche par les gorges du Piémont ; son centre par celle de la Suisse.

La base d'opération de l'armée Prussienne s'étend sur sa gauche jusqu'à Mayence ; sa droite est couverte par l'armée Angloise : donc les opérations, concertées avec les mouvemens de la première, ne peuvent être basées que par la Hollande et les Pays Bas.

Celles-ci paroissent les bases naturelles, qui s'offrent aux puissances mentionnées ci-dessus ; il n'y a que l'armée Russe qui en soit dépourvue dans cette guerre, attendu qu'elle se trouve à une trop grande distance de son pays. La tâche qu'elle a à remplir se présente d'elle-même ; elle doit remplir le grand intervalle, que la nature même des opérations des armées alliées Autrichiennes, Angloises et Prussiennes formera infailliblement. Elle doit être prête à porter des secours à celle d'entre les armées alliées qui en auroit besoin, non pas comme une armée de réserve, mais placée sur la même ligne ; enfin, de pouvoir se porter à droite ou à gauche selon le besoin.

L'offensive des Autrichiens doit être dirigée sur la gauche, et, en partant de son aile gauche, celle des Anglois et des Prussiens sur la droite ; et par conséquent, partant de leur aile droite, il en résulte, qu'indépendamment des autorités militaires, il y a trois grandes masses à disposer, savoir :

1. Une armée combinée Autrichienne sur le Haut Rhin, forte de	165,000
Corps de Bavarois	60,000
Wurtembergeois	25,000
Troupes de Bade	16,000
Do. Darmstadt	8,000
Armée Autrichienne en Italie	70,000
Total	344,000
2. Armée Prussienne et Angloise, consistant en Anglois, Hanovriens, Hollandois	60,000
Prussiens	160,000
Saxons et Hessois	30,000
Total	250,000
3. Armée Russe, forte de	200,000

Les bases de ces armées sont données ; leur objet d'opération est Paris, et la masse de l'armée Françoise par-tout où elle se présentera. En conséquence de ces principes, l'armée Prussienne feroit un mouvement sur sa droite, et l'armée Autrichienne sur sa gauche, aussitôt que l'armée Russe seroit arrivée ; l'opération principale ne peut cependant commencer avec avantage, avant que 50,000 Russes n'aient rejoint l'armée Prussienne auprès de Coblentz, et que le même nombre n'ait fait sa jonction avec l'armée Autrichienne auprès de Manheim.

Le gros de l'armée Russe se porteroit en marches forcées sur Mayence et Coblentz ; et quand la tête de leurs colonnes y sera arrivée, on sera à portée de juger, si c'est sur la droite que le corps Anglo-Prussien, ou sur la gauche que le corps Autrichien aura le plus besoin de son appui.

Tels sont les principes généraux sur lesquels il faut tomber d'accord avant d'ouvrir la campagne.

Pour les détails des opérations, pour les moyens les plus propres à attendre le but général, il faut s'en remettre à l'expérience et aux lumières des quatre généraux en chef ; et eux-mêmes ne pourront les déterminer, que quand leurs forces seront réunies, qu'ils connoîtront celles des ennemis, et les positions qu'ils auront occupées.

Cependant ces principes généraux devroient être dictés par leurs Souverains respectifs aux quatre généraux en chef, pour leur direction générale.

Il résulte toutefois de cet exposé, qu'une opération offensive ne peut être ouverte avant le 16 de Juin. Tout ce que l'ennemi pourroit vouloir entreprendre jusqu'à cette époque, devroit être soumis aux mêmes principes que nous venons d'établir par rapport à l'offensive, c'est-à-dire, qu'un corps de troupes, attaqué avec supériorité, se retireroit sans se compromettre, jusqu'à ce que tous les autres eussent fait des démonstrations énergiques pour le dégager.

Si peut-être des raisons majeures engagent S. M. l'Empereur de Russie à désirer la réunion des forces Russes entièrement sur un point, ou sur la droite ou sur la gauche, sans accéder au détachement proposé de 50,000 hommes, on croit que cela n'attaqueroit pas essentiellement les principes généraux établis dans ce mémoire, pourvu que le total de cette armée occupe au plus tôt la position qu'on avoit indiquée en première ligne à l'armée de 100,000 hommes.

Considerations upon the military operations that may take place at different periods, by the Prussian General Knesebeck.

Vienne, ce 18 Avril, 1815.

Par les mémoires ci-joints on a tâché de montrer :

1. La nécessité de donner derechef de l'ensemble aux opérations des différentes armées ;

2. De bien distinguer les époques, afin de ne pas se tromper sur le calcul des forces de l'ennemi.

Essayons maintenant quelques considérations sur ces opérations mêmes.

L'époque, où un mouvement isolé et rapide pour le soutien de Paris auroit pu produire un grand résultat, paroît être passée.

Cette opération n'étoit bonne qu'aussi long-tems que le Roi de France étoit à Paris, et que Paris se maintenoit. La célérité de Buonaparte, et la déchéance complette de l'armée Française, l'a fait manquer.

Une autre question se présente pour le moment, savoir :

Si l'on doit rester passif jusqu'à ce que l'armée Autrichienne sera arrivée sur le Rhin ; ou si les opérations doivent commencer avec les forces rassemblées déjà ; savoir donc avec 50,000 hommes qui se trouvent déjà sur le Haut Rhin, 50,000 Prussiens sur la Meuse, 43,000 de l'armée Anglo-Belgique.

Les raisons qui parlent pour une telle offensive à l'instant, sont :

1. De soutenir le parti Royaliste du Midi de la France et de la Vendée, avant que Buonaparte parvienne à le supprimer.

2. D'empêcher que Buonaparte ne profite pas de l'intervalle pour consolider son gouvernement, et gagner l'opinion de la nation, comme celle de l'armée s'est déjà prononcée pour lui.

Il n'y a pas de doute que ces deux raisons sont d'une très grande conséquence ; mais ceux qui s'y opposent ne sont pas moins fortes.

1. Il faut se demander, si l'entrée des armées alliées sur le sol Français n'éveillera pas la nation et la ralliera autour de Buonaparte, au lieu de l'éloigner de lui.

2. Le mémoire B. montre que la force disponible de Buonaparte égalera la nôtre jusqu'à la fin de Mai ; savoir, qu'il pourra paroître en campagne encore avec 120,000 hommes, après avoir laissé

des garnisons dans les places fortes, et des corps pour combattre la Vendée, le Midi, et observer Paris.

A cela il faut compter, que les forteresses, que les alliés trouveront à l'instant qu'ils auront passé les frontières de la France, et qu'ils doivent nécessairement bloquer ou assiéger, affoibliront tellement leurs armées, que Buonaparte en se concentrant derrière ces forteresses leur sera prépondérant en forces. Si on ajoute à cela que les alliés, par la situation géographique de la France, manœuvrent sur le circuit du cercle, et que Buonaparte a ses forces concentrées dans le centre; la situation militaire sera si défavorable pour les armées alliées, s'ils entrent en France sans forces suffisantes, qu'une telle opération, autant que les raisons alléguées semblent l'exiger, a trop de chances défavorables, qu'elle pourroit être conseillée autrement, que dans le seul cas, que la Suisse, en joignant ses forces à celles des alliés, permettroit un libre passage à l'armée du Haut Rhin, et oue cette expédition, qui se dirigeroit alors sur Lyon, seroit en même tems soutenue directement par la marche des troupes du Roi de Sardaigne sur Grenoble et Chambéry, et indirectement par les manœuvres des armées de Blucher et de Wellington, qui auroient la tâche d'attirer les forces de l'ennemi de leurs côtés, et de les occuper sans pourtant s'engager autrement à un combat général, qu'à des chances très favorables pour eux.

Telles sont les considérations qui se présentent pour les opérations qui pourroient avoir lieu pour le moment; celles de l'avenir semblent devoir être bien distinguées pour les deux époques marquées dans le mémore B. savoir celle au commencement du mois de Mai, ou quatre semaines plus tard.

La première époque demandera beaucoup plus de circonspection pour les mouvemens que la seconde, quoique le plan en général paroît pouvoir rester le même.

Devoit-on se décider à ne rien entreprendre pour le moment, mais d'attendre jusqu'à ce qu'on pourra entrer en France, en forces, de toutes parts, il paroît que voici doivent être les lignes fondamentales d'une telle opération.

Battre les armées de Buonaparte, délivrer la nation Française du joug sous lequel elle gémit, tel est le but de la guerre.

Tomber sur l'armée Buonapartienne avec tant de forces que possible ; donc, diriger les mouvemens des différentes armées alliées de manière que jamais une d'elles risque d'être accablée séparément ; mais au contraire, que plusieurs doivent toutefois se trouver ensemble, et, s'il est possible, *réunis* au jour de bataille générale ; voilà le moyen d'atteindre ce but. Il résulte de cette considération, que si pour destituer Buonaparte, Paris doit être derechef l'objet que les armées alliées se proposent, ils doivent se trouver sur la même hauteur avant de commencer un mouvement combiné sur cette capitale.

Il semble donc que *l'armée de Wellington* doit prendre position entre Enghien, Halle, et Gemappe, tenant des postes d'observation à Charleroi et sur sa droite jusqu'à Ostende.

Cette armée doit regarder Anvers comme le point duquel ses opérations doivent partir et où elle doit s'être réservé et préparé un asile au cas d'une stricte défensive ; enfin Anvers doit être en Hollande pour l'armée Angloise ce qu'étoit Lisbonne pour elle en Portugal.

Au cas qu'elle se voit attaquée par des forces supérieures, elle se retire sur cette direction, et y prend position jusqu'à ce que les opérations des autres armées viendront la dégager.

L'armée de Blucher prendra position sur la rive droite de la Meuse, entre Namur, Huy, et l'Ourte.

Cette armée s'étant éloignée de Mayence, prendra pour le moment Juliers ou Wesel pour place d'armes.

Les circonstances que les capitaines expérimentés de ces deux armées jugeront le mieux sur les lieux, leur indiqueront ce qu'il y aura à faire, et on laisse à leur sagesse d'en profiter.

On croit cependant devoir les prévenir, que jusqu'au commencement du mois de Juin, l'armée du Haut Rhin ne pourra pas être rassemblée, ni passer cette rivière en forces.

Le fardeau de la guerre pesera donc jusque-là seul sur les forces reúnies sur la Meuse, et le soutien de l'armée du Haut Rhin devra se borner à des diversions ou vers le Midi de la France ou vers la Lorraine.

Des raisons majeures, comme par exemple la vraisemblance d'une contre-révolution à Paris, ou la certitude que l'ennemi, ayant été dans la nécessité de faire de fortes détachemens pour le Midi, ne se trouveroit pas en force du côté des Pays Bas, peuvent donner la possibilité de battre un corps d'armée de l'ennemi, ou de surprendre une des places fortes. Mais si cependant ces raisons ne détermineroient pas les deux armées à prendre à l'instant une vive offensive, il paroît que pour le moment leurs opérations doivent se borner à une défensive active, et de se soutenir réciproquement jusqu'à ce que l'armée du Haut Rhin pourra lier ses opérations aux leurs.

Quand les forces de l'ennemi tomberoient sur l'une de ces armées, sans que l'autre seroit pressée, celle-ci manœuvreroit en attendant sur le flanc de l'ennemi. Par exemple, quand l'armée de Wellington seroit contrainte de se retirer sur Anvers, et l'armée de Blucher pas pressée en même tems, celle-ci s'avanceroit sur le flanc de l'ennemi pour dégager l'armée de Wellington, avec recours de ne pas trop s'éloigner de la Meuse et des points de Namur et de Liège. De même, quand l'armée de Blucher devroit être menacée, l'armée de Wellington passeroit la Meuse pour soutenir Blucher. Si l'ennemi se porteroit avec toutes ses forces du côté de la Moselle, les deux armées marcheront à la gauche sur Luxembourg et tâcheront de le couper de ses ressources. En même tems un mouvement semblable se fera du côté de Manheim sur Trèves par l'armée du Haut Rhin.

Dans cette position les deux armées resteront jusqu'à ce que l'armée du Haut Rhin passera le Rhin. Quand le moment de ce passage sera venu, les armées de Blucher et de Wellington tâcheront de le faciliter par un mouvement offensif de leur côté.

L'armée du Haut Rhin continuera, en attendant, de se rassembler sur les lieux indiqués. Le moment de son passage étant venu, elle se rassemblera vîte sur un point, jettera des ponts et passera cette rivière, d'après les circonstances ou à Bâle ou entre Huninguen et Brisach, attirant l'attention de l'ennemi du côté de Spire par un corps qu'elle tiendra de ce côté. Le point d'appui de l'armée du Haut Rhin doit rester derechef sur la Suisse, sans pourtant y passer qu'avec consentement du gouvernement Suisse. Mais comme il est indispensable pour l'armée Autrichienne d'avoir une communication directe par la Suisse avec l'Italie, ainsi qu'il est de la plus haute conséquence et pour les opérations militaires en général, et pour la sureté de la Suisse elle-même, d'avoir un libre passage par Bâle et Genève, on entamera une négociation avec le gouvernement Suisse, pour obtenir une route militaire entre la Souabe et l'Italie, et le passage par les deux points indiqués.

La ligne d'opération de cette armée sera Bâle, Béfort, Langres, Muhlhausen, Epinal.

D'après cette esquisse on verra que les armées alliées ne formeront jusqu'à l'arrivée de l'armée Russe que deux grandes masses ; l'une groupée sur la Meuse, l'autre du côté de la Suisse. La situation des circonstances a amené cette position ; et sans vouloir exposer l'armée de Wellington à un echec, il ne faudra rien y changer. Aussi se pourra-t-il que l'ennemi par-là se voit forcé de former de son côté de même deux armées ; donc, de partager ses forces. Mais s'il ne le fait pas, la trop grande distance entre la Meuse et le Rhin lui donne l'avantage de manœuvrer long-tems sous la protection de ses forteresses et du Rhin, du côté de Strasbourg, pendant qu'il pourra tomber avec prépondérance sur l'armée de la Meuse ; et s'il devroit reússir à la battre, de l'achever entièrement avant qu'elle pourra être soutenue.

Ces considérations n'échapperont pas sans doute aux illustres capitaines qui commandent les deux armées de ce côté là, et les détermineront à ne rien hazarder.

Si l'ennemi vouloit profiter de la lacune qui jusqu'à l'arrivée des Russes se trouve entre l'armée du Haut Rhin et de la Meuse, et se jeter dans cet intervalle, il semble qu'il faut être bien d'accord de se porter sur ses communications de toutes parts.

Voilà, à ce qu'il paroît, la disposition générale jusqu'à l'arrivée des réserves et de l'armée Russe. Si les circonstances n'ont pas changé jusque-là, alors un mouvement général pour l'intérieur de la France pourra se faire avec assurance de tous côtés.

En attendant on aura soin de préparer à toutes les armées un train d'artillerie de siège, d'accélérer les marches des troupes en arrière, de les former en corps avant qu'ils passeront le Rhin, et de bien préparer les moyens pour rester, pendant toute la guerre, toujours au grand complet.

L'armée d'Italie ne peut entrer pour le moment dans ce calcul des opérations, et doit agir séparément jusqu'à ce que peut-être à l'avenir elle pourra lier ses opérations directement à ceux des autres armées.

Vienne, 24 Avril, 1815.

D'après les mémoires successives que le soussigné a eu l'honneur de soumettre aux yeux des illustres Souverains, reste encore à faire l'esquisse, de quelle manière qu'il faudra manœuvrer, quand le moment sera venu, de marcher vers Paris.

La situation de la France présente deux opérations pour atteindre ce but :

L'une, les alliés ont suivi dans la dernière campagne, en s'avançant avec leurs plus grandes forces par les routes de Langres et de Dijon ;

L'autre peut se faire par la droite, en portant les plus grandes forces entre la Marne et l'Oise. Considérant que les armées de Blucher et de Wellington partant de Mons et Namur n'auront à faire que la moitié de chemin que ceux du Rhin, il paroît qu'il faudra donner la préférence à la seconde opération.

Si l'on s'y devroit résoudre, voici à ce qu'il paroît doivent être les dispositions.

Les corps de **Wrede** et du Prince Royal de Wurtemberg doivent marcher sur la Sarre ; l'armée Russe s'y portera de même aussitôt que possible.

L'armée Autrichienne restera sur le Haut Rhin. Le quartier-général des Souverains sera pris à Fribourg : on tâchera de répandre de toutes parts les bruits, qu'on suivra à-peu-près le même plan de campagne que l'année passée ; que la grande armée s'avanceroit derechef sur la route de Basle et Langres ; qu'elle seroit secourée par l'armée d'Italie et les Suisses ; que les Anglois auroient insisté de faire le siège de Dunkerque, ce qui contraindroit Blucher de rester sur la défensive, et de faire une guerre méthodique ; qu'il en étoit furieux, etc. etc. S'il est possible, il faut vendre de telles nouvelles et un tel plan à un des émissaires de Buonaparte, et en général rien négliger pour attirer les forces de Buonaparte vers les frontières de la Suisse ou de l'Italie.

Si l'on réussit par ces stratagêmes à détourner les forces militaires de Buonaparte de Paris, et de les attirer sur le Haut Rhin, alors il faut vîte réunir les armées du Haut Rhin avec celle de la Russie, ce qui feroit—

Armée du Haut Rhin :

Colloredo	40,000
Hohenzollern	36,000
Réserve	50,000
Wrede	60,000
Prince Royal de Wurtemberg	50,000
	236,000
L'armée Russe	120,000
En tout	356,000

et marcher à lui, pour lui livrer bataille, ou l'occuper et forcer de rester sur le Haut Rhin, pendant que Blucher et Wellington se porteront brusquement sur Paris.

Si on décompte de ces 350,000 hommes cinquante, pour observer les forteresses de l'Alsace, on garderoit toujours 300,000 pour marcher sur Buonaparte, et lui livrer bataille, et Wellington et Blucher exécuteroient le manœuvre sur Paris avec 120,000.

Si on ne devroit pas réussir à attirer la plus grande masse des forces de Buonaparte vers la Suisse, l'Italie, ou le Haut Rhin ; l'alternative se présente—ou, que Buonaparte, se voyant menacé de Wellington et Blucher, marche vers eux avec des forces supérieures ; ou, qu'il attend dans un cercle resserré autour de Paris, (à-peu-près à la hauteur de Péronne, Laon, Rheims, Châlons, Troyes,) les manœuvres des alliés.

Dans le premier cas Wellington et Blucher doivent avoir la liberté de disposer des corps de Wrede et du Prince Royal de Wurtemberg, et pour les attirer directement à eux, et pour les faire marcher dans le flanc de l'ennemi.

Dans le second cas, que Buonaparte devroit rester dans le cercle marqué, pour attendre jusqu'à ce que les manœuvres des alliés se soient entièrement développés, voilà ce qu'il paroît qu'il faudroit faire :

se concentrent sur la Sarre, du côté de Deuxponts.	Les corps de Wrede de . . . et du Prince Royal de Wurtemberg .	60,000 50,000
	En tout, de	110,000

ou passe le Rhin à Manheim, se portant premièrement sur la Sarre et de là par des marches rapides sur Stenay. { L'armée Russe de 120,000 passe le Rhin à Oppenheim, se dirige derrière l'armée Bavaroise par Kreutznach, Birkenfeld, Trèves, à Luxembourg.

L'armée Autrichienne de 125,000 passe le Rhin entre Strasbourg et Bâle. Chaque armée destine un corps de vingt jusqu'à trente mille hommes, qui restera en arrière d'elle, pour contenir le pays, observer les forteresses, et soigner l'approvisionnement des armées. Tout ce qu'il y a de landwehr disponible, se joigne à eux. Cette disposition faite, les opérations commencent.

L'idée générale est—

1. Qu'on présente à l'ennemi trois masses à-peu-près égales, dont le centre est destiné de se porter d'après les circonstances ou sur la droite, ou sur la gauche, et de renforcer de cette manière, par un mouvement rapide, une des ailes, pour lui donner une telle prépondérance de forces qu'il pourra livrer bataille à l'ennemi avec l'espoir de la victoire :

2. Si donc ce mouvement doit avoir lieu sur la droite, les armées Russes, Prussiennes, Angloises et Bavaroises tâchent de se réunir sur la Meuse aussi vîte que possible ; réunies, ils chercheront l'ennemi pour lui livrer bataille, ou marcheront brusquement sur Paris, tâchant de le battre s'il s'y oppose, ou de se tourner sur leur gauche, si l'ennemi cherche de les prendre en flanc par Châlons, ou en longeant la Meuse, manœuvre auquel il faudra s'attendre si Buonaparte est resté concentré dans le cercle de Troyes, Châlons, et Rheims :

3. Que le Prince Royal de Wurtemberg entretienne les communications entre ces armées et l'armée Autrichienne, et que celle-ci manœuvre dans le flanc de l'ennemi, cherchant à l'attirer de son côté, de le détourner du côté de Paris, ou de le suivre s'il se tourne vers les armées de Wellington et de Blucher.

Pour cet effet, l'armée Autrichienne s'avancera premièrement sur

Langres, le Maréchal Wrede sur Verdun, le Prince Royal de Wurtemberg sur Nancy, Toul, et Commercy; l'armée Russe en tournant Sarre-Louis, Thionville, Longwy, sur Stenay; l'armée de Blucher sur Mezières; Wellington sur Chimay. Chaque armée adopte en principe, de surprendre, s'il est possible, sur son chemin, quelques places fortes, et de ne pas s'engager avec des forces supérieures.

Si l'ennemi tâche de percer au centre, le Prince Poyal de Wurtemberg se replie, et trouvera dans le cas le plus malheureux toutefois des asiles sûrs à Mayence ou Luxembourg, pendant que les autres armées se porteront sur le flanc de l'ennemi pour le battre ou le prévenir à Paris.*

The sentiments of the Duke of Wellington, then at Brussels, were earnestly solicited; and I have reason to believe that he gave them in the following terms; though I cannot vouch positively for their accuracy in all points. The statement hereafter detailed was, I know, communicated to the military conference before mentioned.

> I saw Clarke yesterday, and he told me that a person of the war-office, upon whom he could depend, had informed him that on the 30th of April the enemy's regular army amounted to 139,000 men, and the guards to 25,000. *Gendarmerie* and national guards raised, and expected to be raised, would make it 280,000; this was the utmost expected.
> Bournonville, who ought to know, told, me this day, that we ought to reckon that the enemy had an effective force of 200,000 men. He says the king had 155,000 when he quitted Paris, and that he had granted above 100,000 *congés*, which had been called in; but that not above half could be reckoned upon as likely to join. I understood, likewise, that there were above 100,000 deserters wandering about France.
> In reference to these different statements I beg to observe, that Clarke speaks from positive information; Bournonville from conjecture. According to Clarke's account, the army gained in strength only 3000 men in the last fifteen

days; but then it must be observed that the guards have gained about 19,000; being the difference between 6000, which they were, and 25,000, which they are now.

In respect to periods of commencing operations, I had adopted the opinion that it was necessary to wait for more troops as far back as the 13th of April. After, however, we shall have waited a sufficient time to collect a force, and to satisfy military men that their force is what it ought to be, to enable them to accomplish the object in view, the period of attack becomes a political question, upon which there can be no difference of opinion. Every day's experience convinces me that we ought not to lose a moment which could be spared.

I say nothing about our defensive operations, because I am inclined to believe that Blucher and I are so well united and so strong, that the enemy cannot do us much mischief. I am at the advanced post of the whole; the greatest part of the enemy's force is in my front; and, if I am satisfied, others need be under no apprehension.

In regard to offensive operations, my opinion is, that however strong we shall be, in reference to the enemy, we should not extend ourselves further than is absolutely necessary, in order to facilitate the subsistence of the troops. I do not approve of an extension from the channel to the Alps; and I am convinced that it will be found, not fatal, but only that the troops at such a distance on the left of the line will be entirely out of the line of the operations. We are now, or shall be shortly, placed on the French frontier in the form of an *echelon*; of which the right, placed here, is the most advanced of the echelons, and the left, upon the Upper Rhine, is the most retired. Paris is our object; and the greatest force, and greatest military difficulties, are opposed to the movements of the right, which is the most advanced part of our general line. Indeed, such force and difficulties are opposed to us in this part, that I should think that Blucher and I cannot move till the movements of others of the allied corps shall have relieved us from part of the enemy's force opposed to us. Then it must be observed, that we cannot be relieved by movements through Luxembourg. In my opinion the movements of the allies should begin with the left, which should cross the Rhine between Bâle and Strasbourg.

The centre, collected upon the Sarre, should cross on the day when the left should be expected to be at Langres.

If these movements should not relieve the right, they should be continued; that is to say, the left should continue its movements on both banks of the Marne, while the centre should cross the Aisne; and the distance between the two bodies, and between each and Paris, should be shortened daily.

But this last hypothesis is not probable: the enemy would certainly move from this front upon the earliest alarm of the movements on the Upper Rhine, and the moment that he did move, or that the operations be practicable, Blucher's corps and mine should move forward, and the former make the siege of Givet, and the latter of Maubeuge; and the former likewise aid the movement of the centre across the Meuse.

If the enemy should fall upon the centre, it should either retire upon Luxembourg, or fight, according to the relative strength; and, in either case, Blucher should act upon the enemy's communications upon the Aisne.

But the most probable result of these first movements would be the concentration of the enemy's forces upon the Aisne; and accordingly we hear of the fortification of Soisson and Laon, of an entrenched camp at Beauvais, &c. We must in this case, after the first operation, throw our whole left across the Marne, and strengthen it if necessary from the centre and left. It should march upon Paris between the Seine and the Marne, while the right and the centre should either attack the enemy's position upon the Marne, or endeavour to turn its left; or the whole should co-operate in one general attack upon the enemy's position.

I come now to consider the strength required for these operations. The greatest strength the enemy is supposed to have is 200,000 men effective, besides national guards for the garrisons; of this number it can hardly be believed that he can bring 150,000 to bear upon any one point.

Upon this statement let our proceedings be founded. Let us have 150,000 men upon the left, and 150,000 upon the right, and all the rest, whatever they maybe, in the centre; or, after a sufficient centre is formed in reserve for the right, left or centre, as may be most convenient for their march and subsistence, and I will engage for the result, as they may be thrown where we please. Let us begin when we shall have 450,000 men. Before the Austrians upon the left will be at Langres, the Russians will have passed the Rhine, and the whole Prussian army will be in line.

These are my general ideas, which I don't think differ much from General Knesebeck's. Mind, when I think of the siege of Givet and Maubeuge, I don't mean by the whole of the two armies of the right, but to be carried only by detachments from them. The centre should besiege Sedan, which is not strong or garrisoned, and observe Longwy, Thionville, and Metz. The left will have to observe Huningen and the fortresses in Alsace.

In regard to the force in Piedmont, I confess that I wish that the whole of the Austrian army in Italy were entirely employed against Murat, with the exception of the garrisons. Murat must be destroyed early, as he will hang heavily upon us.

If any force should be employed from Piedmont, its operations should be separate from those of the great confederacy. They cannot be connected without disconnecting those of, what I have hitherto considered the left, from the remainder of our great line; however, they may be calculated to aid that left, particularly by being directed upon

Chamberry, or by keeping that post in check;—their basis is, however, different, and cannot easily be otherwise.

God knows whether the allies will allow their forces to be divided as I suppose, and particularly whether the Prussians will act in two corps, one under Blucher here, and another from Luxembourg, with the centre; or whether the other allies will like to commence till the whole Russian army is in reserve: but I am convinced that what I have proposed, is so clearly the plan of operations, that I don't doubt it will be adopted with but little variation.

Statement of the Duc de Feltre.

L'état des forces de l'armée Française, tel qu'il m'a été communiqué par un employé de la guerre, était le premier de ce mois porté à 200 mille hommes effectifs ; mais les hommes qui devoient compléter les ladres des régimens, pour produire ce nombre, n'étoient pas encore répartis dans leur corps respectifs, et leur complétement exige encore trois semaines.

Le matériel de la guerre, le train d'artillerie, les chevaux, les fusils, manquoient en grande partie : aussi à peine évalue-t-on la cavalerie actuellement montée à 20,000 hommes. Cependant, on voit presque tous les jours arriver une petite quantité de remontés, qu'on envoie des provinces.

Quoiqu'il n'ait pas encore osé rendre un décret pour faire revivre la conscription, il a néanmoins envoyé aux préfets des départemens l'ordre de faire rentrer dans l'armée tous les hommes qui ont servi, et d'employer en outre le moyen de procurer le plus grand nombre d'hommes possible par une espèce d'enrôlement volontaire, mais qui en effet devient coercitif.

Lignes occupées par l'armée Française.

Toute l'armée est repartie en six divisions ou corps d'armée.

La première s'étend sur la ligne de Lille, Douay, Arras, &c. et est commandée par le Général Excelmans.

La seconde va depuis Calais jusqu'à Dunkerque, sous les ordres du Général Beil.

La troisième, commandée par le Général d'Erlon, est tracée depuis

Dunkerque jusqu'à Verdun.

La quatrième s'étend depuis Verdun jusqu'à Landau, sous les ordres du Général Lobau.

La cinquième, commandée par le Général Girard, va jusqu'à Strasbourg.

La sixième est confiée au Maréchal Suchet, et s'étend jusqu'à Huningen : c'est à tort que les journaux ont donné ce commandement au Maréchal Ney.

Sur toute la route depuis Paris jusqu'à Péronne, je n'ai pas rencontré un seul soldat, un seul chariot de munitions, ou tout autre objet qui indiquerait des préparatifs militaires. A Péronne, qui nage pour ainsi dire au milieu des eaux, il n'y a qu'un seul bataillon ; le huitième régiment de dragons, qui y était, est parti pour Lille le 5. Je n'ai apperçu que deux pièces de canon dans la partie de la place où je suis entré.

On travailloit à des batteries à Cambray, et les palissades devant la porte de Bouchain n'avaient été commencées que depuis quelques jours. La porte de sortie étoit déjà condamnée le sixième. La garnison était composée de deux régimens d'infanterie et d'un régiment d'artillerie. Il paraît que toutes ces places manquoient de canon de gros calibre; car je n'ai vu en batterie que de pièces de campagne. Valenciennes, qui est dans un bon état de défense, ne renferme que 4000 hommes de garnison, dont le premier régiment d'infanterie ou régiment du roi, et le septième de hussards, font partie.

The scientific report made by the Duke of Wellington, on the most judicious mode of conducting the military operations in 1815, is so clear and explicit, and the reasoning so conclusive, that I hope I shall stand excused with the high authority from whom it emanates, if I should have trenched in any manner on communications within my knowledge, for the benefit of the profession, the British army, and posterity. And as these sentiments are in the possession of the cabinets and councils of the different powers, they are no doubt in the hands of many, and in the archives of the chancellerie of Europe.

My present offering to my companions in arms now closes. If they kindly approve my labour, I may in another year or two, if I should find leisure, once more appear before them.

Appendices

Appendix 1

From Baron Hardenberg, Toplitz, 29th of September, 1813. Acknowledging how much the exertions of the Prussians were owing to England's aid.

Le Chancelier d'Etat soussigné a l'honneur de mettre sous les yeux de son auguste Souverain les offices que Monsieur le Lieutentant-Général Stewart, Envoyé extraordinaire, Ministre Plénipotentiaire de Sa Majesté Britannique, a bien voulu lui communiquer en date du 23 et 27 de ce mois: Sa Majesté y retrouve avec une vive satisfaction les marques précieuses de l'intérêt et de l'amitié active de Son Altesse Royale le Prince Régent. Il sera beau de devoir le triomphe de la grande cause à l'union intime des premières puissances de l'Europe et aux efforts réunis de leurs peuples. Ceux de la Prusse surpassent de beaucoup nos moyens. Il lui deviendroit impossible de soutenir cette lutte pénible, si elle ne trouvoit, à côté des ressources que lui offre l'enthousiasme des habitans, celles que lui fournit l'Angleterre, et qui deviennent toujours plus urgentes à mesure que les événemens se développent.

Sa Majesté, en m'autorisant d'exprimer ses sentimens à Son Excellence Monsieur le Général Stewart, m'a chargé de lui témoigner en même tems combien elle est reconnoissante des fournitures en armes et munitions que S. A. R. le Prince Régent a fait mettre à la disposition du Roi, sans en déduire le montant sur les subsides.

Le Roi a été extrêmement sensible à cette nouvelle marque de l'intérêt de S. A. Royale: il le mérite par l'affection sincère qu'il porte à ce Prince.

Le soussigné a l'honneur d'offrir à Monsieur le Général Stewart l'assurance réitérée de sa plus haute considération.

HARDENBERG.

Toplitz, le 29 Septembre, 1813.

A Statement of Ordnance, Arms, Ammunition, and Military Stores, supplied by Great Britain for the Russian, Prussian, and Swedish Governments, 1813.

Pieces of ordnance complete, with carriages and necessary stores for the field; rounds of ammunition, with a suitable quantity of powder, waggons, &c.	Stand of arms, with 18,231,000 rounds of ball-cartridges; 23,000 barrels of powder, flints, &c.	Swords, sabres, and spears complete	Drums, trumpets, bugles, and cavalry standards
218	124,119	34,443	624

Suits of clothing complete, with great-coats, cloaks, pelisses, and overalls	Yards of cloth of various colours	Boots and shoes, with a proportionate quantity of leather	Blankets	Linen shirts and drawers	Pairs of gaiters	Pairs of stockings
150,000	187,000	175,796	114,000	58,800	87,190	69,624

Sets of accoutrements	Knapsacks complete	Saddles complete, with blankets	Caps and feathers complete	Forage caps	Stocks and clasps	Shoe-brushes, combs, and black-balls	Gloves and bracers
90,000	63,457	14,520	100,000	22,000	14,000	140,000	3,000

Great-coat straps, brushes, pickers, sponge, &c. &c.	Flannel shirts, gowns, caps, and trowsers	Sheets, paillasses, coverlids, &c. &c.	Haversacks and canteens complete	Lbs. of biscuit and flour	Lbs. of beef and pork	Gallons of brandy and rum
20,000	5,000	14,000	5,000	702,000	691,360	28,025

Marquees, Tents, Forage Carts, and necessary Camp Equipage; Surgical Instrument Cases, Medicines, and all necessary Hospital Stores.

Appendix 2

OBSERVATIONS ON THE TRADE BETWEEN GREAT BRITAIN AND PRUSSIA AT THE PERIOD OF THE RUSSIAN TREATY WITH GREAT BRITAIN IN 1813

Immediately after the declaration of war against France a proclamation was issued prohibiting altogether the importation of the produce of the soil and manufactures of that country; and allowing, without any restriction, the importation of British goods at the lowest duties which had existed previous to or after the war of 1806.

It is to be observed, that after the peace of Tilsit, and exclusively with a view to the trade carried on with England during the three first years that followed this event,— trade kept open to a large extent, in spite of the French interference; almost every article of foreign growth and manufacture formerly prohibited was allowed to be imported upon paying a certain percentage: so that the manufactures that may at this time be imported from England into Prussian ports, and by way of transit be conveyed to the adjacent countries through her provinces, are far more numerous than they were formerly, before the old regulations were repealed.

Unfortunately, the right of regulating the duties, which in some instances did not appear applicable to present circumstances, was granted to a gentleman at the head of the board of public revenue, who, from want of information and judgment, committed the grossest mistakes, and excited the well-founded complaints of our trade. His only end was to create a revenue; and he was little aware that his regulations not only defeated the king's intentions to give the greatest activity to British trade in our ports, but likewise destroyed the revenue which would have arisen from it. These measures raised a general cry, especially in East Prussia; and the petitions of the estates of that province, and of the city of Konigsberg, procured redress, though not the punishment of the author of the mischief. An exorbitant duty was thus imposed upon the exportation of wheat, which we succeeded in having repealed, and that which was in force in 1806 was restored. That year having been an abundant harvest in England, with very little importation from the Baltic, the duties upon exportation, too much fluctuating according to our old system, were very low. This is not alleged as a service rendered to England, although such reductions of foreign duties may have some influence upon the price of corn at London. It was chiefly intended for the relief of our own country, where the proprietors, for several years, had suffered from exceeding low prices. But such a system cannot fail to encourage the trade upon both sides, as we cannot possibly import without exporting.

The mistake committed operated for some time, and trade was very dull. Fortunately the military government of East Prussia having the produce of the customs assigned for the armaments, took upon themselves to reduce, the duties upon colonial produce below the ancient rate; and this has completely succeeded in attracting British ships to our ports. In the course of the month of May upwards of 120 English ships, charged with colonial produce, arrived at the port of Memel alone. The value of their cargoes far exceeds the sum granted by Great Britain to Prussia as a subsidy: and if our government take care to favour the British trade with our ports, and the events of the war do not prove quite unfortunate, the exchange of England, notwithstanding the subsidies paid, must improve, as far as it depends upon the balance of trade in the Baltic.

The sufferings of these last six years have produced every where the conviction that a full and free trade with Great Britain is indispensable to the prosperity, nay to the preservation of every country bordering on the sea. All sensible men are of course more disposed than ever to adopt such commercial regulations as may be beneficial to British trade above that of any other country. Such regulations might be entered into with Prussia as a permanent national system, provided Great Britain would consent to repeal some of those laws which affect the Prussian trade in a manner certainly not contemplated towards a friendly nation. Our complaints are chiefly directed against the duty upon the Baltic timber, imposed in 1810, and against those which exclude the Silesian linens from the American markets, without benefiting the Irish linen trade: all the other objects are of less consequence. We, on our side, provided we regain our national independence, may, without hurting our interests, grant such privileges to British trade as, in an exceedingly short time, would amply repay all the assistance granted to us in this contest; and, at the same time, promote an intimate communication between both nations, which, in an age tending to establish public opinion as a political power, will be the best security for a permanent alliance.

It is to be understood that no man will sacrifice the interests of his own nation to that of any other; but a Prussian statesman who in several instances would think it necessary to preserve protecting duties for the manufactures of his own country may, at the same time, exclude the prohibiting system altogether, and secure to British merchandise, both colonial and manufactural, such advantages above those of any other nation as, in his country, would make their admission merely nominal in most provinces.

Appendix 3

HEADS OF THE ARRANGEMENT TOUCHING
THE ARMISTICE AND NEGOTIATIONS

The Duke of Bassano on the 29th of June declared Buonaparte's satisfaction that the delay in the negotiation was not to be attributed to Austria, and that he was in possession of full power for negotiating a convention towards entering into a negotiation for peace. Count Metternich stated, his object was to fix and ascertain Buonaparte's acceptance of the mediation of Austria. The Duke of Bassano sends a project of convention, and proposes a congress either at Prague or Vienna, to which England, the King of Spain, the Regency at Cadiz, and all the powers engaged in the war, *dans les masses,* might send plenipotentiaries; and that the negotiations might continue, like those of Munster, Nimeguen, Ryswick, Utrecht, and Osnaburg, although any of the powers should think it advisable to put an end to the armistice. The articles in this project were very artfully drawn up, in order to establish a separation of interests on the part of Austria from the allies, and to declare that that power did not interfere *"comme arbitre, mais comme médiatrice armée et parfaitement désintéressée."* Count Metternich rejected this project, upon which the Duke desired to recall it; but Count Metternich refused to return it, declaring his intention eventually to print it. Count Metternich informs the Duke of Bassano that the Emperor of Russia and King of Prussia have accepted the mediation of Austria, and are ready to submit to arbitration: he therefore desires to know if Buonaparte is ready to do the same.

A military report is now sent from Prince Schwartzenberg to the Emperor Francis, dated Brandeis, 28th of June. Its object was to demonstrate the expediency of prolonging the period of negotiation to the 10th of August, for the following reasons:

The Bohemian army would not be more than entirely complete on the 20th instant. The vast and unexpected preparations of France render an increased armament on the part of Austria necessary; therefore every unappropriated regiment of the line, the landwehr, and the Hungarian insurrection, must be called out and put into activity. Supposing the difficulty of supplying them with necessaries and clothing to be got over, yet it was impossible to bring the most distant regiments from the south-east provinces to Znain and Presburg before the 14th of August, and the other troops in proportion.

Besides the troops raised in Bavaria, 66,000 men under the Viceroy had passed the Tagliamento, and large reserves were assembled at Wurtzburg and Fulda. As these measures directly menaced Vienna and Gratz, it was necessary to assemble force to cover them, (Klagenfurth was the place proposed,) and a lesser force nearer to Vienna. It was absolutely necessary that these measures should be carried into effect without making any detachments from the Bohemian army. Carriages could not be procured in time to supply Russia with the provisions which she had desired to receive from Bohemia for a particular service; and as the extension of the French line on the Elbe might render it expedient that part of the allied army should move into Bohemia, it was most desirable that there should be sufficient time to prepare means of supplying such force; and that in the mean time the wants of the allies may be supplied from Galicia.

A convention was then signed the 30th of June by Count Metternich and the Duke of Bassano, the heads of which were as follows:

Art. 1. Austria offered her mediation.

Art. 2. France accepted the mediation.

Art. 3. Plenipotentiaries on the part of Austria and France, and also Russia and Prussia, were to assemble at Prague on or before the 5th of May.

Art. 4. The period limited for negotiation, *viz.* 20th of June, being too short, the Emperor and King will agree to extend the same to the 10th of August; and the Emperor of Austria reserves to himself to endeavour to obtain the accession of the Emperor of Russia and King of Prussia to this prolongation.

Art. 5. Ratifications were to be exchanged within four days. The Emperor Francis ratified the convention, agreeing to prolong the "*terme obligatoire de négociation*" to the 10th of August.

This ratification was so worded as not to render any communication necessary on the part of Russia and Prussia. Count .Metternich's first and principal object was to urge the expediency of prolonging the period of negotiation to the 10th of August, for reasons stated in Prince Schwartzenberg's report. 2nd, He was desirous that Count Stadion should accompany the Emperor to Trachenberg, who was to be instructed to use his utmost to strengthen and decide the Prince Royal of Sweden in his intentions to co-operate with the allies. Count Metternich now declared that the Emperor Francis' determination was to support the justice of the cause for which the Emperor Alexander had employed such great resources (*beaux moyens*).

It was then strongly urged in favor of the prolongation of the term, that the French would not benefit by it, because their preparations would be complete by the 20th inst.

The Emperor of Russia had not stated his determination respecting the prolongation of the term to the 10th of August, and it was supposed he would not do so until after the conferences at Trachenberg.

Appendix 4

CONDITIONS OF EQUIPMENT OF THE HANSEATIC LEGION
AND OTHER CORPS

The Hanseatic legion, consisting of cavalry, artillery, and infantry, agrees under the following conditions to enter into the service of His Britannic Majesty under the present state of affairs in the north of Germany:

1st. The Hanseatic legion is to receive the same pay as the Hanoverian levies from Great Britain, and is to serve during the war on the continent of Europe.

2nd. The Hanseatic legion agrees while in the pay of Great Britain to serve under the orders of the general or other officer who may be appointed by His Royal Highness the Prince Regent in the same manner as the Electoral troops.

3rd. The legion is to retain its denomination and establishment, but is to be subject to such dislocation in its formation as may be necessary for the improvement and amelioration of its discipline, or the general interests of the service which the general officer commanding may deem necessary.

4th. Should the Hanseatic towns become again free, the legion shall continue under the immediate orders and service of His Britannic Majesty no longer than is necessary to form an arrangement with the Hanseatic government for its return ; but, until such arrangement be formed, the corps will continue to serve on the footing prescribed in the foregoing conditions.

5th. In case of vacancies or promotions in the officers, the same shall be conducted according to the manner now practised in the Hanoverian levies, so long as the legion remains in British pay.

6th. The British government will keep the legion equipped in like manner with the Hanoverian levies.

7th. The general officer commanding on the part of Great Britain is to have the right of appointing officers to superintend and improve the discipline of the corps.

8th. Officers and men who may become incapable of further service by wounds shall receive the same pension or allowances as are granted to His Majesty's Electoral troops, until the Hanseatic towns become liberated, and shall be enabled of themselves to provide for them.

Goldberg
21st July, 1813

Appendix 5

COPY OF A LETTER FROM LORD CASTLEREAGH TO
HIS ROYAL HIGHNESS THE PRINCE ROYAL OF SWEDEN
DATED LONDON, MARCH 23RD, 1813.

Sir,

In transmitting, by the Prince Regent's command, the enclosed letter, I cannot refrain from expressing to your Royal Highness my grateful sense of your reception of General Hope's mission; of the cordiality with which your Royal Highness's influence was employed to smooth every difficulty, and to combine the cause of Sweden with the great cause in which her true interests must ever be indissolubly bound up.

General Hope has conveyed to me the substance of the many interesting and confidential conversations he was permitted to hold with your Highness. He has further flattered me by repeating the gracious notice your Royal Highness was pleased to take of my endeavours to unite the councils and interests of our respective states. I trust the auspicious prospect which awaits your Royal Highness's approaching operations may enable me, in the discharge of my public duties, more intimately to cultivate your Royal Highness's confidence, and to deserve your esteem. My first wish is to see your Royal Highness at the head of a powerful army, liberated from all the embarrassments of a first lauding, and enabled, without the necessity of losing much precious time in securing your rear, to take that prominent station in the advanced operations of the allied armies to which your name and services, in the expectation of. Europe, at this moment destine you.

The magnificent career of the Russian troops, sweeping everything before them, in the midst of a severe winter, from Moscow to the Elbe, has opened to your Royal Highness new facilities. The combinations required to assemble your army from distant points may now, I trust, be brought within narrow limits, and the Russian auxiliary force be saved the inconvenience of an embarkation. If Denmark should still refuse to accommodate to the general interests (which seems impossible), I trust your Royal Highness will soon extinguish that portion of her military resources which is to he found in her continental provinces, and which can alone, whilst Zealand is blockaded, give any jealousy to your movements. I shall deeply lament this, or any other delay which may retard the moment when your operations may assume a more enlarged character.

General Hope has represented, with the zeal which your Royal Highness knows so well how to inspire, your Royal Highness's sentiments on several detailed suggestions which it was your wish to have considered by His Majesty's government. Upon all the most prominent in importance, and which are the most pressing in point of time, as connected with your first movements, I hope your Royal Highness will find Mr. Thornton already instructed. I shall not lose sight of any suggestions which come recommended by the sanction of either your Royal Highness's wishes or judgment; and when it is not acted upon, you will, I am sure, attribute it to the variety of the many services that at this moment press upon the resources and military force of Great Britain.

Entreating your Royal Highness to accept the tribute of my respectful good wishes for your personal glory and prosperity, in which I consider the best interests of the world to be at the present moment largely involved, I remain, with great deference and consideration,

Your Royal Highness's most obedient
And most humble servant,
(Signed) *Castlereagh*

Appendix 6

Convention signed at Trachenberg, 12th of July, 1813, as a basis for the Operations of the Campaign.

Il a été convenu d'adopter pour principe général, que toutes les forces des alliés se porteront toujours du côté où les plus grandes forces de l'ennemi se trouveront : de-là il s'ensuit :

1. Que les corps qui doivent agir sur les flancs et à dos de l'ennemi diviseront toujours la ligne qui conduit le plus directement sur la ligne d'opérations de l'ennemi.

2. Que la plus grande force des alliés doit choisir une position qui la mette à même de faire face partout où l'ennemi voudra se porter. Le bastion saillant de la Bohême paroît donner cet avantage.

Suivant ces maximes générales, les armées combinées doivent donc avant l'expiration de l'armistice être rendues aux points ci-dessus énoncés, savoir :—

Une partie de l'armée alliée en Silésie, forte de 98,000 à 100,000 hommes, se portera quelques jours avant la fin de l'armistice par les routes de Landshut et de Gratz sur Zoung, Bunzlau, et Brandeis, pour se joindre dans le plus court délai à l'armée Autrichienne, afin de former avec elle en Bohême un total de 200,000 à 220,000 combattans.

L'armée du Prince Royal de Suède, laissant un corps de 15 à 20,000 hommes contre les Danois et les Français en observation vis-à-vis de Lubeck et de Hambourg, se rassemblera avec une force à-peu-près de 70,000 hommes dans les environs de Trauenbrutzen, pour se porter au moment de l'expiration de l'armistice vers l'Elbe, et passer ce fleuve entre Torgau et Magdebourg, en se dirigeant de suite sur Leipzig.

Le reste de l'armée alliée en Silésie, fort de 50,000 hommes, suivra l'ennemi vers l'Elbe. Cette armée évitera d'engager une affaire générale à moins qu'elle n'ait toutes les chances de son côté. En arrivant sur l'Elbe, elle tâchera de passer ce fleuve entre Torgau et Dresde, afin de se joindre à l'armée du Prince Royal de Suède ; ce qui fera monter celle-ci à 120,000 combattans ; si cependant les circonstances exigeroient de renforcer l'armée alliée en Bohême, avant que l'armée de Silésie se joigne à celle du Prince Royal de Suède, alors l'armée de Silésie marchera sans délai en Bohême.

L'armée Autrichienne, réunie à l'armée alliée, débouchera d'après les circonstances ou par Eger et Hoff, ou dans la Saxe, ou dans la Silésie, ou du côté du Danube.

Si l'Empereur Napoléon, voulant prévenir l'armée alliée en Bohême, marchoit à elle pour la combattre, l'armée du Prince Royal de Suède tâchera par des marches forcées à se porter aussi vîte que possible sur les derrières de l'armée ennemie : si au contraire l'Empereur Napoléon se dirigeoit contre l'armée du Prince Royal, l'armée alliée prendroit une offensive vigoureuse, et marcheroit sur les communications de l'ennemi pour lui livrer bataille ; toutes les armées combinées prendront l'offensive, et le camp de l'ennemi sera leur rendezvous.

L'armée de réserve Russe sous les ordres du Général Benningsen s'avancera de la Vistule par Kalish vers l'Oder dans la direction de Glogau, pour être à portée d'agir suivant les mêmes principes, et de se diriger sur l'ennemi, s'il reste en Silésie, ou de l'empêcher de tenter une invasion en Pologne.

Appendix 7

Déclaration Autrichienne, Août, 1813.

Le soussigné, Ministre d'état et des affaires étrangères, est chargé par un ordre exprès de son auguste Maître, de faire la déclaration suivante à S. E. Monseigneur le Comte de Narbonne, ambassadeur de S. M. l'Empereur des François, Roi d'Italie.

Depuis la dernière paix, signée avec la France en Octobre 1809, S. M. I. a voué toute sa sollicitude, non-seulement à établir avec cette puissance des relations d'amitié et de confiance, dont elle avoit fait la base de son système politique, mais à faire servir ces relations au maintien de la paix et de l'ordre en Europe. Elle s'étoit flattée que le rapprochement intime, cimenté par une alliance de famille contractée avec S. M. l'Empereur des François, contribueroit à lui donner sur sa marche politique la seule influence qu'elle soit jalouse d'acquérir, celle qui tend à communiquer aux Cabinets de l'Europe l'esprit de modération, le respect pour les droits et les possessions des états indépendans, qui l'animent elle-même.

S. M. I. n'a pu se livrer long-tems à de si belles espérances. Un an étoit à peine écoulé depuis l'époque qui sembloit mettre le comble à la gloire militaire du Souverain de la France, et rien ne paroissoit plus manquer à sa prospérité, pour autant qu'elle dépendoit de son attitude et de son influence au dehors, quand de nouvelles réunions au territoire François, d'états jusqu'alors indépendans, de nouveaux morcélemens et déchiremens de l'Allemagne, vinrent réveiller les inquiétudes des puissances, et préparer, par leur funeste réaction sur le nord de l'Europe, la guerre qui devoit s'allumer en 1812 entre la France et la Russie.

Le Cabinet François sait, mieux qu'aucun autre, combien S. M. l'Empereur d'Autriche a eu à cœur d'en prévenir l'éclat par toutes les voies de conciliation que lui dictoit son intérêt pour les deux puissances, et pour celles qui devoient se trouver entraînées dans la grande lutte qui se préparoit. Ce n'est pas elle que l'Europe accusera jamais des maux incalculables qui en ont été la suite.

Dans cet état des choses S. M. l'Empereur ne pouvant conserver à ses peuples le bienfait de la paix, et maintenir une heureuse neutralité au milieu du vaste champ de bataille qui de tous côtés environnoit ses états, ne consulta, dans le parti qu'elle adopta, que sa fidélité à des relations si récemment établies, et l'espoir qu'elle aimoit à nourrir encore, que son alliance avec la France, en lui offrant des moyens plus sûrs de faire écouter les conseils de la sagesse, mettroit des bornes à des maux inévitables, et serviroit la cause du retour de la paix en Europe.

Il n'en a malheureusement pas été ainsi : ni les succès brillans de la campagne de 1812, ni les désastres sans exemple qui en ont marqué la fin, n'ont pu ramener dans les conseils du gouvernement François l'esprit de modération qui auroit mis à profit les uns, et diminué l'effet des autres.

S. M. n'en saisit pas moins le moment où l'épuisement réciproque devoit ralentir les opérations actives de la guerre pour porter aux puissances belligérantes des paroles de paix, qu'elle espéroit encore voir accueillir de part et d'autre avec la sincérité qui les lui avoit dictées.

Persuadée, toutefois, qu'elle ne pouvoit les faire écouter qu'en les soutenant des forces qui promettroient au parti avec lequel elle s'accorderoit de vues et de principes, l'appui de sa coopération active pour terminer la grande lutte; en offrant sa médiation aux puissances, elle se décida à l'effort pénible pour son cœur d'un appel au courage et au patriotisme de ses peuples. Le congrès proposé par elle, et accepté par les deux partis, s'assemble au milieu des préparatifs militaires, que le succès des négociations devoit rendre inutiles, si les vœux de l'Empereur se réalisoient, mais qui devoient, dans le cas contraire, conduire par de nouveaux efforts un résultat pacifique, que S. M. eût préféré d'atteindre sans effusion de sang. En obtenant de la confiance qu'elles avoient vouée à S. M. le consentement des puissances à la prolongation de l'armistice que la France jugeoit nécessaire pour les négociations, l'Empereur acquit, avec cette preuve de leurs vues pacifiques, celle de la modération de leurs principes et de leurs intentions. Il y reconnut les siens, et se persuade, de ce moment, que ce seroit de leur côté qu'il rencontreroit des dispositions sincères à concourir au rétablissement d'une paix solide et durable. La France, loin de manifester des intentions, n'avoit donné que des assurances générales, trop souvent démenties par des déclarations publiques, qui ne fondoient aucunement l'espoir qu'elle porteroit à la paix sur les sacrifices qui pouvoient la ramener en Europe.

La marche du Congrès ne pouvoit laisser de doute à cet égard. Le retard de l'arrivée de MM. les Plénipotentiaires François sous des prétextes que le grand but de sa réunion auroit dû faire écarter, l'insuffisance de leurs instructions sur les objets de forme, qui faisoient perdre un tems irréparable, lorsqu'il ne restoit plus que peu de jours pour la plus importante des négociations, toutes ces circonstances réunies ne démontroient que trop que la paix, telle que la vouloient l'Autriche et les Souverains alliés, étoit étrangère aux vœux de la France; et pour ne pas s'exposer au reproche de la prolongation arbitraire de la guerre, en faisant la proposition d'une négociation, elle vouloit en éluder l'effet, ou s'en prévaloir peut-être uniquement pour séparer l'Autriche des puissances qui s'étoient déjà réunies à elle de principe, avant même que les traités n'eussent consacré leur union pour la cause de la paix et du bonheur du monde.

L'Autriche sort de cette négociation, dont le résultat a trompé ses vœux les plus chers, avec la conscience de la bonne foi qu'elle y a portée. Plus zélée que jamais pour le noble but qu'elle s'étoit proposé, elle ne prend les armes que pour l'atteindre de concert avec les puissances animées des mêmes sentimens.

Toujours également disposée à prêter les mains au rétablissement d'un ordre de choses qui, par une sage répartition des forces, place la garantie de la paix sous l'égide d'une association d'états indépendans, elle ne négligera aucune occasion de parvenir à ce résultat désirable; et la connoissance qu'elle a acquise des dispositions des Cours devenues désormais ses alliés, lui donne la certitude qu'elles coopéreront avec sincérité à un but aussi salutaire, en déclarant, d'ordre de l'Empereur, à M. le Comte de Narbonne, que ses fonctions d'Ambassadeur viennent de cesser de ce moment. Le soussigné met à la disposition de Son Excellence, ainsi que de S. E. M. le Duc de Vicenze, les passeports dont elles auront besoin pour elles et leur suite.

Les mêmes passeports seront remis à Monsieur de la Blonde, chargé-d'affaires de France à Vienne, ainsi qu'aux autres individus de l'ambassade.

Le soussigné est également chargé de prévenir S. E. M. le (
que S. M. l'Empereur, fidèle à l'engagement éventuel verbalemen
l'Empereur Napoléon et le soussigné lors de son séjour à Dre
ne faire commencer les hostilités qu'après le terme de six jours révol
Il a l'honneur d'offrir à cette occasion, etc. etc.

(Signé) M

Prague, le 11 *Août,* 1813.
A S. E. M. le Comte de Narbonne, Ambassadeur de S. M.
l'Empereur des François, Roi d'Italie.

Appendix 8

PUBLICATION OF CENTRAL COMMISSION

Their Majesties the Emperor of Russia and the King of Prussia have been pleased to resolve upon the establishment of a council of administration of the combined powers for the North of Germany, in order to bring unity, coherence and harmony into the management of public affairs in that country. This council of administration has particular instructions to communicate with the different existing governments on every subject which has reference to policy, finances, arming of the people, and on all things which may contribute to the security, the support, and increase of the armies engaged in the conflict for the restoration of the independence of Germany.

All public officers, and the inhabitants of the North of Germany, are enjoined to comply with the dispositions of the said council of administration.

Their Majesties have been pleased to nominate Charles Baron de Stein president of this council.

At the head-quarters, Kalisch, the 26th March, (6th April) 1813. In the name of their Majesties the Emperor of Russia and the King of Prussia,

(Signed) *Prince Kutusoff Smolensko*
General, Field-Marshal
Commander-in-Chief of the Combined Armies

Evaluation approximative des Armées des Puissances Belligérantes.

I.—ARMÉE FRANÇOISE.

1. Grande Armée sur le Bober, et celle à Dresde	120,000
2. Corps de Davoust, Vandamme	17,000
3. Corps détachés à Leipzig, Wurtzburg, Frankfurt, &c.	23,000
4. Anticipation sur la levée de 1814, en marche	40,000
N.B. Les autres 40,000 en seront apparemment envoyés en Espagne.	
5. Vieilles troupes qui l'on retire d'Espagne	50,000
6. Garnisons Françoises dans les forteresses, non compris dans les troupes des contingens que se trouvent dans les mêmes forteresses :	
A. Dantzig 15,000	
B. Stettin 7,000	28,000
C. Glogau 3,000	
D. Custrin 3,000	
Total, François	278,000

II.—*Contingens Allemands.*

Transportés		278,000
1. Saxons		20,000
2. Bavarois, à l'armée	8000	
en Bavière	12,000	20,000
3. Wirtemburgeois		6,000
4. Badois		5,000
5. Nassau		1,800
6. Frankfort		1,800
7. Wurtzburg		2,000
8. Valdeck, Reuss, Ysenbuchen, Hohenzollern, Meiningen, Lippe		24,000
Total		358,600

Transportés	358,000

III.—*Troupes Italiennes et étrangères.*

1. Troupes Italiennes à Milan, sur l'Isonzo, Verona, &c. &c.	45,000
2. Napolitains	6,000
3. Suisses	8,000
IV. Gardes Nationales Bavaroises en activité	20,000
V. Polonois	12,000
VI. Garnisons Polonoises à Modlin et Tauck, &c.	10,000
Grand Total	459,600

(Non comprises les troupes en Espagne et dans l'intérieur de France.)

Armée des Alliés.

I.—Russes.

1. Russes en Allemagne, y compris les renforts qui arrivent sous le Général Labanoff, et qui ne les ont pas joint encore	130,000
2. Troupes Russes qui doivent bloquer les forteresses de Dantzig, Modlin, et Tauck	30,000

II.—Prussiens.

Y comprise la landwehr enrégimentée, mais pas le landsturm, et la landwehr de réserve, au moins	180,000
3. Suédois	12,000
4. Mecklenbourgeois et corps francs d'Hanovriens, à-peu-près	8,000
Total	360,000

Il y a encore des Russes en Pologne et Lithuanie	40,000	
Milice sous le Comte Tolstoy	80,000	
Total	120,000	

Transportés	360,000

Autrichiens.

1. Armée autre en Bohême	115,000
2. L'Armée en Illyrie, sur les frontières de l'Italie	45,000
Grand Total	520,000

Sans compter 50,000 de landwehr en Bohême, ni les armées de Galicie et de Hongrie.

Etat des Forces des Alliés, transmis comme minimum par M. le Chancelier Baron de Hardenberg à son Excellence M. le Comte de Metternich.

		Rectifications que l'Empereur y a ajoutées.	
Russes en Silésie	80,000	Russes en Silésie	112,000
Troupes réglées Prussiennes	40,000	Do.	40,000
Landwehr choisie et exercée	30,000	Do.	30,000
En Silésie	150,000		182,000

Corps du Prince Royal de Suède.

Suédois, selon le Prince Royal . . 30,000 comptés seulement à .	25,000	
Bulow	25,000	
Walmöden . . .	11,000	
Woronzoff . . .	4,000	85,000
Tauenzeiu . . .	6,000	
Légion Allemande . .	6,000	
Dans 15 jours elle sera de . . 8,000		
Russes à ajouter (C'est le corps de Winzingerode déjà donné au Prince Royal) . .	8,000	
Transp.	235,000	Transp. 267,000

Transportés	235,000	Transportés	267,000
Réserves Russes.			
Tolstoy	40,000	Tolstoy entre Gitomie et la Vistule	60,000
D'Orloff	14,000	D'Orloff entre Bialistock et la Vistule	40,000
Labanoff	30,000	Labanoff, se dirigeant sur la Waitha	70,000
Réserves Prussiennes.			
Restes de la Landwehr .	90,000	Réserves de la Landwehr . .	90,000
	409,000		527,000
Autrichiens.			
Troupes réglées en Bohême et ailleurs	150,000	. . . . .	150,000
Réserves Autrichiennes . .	100,000	. . . . .	100,000
	659,000		777,000

Note from the Chancellor Hardenberg to Lieutenant-General Sir Charles Stewart, dated Frankfort, 4th December, 1813.

Monsieur le Général,

J'ai l'honneur de renvoyer à Votre Excellence les pièces relatives aux principes établis en Angleterre sur les Ordres de Chevalerie étrangers.

Le Roi, mon auguste Souverain, sous les yeux duquel je me suis empressé de les mettre, m'ordonne de vous dire, Monsieur le Général, que c'est pour vous donner une marque publique de son estime distinguée, et particulièrement de sa satisfaction de la valeur et des talens que vous avez déployés à côté de Sa Majesté, dans les différens combats auxquels vous avez assisté, et dans lesquels vous avez versé votre sang pour la cause commune, qu'il vous a décoré de ses ordres de l'Aigle Noir et de l'Aigle Rouge.

Veuillez agréer l'assurance réitérée de tout mon attachement et de ma haute considération.

     (Signé)   HARDENBERG.

Au Quartier-général de Frankfort, le 4 Décembre, 1813.

GENERAL BLUCHER'S DISPOSITION FOR THE ATTACK ON THE 16TH OCTOBER

On the 16th October, at six a. m., the reserve cavalry of all three corps with their horse artillery, is to march: *viz.*—

The reserve cavalry of the corps of D'Yorck on the great road to Leipsic. As soon as it shall reach the cavalry of the advanced guard, the latter are to lead and proceed to Leipsic.

The reserve cavalry of the corps of Count Langeron to march upon Radefeld and Lindenthal. The cavalry of the advanced guard leads them also. But before the march of the cavalry there must be accounts whether the enemy be near Dubin, and whether he occupy Delitsch, &c.

The cavalry of the reserve and advanced guard, and the horse artillery of the corps of Sachen, are to follow the cavalry of the corps of D'Yorck over Schevditz to Leipsic.

Sir C. Stewart will be at the head of this cavalry.

If the enemy should not be in position on this side the Partha, the reserve cavalry of the corps of D'Yorck is to march between Mackem and Gobles.

The reserve cavalry of Langeron's corps, on this side Wettnitz, and the cavalry of the advanced guard, to find the enemy, and show me the situation of the enemy, either behind the Partha, or on the road to Dubin.

The whole of the infantry to have their provisions ready, so as to be able to march at ten o'clock.

An orderly from each corps is to accompany me; and will carry my orders to the respective commanders.

Letter from General De Gniesenau to Lieutenant-General Sir Charles Stewart

Shows the importance of his having effected the changes narrated in the Prince Royal's march, October 15th, 1813

Le nom du lieu où le Prince Royal de Suède a pris son quartier-général aujourd'hui n'étant pas distinctement écrite dans votre lettre que vous m'avez fait l'honneur de m'adresser aujourd'hui, et ne pouvant pas trouver un tel nom sur la carte, je prends la liberté de vous adresser cette lettre pour vous prier de la faire parvenir au Prince. Elle contient la disposition pour notre attaque, et la demande au Prince en quelle manière il compte co-opérer demain.

En persuadant au Prince de changer la direction de sa marche, vous avez rendu, M. le Général, un service éminent à la bonne cause, etc.
Général de Gniesenau.
A S. E. le Lieutenant-Général Sir Charles Stewart.
Gross Rugel
Octobre 15

Lord Castlereagh's Letter expressing the Prince Regent's approbation of Sir Charles Stewart's conduct both political and military

Foreign Office
November 30, 1813
Sir,
The laudable activity which has marked your official correspondence down to the present period, precludes my adverting to the variety of topics which have been treated of in your dispatches.

I must, therefore, in conveying to you the Prince Regent's

most gracious approbation of your conduct, as well in discharge of your political as your military duties, apply myself to the series of important events which have taken place since you left Toplitz; in all of which His Royal Highness has had occasion to applaud, not less your zeal for his service than the judgment and ability with which you have conducted yourself under the most trying circumstances.

I am, with great truth and regard, Sir,
Your most obedient humble servant,
Castlereagh
Lieutenant-General
The Honourable Sir Charles Stewart, K. B.

The Prince Regent's permission for Sir C. Stewart to accept and wear the Swedish Order of the Sword, conferred on him after the battle of Leipsic

Foreign Office
December 21st, 1813
Sir,

I have received and laid before His Royal Highness the Prince Regent your dispatch, No. 127, of the 28th of October last, transmitting a letter from the Prince Royal of Sweden to you, in which His Royal Highness is pleased to express his intention of recommending to His Swedish Majesty, that the dignity of a Commander Grand Cross of the Swedish military Order of the Sword should be conferred upon you, in testimony of the high sense entertained of the zeal, talents, and valour displayed by you in the memorable battles near Leipsic, on the 18th and 19th of October in this year.

I have now the satisfaction to acquaint you, that His Royal Highness the Prince Regent has been graciously pleased to permit you to accept and wear the order in question; and I beg leave to convey to you my sincere congratulations upon the occasion.

I am, with great truth and regard, Sir,

Your most obedient humble servant,
Castlereagh
To Lieutenant-General
The Honourable Sir C. W. Stewart, &c. &c. &c.

Letter to Sir Charles Stewart sending the Order of the Garter to the Duke of Wellington

College of Arms
March 10th, 1813.
Sir,
I have the honour to enclose the Royal Warrant, under the sign-manual of the Prince Regent, and the signet of the Most Noble Order of the Garter, bearing date the 5th instant, authorising you to deliver unto his Excellency the Marquess of Wellington, knight of that most noble order, the Gold George, and Garter of blue velvet, with gold letters, buckle and pendant; which ensigns are herewith transmitted to you for that purpose.

I have, at the same time, to request your obliging care of the packet addressed to His Excellency, which I also enclose, and which contains the Royal Warrant, signifying his election into the Order. I beg leave to observe that there is not any prescribed ceremony for the delivery of the ensigns transmitted to the Marquess; as I have communicated in my dispatch to His Excellency.

You will have the goodness to transmit me a line acknowledging the receipt of this letter, and of the ensigns; and I have the honour to be, Sir,
Your most obedient, humble servant,
Isaac Heard, Garter
Major-General the Hon. Sir Charles William Stewart, K.B., &c. &c. &c

Memoir from General Walmoden, Dannewitz, November 1813.

A l'ouverture de la campagne au mois d'Août le Maréchal Davoust peut avoir eu 25 à 26,000 Français, et a reçu par détachemens des renforts jusques vers la mi-Septembre ; ils ont en partie compensé les pertes qu'il a éprouvées : elles se montent à-peu-près à 2500 prisonniers ; 1500 tués, blessés, et mis hors de combat : il peut avoir 5 à 6000 hommes dans les hôpitaux, et avoir reçu près de 4000 hommes de renfort pendant le tems que sa communication a été ouverte avec le Weser. Il résulte de là qu'il peut encore disposer de 20,000 hommes de toute arme. Le corps auxiliaire Danois étoit de 15,000 hommes ; il peut être réduit par les maladies et autres pertes à 11 à 12 mille hommes. Trente mille combattans au moins sont donc encore sur ce point dans une des plus fortes positions possibles ; Lubeck à l'abri d'un coup de main ; la ligne de la Stecknitz facile à défendre ; l'Elbe sur le flanc ; Hambourg, qui est devenu une place forte, Brendsbourg et Gluckstadt, sur les derrières, des positions intermédiaires derrière la Bille et la Trave ; plus loin le canal de l'Eyder. Je ne puis juger des intentions des Danois :—ils ont proclamé jusqu'à présent une guerre défensive ; et, quoiqu'ils aient accompagné Davoust à Schwerin, elles peuvent être restées équivoques : c'est à cela, je suppose, qu'est en partie due l'inactivité du Maréchal ; peut-être aussi à l'incertitude, dans laquelle d'un moment à l'autre il pouvoit être sur les renforts qui pouvoient m'arriver, et auxquels je lui ai donné lieu de croire autant que possible par des mouvemens offensifs sur différens points. Effectivement, il étoit difficile qu'il supposât qu'un point aussi important pour les opérations fût gardé si faiblement qu'il l'a été, surtout dès le moment où, abandonnant, après la défaite de la division Pécheux, la rive gauche de l'Elbe, il m'obligea de détacher, pour ne pas perdre les fruits du combats, en ne pas entravant autant que possible ses communications directes avec Magdebourg et la grande armée. Il pousse ensuite l'inactivité et la pusillanimité jusqu'à laisser emporter Bremen par mes détachemens ; et cette conduite a établi une sécurité à son sujet qui paroit encore avoir prévalu, quand on a simplement fixé un corps d'observation de 25,000 hommes pour le contenir. Encore reste-t-il à savoir, si ce corps doit observer et la Stecknitz et la rive gauche de l'Elbe, où un autre corps est destiné sur ce dernier point tout-à-fait séparé devant Harbourg et Zottenspeicker. Mais la situation doit changer : cette crise doit, ou entraîner le Dannemark dans la coalition, ou l'attacher irrévocablement aux intérêts de la France ; et la situation militaire sur ce point va présenter deux points de vue. Davoust, abandonné à ses propres forces, doit se jetter dans Hambourg, où il faudra bloquer près de 20,000 hommes, ou il sera soutenu par les Danois, qui alors doivent se renforcer, et par une armée qu'ils peuvent augmenter à volonté, menacer les alliés sur des points où déjà un grand rassemblement des forces ennemies ne laisse pas que de donner, sinon des inquiétudes, au moins de fixer l'attention. Mais supposé même que les Danois restent à leur système Français et défensif en même tems, quelles peuvent être les opérations d'un corps isolé de 25,000 hommes à eux opposé ? Il ne pourra jamais s'établir au-delà Stecknitz ; car s'il parvenoit momentanément à la passer, il n'y auroit pas une position au-delà de cette rivière, où ce corps de 25,000 hommes, entouré des places fortes de l'ennemi, pourroit se soutenir pendant l'hiver. Le tout se borneroit en conséquence à couvrir avec d'autant plus de peine le Mecklenbourg et les frontières de la Prusse, que l'ennemi, tant qu'il savoit les grandes armées proches, pourroit craindre l'arrivée des renforts ; mais à présent, s'il les voyoit engagées dans des opérations lointaines sur le Rhin, pourroit calculer d'après l'inactivité de ces troupes, qu'on n'auroit laissé que ce qui étoit indispensable pour une observation, et baser là-dessus un système offensif, qui, vu la situation des forces sur l'Elbe, pourroit devenir dangereux, par la proximité de

Magdebourg et Berlin, les communications nécessaires aux armées sur la basse Elbe, la situation du pays de Hanovre, où l'organisation militaire exige de la sureté, et enfin par toutes les considérations que pourroit entraîner une diversion puissante. Il me paraît, d'après cela, qu'il faut, avant de décider sur ce point, être assuré du parti que prendra le Dannemark, et le gagner pour la cause, ou le forcer à se détacher de celle de l'ennemi. Hambourg, abandonné à soi-même, ne sera pas pour cela pris de sitôt, vu l'hiver qui s'approche, et qui, sans compter le manque encore existant des moyens, en empêcheroit le siége. Il faut donc s'attendre à un blocus long et difficile; le local protégé par des eaux des inondations, par beaucoup de soins qu'on a mis à le fortifier par une nombreuse artillerie et garnison, et des approvisionnemens considérables, amènera des difficultés et longueurs ; il faudra un corps considérable pour le bloquer, et 25,000 hommes y contiendront à peine 20,000, si l'on veut les restreindre à la place et les empêcher de consolider les moyens de résistance pendant le blocus. Je ne sais quelle sera la suite des démonstrations du Prince Royal : jusqu'ici elles n'en ont encore eu d'autre que de porter l'ennemi à retirer les troupes qu'il avoit en avant de la Stecknitz, à Ratzebourg, aux camps de Ziethen et Schmielau, derrière cette rivière, et à les placer en réserve. Les Danois et Français sont encore mêlés à Lubeck, quoique du reste les premiers ont la gauche, leur gros sur la Trave, les autres la droite, leur réserve avec le quartier-général du Maréchal, à Tchwayenbeck. Molln est une tête-de-pont retranchée : une reconnoissance faite sur ce point a prouvé qu'ils veulent le soutenir ; elle a coûté inutilement cinq officiers et une centaine d'hommes tués et blessés. Si la suite de ces grandes forces déployées n'étoit qu'une démonstration, et qu'après coup on en revînt à une faible observation, il faut supposer que l'ennemi n'en deviendroit pas moins entreprenant ; et vu la situation générale des affaires sur l'Elbe, un manque de précaution sur ce point-ci pourroit la rendre critique.

Le corps d'observation sous mon commandement, qui se trouve en ce moment sur la rive droite, est fort de 12,000 hommes d'infanterie, (Suédois et tout y compris,) et de 3600 hommes de cavalerie, avec 60 pièces de canon,—total, 15 à 16,000 hommes ; la division du Général Tettenborn, forte de 2500 à 3000 hommes d'infanterie et de 1600 hommes de cavalerie, en ayant été détachée. On peut encore compter ici 3 à 4000 hommes de milice Mecklenbourgeoise (landwehr), dont l'organisation n'est point encore tout-à-fait achevée, mais qui pourra être employée dans la quinzaine au plus tard.

S. WALMODEN.

General Gniesenau to Sir Charles Stewart, in which he states his plan for an invasion of Holland, October 31st, 1813.

Fulda, ce 31 Octobre, 1813.

J'ai eu l'honneur, mon cher Général, de recevoir votre lettre datée du 29 à Mulhausen. Les promesses que vous avez bien voulu me faire au sujet d'armes, habillemens, etc. pour les nouvelles levées à faire, font témoignage du point de vue élevé d'où vous jugez les affaires politiques. C'est à présent le moment de faire de grands efforts, s'il en fut jamais.

Permettez, cher Général, que je lève les doutes que vous avez au sujet de la conquête de la Hollande.

Vous dites, mon Général, que notre armée a trop souffert, et que notre nombre est réduit. Cela est vrai. De 39 mille hommes que le corps de d'Yorck étoit composé à l'ouverture de la campagne actuelle, il ne lui reste plus qu'entre 10 à 11 mille hommes. Mais il nous arrive 3 mille hommes de renforts ; aux Russes de notre armée il en arrive 15 mille hommes. Je tâcherai de poster les nouvelles levées dans nos anciennes provinces cédées à la paix de Tilsit, de 20 à 30 mille hommes. Les Hessois probablement se joindront à nous, c'est-à-dire à l'armée de Silésie, parceque l'Electeur préférera de confier ses troupes à M. le Général Prussien. Tout cela composera une armée formidable, qui pourra bien entreprendre la conquête de la Hollande. Même avec ce qui nous reste maintenant, nous tâcherons de faire une tentative, ne fût-ce que pour obliger l'ennemi de disperser ses forces.

En second lieu, si j'ai conçu le plan de conquérir la Hollande, c'est d'après une combinaison que je crois assez juste. Je vais vous la développer.

La France a entre 130 et 140 places fortes dans les guerres qui ont eu lieu jusqu'ici. Buonaparte a laissé sans garnisons la plupart de ces places fortes; ce qui lui a donné la faculté de former de nombreuses armées. Si on le force de mettre garnison dans un grand nombre de ces places fortes, on lui ôtera la possibilité de mettre en campagne une armée assez forte pour nous résister. La Hollande, la Flandre, le Brabant, sont hérissés de places fortes. Si on passe le Rhin, et si on prend la direction sur Maestricht, on tourne toutes les places fortes de la Hollande, et on les isole de la France. L'ennemi alors n'a que deux choses à faire; ou, de jeter au plus vîte tous les conscrits qu'il peut ramasser dans ces places, ou de les laisser sans garnison. Dans le premier cas, nous ne trouverons devant nous une armée capable à nous résister, et nous pourrons percer dans l'ancienne France elle-même, si cela nous convient. Dans le second cas nous pourrons, sans beaucoup de peine, nous emparer des places de la Hollande, et nous nous y formerons une base solide d'opérations. D'après les renseignemens que nous avons reçus, les places de frontière en France sont très mal pourvues de tout ce qu'il leur faut pour se défendre, et peut-être que nous les aurons à bon marché.

Faites, mon Général, la critique de mes projets militaires, je vous en prie, et rectifiez mes idées, si vous ne les trouvez pas assez justes. J'aime à battre le fer tant qu'il est chaud, et de ne donner de relâche à l'ennemi vaincu.

Beaucoup de militaires conseilleroient d'éviter les places fortes, et d'attaquer la France par les côtés qui en sont le moins garnis: mais comme l'ennemi a perdu l'année dernière une armée de 400 mille hommes, et dans la campagne actuelle une autre armée de 300 mille hommes, il faut choisir une place qui le force d'employer toutes ses nouvelles levées dans ses forteresses; et on y parvient en se mettant dans un point central, et où l'on menace un grand nombre de ces places à la fois.

Ayez la bonté, cher Général, de me faire parvenir une autorisation, par écrit de votre main, pour l'officier que je vais envoyer à Stralsund pour qu'on lui remette les armes et effets militaires dont vous parlez dans votre lettre. Il ne faut pas perdre un moment; et il est important d'arranger au plus vîte l'affaire des nouvelles levées. Agréez, mon cher Général, les assurances de mon inviolable attachement.

Le Général de Gniesenau.

General Gniesenau to Sir Charles Stewart, December 13th, 1813.

State of the Prussian army in the month of December, which shows the great want in which they were of every necessary, from their extreme exertions, which Great Britain supplied.

Monsieur le Général,

J'ai eu l'honneur de recevoir votre lettre du 11 de ce mois, et je m'empresse d'y répondre.

Par les nombreux combats que l'armée Prussienne a soutenue depuis la reprise des hostilités, la consommation des armes a été énorme : un grand nombre a été détruit ou laissé sur les champs de bataille ; et, malgré le soin qu'on eut à les ramasser, une partie en a été volée. Les soldats qui n'étaient pas grièvement blessés, prirent leurs armes avec eux ; mais le désordre qui règne dans les nombreux hôpitaux en fait perdre un grand nombre, et les reconvalescens retournent à leurs corps sans armes. De-là vient que dans le corps d'Yorck il se trouve un grand nombre de soldats sans armes. Sur l'effectif de l'armée Prussienne je ne saurois vous donner, mon Général, des informations positives. Vers la fin de l'armistice j'en étais bien instruit, parceque les corps alors étaient au complet, et que je connoissais le nombre des corps ; mais maintenant, que les corps sont divisés en combattans, et que l'effectif des renforts m'est inconnu, j'en suis moi-même très imparfaitement instruit. La seule personne qui soit en même temps en droit et en état de vous en donner des informations, c'est M. de Knesebeck, qui vous donnera loyalement tous les renseignemens là-dessus.

Cette disette des armes m'inquiète beaucoup, et, si la guerre se prolonge au-delà de six mois, nous mettra dans de grands embarras. Toutes les fabriques d'armes de l'Allemagne ne sauroient répondre à la consommation des armes de 600 mille combattans. Tâchez, mon Général, de fixer l'attention de votre gouvernement sur ce sujet ; car sans cela nous aurons les hommes, sans pouvoir les armer.

Si notre passage du Bas Rhin avoit eu lieu, j'aurais tâché de nous emparer des manufactures d'armes qui sont à Liège, et dans les environs de Namur, etc. etc. ; et j'aurois cru de porter un coup mortel au gouvernement Français, en lui ôtant ou paralysant ses manufactures d'armes. Si nous n'établissons pas des magasins d'armes bien fournis, desquels nous puissions tirer ce qui nous faut, nous serons dans de perplexités étranges. Personne n'y pense.

J'ai remarqué en Angleterre que dans chaque comté il y a un arsenal qui renferme les fusils que le gouvernement a prêtés aux corps de Volontaires, à la Milice Locale, etc. ces armes forment un total de 700 à 800 mille fusils. Tout cela était destiné à servir contre une invasion Française. Maintenant cette invasion n'aura plus lieu. Ne seroit-il pas convenable de rendre ces armes, au moins en partie, aux princes d'Allemagne qui en auroient besoin ? Embden seroit une place très propre pour débarquer et emmagasiner ces armes. Veuiller agréer, mon Général, l'assurance des sentimens distingués avec lesquels j'ai l'honneuz d'être,

Mon Général,

Votre très humble et très obéissant serviteur,

R. DE GNIESENAU.

Hochst, le 12 Décembre, 1813.

Numbers of battalions.	Companies.	Squadrons.	STATIONS.	Effective State.		Fighting.	
				Men.	Horses.	Men.	Horses.
66	21	41	Italy	106,001	7,028	75,232	6,029
8	..	..	Dalmatia	7,320	..	6,815	..
11	6½	12	Mentz	15,688	1,723	11,991	1,700
56	41	38	Bohemia	93,759	6,616	64,738	5,220
57	12	27	Moravia	78,786	4,686	53,061	4,375
21	..	73	Gallicia	74,876	13,562	36,090	12,998
38	19	44	Lower Austria	58,206	7,136	37,602	6,607
15	3	2	Upper Austria	17,338	363	10,684	341
10	36	52	Hungary	30,972	9,552	23,302	9,293
15	10	4	Siebenburgen	27,754	2,351	20,726	2,061
19	4	19	Banat, Sclavonia, the Banat and Carlstadt frontiers	43,180	4,380	35,215	4,269
316	152½	315	Total	553,859	56,297	375,459	52,893

Ordnance ready for the field.	
At Prague ....Pieces..	180
Budweis..................................do.....	200
Brunn and Olmutz....................do.....	150
Gallicia...................................do.....	120
Mentz.....................................do.....	24
Italy......................................do.....	126
Total . .	800

Copy of a Letter from the Prince Royal of Sweden to the King of Prussia, Stralsund, June 3rd, 1813.

[*These letters are inserted in the Appendix, to show that the Prince Royal's sentiments, as expressed to Prussia and Russia, gave fair reason to look for his most zealous and cordial exertions.*]

Sire,

Monsieur le Comte de Lurey m'a remis votre lettre, datée de Breslau, le 27 Mai. C'est toujours avec un nouveau plaisir que j'apprends quelques succès en faveur de la bonne cause; et je suis doublement heureux lorsqu'ils sont obtenus par les troupes de Votre Majesté.

Je ne suis sur le Continent, Sire, que pour agir en conformité des traités; c'est sur leur garantie que je m'y suis rendu avec trente mille hommes. Pour accélérer la paix de l'Europe, avec l'établissement d'un équilibre politique, j'ai consenti, sans prétendre renoncer à aucun des droits de la Suède sur la Norvège, à agir offensivement sur les deux rives de l'Elbe, dès l'instant que les troupes promises par V. M. et par la Russie se sont jointes à moi. V. M. doit sentir avec quelle anxiété j'attends et l'arrivée de ses troupes, et l'avis de la ratification du Traité signé à Stockholm par Monsieur de Tarrac. Si, comme je l'espère, elle a eu lieu, j'accepte avec plaisir, et en attendant les troupes que V. M. me destine, le corps que le Général Bulow commande. Dans ce cas je supplie V. M. de vouloir ordonner à ce Général de se rapprocher de Wittemberg, afin qu'il puisse se lier aux opérations que les circonstances commanderont.

La Dannemarc a toujours été à la dévotion de la France; sa politique est parvenue depuis six mois à jetter entre les Cours alliées le soupçon et la méfiance: le voile est tombé plus tard que je ne l'aurai cru; mais enfin ce gouvernement s'est déclaré notre ennemi.

J'attends le retour du Général Comte de Sowenhielm, que j'ai envoyé au quartier-général de Sa Majesté l'Empereur Alexandre, pour me mettre en mouvement.

Je suis, Sire, de Votre Majesté
Le très dévoué Serviteur et bon Frère,
CHARLES JEAN.

Stralsund, le 3 Juin, 1813.

Copy of a Letter from the Prince Royal of Sweden to the King of Prussia, Stralsund, June 4th, 1813.

Sire,

Monsieur de Kaas ayant fait dire au Général Tettenborn et au Général Suédois Boye, que si le Roi consentoit à renvoyer toute discussion sur la Norvège jusqu'à la paix générale, le Roi de Dannemarc mettroit à ma disposition vingt-cinq mille hommes pour agir contre l'Empereur Napoléon ; la connoissance que j'ai de la politique de ce Gouvernement ne me permet point d'ajouter foi à ces ouvertures : mais, pour n'avoir rien à me reprocher, je voulus bien permettre que M. le Baron de Wetterstedt se rendît à Copenhague avec le Général Luchtelin, le Ministre Anglais Thornton, et le Général Hosse. Leur voyage a été tout-à-fait infructueux, la permission de descendre à terre ne leur a pas même été accordée, et les réponses du Roi de Dannemarc ont été déclinatoires. Tout ce qui vient de se passer ne m'étonne pas, mais doit prouver à V. M. et à l'Empereur Alexandre qu'il n'y a pas de sureté pour l'Allemagne, tant que le Roi de Dannemarc ne combattra pas pour notre cause, ou qu'il ne sera pas totalement dépossédé de sa presqu'île. Par cette occupation, nous sommes maîtres de Hambourg, de Lubec, du Mecklenbourg, et du cours de l'Elbe ; et l'Empereur Napoléon a besoin d'une armée de cent mille hommes pour observer mes mouvemens.

Je viens d'apprendre, Sire, que le corps du Général Bulow s'étoit posté sur Osoren : si V. M. n'a pas changé d'avis, et qu'elle le destine toujours à agir avec moi, je la prie de lui donner l'ordre de s'en rapprocher.

Je prie V. M. d'agréer l'expression des sentimens inviolables avec lesquels je suis,

Sire, De Votre Majesté

Le très dévoué Serviteur et bon Frère,

CHARLES JEAN.

Stralsund, 4 Juin, 1813.

Copy of a Letter from the Prince Royal to His Majesty the Emperor of Russia, dated Stralsund, June 10th, 1813.

Extrèmement occupé, il m'a été impossible d'écrire de ma main cette longue lettre ; mais je ne puis, Sire, résister au plaisir de réitérer à V. M. l'assurance que je désire vivement que les circonstances actuelles jettent les bases d'une union éternelle entre la Russie et la Suède. Il faut venger l'Europe, et la sauver. Voilà, Sire, notre vocation : elle sera emplie, j'en atteste les principes de V. M. et les qualités éminens qui ont fixé sur elle mes premiers regards, et les yeux du monde. Que de vœux, que de soupirs, sont dans ce moment pressés vers le camp Impérial Russe ! V. M. I. n'appartient pas seulement à la Russie, mais à l'univers : ce fut le langage que j'ai eu l'honneur de lui tenir, il y a dix mois, et certes les affaires sont loin d'être dans l'état où elles se trouvoient alors. L'Autriche et la Prusse étoient contre vous, Sire : aujourd'hui la Prusse fait cause commune avec V. M. ; l'Autriche est au moins neutre ; et l'Allemagne nous appelle ; elle s'arme, nous attend, et nous conjure de rester unis.

Agréez, Sire, mes vœux et mes sentimens pour tout ce qui vous intéresse.

(Signé) CHARLES JEAN.

Copy of a Letter from the Prince Royal of Sweden to the Emperor of Russia, dated Stralsund, June 10th, 1813.

Sire,

Le Colonel Pozzo di Borgo m'a remis les deux lettres dont V. M. I. avait bien voulu le charger pour moi en date de Schweidnitz, le 30 Mai dernier, et je ne perds pas un instant à y répondre.

En la lisant, Sire, j'ai éprouvé le plus profond chagrin de ce que V. M. I. a pu douter de mon cœur et des sentimens qu'il lui a voués. Croyez, Sire, qu'au milieu même des momens les plus difficiles de nos discussions ni mon amitié sincère pour V. M. I. ni la confiance illimitée que j'ai placée en ses promesses n'ont jamais souffert la moindre altération. Connoissant les immenses ressources de votre Empire, Sire, je m'étois attaché à l'espérance que V. M. trouveroit le moyen de me fournir le corps de troupes stipulé dans nos Traités, parceque cette réunion de forces promettoit à la cause commune les résultats les plus heureux; mais la lettre que V. M. I. vient de m'écrire, en portant ce caractère de loyauté et d'épanchement qu'elle sait si bien exprimer, m'éclaire à la fois sur ce que j'ai à attendre d'elle, et sur la marche que mes devoirs et mon attachement pour V. M. m'indiquent.

Sire, les grands événemens qui se précipitent ne vous permettent plus de revenir sur le passé; que le souvenir d'opinions contraires soit enseveli à jamais! le présent nous appartient; et en fondant une nouvelle époque de confiance mutuelle, il deviendra un nouveau gage d'un avenir heureux. La nouvelle de l'Armistice conclu le 5 de ce mois m'est parvenue hier, et j'attends à tout moment la copie de cet acte. Quelque onéreux qu'il soit, rien n'est perdu, si ce premier pas vers un accommodement avec l'ennemi commun n'est suivi d'un autre plus décisif encore, où il pourroit cimenter, par la plume, les avantages qu'il se sera acquis par l'épée. La position militaire de l'Empereur Napoléon est trop aventurée pour qu'il ne doive tout tenter en faveur de la paix; et sa tactique est plus active dans les négociations que sur le champ de bataille. La fermeté de V. M. I. et celle de S. M. le Roi de Prusse peut déjouer toutes ces tentatives, et l'Europe peut encore être sauvée, si nous parvenons, Sire, à nous vouer à sa défense. Déjà V. M. I. a vu l'ancienne capitale de son Empire consumée par les flammes au milieu des cohortes ennemies, qui étoient venues des bords du Rhin pour la conquérir. En cédant alors aux insinuations pacifiques de l'Empereur Napoléon, V. M. n'auroit aperçu des ruines du Kremlin, que l'Europe dans les fers. Elle résista aux intrigues et aux menaces: la Russie fut délivrée, et les espérances rendues au Continent. Que le même marche dans ce moment soit couronné du même succès! Plus la crise actuelle est importante, et plus la concorde et la persévérance doit devenir l'apanage des Puissances Alliées. Que tout intérêt particulier s'ajourne devant les grands intérêts de la cause dont nous sommes les défenseurs, et mon cœur et mes calculs m'assurent que nous en sortirons avec gloire.

En employant les six semaines que nous laisse l'armistice à renforcer les armées, à concerter nos mouvemens, et à agir encore plus puissamment sur le moral de la Cour d'Autriche, à mesure qu'elle nous verra en état de recommencer la guerre d'une manière efficace, je crois que nous retirerons de cette suspension d'armes une utilité réelle, bien préférable aux chances d'une nouvelle bataille, qui auroit pu amener immédiatement la paix.

Si V. M. I. et le Roi de Prusse sont décidés à remettre encore au sort des armes la grande question de la liberté Européenne, à moins que l'Empereur Napoléon ne se prête à des conditions qui assurent une garantie durable à la pacification, je propose à V. M. I. que si l'armée combinée n'auroit pas reçu des renforts assez considérables avant l'expiration de l'armistice, elle reste derrière l'Oder, jusqu'à ce qu'elle soit égale en nombre à celle de l'ennemi. En attendant je pourrai prendre l'offensive, si V. M. I. et le Roi de Prusse mettent de suite à ma disposition les corps dont l'état suit: en ajoutant à cette force 30,000 Suédois, je me trouverai, à l'ouverture de la campagne, avec plus de 60,000 hommes, non compris un corps de 15,000 hommes que je laisserai pour masquer les Danois et les François à Hambourg et à Lubec. Ce dernier corps réuni au Landsturm du Mulembourg, que le Duc m'a promis de faire lever, aura dans tous les cas sa retraite assurée sur la presqu'île du Darz, que je fais retrancher sur Ribrutz, qui va devenir un bon poste, et enfin sur Stralsund, qui deviendra aussi bientôt, par les ouvrages que j'ai fait construire, une tête-de-pont excellente pour l'île de Rugen. En me portant sur le flanc quartier, ou sur les derrières de l'armée Française, elle sera forcée de se replier pour venir à moi, et l'armée Russe et Prussienne en Silésie et en Pologne sera dégagée d'autant. Celle-ci, suivant alors les mouvemens de l'Empereur Napoléon, pourra profiter d'un moment opportun pour reprendre l'offensive, et le résultat de nos efforts doit devenir funeste à l'ennemi.

C'est ainsi, Sire, que nous devons dissiper les nuages momentanés, qui ont obscurci la sérénité de nos relations; c'est ainsi que le Continent attend encore des forces de votre Empire; et de la loyauté de vos principes, la tranquillité et l'indépendance qu'il réclame. Les peuples de l'Allemagne ne demandent qu'un guide; la Cour d'Autriche ne pourra pas rester indifférente à la vocation brillante que lui présentent à la fois sa propre sureté, sa gloire, ses forces réelles, et les vœux des peuples opprimés. Tous les élémens pour réussir existent encore: séparés, ils ne tourneront qu'au profit de nos ennemis; unis, ils assureront le repos du monde.

Oui, Sire, accepter une paix en ce moment dictée par l'Empereur Napoléon, c'est poser la pierre sépulcrale sur l'Europe; et si ce malheur arrive, il n'y a que l'Angleterre et la Suède qui peuvent rester intactes.

Quelles que soient les déterminations de V. M. I., soit pour la guerre, soit pour une paix générale, je la prie de croire que j'irai en toute occasion au-devant de ses vœux avec une entière confiance. Je crois qu'il est plus important que jamais que nulle divergence d'opinion n'existe entre nous; et pour y parvenir, rien ne me paroît plus propre qu'une entrevue personnelle. La politique est à cette occasion d'accord avec mon cœur; et je serai heureux si V. M. I. et S. M. le Roi de Prusse, en profitant du tems de relâche que donne l'armistice, peut venir à Berlin, ou à tel autre endroit dans ses environs que V. M. I. indiquera. Une heure d'entretien, surtout dans des circonstances aussi pressantes que celles de ce moment, est plus décisive pour la marche des affaires qu'un mois de correspondance.

C'est le Lieut.-Gen. de Skjoldebrand qui aura l'honneur de remettre cette lettre à V. M. I. ayant l'avantage d'être déjà connu d'elle, et possédant toute ma confiance, je prie V. M. de lui accorder la sienne.

Que V. M. I., rassurée sur mes intentions et sur mes plans, comme j'espère qu'elle le sera par cette lettre, n'y voie qu'un motif de plus de persévérer dans la noble lutte qu'elle a entreprise, et qu'elle ne doute jamais de l'amitié inaltérable qui sera toujours indépendante de tous les événemens humains, et de l'attachement sincère avec lequel je suis, etc. etc.

(Signé)   CHARLES JEAN.

Stralsund, 10 *Juin*, 1813.

Corps du Lt.-Gen. Bulow	25,000
———— Comte de Janengsen	6,000
———— Comte de Walmoden	6,000
———— Comte de Woronzoff	4,000
Bataillons séparés, qui pourroient être omis du côté de la Baltique ou de la Finlande	6,000
Total	47,000

Declaration of the Allied Plenipotentiaries.

Châtillon, February 28th, 1814.

Plusieurs jours s'étant écoulés depuis que le projet des Préliminaires d'une Paix générale a été présenté par les Plénipotentiaires des Cours alliées à M. le Plénipotentiaire Français, et aucune réponse n'ayant été donnée ni dans la forme d'une acceptation ni dans celle d'une modification du dit projet; LL. MM. II. et RR. ont jugé convenable d'enjoindre aux plénipotentiaires Français une déclaration distincte et explicite de son gouvernement sur le projet en question. Les plénipotentiaires des Cours alliées pensent qu'il y a d'autant moins de motifs de délai de la part du gouvernement Français à l'égard d'une décision sur les préliminaires proposés, que le projet présenté par eux était basé en substance sur une offre faite par le plénipotentiaire de France dans sa lettre au Prince de Metternich, datée le 9 de ce mois, que le Prince a soumise aux Cours alliées. De plus, les plénipotentiaires des Cours alliées sont chargés de déclarer au nom de leurs Souverains, qu'adhérant pleinement à la substance des demandes contenues dans ces conditions, qu'ils regardent comme aussi essentielles à la sureté de l'Europe, que nécessaires à l'arrangement d'une paix générale, ils ne pourraient interpréter tout retard ultérieur d'une réponse à leur propositions que comme un refus de la part du gouvernement Français.

En conséquence, les plénipotentiaires des Cours alliées, prêts à se concerter avec M. le plénipotentiaire Français à l'égard du tems indispensablement nécessaire pour communiquer avec son gouvernement, ont ordre de déclarer que si, à l'expiration du terme reconnu suffisant, et dont on sera convenu conjointement avec M. le plénipotentiaire de France, il n'était pas arrivé de réponse qui fût en substance d'accord avec la base établie dans le projet des alliés, la négociation seroit regardée comme terminée, et que les plénipotentiaires des Cours alliées retourneroient au quartier-général.

Capitulation of Paris.

Art. 1. Les corps des Maréchaux Ducs de Trévise (Mortier) et de Raguse (Marmont) évacueront la ville de Paris, le 31 Mars, à 7 heures du matin.

Art. 2. Ils emmeneront le matériel de leur armée.

Art. 3. Les hostilités ne pourront recommencer que 2 heures après l'évacuation de Paris, c'est-à-dire, le 31 Mars, à 9 heures du matin.

Art. 4. Tous les arsenaux, ateliers, édifices militaires, et magasins resteront dans l'état où ils se trouvoient avant la présente capitulation.

Art. 5. La garde nationale, ou garde urbaine, est entièrement séparée des troupes de ligne. Elle sera conservée, désarmée ou licenciée selon que les Souverains alliés le jugeront nécessaire.

Art. 6. Le corps de la gendarmerie municipale partagera en tout le sort de la garde nationale.

Art. 7. Les blessés et maraudeurs qui 7 heures après seront encore à Paris seront faits prisonniers de guerre.

Art. 8. La ville de Paris est recommandée à la générosité des Hauts Alliés.

Fait à Paris le 31 Mars, 1814, à 2 heures du matin.

(Signé)

Le Colonel Orloff, Aide-de-camp de S. M. l'Empereur de Russie.
Le Colonel Comte Paar, Aide-de-camp général de S. A. le Feld-Maréchal Prince de Schwarzenberg.
Le Colonel Fabvier, attaché à l'état-major de Son Excellence le Maréchal Duc de Raguse.
Le Colonel Denys, premier Aide-de-camp de S. E. le Maréchal Duc de Raguse.

Conclusion of the Treaty of Paris, April 11th, 1815.

ART. 1. S. M. l'Empereur Napoléon renonce pour lui et ses successeurs et descendans, ainsi que pour chacun des membres de sa famille, à tout droit de souveraineté et de domination, tant sur l'empire Français et le royaume d'Italie que sur tout autre pays.

ART. 2. LL. MM. l'Empereur Napoléon et l'Impératrice Marie Louise conservent ces titres et qualités pour en jouir leur vie durant; la mère, les frères, sœurs, neveux et nièces de l'Empereur, conserveront également, partout où ils se trouveront, le titre de princes de sa famille.

ART. 3. L'île d'Elbe, adoptée par l'Empereur Napoléon pour le lieu de son séjour, formera, sa vie durant, une principauté séparée, qui sera possédée par lui en toute souveraineté et propriété. Il sera donné en outre, en toute propriété, à l'Empereur Napoléon, un revenu annuel de deux millions de francs, en rentes sur le grand livre de France, dont un million reversible à l'Impératrice.

ART. 4. Toutes les puissances s'engagent à employer leurs bons offices pour faire respecter par les barbaresques le pavillon et le territoire de l'île d'Elbe, et pour que dans ses rapports avec les barbaresques elle soit assimilée à la France.

ART. 5. Les Duchés de Parme, Plaisance, et Guastalla seront donnés en toute propriété et souveraineté à S. M. l'Impératrice Marie Louise; ils passeront à son fils et à sa descendance en ligne directe. Le Prince son fils prendra dès ce moment le nom de Prince de Parme, Plaisance, et Guastalla.

ART. 6. Il sera réservé dans les pays auxquels l'Empereur Napoléon renonce, pour lui et sa famille, des domaines, ou donné des rentes sur le grand livre de France, produisant un revenu annuel net, et déduction faite de toute charge, de 2,500,000 francs. Ces domaines ou rentes appartiendront en toute propriété, et pour en disposer comme bon leur semblera, aux Princes et Princesses de sa famille, et seront répartis entr'eux de manière à ce que le revenu de chacun soit dans la proportion suivante, savoir: à Madame Mère, 300,000 francs; au Roi Joseph et la Reine 500,000 francs; au Roi Louis, 200,000 francs; à la Reine Hortense et à son enfant 400,000 francs; au Roi Jérôme et la Reine 500,000 francs; à la Princesse Elisa, 300,000 francs; à la Princesse Pauline 300,000 francs. Les Princes et Princesses de la famille de l'Empereur conserveront en outre tous les biens, meubles et immeubles, de quelque nature que ce soit, qu'ils possèdent à titre particulier, et notamment les rentes dont ils jouissent également comme particuliers sur le grand livre de France ou le Mont Napoléon de Milan.

ART. 7. Le traitement annuel de l'Impératrice Joséphine sera réduit à un million en domaines ou en inscriptions sur le grand livre de France.

Elle continuera à jouir, en toute propriété, de ses biens meubles et immeubles particuliers, et pourra en jouir conformément aux loix Françaises.

ART. 8. Il sera donné au Prince Eugène Viceroi d'Italie, un établissement convenable hors de France.

Art. 9. Les propriétés que S. M. l'Empereur Napoléon possède en France, soit comme domaine extraordinaire, soit comme domaine privé, resteront à la couronne. Sur les fonds placés par l'Empereur Napoléon, soit sur le grand livre, soit sur la banque de France, soit sur les actions des forêts, soit de toute autre manière, et dont S. M. fait l'abandon à la couronne, il sera réservé un capital qui n'excédera pas deux millions, pour être employé en gratifications en faveur des personnes qui seront portées sur l'état que signera l'Empereur Napoléon, et qui sera remis au gouvernement Français.

Art. 10. Tous les diamans de la couronne resteront à la France.

Art. 11. L'Empereur Napoléon fera versemens au trésor et aux autres caisses publiques de toutes les sommes et effets qui auraient été déplacés par ses ordres, à l'exception de la liste civile.

Art. 12. Les dettes de la maison de S. M. l'Empereur Napoléon, telles qu'elles se trouvent lors de la signature du présent traité, seront immédiatement acquittées sur les arrérages dûs par le trésor public à la liste civile, d'après les états qui seront signés par un commissaire nommé à cet effet.

Art. 13. Les obligations du Mont-Napoléon de Milan envers tous ces créanciers, soit Français soit étrangers, seront exactement remplies, sans qu'il soit fait aucun changement à cet égard.

Art. 14. On donnera tous les sauf-conduits nécessaires pour le libre voyage de S. M. l'Empereur Napoléon, de l'Imperatrice, des Princes et Princesses, et de toutes personnes de leur suite qui voudront les accompagner ou s'établir hors de France, ainsi que pour le passage de tous les équipages, chevaux et effets qui leur appartiennent. Les Puissances alliées donneront en conséquence des officiers et des hommes d'escorte.

Art. 15. La garde Impériale Française fournira un détachement de 12 à 1500 hommes de toutes armes, pour servir d'escorte jusqu'à St. Tropez, lieu de l'embarquement.

Art. 16. Il sera fourni une corvette armée, et les bâtimens nécessaires pour conduire au lieu de sa destination S. M. l'Empereur Napoléon ainsi que sa maison; la corvette demeurera en toute propriété à S. M.

Art. 17. S. M. l'Empereur emmenera avec lui, et conservera pour sa garde, 400 hommes de bonne volonté, tant officiers que sous-officiers et soldats.

Art. 18. Tous les Français qui auront suivi S. M. l'Empereur Napoléon ou sa famille, seront tenus, s'ils ne veulent pas perdre leur qualité de Français, de rentrer en France dans le terme de trois ans, à moins qu'ils ne soient compris dans les emplois que le gouvernement Français se réserve d'accorder après l'expiration de ce terme.

Art. 19. Les troupes Polonaises de toutes armes, qui sont au service de France, auront la liberté de retourner chez elles, en conservant armes et bagages, comme un témoignage de leurs services honorables; les officiers, sous-officiers et soldats, conserveront les décorations qui leur auront été accordées, et les pensions affectées à ces décorations.

Art. 20. Les Hautes Puissances alliées garantissent l'exécution de tous les articles du présent traité. Elles s'engagent à obtenir qu'elles soient adoptées et garanties par la France.

Art. 21. Le présent traité sera ratifié.

RETURN OF THE ARMY ASSEMBLED AT DIJON IN 1814.

First Corps.

S. M. Count Colloredo—Division, M. G. Ledener.

			Batts.	Squads.	Men.	Horses.
General Ledener	Major-General Geramb	2 Companies pioneers			300	
		Hussars		12		2400
		Light infantry . .	2		1800	
	Major-General Scheidler	Hussars		8		1600
		Light infantry . .	2		1800	
General Marschall	Major-General Villater	Chevaux légers .		8		1600
		Light infantry . .	1		1000	
	Major-General Salius	1 Regt. of the line	3		3000	
		1 do. do.	4		4300	
Genera Wimpfen	Major-General Lauleen	1 do. do.	3		3000	
		1 do. do.	3		4000	
	Major-General Steinings	1 do. do.	3		3500	
		1 do. do.	3		3500	
	Major-General H.	1 do. do.	4		4300	
		1 do. do.	3		2700	

Second Corps.

General Prince Hohenzollern.

			Batts.	Squads.	Men.	Horses.
General Hardigg	Major-General Vexey	1 Company pioneers			300	
		Hussars		12		2400
		Light infantry . .	2		1800	
	Major-General H. Hardigg	Uhlans		8		2000
		Light infantry . .	2		2000	
General Machurzely	Major-General Volkinan	Hussars		12		2400
		Light infantry . .	1		1000	
	Major-General Veigl	1 Regt. of the line	4		4500	
		1 do. do.	4		4500	

Bandin troops, 16,000 men.

Third Corps.

Crown Prince of Wurtemburg—Prince Philip of Hesse Homburg.

			Batts.	Squads.	Men.	Horses.
General Palombino	Major-General Watze	1 Regiment of the line	3		3,500	
		1 do. do.	3		3,500	
	Major-General Luxem	1 do. do.	4		4,300	
		1 do. do.	4		4,300	
	Major-General Wartensleben	Hussars		12		2,400
Prince E. Hesse Darmstadt					8,000	
Wurtemburgers					25,000	

Fourth Corps.

Field-Marshal Prince Wrede.

Bavarians 65,000

RESERVE CORPS.

Archduke Ferdinand—Prince of Hesse Homburg.

General Prince M. L.	Major-General Pr. Cobourg	4 Companies pioneers		600
	Major-General Cte. Amersberg	2 Regiments cuirassiers	12	1560
		2 do. do.	12	1560
		2 do. do.	12	1560
General Nostitz	Pr. K. Wombung	2 do. do.	12	1560
	General Minsky			
General A. Hardigg	General Derfong	2 do. Uhlans	16	3200
	General Raizecourt	2 do. chevaux légers	16	3200
General Klebelberg	General Pawm	2 do. hussars	26	5200
		1 do. do.	6	1200
		1 do. dragoons	6	1080
General Mariassy	General Stollish	Light infantry	4	3600
	Gen. Stanisacliuch	do. do.	3	3000
Archduke Lewis	General Stutt	Grenadiers	5	5300
	General Benthieu	do.	4	4600
	General Trapp	do.	4	4600
General Prince Alvis Liecht	General Bahong	1 Regiment of the line	4	4600
		1 do. do.	4	4300
		1 do. do.	4	5000
	General Marzery	Grenadiers	2	2500

PRUSSIAN ARMY.

FIRST CORPS.

Marshal Prince Blucher, Commander-in-chief—Lieutenant General de Ziethen.

CAVALRY.

Regiment of Brandenburg dragoons
1st Regiment West Prussian do.
1st do. Silesian hussars
Uhlans of Brandenburg
1st Regiment of Churmark landwehr dragoons
2nd do. do. do.
Lutzow corps of cavalry
Westphalian cavalry

                  3,200

INFANTRY.

Major-General Steinmetz Colonel Hoffman	2nd Regiment of Brandenburg 12th do. of reserve 11th do. of Westphalian landwehr	7,450
Major-General Pirch Colonel Carnall	1st Regiment of West Prussia 1st do. of Berg 2nd do. of Westphalian landwehr	7,450
Major-General Lagow Colonel Ruchell	2nd Regiment of West Prussia 2nd do. of Berg 3rd do. of Westphalian landwehr	7,450
Major-General Henckel Lieut.-Colonel Stutterheim	1st Regiment of reserve 7th do. of do. 4th do. of Westphalian landwehr	6,650
	1st Brigade of Silesian riflemen	900
	2nd do. do. do.	900
		30,800

ARTILLERY.

Twelve Brigades of Artillery		1,620

FIRST CORPS	{ Cavalry Infantry Artillery	3,200 30,800 1,620	} 35,620

SECOND CORPS.

Lieutenant-General Borstell.

CAVALRY.

Major-General Surgas Colonel Thumen Lieut.-Col. Sohr Lt.-Col. Count Schulenber	{ Regiment of Queen's Dragoons do. of Newmark do. do. of Brandenburg Hussars do. of Pomeranian do. do. of Silesian Uhlans 3rd Regiment of Churmark Landwehr Dragoons 4th do. do. do. Elbe Landwehr Dragoons Berg Hussars	
		3,600

INFANTRY.

Major-General Pirch Colonel Tippelskirk	{ 1st Regiment of Pomeranian Lutzow's Corps 5th Regiment Westphalian Landwehr	
		7,500
Major-General Krafft Colonel Zastrow	{ Regiment of Colberg — Regiment of Elbe 1st do. of do. Landwehr	
		7,500
Colonel Schoen	{ 2nd Regiment of Reserve 10th do. do. 2nd do. of Elbe Landwehr	
		7,500
Colonel Langen	{ 9th Regiment of Reserve 11th do. do. 3rd do. of Elbe Landwehr	
		7,500
		30,000

ARTILLERY.

Twelve brigades of Artillery		1,600

SECOND CORPS.	{ Cavalry Infantry Artillery	3,600 30,000 1,600	} 35,200

THIRD CORPS.

Lieutenant-General Thielman.

CAVALRY.

Major-General Dobschutz
Lieut.-Colonel Marvitz
Lieut.-Colonel Watzdorf

One Squadron of Helvetian Dragoons
Regiment of Uhlans of the German Legion
New Regiment of Saxon Hussars
Seven Regiments of Heavy Dragoons
Nine do. of Hussars
Five do. of Uhlans
5th Regiment of Churmark Landwehr Dragoons
6th do. do. do.

3,200

INFANTRY.

Major-General Borke
Colonel Zeplin

Royal Regiment of Infantry
1st Regiment of German Legion
1st do. of Churmark Landwehr

7,500

Colonel Krauseneck
Lieut.-Colonel Kemphen

8th Regiment of Reserve
27th do. of Infantry
2nd do. of Churmark Landwehr

7,500

Colonel Luck

A new Regiment of Saxon Infantry
3rd Regiment of Churmark Landwehr
4th do. do. do.

7,500

Major-General Hobe
Lieut.-Colonel Lettow

2nd Regiment German Legion
5th do of Churmark Landwehr
6th do. do. do.

7,500

30,000

ARTILLERY.

Twelve brigades of Artillery   1,600

THIRD CORPS.
Cavalry   3,200
Infantry   30,000 } 31,800
Artillery   1,600

FOURTH CORPS.

CAVALRY.

2nd Silesian Hussars
Uhlans of West Prussia
Elbe National Hussars
1st Regiment of Newmark Landwehr Dragoons
2nd   do.   do.   do.
1st   do.   of Pomeranian   do.
2nd   do.   do.   do.
1st   do.   of Silesian   do.
2nd   do.   do.   do.
3rd   do.   do.   do.

Eight regiments of Dragoons
Eight   do.   of Hussars
                                                    4,800

INFANTRY.

1st Regiment of Silesian Infantry
1st   do.   Newmark Landwehr
2nd   do.   do.   do.
                                                    7,500
2nd Regiment of Silesian Infantry
1st   do.   Pomeranian Landwehr
2nd   do.   do.   do.
                                                    7,500
6th Regiment of Reserve
3rd   do.   Silesian Landwehr
4th   do.   do.   do.
                                                    7,500
3rd Regiment of Reserve
1st   do.   of Silesian Landwehr
2nd   do.   do.   do.
                                                    7,500
                                                   30,000

ARTILLERY.

Twelve brigades   1,600

FOURTH CORPS. { Cavalry   4,800 }
              { Infantry   30,000 } 36,400
              { Artillery   1,600 }

FIFTH CORPS.

CAVALRY.

2nd Regiment of Dragoons of West Prussia
Regiment of Letthau Dragoons
1st Regiment Life Hussars
2nd   do.   do.   do.
Seven Regiments of Hussars
1st Regiment of West Prussian Landwehr Dragoons
2nd   do.   do.   do.
3rd   do.   do.   do.
3rd   do.   of Pomeranian   do.
7th   do.   of Churmark   do.
4th   do.   of Silesian   do.
5th   do.   do.   do.
                                                    4,800

INFANTRY.

3rd Regiment of East Prussian Infantry
1st   do.   do.   Landwehr
1st   do.   of West Prussian   do.
                                                    7,700

4th Regiment of East Prussian Infantry		
2nd do. of West Prussian Landwehr		
5th do. of Silesian do.		7,700
4th Regiment of Reserve		
6th do. of Silesian Landwehr		
7th do. do. do.		7,700
5th Regiment of Reserve		
7th do. of Churmark Landwehr		
Three do. of Pomeranian do.		7,700
		30,800

ARTILLERY.

Twelve brigades   1,600

FIFTH CORPS. { Cavalry   4,800 }
                { Infantry   30,800 } 37,200
                { Artillery   1,600 }

SIXTH CORPS.

CAVALRY.

Regiment of Silesian Cuirassiers
   do.   of Brandenburg do.
   do.   of East Prussian do.
Four regiments of Cuirassiers
Four do. of Uhlans
6th Regiment of Silesian Landwehr
7th do.   do.   do.
8th do.   do.   do.
1st do. of East Prussian Landwehr
2nd do.   do. do. do.
3rd do.   do. do. do.
4th do.   do. do. do.   4,800

INFANTRY.

1st Regiment of East Prussian Infantry	
8th do. of Silesian Landwehr	
9th do. do. do.	7,500
2nd Regiment of East Prussian Infantry	
10th do. of Silesian Landwehr	
11th do. do. do.	7,500
12th Regiment of Silesian Landwehr	
13th do. do. do.	
2nd do. of East Prussian do.	7,500

	3rd Regiment of East Prussian Landwehr		
	4th do. do. do.		
	5th do. do. do.		7,500
			30,000

ARTILLERY.

Twelve brigades 1,600

SIXTH CORPS. { Cavalry 4,800 } 36,400
{ Infantry 30,000 }
{ Artillery 1,600 }

RESERVE.

CAVALRY.

Regiment of Life Guards
do. of do. Hussars
do. of do. Dragoons
do. of do. Uhlans 1,600

INFANTRY.

1st Regiment of Guards
2nd do. do.
A battalion of Riflemen of the Guards 5,800

Regiment Grenadiers Emperor Alexander
do. do. Emperor Francis
Riflemen of Neufchatel 5,400

11,200

ARTILLERY.

Four brigades 540

RESERVE. { Cavalry 1,600 } 13,340
{ Infantry 11,200 }
{ Artillery 540 }

Remaining Force to be disposed of for Dresden, Torgau, and Posen.

RESERVE. { Two regiments of Silesian Landwehr Infantry
{ One do. of Newmark Landwehr do.
{ One do. of East Prussian Cavalry

RECAPITULATION.

	Cavalry.	Infantry.	Artillery.	Total.	Remarks.
1st Corps	3,200	30,800	1,020	35,020	
2nd do.	3,600	30,000	1,600	35,200	
3rd do.	3,200	30,000	1,600	34,800	
4th do.	4,800	30,000	1,600	36,400	
5th do.	4,800	30,800	1,600	37,200	
6th do.	4,800	30,000	1,600	36,400	
Reserve Corps	1,600	11,200	540	13,340	
For Saxony	900	7,000	..	7,900	
Grand Total..	26,900	199,800	10,160	236,860	

Vienna, April 14, 1814.

Addenda

The following private Letters, written at the time of Napoleon's escape from Elba, by the author, at Vienna, may not be wholly uninteresting ; and they are therefore added to the work.

(The Letter here inserted will show how entirely the Prince Metternich agreed in the Duke of Wellington's military views upon the important subject of the new campaign, which absorbed public attention.)

Vienne, Mai 17, 1815.

Je vous remercie de l'intéressante communication de Lord Wellington. Il y a un mot sur la 5me page que je ne puis lire. Si vous êtes plus heureux que moi, veuillez m'écrire ce que c'est que l'endroit illégible.

Les idées de Milord Wellington sont entièrement les miennes ; et je crois pouvoir répondre que le Prince de Schwartzenberg les partagera également.

Il propose un grand mouvement concentrique ; et il veut que pour que ce mouvement ne soit pas risquant, on attende que l'ensemble des forces soit à la disposition des généraux.

Voilà également ce que nous voulons. Il veut que les armées se placent à telle hauteur qu'elles puissent se prêter la main en cas de revers.

Il ne propose, en un mot, rien d'eccentrique ; et je l'aime aussi peu en fait de questions militaires, qu'en toutes autres.

(Signé)   METTERNICH.

The following Declaration, drawn up by the Plenipotentiaries of the Allied Powers in Congress at Vienna, was ultimately decided on, and promulgated on Napoleon's escape from Elba, and is added as a most interesting document:

Les Puissances qui ont signé le Traité de Paris, réunies en Congrès à Vienne, informées de l'évasion de Napoléon Buonaparte, et de son entrée à main armée en France, doivent à leur propre dignité et à l'intérêt de l'ordre social une déclaration solennelle des sentimens que cet événement leur a fait éprouver.

En rompant ainsi la Convention qui l'avoit établi à l'Ile d'Elbe, Buonaparte détruit le seul titre légal auquel son existence se trouvoit attachée. En reparoissant en France avec des projets de troubles et de bouleversemens, il s'est privé lui-même de la protection des lois, et a manifesté à la face de l'Univers, qu'il ne sauroit y avoir ni paix ni trêve avec lui.

Les Puissances déclarent en conséquence, que Napoléon Buonaparte s'est placé hors des relations civiles et sociales, et que, comme ennemi et perturbateur du repos du monde, il s'est livré à la vindicte publique.

Elles déclarent en même tems, que fermement résolues de maintenir intact le Traité de Paris du 30 Mai 1814, et les dispositions sanctionnées par ce Traité, et celles qu'elles ont arrêtées ou qu'elles arrêteront encore pour le compléter et le consolider, elles employeront tous leurs moyens, et réuniront leurs efforts, pour que la paix générale, objet des vœux de l'Europe, et but constant de leurs travaux, ne soit pas troublée de nouveau, et pour la garantir de tout attentat qui menaceroit de replonger les peuples dans les désordres et les malheurs des révolutions.

Et quoiqu'intimement persuadés que la France entière, se ralliant autour de son Souverain légitime, fera incessamment rentrer dans le néant cette dernière tantative d'un délire criminel et impuissant, tous les Souverains de l'Europe, animés des mêmes sentimens et guidés par les mêmes principes, déclarent, que si, contre tout calcul, il pouvoit résulter de cet événement un danger réel quelconque, ils seroient prêts à donner au Roi de France et à la nation Française ou à tout autre gouvernement attaqué, dès que la demande en seroit formée, les secours nécessaires pour rétablir la tranquillité publique, et à faire cause commune contre tous ceux qui entreprendroient de la compromettre.

La présente Déclaration insérée au Protocole du Congrès réuni à Vienne dans sa Séance du 13 Mars 1815, sera rendue publique.

Fait et certifié véritable par les Plénipotentiaires des huit Puissances signataires du Traité de Paris. A Vienne, le 13 Mars 1815.

Suivent les signatures dans l'ordre alphabétique des Cours :

AUTRICHE.	Le Prince de METTERNICH.
	Le Baron de WESSENBERG.
ESPAGNE.	P. Gomez LABRADOR.
	Le Prince de TALLEYRAND.
FRANCE.	Le Duc de DALBERG.
	LATOUR-DUPIN.
	Le Cte. Alexis de NOAILLES.

GRANDE BRETAGNE.	{ Wellington. Clancarty. Cathcart. Stewart.
PORTUGAL.	{ Le Cte. de Palmella. Saldanha. Lobo.
PRUSSE.	{ Le Prince de Hardenberg. Le Baron de Humboldt.
RUSSIE.	{ Le Cte. de Rasoumowsky. Le Cte. de Stackelberg. Le Cte. de Nesselrode.
SUEDE.	Loewenhielm.

Extract of a Letter

Vienna
March 13th, 1815

If I had had my will, or any responsibility, I should certainly have despatched a messenger to England as soon as the news of Napoleon's flight reached this capital, in order to have put you in possession of the sensations this event has occasioned here, with the speculations it has given rise to, and the probable effect it will have on our still pending operations in Congress.

Before I send off this letter, however, it is probable that many of my hypotheses may be at an end, by the destination of this singular man being ascertained. Nevertheless, to give you the conversation now current here, cannot be entirely uninteresting. It happened that Lord Burghersh's *aide-de-camp,* Captain Aubin, arrived in Vienna on the day of one of the fêtes at court. He was the first proclaimer of the startling news; and Metternich was so alarmed, that he would willingly have kept it secret, at least for that night, in order not to throw a sudden gloom over the *représentations du Théâtre Royal* at court. However, as the populace in the town, and the cabarets had got possession of the intelligence, all notion of keeping the matter concealed was soon at an end. A conference was sitting the same day, with reference, I believe, to the mode of dealing with the King of Saxony. At this meeting the event of the escape came under discussion; and I understand there was an idea of a meeting of the eight Powers, to come to some sort of a declaration or sentiment of general and united hostility on the event.

Whether it was afterwards considered that this had better be deferred until it was known where the game was to be found, or whether it was deemed imprudent to sound the tocsin too soon, I know not; but I understood the above notion was given up, and the Duke of Wellington, Metternich, and Talleyrand, set out to conduct their negotiation with the' King of Saxony at Presburg yesterday, as if nothing had occurred. It is almost difficult to describe to you the various impressions produced on the circle at court by the intelligence of the day. Some, with a degree of seeming indifference and jest, expressed blame and surprise that the English could have let him escape from Elba, the custody of him at that island having been confided to them. Others blustered and rejoiced at it, as an auspicious accident, that must bring all disagreeable differences to a close. Others again dreaded the possible breaking out of a civil war in France, and of the renewed bloodshed and tumult, of which Napoleon's appearing in France would be the forerunner; and finally, others ,speculated on Buonaparte's having made common cause with Murat to rescue the kingdom of Italy.

It is however too true, that the present apparent Quixotical expedition from the island of Elba occasions a general and indescribable expression of fear in every quarter, that their best efforts cannot conceal. I understand that all the great men laughed on reading Lord Burghersh's dispatch; but next to the smile, I believe apprehension and alarm existed to an inordinate degree. Lord Wellington did not see the Emperor before the ball and play took place at court. The Duke, I understand, was very much satisfied with the Emperor of Russia's expressions. It seemed a moment for a general rally, and renewed pledges of union against a common danger. If the phoenix should again rise out of its ashes in Europe, whatever were the difficulties among ourselves, the Emperor declared that we must unite more firmly than ever against any new efforts made by Napoleon; and that we ought now to exert every nerve to carry into the speediest effect all the remaining stipulations relative to the Treaty of Paris.

When the Emperor approached Talleyrand, and observed on the curious fact of the bird having escaped from his cage, which he believed would not have occurred if France had made the payments as stipulated by treaty, Talleyrand is said to have asked him jocosely, if His Imperial Majesty would pay in March what was not due till May. I think Talleyrand has been particularly cheerful since the news. I know not Mr. La Bernarchere's sentiments, the right-hand man of the French *Chancellerie*; and D'Alberg has been ill. I believe they all fear the party against the government in France, if Napoleon should go to the south. In this party, however, there is a schism, unless Napoleon can manage to reunite it. The Empress Maria Louisa has been deeply affected, and has declared that Napoleon must be frantic to compromise in such a manner the interests of his son, without a solid hope of success. Her servants, &c. on hearing the intelligence, gave loose to extravagant demonstrations of joy, leaping, and hurrahing, and saying that Buonaparte would be emperor again, &c.

As to the course Napoleon has pursued, or his plans, there are various conjectures afloat. Naples appears the most likely point where, if acting in unison with Murat, a great force might soonest be collected. But is it probable that Murat would connect himself with him now? It would be the living acting with the dead. And Murat has certainly a better chance with Austria favourably disposed, and with the other powers in a degree passive, than if he were to join in battle-array against them; besides the uncertainty as to what Napoleon might bring into action, and with a knowledge that he must, in all points, yield to his superior direction. Treachery so great as to believe Murat would seduce his old chief, and deliver him up after he fell into his possession, to secure his own object, can hardly be imagined; and yet some think this more probable than that Murat would consent to make common cause in Italy with Napoleon.

The Austrians are naturally alarmed at the idea of the scene of war being in Italy; and yet many say that if Buonaparte should land there, it would be the best means of their becoming extricated from their engagements with Murat; to which the Emperor of Austria, in his own handwriting, stands already pledged.

Next to the speculations as to Italy, Napoleon's return to France is the most prevalent conjecture; and on this head all seem to agree that it would be a most fatal and dangerous attempt, in which much blood must probably flow, and a civil war in the country ensue. With respect to the immediate effect which the event may produce on our proceedings at Congress, I think the first impression was, that it would tend to accelerate them, and bring every point to a conclusion. However, I am not of this opinion. It is not to be expected that an indecisive and theoretical mind like my friend Metternich's, leaning on events, would come to a straight-forward arrangement. Upon Italy, for instance, when there is such an enemy as Napoleon again in the field, and as regards all other unsettled points, I doubt if our approach towards a general pacification will be narrowed. The arrangement as to Parma might become more questionable if Napoleon, by treaty, was not actually confined to Elba, which evidently appears not to be the case.

However, I do not see the necessity of a change; for, after this excursion, it is not very likely that the powers of Europe will allow him to return to the quiet possession of Elba; and if he should close his career elsewhere, all danger will cease with him. The arrangements of Italy, especially the question of Naples, must at present stand still in the hands we have now here. The Austrians are reinforcing, and I believe collecting their army as one of observation. I understand by letters from Paris, that the point of the Valteline, &c. is acceded to by France: there will be therefore no remaining difficulty in winding up the Swiss Cantons when we have directions so to do.

The Austrian and Bavarian differences are still so heterogeneous, that, without the hand of a master, I do not think they will speedily be brought to a settlement. Bavaria has been more yielding on the point of Saltzburg, and in proportion more tenacious as to that of Hanau, which was thrown out for her: but the king of Prussia has made such strong objections to the latter, and the remonstrances of Baden and Wirtemburg are so loud, that unless there is proper foresight to plan the best arrangement for all parties, and decision enough to say it shall be so, when it has been so laid down, I doubt whether the adjustments will ever be arrived at. The arrangements for Germany do not get on; and Count Munster complains of the Prince Royal of Wirtemburg, who has set himself up as the champion of the Mediatizes, and he is opposing violently all efforts for the German constitution.

The reports which Schwartzenberg received last night brought the intelligence of Buonaparte's landing at Cannes, near Grasse. He first made an attempt to re-embark at Antibes, where he was prevented, and then went to Cannes. His Polish lancers made M. de Monaco prisoner, and he was much examined as to the *esprit* reigning in France. He was then suffered to depart; and, going to Nice, gave the information above detailed. These reports came to the Emperor of Russia from Schwartzenberg, while at a party at Prince Esterhazy's; and the Emperor, the King, and all the ladies got the maps, and were planning over the table the various probable enterprises of the great wild beast, as they all now term him; and they seemed all to be affected with the same alarm as the escape of a ferocious animal would inspire.

The French mission here now appear much terrified. I hear they have only two couriers by whom they dare send dispatches. When Talleyrand was told of the possible collusion between the French ships of war and Napoleon before he left Elba, he is said to have actually trembled. I think, however, Mr. Nicholson Stewart's report to Lord Burghersh on this head is possibly the tale of those who are secret adherents to Napoleon.

I have urged the Duke of Wellington very much to send Hardinge to Genoa, to communicate on military points, between Lord William and him, and from thence to go on to the most advanced troops, and join any French corps, if aiding the royal cause, and to report direct to the Duke. I am sure this arrangement would be attended with advantage, and I hope to carry it into effect. I fear Colonel Campbell has got into difficulty by all I learn, and his conduct is much animadverted upon: this I lament, as I accomplished his recommendation.

Vienna
March 16th
Our news from Paris last night of the 9th has quieted a pretty general ferment that prevailed. The Duke of Wellington adopted my plan, and sent Colonel Hardinge off last night. He goes by the way of Zurich, and from thence towards Grenoble, or any other direction that is most advisable. He will correspond with Paris, to forward to London, and with the Duke here. You will, I am sure, prevent his being superseded. If this thing should last, . . . and at all events if Hardinge is up before the curtain drops, he may be of use.

I see no progress here in other points; a great deal of talk, but no acting. The arrangement of armies, planning commands, &c. is without end. I would rather be able to state the progressive *marche* of congress, or of some probable term to our labours. But how does this stand? Prince Metternich places 150 articles—all, as he says, *arretées,* into the hands of the *redacteurs.* They find, on examination of them, that the sole points that are completely finished are our treaty on the Slave Trade, and the line between Prussia and Saxony. The limits on the side of Poland, between Austria and Prussia and Russia are still loose. All the arrangements of Germany are unsettled; even the conclusion of the affair of Genoa cannot yet be put in treaty; and Switzerland is again postponed. Italy likewise opens rather a new face: Prince Metternich argues, that although Napoleon may have broken his treaty for himself, it still holds good for all the other parties. It is circulated also, most absurdly, and I know not on what grounds, that the English ministry are very zealous in Murat's interest.

March 19th
Since writing the foregoing pages, two days since, the aspect of affairs has much changed, and general alarm, almost leading to unaccountable despondency, has taken place. Our accounts from Paris of the 11th mention Napoleon's entry into Lyons; the different troops that have joined him—Garyan and La Beroudiere's corps; also the defection of the garrison at Metz, the garrison of La Force having marched for Paris, &c. All these reports you will probably have already received more accurately.
Consternation has been produced, and I think the Duke of Wellington, who, saw things in a good light at first, has changed to the other extreme. All unite in urging his immediate departure for Belgium, to consolidate the mass of acting force in that quarter. Prince Talleyrand appears to feel his going as his only salvation. I am quite

of opinion he should do so, when the military cabinets here are agreed upon a common system of action. Several and repeated conferences have taken place. Knesebeck, Schwartzenberg, &c. have assisted the Emperor and King, and the Duke has been of immense service. Orders are gone to all the armies. General Nugent sets out for Italy today, and active measures are taken. The Duke's absence from hence, when once the outline of military arrangement is fixed, will not be important. I am satisfied Lord Clancarty will carry on such business as it is possible to accomplish, while Buonaparte occupies every head, and issues forth from every mouth. All our illustrious allies are pressing hard for subsidy, and we are to have a new treaty of Chaumont. I understand the Emperor of Russia, with his usual address, has circulated doubts as to our last declaration against Napoleon, evidently to liberate himself from carrying on an eternal war against France. If she chooses to be governed by a military chief, or even republic, who would execute, on their part, the treaty of Paris? I hope some clear understanding may be insisted upon on this most important point. It is surely not to be endured that there should be a doubt, from our declaration, whether we are called upon not to make war in France until appealed to by the King, much less that we should agree, after such a paper, to let Napoleon reign in Europe, when we have pledged ourselves to have neither *"paix ni treve avec lui;"* and yet last night I heard frequently the language, that if the Bourbons were put down—if the army, and ultimately the nation, received Napoleon, that our declaration was not ratified, and might be arrested, &c. In short, we begin now to be exposed to the same vapours we breathed so much in the winter of 1813 and the spring of 1814. The French embassy, by their fears, will give great encouragement to the alarm. Prince Talleyrand has already announced, if things go bad, he will never go back to France, but will reside in

Germany. It is very well to take this resolution when the time arrives, but to circulate these sort of declarations at the present moment is very prejudicial. Lord Wellington was deeply affected by poor Packenham's death: there never was a greater loss to the. British army. The Duke received papers from Talleyrand by his courier, with an intimation that we had failed at New Orleans. Going out to dinner in a hurry, he put them into his red box, and the two days following he was busy; on the third by accident he looked into the box, found the newspaper of. the 8th, which announced the misfortune, and which for two days he had had shut up, ignorant of the contents. I question much if this failure—the non-ratification—your riots on corn—and Buonaparte's resurrection, will not give you work enough at home. But I have no question of any crisis being replete enough with events, &c. to puzzle or annoy you.

March 27th at night, 1815
I have only time for a few words. The news received this night is as bad as possible. The accounts are of the 20th. The King was on the point of leaving Paris;—the Melun camp all broken up, and there is little doubt of the success of Buonaparte in all quarters.

Vienna
March 29th at night, 1815
I was not in the-way when the last messenger was despatched, and therefore missed the opportunity of writing. Today's intelligence has confirmed Napoleon's entry into Paris—his nomination of his ministry—the King's flight to Lisle—his safe journey as far as Peronne, and all the other details, which you will have heard before this reaches you. Prince Metternich read his accounts at the conference tonight, up to the 21st. Nothing can be worse; and there is a gloom here quite indescribable; it is a most wonderful change in one short month. It may be divided into three

acts;—Buonaparte lands, his attempt is ridiculed, and it is supposed the measures of the police and the first troops that meet him, will put an end to him.—His entry into Lyons next announces that the whole French army are with him, and opposed to the nation.—The last act of his arrival at Paris shows that nearly all France is under his influence; and we must not deceive ourselves in thinking we have an easy task before us. It is true the nation are unaccountable in their acts and feelings; for Ney's renewing his oath of fidelity perplexes sadly a well-regulated honourable mind; and one is lost in amazement at the repeated instances of infidelity in the military chiefs.

You will hear of the attempt to carry off young Napoleon from the King's palace at Schonbrunn. Everything was arranged: young Montesquiou is believed to have been charged with it; and carriages, &c. were to have been in readiness near the Imperial Gardens. This plot was discovered, and the *soi-disant* King of Rome is now separated from the Empress Maria Louisa, and lodged in the palace here.

I am rather out of sorts at all I contemplate. The accounts from France of the 14th are certainly very critical. It appears clear the cause of the Bourbons will not be upheld but by foreign aid, and by the vigour and decision of England; and your own sterling courage, and animated feelings on this head, will do more than any other *appui*. The intelligence from Italy is likewise alarming. Switzerland seems to be behaving well, and the Pays de Vaud and Geneva are showing great determination.

Your return to the head-quarters, if things go on in their warlike shape, will be absolutely necessary: the different parts of the confederacy will be disunited without it, and all seem to look for it. We have as yet no accounts from Hardinge, but we expect them daily. *Adieu.*

The remainder of the authors letters, and all other documents and anecdotes of the congress, and the campaign of 1815, will be probably introduced in a future work.

These letters have been added at this moment chiefly to show the effect created by Napoleon's escape from Elba. And having now placed the readers of these pages in full possession of what passed at Vienna, as to military points, at the above epoch, this short series of letters is concluded by adding the first report received from Sir Henry Hardinge, at Brussels, which will demonstrate what was passing there, and will put on record, in an extraordinary manner, what the first elements and materials were in March 27th, of an army which, under the Duke of Wellington, on June 18th, achieved the battle of Waterloo, entirely defeated Napoleon, and gave a second time peace to Europe.

Brussels
March 27th
I am arrived here, my dear general; and I do not think it likely that Napoleon will make a push in this direction; for although we are not well prepared, either in the number or quality of the troops, yet I should conceive he will attempt to negotiate, and notwithstanding the declaration of the congress, consider its sentiments as no longer applicable to him, having been reinstated without bloodshed, or a civil war, by the unanimous choice of the people; in whose internal affairs foreign powers have declared they are not entitled to interfere, he being ready, on the part of the nation, as its chief, to guarantee the Treaty of Paris, and to abide by all public diplomatic acts of the interregnum. This I suppose to be the course he will take in preference; and I therefore do not in the least enter into the alarms of those who expect him at the head of his imperial guards immediately in Brussels. The dread of such a visit has been so strong and universal, that the greater part of the English have hurried away to the Hague.
The force, I have said, is small, not amounting to 10,000

British, and including Hanoverians of the legion and landwehr, about 28,000, of which 10,000 are regiments for garrisons; and, in point of quality, the British are mostly composed of the 2nd battalion, who, as young soldiers, at their outset in this country, got somewhat discouraged by the Bergen-op-zoom failure; and the Hanoverians, in point of advancement in discipline, about as far advanced as the Portuguese levies the first year of their service. In short, this army has not 10,000 formed soldiers. The Belgian regiments are composed of officers and men who have served under Buonaparte, and who are not in a loyal temper, and therefore almost worse than nothing. They are sent to the rear, and may be sprinkled in the garrisons, until by reinforcements and steady measures the army and people gain confidence, when I have no doubt they may be usefully brought forward. There are also 25,000 Dutch troops on their march, in a raw undisciplined state; and if the Duke personally takes the command of this army, and undertakes any operation at present, I should almost fear he would compromise his reputation; for they cannot move, and far outnumber the made troops.

No very material augmentation can, I understand, be expected from England, and that it will be the middle or end of next month (April) before any American troops can arrive.

The Russians call themselves 80,000 men, and promise for any co-operation 40,000 good troops, at the disposition of Holland and England, in defence of their frontier. The enemy have marched some bodies of troops in this direction; but I believe they are chiefly the garrisons which the King drew out to protect Paris, and which, after betraying him, are on their march to resume their former points. The Prince of Orange is very active and very popular: his plans are however uncertain. The Dutch have the greatest confidence in his military talents; and His Royal Highness is not said to be pleased with the idea of the Duke's being likely to supersede him in the command. Sir Hudson Lowe and Barnes are very anxious for the Duke's arrival. Colborne appears somewhat sick of his situation, and dreads any crisis of affairs under the present state of things. The army is not unlike Lord Rancliff's description of the French pack of hounds—pointers, poodles, turnspits—all mixed up together, and running in sad confusion. Sir Charles Stewart came here this afternoon in consequence of an express which Lowe sent off the day before yesterday, with the news (unconfirmed) that Buonaparte was at Arras; and the King is expected from the Hague tomorrow.

The King of France is at Ostend; and it would seem that he trusts his sentiments of future plans to no one, having taken (and very naturally, from the numerous treasons he has experienced) a suspicious turn of mind. He has, it is said, brought away, in cash and valuables, about five millions sterling! Every one, it is said, lost their head, excepting the Duc d'Orleans, who had a good deal of popularity in the army; but, from the jealousy of the King, every advice and assistance of his is said to have been discountenanced and neglected. He has, by universal consent, the best abilities; and if there is such a thing in France as personal attachment or party to the Bourbons, he possesses it. But I won't enter into farther conversation on this subject, as I must reserve a page for my own operations since I left Basle.

I made my way through the Pays de Vosges to Nancy, where the troops and people had declared for Buonaparte, and hurried from thence to Chalons still hoping to out-march Buonaparte, and to place myself with some royal army, and not quite crediting the rumours I heard from his partisans, of his near approach to Paris. At Chalons I was induced, from a wish to get information, and a necessity of eating, to stop at an inn, where I was very unwillingly obliged to dine with some French officers, who were in great glee at the return of Buonaparte. They had information by express of his being at Paris. I therefore thought it quite time that I should leave such company, and considering the declaration of the congress a declaration of war of Europe against Napoleon, and that the flight of the Bourbons gave me no chance of acting upon my instructions, I determined to make for the frontier before I should be detained. I should tell you, that at most places I was brought before the civil and military authorities, and underwent a good deal of inquisitional examination. I was compelled to drive two stages on the high road to Paris from Chalons, because, when my horses were put to, these troublesome rascally officers asked the road I was about to take. About midnight we got the postilions to drive by a cross road to Rheims, and thence to Mezieres, where I was again detained; thence to Levan; and so across the Duchy of Luxembourg to this place. I found the people, where there were no military, indifferent enough as to the success of either party; but certainly in general preferring Napoleon, or perhaps the change of masters, by which those who are not very well off speculate that by chance they may be better. Buonaparte appears to have acted, and to be now acting, upon the old revolutionary principles of 1793. On his advance from Lyons, he was always one or two marches in front of his troops, his partisans raising the mob of the villages through which he was to pass; and when the multitude were in the fermentation desired, he used to make his appearance, cajoling them in the most familiar terms; and by such means he maybe said to have entered Paris, by the aid of the rabble whom he picked up on the roads he passed along.

Large parties of troops were, however, always in his front, and which, it may be supposed, he contrived by means of emissaries despatched to the chief towns and cantonments of the troops, with regular orders of march, signed by Da-

voust or Bertrand, ordering the troops on certain days to be at fixed places, so that at various places he knew he would meet with support by the junction of such deserters as had obeyed these orders, which were very generally and very artfully distributed throughout the country.
Ever your most affectionate and attached,
H. Hardinge

ALSO FROM LEONAUR
AVAILABLE IN SOFTCOVER OR HARDCOVER WITH DUST JACKET

LIGHT BOB by *Robert Blakeney*—The experiences of a young officer in H.M 28th & 36th regiments of the British Infantry during the Peninsular Campaign of the Napoleonic Wars 1804 - 1814.

NAPOLEON'S RUSSIAN CAMPAIGN by *Philippe Henri de Segur*—The Invasion, Battles and Retreat by an Aide-de-Camp on the Emperor's Staff

SWORDS OF HONOUR by *Henry Newbolt & Stanley L. Wood*—The Careers of Six Outstanding Officers from the Napoleonic Wars, the Wars for India and the American Civil War. Illustrated.

HUSSAR IN WINTER by *Alexander Gordon*—A British Cavalry Officer during the retreat to Corunna in the Peninsular campaign of the Napoleonic Wars.

THE LIFE OF THE REAL BRIGADIER GERARD VOLUME 1 THE YOUNG HUSSAR 1782 - 1807 by *Jean-Baptiste De Marbot*—A French Cavalryman Of the Napoleonic Wars at Marengo, Austerlitz, Jena, Eylau & Friedland.

THE LIFE OF THE REAL BRIGADIER GERARD VOLUME 2 IMPERIAL AIDE-DE-CAMP 1807 - 1811 by *Jean-Baptiste De Marbot*—A French Cavalryman of the Napoleonic Wars at Saragossa, Landshut, Eckmuhl, Ratisbon, Aspern-Essling, Wagram, Busaco & Torres Vedras.

THE LIFE OF THE REAL BRIGADIER GERARD VOLUME 3 COLONEL OF CHASSEURS 1811 - 1815 by *Jean-Baptiste De Marbot*—A French Cavalryman in the retreat from Moscow, Lutzen, Bautzen, Katzbach, Leipzig, Hanau & Waterloo.

RIFLEMAN COSTELLO by *Edward Costello*—The adventures of a soldier of the 95th (Rifles) in the Peninsular & Waterloo Campaigns of the Napoleonic wars.

WITH THE LIGHT DIVISION by *John H. Cooke*—The Experiences of an Officer of the 43rd Light Infantry in the Peninsula and South of France During the Napoleonic Wars.

COLBORNE: A SINGULAR TALENT FOR WAR by *John Colborne*—The Napoleonic Wars Career of One of Wellington's Most Highly Valued Officers in Egypt, Holland, Italy, the Peninsula and at Waterloo.

A VOICE FROM WATERLOO by *Edward Cotton*—The Personal Experiences of a British Cavalryman Who Became a Battlefield Guide and Authority on the Campaign of 1815.

ALSO FROM LEONAUR
AVAILABLE IN SOFTCOVER OR HARDCOVER WITH DUST JACKET

WELLINGTON AND THE PYRENEES CAMPAIGN VOLUME I: FROM VITORIA TO THE BIDASSOA by *F. C. Beatson*—The final phase of the campaign in the Iberian Peninsula.

WELLINGTON AND THE INVASION OF FRANCE VOLUME II: THE BIDASSOA TO THE BATTLE OF THE NIVELLE by *F. C. Beatson*—The second of Beatson's series on the fall of Revolutionary France published by Leonaur, the reader is once again taken into the centre of Wellington's strategic and tactical genius.

WELLINGTON AND THE FALL OF FRANCE VOLUME III: THE GAVES AND THE BATTLE OF ORTHEZ by *F. C. Beatson*—This final chapter of F. C. Beatson's brilliant trilogy shows the 'captain of the age' at his most inspired and makes all three books essential additions to any Peninsular War library.

NAVAL BATTLES OF THE NAPOLEONIC WARS by *W. H. Fitchett*—Cape St. Vincent, the Nile, Cadiz, Copenhagen, Trafalgar & Others

SERGEANT GUILLEMARD: THE MAN WHO SHOT NELSON? by *Robert Guillemard*—A Soldier of the Infantry of the French Army of Napoleon on Campaign Throughout Europe

WITH THE GUARDS ACROSS THE PYRENEES by *Robert Batty*—The Experiences of a British Officer of Wellington's Army During the Battles for the Fall of Napoleonic France, 1813.

A STAFF OFFICER IN THE PENINSULA by *E. W. Buckham*—An Officer of the British Staff Corps Cavalry During the Peninsula Campaign of the Napoleonic Wars

THE LEIPZIG CAMPAIGN: 1813—NAPOLEON AND THE "BATTLE OF THE NATIONS" by *F. N. Maude*—Colonel Maude's analysis of Napoleon's campaign of 1813.

BUGEAUD: A PACK WITH A BATON by *Thomas Robert Bugeaud*—The Early Campaigns of a Soldier of Napoleon's Army Who Would Become a Marshal of France.

TWO LEONAUR ORIGINALS

SERGEANT NICOL by *Daniel Nicol*—The Experiences of a Gordon Highlander During the Napoleonic Wars in Egypt, the Peninsula and France.

WATERLOO RECOLLECTIONS by *Frederick Llewellyn*—Rare First Hand Accounts, Letters, Reports and Retellings from the Campaign of 1815.

AVAILABLE ONLINE AT
www.leonaur.com
AND OTHER GOOD BOOK STORES

ALSO FROM LEONAUR
AVAILABLE IN SOFTCOVER OR HARDCOVER WITH DUST JACKET

THE JENA CAMPAIGN: 1806 *by F. N. Maude*—The Twin Battles of Jena & Auerstadt Between Napoleon's French and the Prussian Army.

PRIVATE O'NEIL *by Charles O'Neil*—The recollections of an Irish Rogue of H. M. 28th Regt.—The Slashers— during the Peninsula & Waterloo campaigns of the Napoleonic wars.

ROYAL HIGHLANDER *by James Anton*—A soldier of H.M 42nd (Royal) Highlanders during the Peninsular, South of France & Waterloo Campaigns of the Napoleonic Wars.

CAPTAIN BLAZE *by Elzéar Blaze*—Elzéar Blaze recounts his life and experiences in Napoleon's army in a well written, articulate and companionable style.

LEJEUNE VOLUME 1 *by Louis-François Lejeune*—The Napoleonic Wars through the Experiences of an Officer on Berthier's Staff.

LEJEUNE VOLUME 2 *by Louis-François Lejeune*—The Napoleonic Wars through the Experiences of an Officer on Berthier's Staff.

FUSILIER COOPER *by John S. Cooper*—Experiences in the 7th (Royal) Fusiliers During the Peninsular Campaign of the Napoleonic Wars and the American Campaign to New Orleans.

CAPTAIN COIGNET *by Jean-Roch Coignet*—A Soldier of Napoleon's Imperial Guard from the Italian Campaign to Russia and Waterloo.

FIGHTING NAPOLEON'S EMPIRE *by Joseph Anderson*—The Campaigns of a British Infantryman in Italy, Egypt, the Peninsular & the West Indies During the Napoleonic Wars.

CHASSEUR BARRES *by Jean-Baptiste Barres*—The experiences of a French Infantryman of the Imperial Guard at Austerlitz, Jena, Eylau, Friedland, in the Peninsular, Lutzen, Bautzen, Zinnwald and Hanau during the Napoleonic Wars.

MARINES TO 95TH (RIFLES) *by Thomas Fernyhough*—The military experiences of Robert Fernyhough during the Napoleonic Wars.

HUSSAR ROCCA *by Albert Jean Michel de Rocca*—A French cavalry officer's experiences of the Napoleonic Wars and his views on the Peninsular Campaigns against the Spanish, British And Guerilla Armies.

SERGEANT BOURGOGNE *by Adrien Bourgogne*—With Napoleon's Imperial Guard in the Russian Campaign and on the Retreat from Moscow 1812 - 13.

AVAILABLE ONLINE AT
www.leonaur.com
AND OTHER GOOD BOOK STORES

www.ingramcontent.com/pod-product-compliance
Lightning Source LLC
Chambersburg PA
CBHW021959160426
43197CB00007B/181